Teaching Today and Tomorrow

A poster from the 1800s commemorating leaders of the public school movement.

Teaching Today and Tomorrow

Charles R. Kniker
Iowa State University

Natalie A. Naylor
Hofstra University

Charles E. Merrill Publishing Company
A Bell & Howell Company
Columbus   Toronto   London   Sydney

Published by
Charles E. Merrill Publishing Co.
A Bell & Howell Company
Columbus, Ohio   43216

This book was set in Helvetica
Cover Design Coordination: Will Chenoweth
Cover Illustration: Laurie Campbell
Production Coordination: Linda Hillis Bayma

Library of Congress Catalog Card Number: 80-84604

International Standard Book Number: 0–675–08034–7

Printed in the United States of America
1 2 3 4 5 6 7 8 9 10—86 85 84 83 82 81

To those great teachers we have had, with special thanks to

Philip Phenix
Robert W. Lynn
Lionel A. Whiston

and our parents

Contents

Contents

PHOTO CREDITS

ACTIVITIES

Listed below are all the activities found in *Teaching Today and Tomorrow*. They are identified by Chapter and number (1-1) as well as by title.

Activities

To the Instructor: There are 50 additional activities included in the Instructor's Manual that accompanies the text. Please contact the publisher and request code number 8034-M. The manual is free upon adoption of the text.

Preface

You as a future teacher may ask yourself the questions: Is teaching for me? What are schools for? Our book, *Teaching Today and Tomorrow*, will attempt to provide enough information for you to answer these equally important questions for yourself. More specifically, this book should help you

- reach an informed decision about teaching as a career
- begin formulating a philosophy of education
- analyze our educational system within society

Teaching Today and Tomorrow should help you meet these objectives with its over 40 self-assessment activities interspersed throughout the chapters. The activities will enable you to help decide about teaching as your career and to formulate and refine a personal philosophy of education. If used, they'll give you the opportunity to participate in class discussions, observe classrooms, talk with educators, etc.

It is our hope that this book will help you develop a philosophy of education and beliefs on the following topics: ˙

- the goals of education   Chapters 6, 11–16, Epilogue
- the curriculum   Chapters 8, 11, and 12
- the role of the teacher   Chapters 2–4, 6, and 7
- perceptions on teaching
  and learning   Chapters 6 and 7

- educational policies   Chapters 7–16, Epilogue

You'll find that this book is systematically structured in the same way in which you'll approach your decision about teaching as a career. First and foremost, college students are likely to be concerned about themselves and their futures. Second, when students think about teaching, they envision themselves as instructors in front of classrooms. Third, students gradually see that teachers are more than conveyors of knowledge or friend of pupils—they are agents for society and members of a social organization. Fourth, prospective teachers wonder how the "system" can be changed and how they can offer to their students the best possible learning environment. Thus, students want to know what the likely trends in education will be.

Since we know you can examine the table of contents, we would like to present the parts of the book in brief.

Part 1—has the students examine their own attitudes toward teaching and personal priorities. Discusses teacher's roles and the kind of people involved in teaching.

Part 2—describes the teaching process and the teaching profession.

Part 3—alerts students to the "rules of the game," and the teacher's role within the social system.

Part 4—pictures the concerns of education in the future.

Because there's a good deal of material to digest here, you'll find the book enlivened with numerous cartoons and photographs that speak to some of the issues in education today. Additionally, we confront such complex issues as Who should control the schools? directly within the text itself.

We hope the arrangement of the book, the activities, and the information about the school and other educational agencies in American society will blend successfully in helping you answer the questions: Is teaching for me? What are schools for? We are convinced that if you commit yourself to an honest self-appraisal, regardless of your final decision, you will benefit not only yourself but also tomorrow's students.

Charles R. Kniker
Natalie A. Naylor

Acknowledgments

Even the experience of writing other books did not prevent our surprise at the tally of names of persons who contributed to the preparation of *Teaching Today and Tomorrow.*

We cannot list all those who provided us with encouragement, suggestions or support. Numerous permission editors and officials at schools and state and federal education agencies gave generously of their advice and resources. A special word of thanks must go to the hundreds of Education 204 students at Iowa State University who, during the past 5 years, used various portions of the self-assessment approach and provided the authors with constructive criticisms. To these and others unnamed, you are not forgotten.

The following persons we wish to acknowledge because they made special efforts to aid us.

Those who reviewed the total manuscript and/or advised us in the initial stages of writing included Gene Larson, Ellen Look, Paul Rosewell, Thomas Hunt, and Dorothy Ruettgers.

Those graduate assistants who taught the introductory course at Iowa State and provided activities for the book—John J. Woods, Karen Willis, Kent Koppelman, and Linda Wilson.

Those who read and reacted to one or more chapters— Trevor Howe, Wallace Schloerke, Orrin Nearhoff, Gary Phye, William Wolansky, J. Stanley Ahmann, George Kizer, Shirley Wood, Frank Schabel, Elaine McNally Jarchow, Walter Hart, Al Kahler, Robert Thomas, Connie Earhart, Charles Rankin, Thomas Kelley, Jane Power, Charol Shakeshaft, Raymond Sheele, Mary Anne Raywid, and Madelyn Issacs.

Our college administrations were most supportive of the efforts that went into this book. Especial thanks go to Dean Virgil Lagomarcino and Associate Dean Harold Dilts (of the College of Education) at Iowa State University and Dean David Christman and Ignacio Gotz of (New College) Hofstra University.

The authors wish to thank the editorial staff of Charles E. Merrill, notably Fred Kinne, William Lochner, and Tom Hutchinson, who sought to ensure the best possible manuscript. Our personal responsibilities were as follows: Charles R. Kniker conceived the idea for the book, outlined all the chapters, and wrote most of the chapters. Natalie A. Naylor wrote Chapters 5, 9, and 12 and helped revise other chapters.

Lastly, to Eleanor, Ted, and Tim—your patience and understanding are appreciated, as always.

Teaching Today and Tomorrow

Part 1
You as a Teacher

Each person has only one genuine vocation—to find the way to himself.

Hermann Hesse

Is it appropriate to begin a book about schooling and teaching as a career by asking you to make a straightforward personal evaluation? We think so. Society wants learners to become self-sufficient persons who share their knowledge, apply their skills, defend their convictions, tolerate diversity, and work effectively with others. How can that be accomplished unless educators are purposeful and competent?

WHO ARE YOU?
A SELF-ASSESSMENT

The first chapter asks you to examine yourself, beginning with activities that consider your assets, needs, and beliefs. You may choose to perform one or more activities that focus on your feelings about family, friends, and associates. In so doing, you may discover how well you function in groups, which is important for teachers to know. The last part of the chapter suggests activities to help you recognize your feelings about schools.

The primary reason for the extensive number of activities in the first chapter is to provide you with benchmarks to which you can refer as you progress in the course. By reviewing these early activities you may be able to chart the changes in your attitudes and opinions about schooling and teaching.

WHAT'S EXPECTED OF TEACHERS?

Chapter 2 emphasizes what society *expects* teachers to be today. Many of the current expectations of teachers are vestiges of historical images, factual as well as fanciful. Besides looking at the job demands and daily routines of instructors today, the chapter explores predictions about schooling which may help you anticipate what teaching may become during your professional lifetime.

WHO ARE TODAY'S TEACHERS?

Part 1 closes with a discussion of who teachers *are*. What generalizations can be drawn about the more than 2 million elementary and secondary teachers in American schools? What are their motivations

---

Historical quotations are given accurately. The authors are conscious of the sexist language some may contain.

for teaching? What are their social backgrounds? Are they clustered in certain age groups? Do they hold similar political views?

After Chapter 3 examines the reasons people teach, their demographic patterns, and personal attributes, it focuses on what teachers are doing today. What satisfactions and frustrations are teachers experiencing? What do students think of teachers? What is the classroom climate?

ISSUES OF PART 1

Part 1 asks you to consider your value system and what is expected of teachers as *persons*. Because teaching is a profession that requires interaction, it demands individuals who are people oriented. We hope that Part 1 aids you in beginning a systematic evaluation of the decision to teach.

The issues in Part 1:

1. Are you intellectually and emotionally suited to be a teacher?

2. Are current community expectations for teachers realistic?

3. Are the best teachers recruited and retained in the classroom?

4. Are you the type of person who will be compatible with other teachers?

1

Who Are You?
A Self-Assessment

*There's only one corner of the universe
you can be certain of improving, and that's
your own self.*

Aldous Huxley

*What it lies in our power to do, it lies in
our power not to do.*

Aristotle

To assess your interest in teaching, you
need a clear picture of your personal goals
and abilities. While there can be no guarantee that self-assessment will make you
a good teacher, common sense suggests
it may be immensely helpful.

Chapter 1 begins with a rationale for the
self-assessment approach used in this
book. Some suggestions are given to help
you get the most from the activities. Most
of the chapter is devoted to activities that
help you learn more about yourself.

The tone of the chapter is personal; we
do not include the data that you will find in
other chapters, which will focus more directly on educational issues.[1] The issue in
this chapter is Am I interested in becoming an educator? Or it might be phrased,
Am I suited to be a teacher?

In this and every chapter, we shall conclude the introduction with a paragraph
containing several objectives that focus
on the most important aspects discussed.
After you have completed Chapter 1, you
should be able to (1) more fully understand
yourself as a person and (2) describe

Chapter One

several strengths and needs you have in your relations with others.

SELF-ASSESSMENT

Why Self-Assessment?

Consider the decisions you have made that have given you the greatest satisfaction. What made you comfortable with the outcomes? In all likelihood, you felt confident about the process of reaching a choice because it included the following:

● sufficient and accurate information;

● a clear understanding of the alternatives and their consequences;

● adequate time to reach a decision; and

● responsibility for making the decision yourself.

Higher education should enhance your chances for making good decisions. You should learn skills that enable you to gather information more effectively, weigh alternatives, become sensitive to the wants and needs of others as well as yourself, and increase your actual decision-making opportunities while you are in college.

Most undergraduate students spend a lot of time weighing career options. Your consideration of a teaching career should be treated seriously and directly. Thus, you will find numerous activities integrated with the text to give you sufficient information, a clear understanding of alternatives and consequences, and adequate time to decide about teaching as a career. We encourage you to do as many of the activities as you can, but we do not expect any reader to attempt all of them.

The key to successful decision making is that it must be *your* responsibility. As helpful as parents, friends, teachers, and counselors may be, they will not have to live with your decision.

Your teacher education faculty should

help you by providing a realistic picture of teaching, including the latest data about teaching opportunities. Considering that the annual dropout rate for teachers approaches 7%, we need to alert you to the problems, as well as the promises and rewards, of teaching. There are limitations to what we can do, however. Predicting how well you, or any other teacher education candidate, will do in the classroom, is an inexact science.

For both psychological and ethical reasons, then, it is preferable that you do a self-screening. Moreover, it is an all win/ no lose situation. If you are certain that teaching is for you, and you confirm that feeling, you will boost your confidence in your future career. If you find that teaching is not for you, you will avoid wasting time and money, and spare future students from an unhappy situation. These activities may reveal that teaching is a possibility for you, but that you need to reconsider what age level or type of school is best.

You may not be able to reach a firm decision about teaching by the time the course ends; additional classes and field experiences may be necessary. The self-assessment approach can carry over; you can use the techniques and activities described throughout the book to evaluate future experiences.

Some Hints for a Self-Assessment

Like forest rangers in lookout towers triangulating the location of a fire, the activities in the text help you to pinpoint your values. In time, you should learn whether you have shifted your points of view on a number of educational issues, and you can determine your intensity about them.

To get the most from self-assessment, consider these suggestions:

1. *Reexamine each activity.* Keep your responses to all activities and review them later in the course. Then either repeat them or at least read through them and note how your answers have changed.

Ask yourself, for example: Have I expanded my contacts? Have I enlarged my circle of friends? Am I more comfortable now with people from different cultures? Can I give more specific reasons and examples when I explain my philosophy of education? Did I change what I said I would change?

2. *Be as honest and specific as possible.* While you may feel that some of the activities you do are for your professor, they are really for you. You may fool your instructor, but you are unlikely to deceive yourself. Part of being honest is being as specific as possible. Taking a casual approach to the activities will waste your time. Whenever possible, indicate changes you expect if you meet the activity's objective.

When you review the activities at the end of the course, ask yourself: Am I enthusiastic about education? Is there a discrepancy between what I say is important and what I usually do? Am I comfortable when I share what I have written?

3. *Engage in a variety of activities.* Some activities should be done quickly, as snapshots of your outlook on life. Others are designed to help you assess how well you work with others. Another cluster of activities, more typical of conventional class assignments, asks you to write a report about a famous educator, read or review a book on an educational issue, or take a field trip. By experimenting with various activities, you are likely to improve awareness of yourself.

The self-assessment forms at the end of each Part are a good place to reflect on the variety of activities you have done. When you complete each Part, think about the activity or activities you chose to do: Do I have the curiosity to try some really different kinds of activities, or do I stick with the traditional or easy ones? (What

does that tell me about my willingness to engage in time-consuming and demanding projects that teachers often have?) Am I a conservative person? Do I prefer paper-and-pencil activities, or activities that require me to talk with others? Am I an introvert or an extrovert?

4. *Evaluate your comments.* How forceful were they? Do they reflect your position, or are they a carbon copy of the opinions you've heard from others? Would many of your comments wither under close scrutiny?

Categorize your comments. How many are factual statements? How many are platitudes? Do you have a tendency to overpower people with evidence? ("The data say . . ." or, "Most Americans practice . . ." or, "History teaches us. . . .") What impact does that have on students if a teacher uses a lot of information?

How often do your activities reflect attitudes you hold? ("I believe most students really want to learn." Or, "I wouldn't trust . . ." or, "Grades are overemphasized in school.") Do you attempt to persuade others rather than prove your point of view with data? Do you tend to overpower those with different points of view by discrediting their opinions? What implications can you see in this for a teacher? Should teachers refrain from giving their own opinions? Should they freely share their views?

How many of your comments are "action" statements? ("I wrote a letter to . . ." or, "When my teacher said that, I had to . . ." or, "After I saw how Maria was treated, I. . . .") Are you a contemplative person? Are you impulsive? How important is it for teachers to be active in their communities?

As you complete the self-assessment forms and the activities, note what type of person you are. Who is your model for teaching? Do you tend to take the same role in most group situations—consensus-seeker, maverick, leader, supporter?

5. *Share your findings.* As we have stated, *you* should assess who you are and what career you should pursue, but you can see whether others perceive you the same way. Some activities will lend themselves to group projects. You may decide to try some with your classmates or family. You may wish to have a close friend write a candid assessment of you. Your instructor may offer comments, too.

Questions you could ask others about yourself include: What does this activity show me to be? What are my best talents? If I had to improve one characteristic, which should it be? What about me surprises you the most?

By using these steps, you enhance the value of the activities. We do not suggest that you answer all of the above questions in each activity. We merely want to promote the concept of systematic self-examination, which we believe will benefit you now and throughout your life.

UNDERSTANDING WHO YOU ARE

Evidence suggests that effective teachers have clearly defined personal goals and teaching styles that are modeled after specific individuals who have influenced their lives.[2] Moreover, they are enthusiastic about their specialty, and they enjoy working with young people.

How well do you know yourself? Are you committed to certain goals in life? Are there places you want to visit or experiences you wish to have before you begin a career? Will you consciously plan to be like certain teachers you have had? How do you feel about working in a school? Or teaching outside the traditional classroom?

You as an Individual

The activities in this section and the two that follow may help you answer the questions just posed. Read through all of them and select the one(s) which will be most helpful to you.

ACTIVITY 1–1
Identity Tag

This is most appropriate for the first day of a class. If at all possible, share it with others, even if you do not do it in class.

Instead of making a typical name tag, create a tag on a 3-by-5 index card which contains the following items:

1. the name you wish to be called in class;
2. a symbol of a hobby or avocation;
3. a symbol of your favorite place; and
4. a symbol of the most special event you hope will happen to you in the coming year.

After drawing your tag, write your answers to these questions:

1. How similar will I be to others (in my class or group)?
2. Does the tag reveal that I am an ordinary, exciting, or special type of person?
3. Would my tag have been the same a year ago?
4. (answer at the end of the course) Would I now change anything on the tag?

The previous activity may not offer enough space for comments about yourself. The one that follows could be considered an interview that you hold with yourself. Al- though the questions are general, a num- ber of them revolve about skills expected of teachers.

ACTIVITY 1–2
Personal Profile

Respond to the questions below. Put your answers aside until the end of the course, then reexamine your responses and note how you have changed.

How Well Do I Understand Myself?

Strengths

1. What do I do best? In what am I most accomplished? Cite an illustration.
2. What skills need I improve?
   a. skills
   b. reasons for improving them
   c. my plan for improving them (estimate of time, methods and expenses required)
3. Which person(s) have most influenced my life? In what ways and to what extent?
4. What group(s) have most influenced me? Give an example or two.
5. If I met myself, what would I think?

Needs

6. What personality traits do I need to improve?
7. What has been the biggest disappointment in my life?
8. What are some of my failures? How have I overcome them?

How Well Do I Understand Others?

Relationships

9. What single term best describes my relationship with others? Why did I choose that term?
10. Generally, with which sex do I feel most comfortable?
11. How easy or hard is it for me to forgive others?
12. How do I behave when I don't get my way?
13. How do I usually take criticism? How do I usually give criticism?

Teaching-learning situations

14. Am I a good listener?
15. Can I easily place myself in another's position?

16. Am I patient?
17. Do I enjoy explaining things to persons who have a hard time understanding?
18. Who were my favorite and least favorite teachers?
　　a. What did I most like/dislike about those teachers?
　　b. If I were teaching now, how would I try to be like, or different from, those teachers?

The Future

19. What are some things that I feel need to be changed in my life? In schools?
20. What doubts do I want to resolve in the near future?
21. (at the end of the course) Looking back, how have I changed since I wrote this? What are my feelings about these changes?

Source: Karen Willis, "A Self-Assessment," in Charles R. Kniker and John J. Woods, *Schooling in American Life* (Ames. Iowa: Iowa State University, 1979) pp. 45–46.

Cartoon by Richard Weiss, reprinted with permission from *Colloquy,* October 1971. Copyright © 1971 by United Church Press.

Dick & Jane

Do you remember Dick and Jane?
See how they look now.
"Things certainly have changed," said Dick.
"They certainly have," said Jane.
Change, change, change.

You and Others

Reflect for a moment on the many influences that mold our beliefs and attitudes, our food tastes and literary classics, our local and national priorities. In short, think of the many individuals and groups that have socialized you.

Despite talk about the decline of the family, few authorities discount its significance for setting many lifelong patterns.[3] For most individuals, characteristics like creativity, modesty, and sociability are set in the family and only rarely modified to any great extent.

While this book focuses on the school as a socializing agency, numerous other social agencies have molded our musical preferences, clothing styles, attitudes about other countries, and feelings about schooling. A substantial number of Americans indicate they hold membership in a religious organization. Civic groups such as service clubs (Lions, Rotarians, and Elks) and scout troops claim large memberships. Corporations and the military as well as schools operate extensive training programs. Local governments operate facilities such as libraries and museums.[4]

Increasingly, we are realizing the powerful role of the mass media. The media shape our values, dreams, and fears as well as provide us with heroes and villains. With American children now likely to spend more hours watching television than being in the classroom, we can comprehend why television has been called "the third parent."

As you interact with these social agencies, peer groups, and your family, you begin to perceive yourself as a group member. While you are perhaps a leader in some organizations and a follower in others, you are likely to have certain patterns of response that are consistent from one group to the other, whether in a religious organization, a club, or among friends.

Using the following activities, you may gain some insight into your behavior in groups. Such insight should help you if you decide to teach, because you will have to work in many groups—curriculum committees, student clubs, faculty-administration groups, and so forth. These activities are merely exploratory. There are no right or wrong responses.

ACTIVITY 1–3
How I Feel and Act in Groups

Complete these sentences without previously discussing the topic with others. If then possible, share your statements with others.

1. When I enter a new group I feel _____.
2. I begin to relax in a new group when _____.
3. I feel most helpless in a group when _____.
4. When individuals in my group remain silent I feel _____.
5. I most enjoyed _____ (what group?)
6. Currently, I am most active in _____.
7. I've had poor experiences working with _____ (children or older people; jocks or socialites; blacks, whites, or Chicanos).
8. When I'm a group leader, I am _____.
9. As a group leader, I am most tense when _____.

Chapter One

10. What will make me proud of my group is _____.
11. When someone in the group is hurt, I usually _____.
12. When there is a conflict in the group, I usually _____.
13. What would cause me to resign as a group leader is _____.
14. Generally speaking, my role in most groups is that of a _____.

Reflecting on your statements, respond to these questions: Are you an active member of the groups you have joined? Do you have a tendency to move from group to group? Do you find your answers to the questions similar to those given by others? Are there specific groups with which you are very comfortable? Very anxious?

Source: Douglas F. Risberg, St. Cloud, Minn. St. Cloud University, Center for Educational Change.

Certain people have been more significant in shaping your life than others. What was it about these persons that most influenced you? Would you want to emulate them in your relations with young people?

ACTIVITY 1–4
Hall of Fame

1. Write a brief description of the three to five individuals who have most influenced your life. (Describe their outstanding characteristics rather than the specific ways they changed your life.)
2. If you have not included any famous persons in your descriptions, comment briefly along the same lines on several well-known figures you admire.
3. Questions for now and when you review this activity:

Are the characteristics these people display qualities which good teachers usually have? (See Chapters 2, 3, and 6.)
Do I especially admire people who come from certain vocations, e.g., music, athletics, business, religion, education?
Are all of the individuals named from the same ethnic or racial group? If so, what does that say to me?
To what extent have I modeled my behavior after one or more of these persons?

You and Schooling

The fact that you are in college suggests you did reasonably well in school. It is likely you thoroughly enjoyed grade school and high school and thrived on numerous extracurricular opportunities. You may be attracted to teaching because it involves working with a lot of people, a repeat of what you did in school. Or you may have been turned on to a subject by a favorite teacher and now want to share that enthusiasm. Possibly, you find the process of inquiry—dissecting and discussing ideas—so exciting that you can hardly wait to be a teacher.

On the other hand, your memory of school may be bittersweet, equally filled with positive and negative recollections. To you, school had occasional moments when classwork and extracurricular events were meaningful; other times, school was

Teachers are often group leaders. They also are members of many groups.

boring. When you reflect on the knowledge, skills, and friendships that you gained from school, you immediately think of the price you had to pay—the hours of study, the anxiety of tests, the hassles from administrators and teachers and some students.

You may have an even less positive impression of schooling. William Shakespeare's description of a student of another era, "The whining schoolboy, with his satchel / And shining morning face, creeping like snail/Unwillingly to school," could have been you. Somehow you managed to survive school, and perhaps now you see your mission in life as a reformer of a dehumanized system of instruction.

The following activity may help you discover more precisely how you feel about the institution which, from September to June, houses approximately one of four Americans. There will be other activities in Chapters 2 and 3 to help you focus on your attitudes about schooling.

ACTIVITY 1–5

How I Feel About School

If you had to select an object that to you symbolized school, what would it be?

- An alarm clock: "School is meeting one deadline after another."
- A circular piece of yellow construction paper: "School made me feel warm all over."
- A golf tee: "School teed me off."

Or, if you were to construct a model or collage that illustrated your general attitude toward school, what would you attempt to convey?

- A model of a rat maze: "That's all it was—a rat race."
- A collage of pictures showing fraternity/sorority parties: "Now that's where I really got an education."

If you have the chance, compare your object or model with those that others in your class have brought or created. Are they generally positive or negative in tone? If you can't do this in a class, display your object where others can see it. Invite their reactions, and ask them to share their opinions about schooling.

We believe that all teachers have an operational philosophy of education; that is, they have formed, based on their experiences, a system of beliefs about schools. They have opinions about how trustworthy and diligent students are, what the curric-

Chapter One

From "Children," a Pictorial Archive from 19th Century Sources. Dover Publications, Inc., New York.

Examine your views on schooling in a systematic way.

ulum should be, which discipline techniques are most effective. As a veteran of schooling, you have similar opinions. Do your ideas form a cohesive and defensible pattern? Use this course to find out.

SUMMARY

It is important for prospective educators first to know themselves and then to weigh carefully their career options. College years are natural ones to consider vocations.

A much-beloved guidance counselor said after she retired, "I started out as a home economics teacher. I found out after several years of teaching that I was more interested in how the students turned out than how their recipes turned out." Precisely. We, too, are interested in how you

are going to turn out. Begin your study of the educational world by gaining some insights into yourself, your relations with others, and your feelings about school.

NOTES

1. John Martin Rich, *Conflict and Decision: Analyzing Educational Issues* (New York: Harper & Row, 1972), pp. 1–25, has an excellent description of what constitutes an educational issue and what steps can be taken to ensure that issues are thoroughly discussed.

2. See the discussion on teacher effectiveness in Chapter 6. See also Thomas L. Good et al., *Teachers Make a Difference* (New York: Holt, Rinehart and Winston, 1975).

3. See the following special issue on this topic, "Families and Communities as Educators," *Teachers College Record* 79, no. 4 (May 1978), especially the articles by Leichter, Getzels, Cremin, and Hobbs.

4. Lawrence A. Cremin, *Traditions of American Education* (New York: Basic Books, 1977).

Cartoon by Herbert Goldberg in *Phi Delta Kappan.* November 1972, p. 157. Reprinted with permission.

"You're always quoting from Aristotle, Plato, Socrates, Juvenal, Cicero— when are you going to quote something from your own head?"

FOR FURTHER STUDY

Becvar, Raphael J. *Skills for Effective Communication: A Guide to Building Relationships.* New York: John Wiley, 1974.

Curwin, Richard, and Fuhrmann, Barbara S. *Discovering Your Teaching Self.* Englewood Cliffs, N.J.: Prentice-Hall, 1975.

Greene, Mary, and Rubinstein, Bonnie. *Will the Real Teacher Please Stand Up?* Pacific Palisades, Calif.: Goodyear Publishing, 1972.

Greene, Maxine. *Existential Encounters for Teachers.* New York: Random House, 1967.

Jersild, Arthur. *In Search of Self.* New York: Teachers College Press, 1952.

Marshall, John P. *The Teacher and His Philosophy.* Lincoln, Neb.: Professional Education Publishers, 1973.

2

What's Expected of Teachers?

No limit can be set to the power of a teacher, but this is equally true in the other direction: no career can so nearly approach zero in its effect.

Jacques Barzun

What is it like to be a teacher?

You have some idea, to be sure. You've been in enough classrooms to form an impression of the teacher's role and duties. Perhaps you have friends or relatives who are teachers, and they have given you additional insights into the demands and rewards of the occupation. In high school you may have been a volunteer tutor or joined Future Teachers of America to learn about a career as an educator.

Even with such experiences, do you really know what is involved in a teaching career? Do you have accurate information about the historical roles and status of teachers? Do you comprehend the subtle and not-so-subtle pressures on teachers to conform to community standards? Do you perceive the changing shape of American education, so that you can reasonably predict the characteristics tomorrow's teachers will need?

The major purposes of this chapter are to help you recognize the profiles of educators expected now and in the future and to help you evaluate whether you fit within the parameters of that profile. As you examine the past roles of teachers, current expectations, and probable future responsibilities, you may also consider the educational issue: Are current community expectations for teachers realistic?

Chapter Two

Cartoon by Herbert Goldberg. Reprinted with permission.

"Oh dear, you just can't get away from P.S. 202!"

After you have completed Chapter 2, you should be able to (1) summarize the five historical roles of teachers, (2) list three current expectations of teachers, and (3) project possible changes in future roles of teachers.

HISTORICAL ROLES

Your images of past teachers may be largely the result of accounts you have read in novels, or seen in movies or on television. There are numerous written tributes to great teachers, from Cotton Mather's reverent recollection of Ezekiel Cheever of the Boston Latin School to William Saroyan's glowing description of Miss Hicks, the Ancient History teacher.[1] The movies have pictured the schoolmarm as consistently innocent and selfless, while early television shows depicted several bumbling but good-natured educators such as "Mr. Peepers" and "Our Miss Brooks."

You may recall as many—perhaps more—unflattering accounts that portray teachers

as humorless individuals who are powerless outside the classroom as well as incompetent inside it. This view is tersely expressed in George Bernard Shaw's adage, "He who can, does; he who cannot, teaches." (Shaw, as many do not remember, later changed this to: "He who can think, teaches.") Washington Irving's Ichabod Crane and the teachers in Mark Twain's novels are impractical, overbearing malcontents with little community prestige.

Teaching has been both a pinnacle of respect and a vocational way station. In the colonial period, it was a temporary job for ministers waiting for a parish assignment. In the 1800s, when credentials and references were hard to check, it was sometimes a refuge for alcoholic merchants and unemployed factory hands. In the early 1900s, teaching was the first rung up the social ladder for children of immigrants.

The point is that it can be dangerous to draw generalizations about the historical roles of teachers, even when conclusions are based on accounts by teachers and

As the nation expanded, the need for education and the demand for good teachers increased.

their contemporaries. As Willard Elsbree noted about the colonial schoolmaster:

> He was a God-fearing clergyman, he was an unmitigated rogue; he was amply paid, he was accorded a base pittance; he made teaching a life career, he used it merely as a steppingstone; he was a classical scholar, he was all but illiterate; he was licensed by a bishop or colonial governor, he was certified by his own pretensions; he was a cultured gentleman, he was a crude-mannered yokel; he ranked with the cream of society, he was regarded as a menial. In short, he was neither a type nor a personality, but a statistical distribution represented by a skewed curve.[2]

As you consider the following roles of teachers, note how they overlap current expectations. Do not assume, however, that all or most teachers in any period of the country's history met all of these roles.

Classroom Manager

Above all else, teachers stand as the symbol of adult rules and regulations. They are expected to teach students how to behave. To learn to accept authority is never easy, and as *The Hoosier Schoolmaster* revealed, parents were not too surprised when their sons occasionally challenged teachers to a fight. A common theme in illustrations of other eras is that of a teacher physically disciplining a student.

Teachers of the past knew that being a disciplinarian was their chief responsibility. To lose authority over the students was the ultimate disgrace. Willard Waller's research in the 1920s reported that a common experience among teachers was a recurrent dream of losing control in the classroom. Even student accounts about favorite teachers of bygone years highlight their strictness and aloofness rather than their compassion and friendliness.[3]

Chapter Two

The disciplinarian, or classroom manager role, in summary, is the most consistently mentioned expectation society has held for teachers.

Moral Example

Teachers have not only been expected to teach children how to behave, they were supposed to be models of the best behavior. Often, it has been assumed that they would be active church members, or at least support the dominant religious practices of the community. Well into the nineteenth century, school districts kept taxes low by having teachers "board round" with the families of the children they taught, and such a practice made the teachers' moral behavior highly visible. As one teacher wrote in her diary in 1850: "We were cautioned against disturbing the family with whom we are stopping by talking late or making any noise; we were to remember that our life was constantly subject to the inspection of those around us."[4]

One of the reasons women outnumbered men teachers by the 1860s was the moral influence that they were expected to exert on children. In the mid-nineteenth century, several organizations recruited women teachers for the West, hoping that their feminine virtues would civilize the barbaric frontier. Further, districts could hire women for one-half or one-third the salary paid to men. Thus, economics determined the women's numerical superiority.

That teachers have been expected to be moral examples can be documented by codes of behavior that school committees prepared for their employees. Here is part of a contract in North Carolina in the 1920s:

> I promise to take a vital interest in all phases of Sunday School work donating of my time, service and money without stint for the benefit and uplift of the community.

> I promise to abstain from dancing, immodest dressing, and any other conduct unbecoming a teacher and a lady.

> I promise not to go out with any young man except as it may be necessary to stimulate Sunday School work.

> I promise not to fall in love, to become engaged or secretly married.

> I promise to remain in the dormitory or on the school grounds when not actively engaged in school or church work elsewhere.

> I promise not to encourage or tolerate the least familiarity on the part of my boy pupils.

> I promise to sleep eight hours a night, to eat carefully, and to take every precaution to keep in the best of health and spirits in order that I may be better able to render efficient service to my pupils.

> I promise to remember that I owe a duty to the town people who are paying my wages, that I owe respect to the school board and the superintendent that hired me, and that I shall at all times, consider myself the willing servant of the school board and the townspeople.[5]

While some communities today have relaxed their standards and will tolerate a teacher's visit to a local bar or look the other way when the teacher has an extra-marital affair, they are still likely to pressure teachers to resign if their personal conduct is viewed as detrimental to their classroom effectiveness—for example, dating a student or using a drivers' education car for personal business. A practicing homosexual or a single person who lives with someone of the opposite sex may find it difficult to be hired or to receive tenure in some districts.

School officials still can exercise some control over the personal lives of teachers. Courts have generally upheld the practice of requiring teachers to live within the boundaries of the district (to patronize local merchants and to help the tax base of the district).

Teachers have been expected to maintain control of their classrooms, to be moral examples, to know and promote the basics, to encourage student interest in a wide range of fields, and to have a variety of skills. Which of these is most important today?

Instructor in the Basics

The basic curricula in American education have been reading, writing, spelling, and arithmetic. Many nineteenth century teachers were rehired or fired on the last day of the school year, when the school board members and parents came to a public exhibition where students displayed their knowledge of the basics. No wonder teachers stressed memorization and rote recitation. A leading educator of the era noted: "Many teachers seemed to suppose their whole duty consisted in filling children's heads with words. The child who could commit the greatest number of verses or pages to memory in a given time, was considered the best scholar."[6]

Teachers could feel some pride, however, when members of the community asked them to apply some of their knowledge. A teacher in rural Iowa in the 1920s recalled: "My strongest line was mathematics and I was often asked to measure cribs of corn for some farmer in my neigh-

Chapter Two

borhood. . . . I took the older pupils with me and had them learn to measure, too. . . ."[7]

The call for instruction in the basics, so often heard today, is thus not new. But now, as then, there are questions: Which subjects are "basic"? How can student competence be measured? How effective is the teacher's instruction? (See Chapters 12, 11, 7, and 6, respectively.)

Guide to Culture

America's independence in the late 1700s and the immigrants who came to the new country in the 1800s spurred the growth of the common or public schools. Teachers were expected to make good citizens of the newcomers by inculcating such values as patriotism, respect for property, punctuality, cleanliness, and manners.

The teachers themselves were often second-generation immigrants who, ruthlessly at times, purged students of their heritages. Pupils who were slow to lose their dialects were ridiculed by the teachers as well as fellow students. To aid assimilation, some educators anglicized the given names and abbreviated the surnames of students.

At best, teachers helped move their charges from lives of poverty and poor health to respectability and middle-class values, which enabled the graduates later to assume positions of authority. From such mentors, students were introduced to worlds of thought, music, food, and vocations that they had not imagined. Accounts from immigrants and minority group members report that the path of instruction offered by their cultural guides had many painful steps. Leonard Covello, an Italian immigrant, described such experiences in his autobiography, *The Heart is the Teacher,* while Mary Antin's *The Promised Land* mirrors the plight of a Russian-Jewish immigrant. *Up From Slavery*, by Booker T. Washington, recounts the educational journeys of a native-born black.[8]

Jack (or Jill) of All Trades

A number of factors already evident in the colonial world—a teacher shortage, a simple curriculum, the isolation of communities, and low wages—contributed to the public's perception that most educators were likely to be a jacks-of-all-trades, and masters of none. As more settlers arrived in the 1600s, towns needed teachers, and they were prone to accept anyone who had, or claimed to have, even a modicum of learning. Teaching did attract some individuals with college training, such as Harvard graduates, but they were often ministers who were waiting for a new pastoral assignment. The curriculum was not extensive, and it was assumed that the teacher could handle all subjects. As new disciplines were formed, it was expected that the teacher would add them to his or her repertoire. In remote villages, teachers were often asked to assume responsibilities beyond those in the classroom. The low pay often forced even the most dedicated teachers into offering private lessons after school hours or taking a second job.

Taking account of these factors, we do not find this 1661 contract of a colonial schoolmaster surprising. He was expected to do the following:

1. act as the court messenger
2. serve summonses
3. conduct certain ceremonial church services
4. lead Sunday choir
5. ring bell for public worship
6. dig graves
7. take charge of school
8. perform other occasional duties.[9]

By the 1860s, teaching had become more of a profession. It was common to find widely published lists of regulations that local school districts could ask their teachers to observe. One such list contained 31 directives for the teachers, including the following: keep records for the school district, check the ventilation of the building, supervise janitorial work, and send monthly reports to the parents. Several regulations, it would appear, reflect teacher abuses of their position:

18. Teachers shall not appropriate to themselves, in the school, or within the hours thereto belonging, any portion of time for their own reading, writing, or business; nor shall they engage in any other business which, in the judgment of the Board of Directors, will interfere with or be inconsistent with the performance of their duties.

19. Teachers shall not engage in any other teaching, or give private lessons, before 6 o'clock P.M., Saturdays excepted.

23. Teachers shall not sell books and stationery to pupils. . . .[10]

In the tradition of Laura Ingalls Wilder's teacher in *Little House on the Prairie*, teachers in one-room schools well into the twentieth century continued to be carpenters, musicians, counselors, janitors, scientists, doctors, and on occasion, cooks. Besides teaching the academic subjects, they were often asked to play the organ, lead the school glee club, and read Bible stories. Penmanship, hygiene, art, and physical education were added to their list of subjects to teach. In twentieth-century city schools, teachers were expected to do similar things, such as helping students with craft projects, advising student clubs, and patrolling school playgrounds.

This heritage of being a jack-of-all-trades continues today. While teachers at the secondary level are more specialized, elementary teachers continue to instruct in a myriad of fields. To a lesser extent, teachers are asked to be involved in community affairs. Even though communities may not like it, they continue to acknowledge and accept the fact that the low pay teachers receive prompt many to moonlight.[11] Based on these factors, do you agree that the teacher's role as a generalist, a jack-of-all-trades,

continues? Or do you feel it has significantly diminished?

CURRENT EXPECTATIONS

Many observers claim that none of the roles has disappeared, although they might concede that some have diminished in importance. Historian Michael Katz, for example, has stated that the schools have not changed their purposes since the 1880s, hence teachers do virtually the same things today. The concerns of the public about public education, as expressed in the annual Gallup polls, center around lack of discipline in the schools and the need for basics—hardly new ideas.[12]

Others argue that the role of the teacher is changing. They use sociological data, literature, and television programs about teachers as evidence that teachers have a decidedly different emphasis today. They are no longer primarily transmitters of the society's values, but change agents for a better society.[13] According to these analysts, today's teachers should be more involved with students personally, more active politically, and more professionally competent.

As you debate whether teachers of today are seen in the same light as teachers were in days past, bear in mind one other issue: Has the *status* of teachers changed markedly from 50 or 100 years ago? Are teachers today held in any greater esteem than were their counterparts a century ago? (If you have friends who were educated abroad, it might be interesting to ask them about the prestige of their teachers.)

To Be Personally Involved

Literature for teachers today commonly concerns humanizing the classroom (see Chapter 13). Books and articles by and for teachers stress the crucial importance of

Chapter Two

recognizing the individual needs of students. Many education textbooks regard a good self-concept in children as the highest goal of teaching, because students who have poor self-images have greater difficulty learning. The development of the open school and a flexible curriculum are signals that teachers should be very conscious of the special learning needs of students.[14]

Teachers are urged to be much more conscious of the motivations and feelings of students about schooling. For the academically successful student, school is a pleasant place. For the marginal student, school becomes an increasingly frustrating experience. Much of formal education is seen by students, regardless of performance level, as a series of repetitive tests and small steps of learning.[15]

Some researchers hold that there is a growing attitude of alienation among students toward schooling and their teachers. In years past, this attitude may have been most prevalent among children from lower socioeconomic backgrounds, but such an attitude is now expressed by students from all socioeconomic levels. If that is true, keeping students interested in school work may be the major challenge facing teachers today. Some studies disagree with this finding. They suggest that most students have a positive attitude about their teachers as well as their schools.[16]

The more recent television series involving teachers show them to be quite concerned about student attitudes toward school as well as about life in general. David Hartman in "Lucas Tanner," Gabe Kaplan in "Welcome Back, Kotter," and Ken Howard in "The White Shadow" are heavily involved in the personal lives of students.

Do such depictions of teachers foster a new, unrealistic stereotype about them? Can or should teachers spend so many hours with the students? Do most real-life teachers have the skills to help students solve their nonacademic problems? Are the images of these teachers too ideal? What legal difficulties await the teacher who intervenes in the lives of his or her students?

To Be Politically Active

Television news programs, more than situation comedies, alert us to the growing political activism of teachers. Commentators pointed out that teachers constituted the largest block of delegates at the 1980 Democratic Party convention. Teacher union efforts for and against the forming of a U.S. Department of Education, as well as strikes for higher pay and better benefits, also made the news. Teachers have become effective campaigners at federal, state, and local levels. At both the national and state levels, teacher organizations are among the most effective lobbyists. (See Chapter 5.)

While few would challenge the right of teachers to be active in the political process outside the classroom, there is more concern about teachers instructing impressionable children in their personal political beliefs. Court cases regarding the academic freedom of teachers (also discussed in Chapter 5) have underscored the principle that educators, like students, do not check their constitutional rights at the schoolhouse door. They are entitled to present students with challenging and unconventional ideas if they are germaine to the subject of the class.

Some critics of the schools, like Jonathan Kozol, believe that teachers have not gained much freedom from political orthodoxy, in or out of the classroom. Kozol believes that the fundamental purpose of the school system in America is to indoctrinate students in the existing social order. In his opinion, teachers must mold students into "eager consumers, obedient servants, and if need be, willing killers."[17] Those who agree with Kozol point out that it hasn't been so many years ago that new teachers being interviewed for jobs were asked how they felt about communism. During the Vietnam War, many university students demonstrated against the American involvement in Asia. When some of these students completed their teacher education programs and applied for their certificates, a special review committee in California declared that even those who only had been detained after demonstrations were not "stable enough" to teach. (That decision later was overturned after pressure by state teacher organizations.) In midwestern towns and eastern cities, some untenured teachers who participated in Vietnam protests found that their contracts were not renewed.[18]

In summary, teachers are more active politically today, but they operate in the mainstream. Schools, almost by definition, are rather conservative institutions and expect to inculcate the young in generally accepted modes. It is acceptable for teachers to campaign for Democratic or Republican candidates (and even some independents), but probably not for the Communist party. It is doubtful many superintendents would knowingly hire an ar-

dent Nazi. In the classroom, the teacher is entitled to academic freedom, and may volunteer political sentiments when asked by students, or may engage the students in a debate about a political matter that is pertinent to the discipline.

To Be Professionally Competent

Training programs for teachers were sufficiently rigorous by the early 1900s that there was a general consensus that teaching was a profession. As John Dewey, the leading philosopher and educator of that era explained, "All other reforms (in education) are conditioned upon reform in the quality and character of those who engage in the teaching profession." Today, the U.S. Census Bureau identifies teaching as one of approximately 50 professions.[19]

Professions, generally, are considered to have two central foci—academic preparation and a social mission. Those who believe teaching deserves the status accorded to professions point out that teachers need to be intelligent persons who take a substantial period of specialized training, and who become experts in interpersonal relations. The curriculum for teachers has expanded remarkably. The complexity of learning requires that future teachers be

Teachers recognize the needs of students; they would like the public to recognize their professional needs.

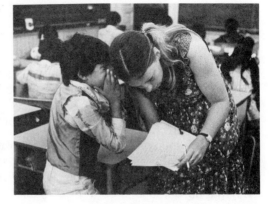

competent in lesson planning, test construction, evaluating and recording information, identifying appropriate motivational and disciplinary techniques, locating appropriate media, diagnosing learning disabilities, and integrating children with special needs into the classroom. Like medicine, the number of specialized degree programs has increased for teachers.[20]

In addition, teaching has been a pioneer in requiring its practitioners to upgrade their skills. Numerous states require teachers to attend accredited graduate programs or in-service workshops before their certificates can be renewed. Increasingly, states are reducing the time period for which the teacher's initial and renewed certificates are valid. The era of lifelong certificates is passing.[21]

Teaching, like other professions, offers "a unique, definite, and essential social service." In the case of teachers, they serve the interests of the public, for which they receive a modest salary. Because of the special nature of the relationship between the teacher and student, somewhat like the relationship of the doctor and patient, or lawyer and client, much latitude is given to the judgment of the professional in determining best how to serve those with whom he or she works. Teachers, therefore, would like to see more authority on educational policy matters given to their organizations. While teachers recognize administrators' legal responsibilities, they believe that student learning would be enhanced and teacher morale improved if educators had parity with administrators in making school-related decisions.[22]

Not everyone is convinced that teaching is a profession. These critics point to its lack of a specialized body of knowledge (borrowed from so many other fields—psychology, sociology, and the traditional disciplines), its short period of training (compared to other professions), its low status and pay, and perhaps most importantly, its inability to set its own standards and be responsible for its own actions, individually and collectively. In addition, some argue that it is relatively easy to become a teacher, and the profession suffers from a chronically high turnover rate.[23]

Do you believe that teachers today see themselves, and are viewed, as professionals? Are you convinced that teachers can rightly claim that they have subject-matter expertise, that they have special skills in teaching, and that they do have a vital social function? If so, why is their compensation low, and why has society resisted efforts to give them greater control of their profession? Recall the other two current expectations and the historical roles. Are these roles realistic for tomorrow's teachers?

ACTIVITY 2–1

Interview an Educator

Interview a classroom teacher, a school administrator, or a counselor about teaching as a career. (It may be beneficial to interview two educators, one who loves his or her work, and one who is disenchanted.)

Among the questions you might ask are these:

1. What are the social roles of the teacher in this community?
2. Is teaching a satisfying career today? In what specific ways? What are the drawbacks?
3. What rewards other than financial do teachers receive?
4. What does it take to be a good teacher?

5. What is the future going to be like for classroom teachers?

6. What is the future going to be like for students?

When you write your report, be sure to include your reactions to the comments made by your interviewee(s). Do you agree or disagree with their statements?

FUTURE ROLES

Will teachers of tomorrow have the same roles as today? Some teachers prefer similar roles. Others hope for changes. Should you go into teaching, you will have control over the roles you choose, and as Charles Silberman advises, you should begin to think about them now.

> To be sure, teaching has its share of sadists and clods, of insecure and angry men and women who hate their students for their openness, their exuberance, their color or their affluence. But by and large, teachers, principals, and superintendents are decent, intelligent, and caring people who try to do their best by their lights. If they make a botch of it, and an uncomfortably large number do, it is because it simply never occurs to more than a handful to ask *why* they are doing what they are doing—to think seriously or deeply about the purposes or consequences of education.[24]

Look at this collection of predictions about education in America between now and the year 2000. What inferences can you draw that will affect your possible teaching career? You will note that the projections, gathered from a variety of sources, do not entirely agree.[25]

1. The school year will be extended from the current 180 days to 200 days. The expense of large school plants will dictate year-round use of buildings. Teachers will receive 11-month contracts. To avoid boredom, teachers will rotate teaching assignments from semester to semester, thus requiring preparation in several areas.

2. Experiments in organizing student learning will continue. Some schools will structure learning in competency-based modules; that is, students will demonstrate their mastery of skills in mathematics, reading, and spelling through demonstrations rather than paper-and-pencil tests. In some systems, instruction will be organized in more flexible units of time. Learning will be ordered less sequentially, with students moving rapidly from one subject to another. Educators will be expected to orient learning to the individual.

3. States will amend their laws governing required studies to allow for alternatives in education. Parents will have more choices on where to send their children, which means that schools are more likely to have clearly defined philosophies of education. Some will be rigidly organized; others will be modeled after free schools like Summerhill (see Chapter 15). Renewed interest will be shown in schools that have a religious orientation. Teachers must have clearly developed philosophies of education, and school officials will monitor teachers' presentations closely.

4. The technological needs of American society, plus dissatisfaction with standardized test scores, will result in great attention to the basics for another decade. Teachers will have to drill students and be firm disciplinarians.

5. The world as a "global village" will increase pressure to teach foreign languages and to educate students in a number of locales. Field trips, study abroad, and student exchange programs will become more popular. Instructors will be expected to have knowledge of several

Chapter Two

foreign cultures and serve as tour directors on a regular basis.

6. The evaluation of educational performance will shift from paper-and-pencil tests to computer-scored examinations. Teachers will use computers in the classroom to teach problem-solving skills and to help students make career projections, besides using computers for evaluation and record-keeping purposes. In addition, teachers will use computer technology to diagnose students' learning disabilities.

7. There will be greater emphasis upon nonprint educational materials. Teachers will have to become experts in the use of various media in the classroom. Moreover, other educational agencies will assume functions formerly done by the schools. For example, libraries will become more automated and have educational materials that will supplement those in schools. Thus, teachers will have to work more closely with other institutions, for example, in arranging phone hookups so students may hear the recorded voices of famous people that are stored on tape at the library or a museum.

8. As the population in the 5- to 21-year-old age group drops, schools will offer more instruction for special groups and nontraditional students. Programs for preschoolers will be expanded, and offerings for adults will be initiated. Some courses will be cross-generational. Within the traditional school-age population, the regular classroom teacher will have more students with special needs (see Chapter 13 for a discussion on mainstreaming). Educators will be retrained to work with the diverse populations that the schools will be serving.

9. With declining enrollments, fewer teachers will be needed in K-12 classrooms. Those retained and hired will either have to be willing to handle a variety of assignments or become specialists, for example, a learning disabilities teacher. For

those not willing or able to coach, advise, or counsel in schools, careers in service fields may be real alternatives. The Peace Corps is a prototype community service program, coordinating projects that need teachers for hospitals (patient education), community health agencies, environmental studies experiments, and day-care centers.

10. State and federal government will assume even greater control of formal education. An important component of such a trend will be regional and national competency examinations (see Chapter 7). Teachers will be evaluated increasingly on how their students rank on such tests. Educators will be correspondingly less inclined to provide a liberal arts education measured by essay exams and more predisposed to "teach to the test." Some will moonlight as coaches of students taking standardized tests.

11. As a reaction to the violence and alienation in society, schools will expect teachers to discuss moral decision making in the classroom. Teachers will have to learn techniques for teaching in the affective domain (values, attitudes, emotions). Parent groups will become more concerned about the teachers as role models.

12. How individuals learn will receive increased attention. Experiments to modify human behavior will be performed, using chemicals and electrical currents. (Even now hundreds of thousands of students are given prescription drugs to calm them, presumably to enhance their learning.) School teachers will be asked to participate in such experiments.

13. The energy crisis, coupled with inflation, will bring on a resurgence of interest in small school districts (as opposed to the trend to consolidate school systems). The chances for teachers having students from several grade levels in their classes will increase. Team teaching will become

In addition to classroom duties, teachers have, and will continue to have, responsibilities such as sponsorship of school newspapers and yearbooks. What activities would you be willing to sponsor?

more popular as more schools combine classes and experiment with open classrooms.

14. There will be more instruction in homes and businesses and less in schools. Homes will have mini-computers, cable television, and video playback systems, while businesses will expand their employee training programs. Teachers will have less direct contact with students, instead preparing materials for audio- and videotapes to be used by students at their leisure. More of the teacher's time in class will be spent tutoring students.

ACTIVITY 2–2
Teaching in Schools of the Future

What are your reactions to these potential trends?

1. List those projections you feel will happen on a wide scale. Which projections are least likely? Why?
2. Explain your feelings about each of these changes. What is appealing or disturbing about them?
3. Can you think of other possibilities that are likely to occur in the schools? (Readings in the "For Further Study" section will help you to answer this question.)
4. Are any of these changes so inhibiting that they would prevent you from teaching?

Source: Modified from an activity that appears in Charles R. Kniker and John J. Woods, *Schooling in American Life* (Ames, Iowa: Iowa State University, 1979).

SUMMARY

By acquiring an overview of the roles of teachers, historically and currently, and by looking at directions schools may take, you can begin to raise significant questions for yourself about teaching as a career.

Everyone who first considers teaching fantasizes about what it is like to be a teacher. It is easy to forget that teachers do not operate in a vacuum. Just as you will bring certain images about teaching to the classroom, so will your students. You will also be confronted by the expectations of parents and the community. Part of your success as a teacher will depend upon your reaction to all of these expectations.

You must ask yourself: Can I be comfortable as a classroom manager, a moral example, an instructor in the basics, a guide to culture, and a Jack or Jill of all trades? Are you the type of person who will be personally involved with students, politically active, and concerned about professional competence? Do you anticipate that the future will be the same or different?

The focus should be on the present. The prime question to face as you explore whether you want to teach, or what type of teacher you will be is, Are current community expectations for teachers realistic?

NOTES

1. Elizabeth P. Gould, *Ezekiel Cheever, Schoolmaster* (Boston: The Palmer Co., 1904); William Saroyan, *The Human Comedy* (New York: Harcourt, Brace, and Co., 1943), pp. 51–61.

2. Willard S. Elsbree, *The American Teacher* (New York: American Book Co., 1939) pp. 123–24.

3. Willard Waller, *The Sociology of Teaching* (New York: John Wiley & Sons, 1967; originally published in 1932), pp. 401–5; Edward Eggleston, *The Hoosier Schoolmaster* (New York: Sagamore Press, 1957 ed.). For accounts about teachers see Abraham Blinderman, *American Writers on Education before 1865* and *American Writers on Education after 1865* (Boston: Twayne Publishers, 1975, 1976); Don C. Charles,

"The Stereotype of the Teacher in American Literature," *Educational Forum* 14, no. 3 (March 1950): 299–305.

4. Quotation found in Elsbree, *American Teacher*, p. 202.

5. Quoted by Waller, *Sociology of Teaching,* p. 43.

6. Samuel Hall, *Lectures on School-Keeping*, 1829 (New York: Arno Press, 1969), p. 126. Hall began the first teacher training school in the country, and urged that teachers concentrate on building understanding and thinking processes.

7. Amy Ambrose Cash, teacher in Lenox, Iowa. Letter in the file of Charles R. Kniker.

8. Leonard Covello, *The Heart is the Teacher*, 1958, reprinted in paperback under the title *The Teacher in the Urban Community* (Totowa, N.J.: Littlefield, Adams, 1970); Booker T. Washington, *Up from Slavery*, 1901 (available in many editions); Mary Antin, *The Promised Land* (New York: Houghton Mifflin, 1912).

9. John H. Best and R.T. Sidwell, *The America Legacy of Learning* (Philadelphia: Lippincott, 1967), pp. 46–47.

10. *Adams School Register* published in St. Charles, Ill. 1862.

11. Diane Divoky, "Moonlighting: Occupational Hazard or Benefit?" *Learning* 7, no. 3 (November 1978): 40–46.

12. Michael Katz, *Class, Bureaucracy, and Schools: The Illusion of Educational Change in America* (New York: Praeger, 1971), pp. xvii–xxvi. The Gallup polls on education are reported each year in a fall issue of *Phi Delta Kappan*.

13. Dan C. Lortie, *Schoolteacher* (Chicago: University of Chicago Press, 1975); Frances Markham Briggs, *The Changing Concept of the Public School Teachers as Portrayed in American Novels* (Chapel Hill: University of North Carolina Press, 1962); Leslie Rich, "The Teacher As Change Agent," *American Education* 9, no. 7 (August-September 1973): 9-13; Dean M. Laux, "A New Role for Teachers?" *Phi Delta Kappan* 46, no. 6 (February 1965): 265–68.

14. T. Robert Bassett, *Education for the Individual: A Humanistic Introduction* (New York: Harper & Row, 1978).

15. Benjamin S. Bloom, *Human Characteristics and School Learning* (New York: McGraw-Hill, 1976).

16. Charles M. Fair, "The Reluctant Student: Perspectives on Feeling States and Motivation," in *Feeling, Valuing, and the Art of Growing: Insights into the Affective*, ed. Louise Berman and Jessie A. Roderick (Washington, D.C.: Association of Supervision and Curriculum Development, 1977), pp. 127–43; John J. Woods, "Student Attitudes Toward School as Revealed in Questionnaires" (Ph.D. diss., University of Missouri, 1978).

17. Jonathan Kozol made these remarks in a speech to the National Education Association in 1972. He made similar comments in *The Night is Dark and I Am Far from Home* (Boston: Houghton Mifflin, 1975).

18. For examples of teachers who did get into trou-

ble because of their outspoken political and educational stances, see Pat Michaels, "Teaching and Rebellion at Union Springs," *No More Teachers' Dirty Looks* 52, no. 5 (January 1971): 262–66; Jonathan Kozol, *Death at an Early Age* (Houghton Mifflin, 1967); Pat Conroy, *The Water is Wide* (Boston: Houghton Mifflin, 1972). The Conroy book was the basis of the movie *Conrack.*

19. John Dewey, quoted in James Koerner, *The Miseducation of American Teachers* (Boston: Houghton-Mifflin, 1963), p. xii. For an overview, see American Association of Colleges for Teacher Education, *Educating a Profession* (Washington, D.C.: American Association of Colleges for Teacher Education, 1976).

20. For a discussion of the topic, see such sources as Myron Lieberman, *Education as a Profession* (Englewood Cliffs, N.J.: Prentice-Hall, 1956), pp. 1–6; National Education Association, Division of Field Service, "The Yardstick of a Profession," *Institutes on Professional and Public Relations* (Washington, D.C.: National Education Association, 1948), p. 8; and Martin Haberman and T. M. Stinnett, *Teacher Education and the New Profession of Teaching* (Berkeley: McCutchan Publishing Co., 1973), pp. 77–85.

21. Elizabeth Woellner, ed., *Requirements for Certification of Teachers, Counselors, Librarians, Administrators for Secondary Schools, Junior Colleges* (Chicago: University of Chicago Press, 1980); M.L. Cushman, *The Governance of Teacher Education* (Berkeley: McCutchan Publishing Co., 1977).

22. Ragha P. Mathar, "Educators as Public Servants," *Education* 98, no. 3 (March-April 1978): 280–85.

23. Kevin Ryan, *Teacher Education*, 74th Yearbook of the Society for the Study of Education (Chicago: University of Chicago Press, 1975).

24. Charles E. Silberman, *Crisis in the Classroom: The Remaking of American Education* (New York: Random House, Inc., 1970), pp. 10–11.

25. Dwight W. Allen, "The Future of Education— Where Do We Go From Here?" *Journal of Teacher Education* 26, no. 1 (1975): 41–46; "Happy Holidays: The Year 2000," *Senior Scholastic* 107, no. 8 (December 16, 1975): 4–5; Harold G. Shane, "America's Next 25 Years: Some Implications for Education," *Phi Delta Kappan* 58, no. 1 (September 1976): pp. 78–84.

FOR FURTHER STUDY

Hipple, Theodore W., ed. *The Future of Education: 1975–2000.* Pacific Palisades, Calif.: Goodyear Publishing Co., 1974.

Landau, Elliott; Epstein, Sherrie L.; and Stone, Ann P., eds. *The Teaching Experience: An Introduction to Education Through Literature.* Englewood Cliffs, N.J.: Prentice-Hall, 1976.

Lindley, J. Stiles, ed. *The Teacher's Role in American Society.* The 14th Yearbook of the John Dewey Society. New York: Harper and Brothers, 1957.

National Education Association. *Schools are People: An Anthology of Stories Highlighting the Human Drama of Teaching and Learning.* Washington, D.C.: National Education Association, 1971.

Pullias, Earl V., and Young, James D. *A Teacher is Many Things.* 2nd ed. Bloomington, Ind.: Indiana University Press, 1977.

Wagshcal, Peter H., ed. *Learning Tomorrows.* New York: Praeger Publishers, 1979.

3

Who Are Today's Teachers?

What the teacher is, is more important than what he teaches.

Karl Menninger

This chapter moves from the misty fantasies about teachers to concrete realities about them and their careers. By closely examining the types of individuals who become teachers, you may gain insights into your own motivations for considering this vocation.

The first segment of the chapter details the reasons given by teachers concerning their career choice. Some studies suggest psychological factors that draw individuals to a teaching career. Other studies indicate that educators are influenced by the advice or impact of an important person in their lives. Certain social and material benefits of teaching also attract some teachers.

Just as there are different reasons given by teachers for becoming educators, so there is a diversity of backgrounds. Histor-

ical evidence, sociological studies, and surveys are used to construct a profile of today's educators. Using this data, we want to dispel some of the stereotypes mentioned in the previous chapter. The second part of this chapter reviews demographic data regarding age, sex, marital status, social class background, ethnic origin, and geographic distribution of teachers.

The third portion of the chapter highlights the personal attributes and interests of teachers. Political and social affiliations, their sports and hobbies, and their academic abilities and reading preferences will be covered. The implication of the data is that the similarities regarding these attributes and interests are more than mere chance.

Two issues are raised in this chapter—one personal, one professional. When you complete the chapter you should have some answers to the question: Am I like many who are teachers today? The response may raise other personal questions: If I am like most teachers, then can I assume that I will be compatible in most educational situations? If I am not, does it mean that I should not think about becoming a teacher?

The implicit professional issue of the chapter is, What can be done to ensure that the best teachers will be recruited and retained in the classroom?

After you have completed this chapter you should be able to (1) cite at least three reasons why others have chosen teaching as a career, (2) describe what types of individuals usually become teachers, (3) identify personal attributes of teachers, (4) state at least two factors that promote teacher job satisfaction and two factors that diminish it, and (5) determine whether you are like the majority of individuals who are teachers.

REASONS PEOPLE TEACH

It is easy to compile an extensive list of reasons for one to engage in a teaching career. When analyzed, however, they fall into three broad categories— psychological, social, and material. The purpose of this section is to identify and compare the types of motivation behind your consideration of a teaching career rather than select the one or two specific factors that influence you.

ACTIVITY 3–1
Why Teach?

The questions below may help you understand why you are exploring teaching as a career. This activity will be enhanced if you reconsider your written responses toward the end of the course.

1. What are your reasons for wanting to be a teacher?
2. Can you identify any individual or incident that led you to want to teach?
3. Do you like to spend time with young people? Which particular age group do you prefer to work with?
4. What makes the experience of working with children or young adults satisfying for you?
5. What talents and knowledge do you have that you can share with students?
6. What are your attitudes about working with students of different racial, ethnic, or social class backgrounds?
7. Are you attracted to teaching because there is a particular group you would like to work

with, such as the emotionally disabled? Have you ever worked with students who will have special educational needs? Are you a patient person?

8. Are there any additional reasons for your interest in teaching?

Source: Many of these questions were modified from Herb Kohl, "Why Teach?" *Teacher* 94, no. 3 (November 1976): 73–79.

Psychological Influences

When we discuss the importance of early life experiences and the power of the family to set lifelong trends, we must acknowledge that patterns established in childhood can influence ultimate career decisions. Some children develop fantasies about teaching that they later "live out" when they become educators. Some research indicates that teachers tend to be individuals who were active talkers, moralizers, and manipulators as children. Numerous reports indicate that many teachers had parental or familial models that they wanted to emulate when they became adults.[1]

All human beings have emotional needs. In our interactions with others we attempt to meet our needs, which, of course, can be done constructively or destructively. The needs mentioned here are not unique to teachers, but they are frequently observed in classroom interactions. Teachers seek a lot of *affection*. They want to be admired and respected, and they relate best to students who respect them personally and professionally. Some teachers like *order* and *authority* status. They are comfortable when they control a classroom and determine rules and policies. Conversely, in many ways teaching is appropriate for individuals who prefer *dependence*. They like a system in which someone else (the principal) will handle major decisions. Routines are clear, and one soon learns how to act to get along. In short, some individuals do not want to take risks, and the school can be a place where risks are minimized. Similarly, the classroom offers a captive audience for those individuals who like to perform, i.e., need *attention*.[2]

Another very natural reason some individuals are attracted to teaching is that they enjoyed school. They had positive experiences in the classroom as well as in extracurricular activities. Such events as school dances, theatrical plays, and field

Reprinted with permission from "Values and Schools," cartoon essay by Elsa Bailey, *Colloquy*, January 1970. Copyright 1969 by United Church Press.

AH DON'T CARE *WHAT* THEY TOLD YOUALL UP NAWTH. YOU'RE GOING TO *STAND THERE* IN THAT CORNER UNTIL YOUALL ADMIT THE SOUTH WON THE WAR.

Chapter Three

trips in the spring were and are exciting to them.

Humanitarian Influences

A National Education Association survey found that the three most frequently stated reasons teachers give for their vocational choice are social or humanitarian. "Desire to work with young people" was most often cited, followed by the "value of education to society." These were chosen equally by men and women, and consistently by various age groups of teachers. Predictably, secondary teachers were more likely to indicate an interest in their subject field (and a belief in its importance for society's benefit) than were elementary teachers.[3]

There are cultural influences which may cause you to consider teaching as a career. Some families have a tradition of sons and daughters going into so-called service vocations—nursing, teaching, medicine, social work, the ministry, and law. Traditionally (but changing rapidly), parents have frequently recommended the teaching profession to their daughters as a most appropriate career.[4]

For some, a career in teaching may be a chance to continue a talent or field of study that otherwise might be thwarted. Individuals who dreamed of a career as a professional musician or a star on Broadway, for example, may find such aspirations impossible. They turn to teaching as a vehicle with which they can continue their interests. Also, there are teachers who reject jobs in industry or the laboratory because they find greater satisfaction in teaching others new skills.[5]

Material Influences

Material influences mean work-related conditions rather than material benefits or remuneration. For example, ostensibly short hours, little weekend work (except coaching and grading papers), numerous holiday breaks, and a long summer vacation attract many to teaching.

The salary level of teachers is not par-

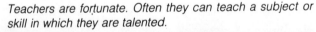

Teachers are fortunate. Often they can teach a subject or skill in which they are talented.

ticularly high compared with some other occupations requiring a similar amount of education and training (see Chapter 5). Historically, many women found salaries in teaching higher than in other fields open to them.

A career in education can be a form of security. Job termination is comparatively common in industry, but teaching offers tenure for the experienced teacher. Few teachers are fired, although school districts are increasingly faced with declining enrollments, which may bring teacher layoffs. A related factor is that salary increases in

teaching are based on clearly known criteria—years of experience and academic credits.

For a few people, teaching offers another benefit. It can be a job that has easy entry and reentry, enabling a person to leave the classroom to try another career, and return should that not succeed. This benefit may be less available, however, when there are many more teachers than openings in the field.

Some of these factors could be either positive or negative. The long summer break may be seen as either a vacation or

ACTIVITY 3–2

My Vocational Heritage

Complete the chart below to aid you in discerning the vocational and educational roots and values which you have received from your family. You may wish to redesign the diagram to include the occupations of additional relatives (uncles, cousins). In the "A" space, place the primary vocation. The "B" space is for the formal schooling the individual has received.

After you have filled in the chart, discuss these questions:

1. What vocational and educational patterns did you discover?
   a. Is your family clustered in certain vocations, i.e., business, labor, professional, "service"?
   b. Has the level of schooling increased from one generation to the next? If so, what factors best explain the change?
2. What impact has your family had upon your vocational choice?
3. What would you say to your own children or students about how much schooling they should have and what career choices they might make?

Paternal		Maternal	
Grandfather	Grandmother	Grandfather	Grandmother
A._____	A._____	A._____	A._____
B._____	B._____	B._____	B._____

Father	Mother
A._____	A._____
B._____	B._____

Sibling:_____	YOU	Sibling:_____
A._____	A._____	A._____
B._____	B._____	B._____

a financial drawback, since many districts pay only during the months of actual teaching. The security that some relish will be regarded as too stifling by others. In summary, you must weigh carefully the various material benefits of teaching since, like many other professions, the advantages are not all that clear-cut.

TEACHER BACKGROUND

Just who does go into teaching?

In Chapter 2 you learned that there are many stereotypes about educators, and that such expectations, reinforced by nostalgic accounts, television portrayals, and the rhetoric in professional journals, may distort the realities about teachers. The number of reliable studies about teachers is small. Often, those who have written about teachers are educators themselves. Deliberately or unintentionally, they tend to show teachers in the best light. Some, who sincerely want to upgrade the profession, depict teachers as financially poor but sincere individuals who have been inadequately prepared and rewarded. More rigorous historical and sociological studies did not begin until the twentieth century.[6]

Most of this section will focus on the sociological data regarding the background of teachers in the 1970s. However, it is vital to develop some comparisons with teachers of previous decades and centuries, and the opening segment provides an historical overview that focuses upon the socioeconomic status and ethnic patterns of the teaching force.

A word of caution about the sources used throughout this chapter: much of the data on the social, economic, and personal background of teachers is based on information collected by the National Education Association or other professional education groups. You should remember that surveys of this sort may be written in such a way as to gain support for the sponsoring organization's goals and stated positions. Further, the NEA studies are not representative of all teachers (more than 70% of the respondents are NEA members). Moreover, most education questionnaires compare teachers with each other and not to other professional groups. For example, later in the chapter where teachers' political views are examined, it is not known whether the teacher's perception of themselves as "conservative" is similar to the perceptions social workers or doctors have about their political outlook.

Profile of Educators of the Past

Why is it important to have an understanding of historical, socioeconomic, and ethnic data regarding teachers? Isn't how you relate to your students, fellow teachers, and administrators, more significant than your parents' social status? Certainly it is, but the reality is that just as your temperament is related to your biological makeup, so some of your actions reflect your cultural heritage.

Social scientists have demonstrated, for example, in rather convincing fashion, that social class is one (if not the major) determinant of the extent of formal schooling individuals are likely to attain and the types of positions they hold. More specifically, there is much evidence to suggest that how well or poorly teachers and their students interact is highly related to their respective social classes. Similarly, the social class background of a teacher can have a major effect on how the teacher relates to other staff members, the administration, and likely, the school board.[7]

Moreover, social class differences are revealed in numerous ways that have classroom implications. Language patterns vary among social classes as they do among ethnic groups. The number of words in the vocabulary, the complexity of sentences, and the organization and presentation of problem-solving techniques are different from class to class. The use of force for disciplining likewise varies, as does the condoning of certain vulgar words. A teacher from an upper-middle-class background may be more offended by the students' use of incorrect grammar or particular four-letter words than will a teacher from a lower-middle-class home. Conversely, a teacher from a lower-class family who is teaching in an upper-middle-class school may believe in disciplining by spanking or shaming the students, techniques not as frequently employed by upper-middle-class parents.

Social class background can also have an impact on teacher-teacher and teacher-administrator or school board relationships. Elementary teachers may be alienated from secondary teachers in a district because of the likelihood that the elementary teachers come from a lower-class background. Administrators, as a group, tend to come from a lower social class than do teachers. This implies that the administrator, more concerned than the teacher about social standing in the community, is more likely to defend the status quo. Similarly, since studies confirm that the social standing of school board members is predominantly upper-middle-class, policies set by the board members are most likely partial to that class.[8]

To repeat, generalizations must be made cautiously, especially in their application to individuals. At this point they are used to help us understand some of the broad dynamics that occur in the classroom and school system. Two generalizations are underscored in this and succeeding sections: teaching is a solidly middle-class occupation, and it provides a route for upward social mobility for those from lower social classes.[9]

In the colonial world, it was common for ministers to teach. But many other individuals taught also, and it is difficult to generalize about their social class background. Teachers were usually impoverished economically. As a seventeenth-century rector of Annapolis noted, when ships arrived from England carrying indentured servants, the schoolmasters among them did not bring as good a price as weavers, tailors, or other tradesmen.[10]

When the new nation emerged in the 1790s, most teachers came from the lower-middle class. Such forces as urbanization, secularization, and school expansion (both in total school enrollments and in the settlement of the West), changed the profile of the American teacher. Increasing numbers of women became teachers. Because women were hired at lower wages, the financial status of teachers compared with other working groups did not improve and, in fact, may have declined. During the middle and latter part of the nineteenth century, teachers were paid wages approaching those paid to skilled artisans and common laborers, but were below the incomes of ministers, physicians, and lawyers.[11]

Twentieth-century studies note that 30% to 40% of the teachers surveyed indicated their fathers were blue-collar workers. Comparing data relative to teachers in the 1930s and 1940s with data relative to teachers in the 1910s and 1920s, it appears teachers of the earlier period were from slightly higher social origins. An extensive study published in 1941 revealed that 26% of the teachers surveyed had fathers who owned small businesses, 18% had fathers who were day laborers, and 4% had fathers who were professionals. The largest percentage of teachers in that survey came from farm families. More recent surveys indicate a severe drop in the farm-family category (greater than the decline in farm population), and an increase in those whose fathers are from professional ranks. Further, studies in the twentieth

Chapter Three

In the late nineteenth and early twentieth century many students were children of immigrants. A significant number would become teachers some day.

century suggest that there are differences between the social class backgrounds of men and women educators. In 1971, for example, 44% of the men teachers had fathers who were unskilled, semi-skilled, or skilled workers, compared to 29% of the women teachers. Thus more men than women come to teaching from lower status backgrounds.[12]

From the foregoing data, it appears that teaching is an anomaly; it has relatively high respectability, i.e., prestige, but offers low income. Perhaps there is no better illustration of teaching's aura of respectability than the frequency with which immigrants turned to a career in teaching as the vehicle for their children to escape the poverty of the ghettos.

This was a phenomenon evident by 1900, especially in the cities. As public school enrollments in the cities increased, teachers were likely to be recruited from the ethnic groups that dominated the neighborhoods. Forty-four percent of urban teachers were second-generation immigrants whose families had come from Britain, Germany, and Canada.[13] In the West, large numbers of Scandinavians and other northern Europeans were added to instructional staffs.

Beginning in the early decades of the twentieth century, and escalating after World War II, Jewish and Italian-American teachers emerged in greater numbers in the cities, together with second- and third-generation Poles and Greeks. Although the numbers were small, there were increases in teachers from Chinese, Japanese, and other Asian backgrounds after World War II. The growing enrollments of Hispanics and Chicanos have been accompanied by an increase in the number of teachers from those ethnic backgrounds.[14]

In the early nineteenth century, many

American Indian tribes had high literacy rates and their own systems of education. In the antebellum period, missionary groups attempted to convert the so-called savage Indians, and the use of Indian teachers was discouraged. By the 1880s and 1890s, the federal government used boarding schools, administered by the Bureau of Indian Affairs (BIA), to destroy tribal society. Indian children were routinely taken from families and tribes and educated at distant schools, where they were punished if they spoke their native language or sang Indian songs. In the 1930s, a gradual softening of that position began. Currently, BIA schools (there are 224 of them, with 41 other schools educating Indian students on a contract basis) give preference in hiring to Indian teachers. Most Indian teachers do work in such schools.[15]

After the Civil War, southern states established separate schools for blacks. Likewise, church denominations founded black colleges in the South. Deprived of entering other professions, graduates of the black colleges often became teachers. By the end of the 1920s, an estimated 50,000 black teachers were employed in the District of Columbia and 17 states that had mandatory segregation. The migration of blacks to the North in the twentieth century was followed by increasing numbers of black teachers in northern schools. Yet blacks, like other minority groups, experienced job-ceiling pressures, i.e., they were denied training for and access to certain professions that whites were receiving. For example, when desegregation was enforced by the courts in the 1950s and 1960s, a number of black schools in the South were closed. The newly integrated schools hired white teachers, including inexperienced ones, over blacks who were experienced.[16]

In summary, teaching has been an avenue for ethnic and minority youth to im-

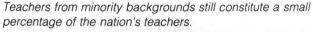
Teachers from minority backgrounds still constitute a small percentage of the nation's teachers.

Chapter Three

Table 3–1.
Percentage of teachers by racial groups by region and size of district

| Racial groups | Total | Region | | | | Size of district (by student enrollment) | | |
		Northeast	Southeast	Midwest	West	25,000 & over	3,000– 24,999	2,999 & less
Black	8.4	6.1	19.3	3.6	4.4	15.2	7.6	3.1
White	90.2	93.6	80.3	96.2	90.5	81.4	91.9	95.7
Indian	0.3	0.0	0.2	0.0	1.0	0.2	0.2	0.4
Asian	1.1	0.3	0.2	0.2	4.1	3.1	0.3	0.7

Source: National Education Association, *Research Memo, Nationwide Teacher Opinion Poll, 1979* (Washington, D.C.: National Education Association, 1979), p. 10.

prove their social standing. One illustration of this is that minority students, much more so than whites, will have a higher percentage of degrees in education. More importantly, as Table 3–1 indicates, minority and ethnic teachers often teach in schools serving predominantly the children of their own background. The first generation of ethnics is likely to live in a neighborhood that is comprised of its own heritage, but by the third generation, the teachers may be instructing a more diverse student body.

Age

Clearly, teaching is a profession for the young. The largest group of teachers is the under-30 category, and the smallest group is comprised of those 50 years and older. (See Figure 3–1.)

These figures, compared with data from the 1960s and 1970s, deserve further analysis. The average age of teachers declined from 41 in 1960–61 to 33 in 1975–76. In the 1980 NEA study it rose to 36. The median number of years of teaching ex-

Figure 3–1.
Age groups and years of experience of teachers

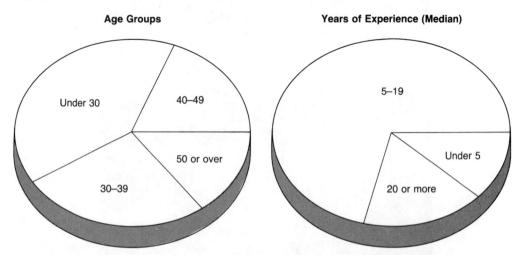

Age Groups

Under 30
40–49
50 or over
30–39

Years of Experience (Median)

5–19
Under 5
20 or more

Source: National Education Association, *Research Memo* (Washington, D.C.: National Education Association, July 1980), pp. 2–3.

Cartoon by Kaufman, Master's Agency. Reprinted with permission.

"Hawkins, you've been with us a long time . . ."

perience dropped, from 11 years in 1961 to 8 years in 1976. In 1980 it rose again to 11. What will be the trends of the future? Will the stress on teachers (discussed later in this chapter) force experienced educators from the classroom? On the other hand, will an inflationary economy keep more persons with experience in the classroom and thereby continue the trend of rising average age of teachers? Will the perceived teacher surplus and/or declining student enrollment reduce the number of job opportunities for new teachers?[17]

Sex

In 1980, 68% of the teachers in America were women. In 1929–30, by contrast, approximately 75% were women, and in 1919–20, it was even higher, 86%. As these figures indicate, the general trend is for more men to enter teaching. At the elementary level, men constitute almost 10% of the educators, whereas at the secondary level, they hold 60% of the positions. In 1977, however, the percentage of male teacher-education graduates had dropped to 30%, which was similar to the percentage of men going into teaching in 1973–74

(during the Vietnam years), but lower than the 44% male enrollment in 1962–63.

Women and men teachers have nearly equal amounts of teaching experience and work the same number of hours per week. (Teachers, incidentally, average about 48 hours of work per week, including work at home.) Men, however, receive higher income from teaching than women. In 1980 the mean salary men received was $16,976, approximately $2,060 more than women teachers received. The men are not paid more initially, but they are more likely to have advanced degrees (see Table 3–2). They are also more likely to take on assignments (such as coaching) that provide additional income.[18]

Marital Status

Most teachers are married. According to 1979 data, 73% of all teachers are married. Another 10% are widowed, separated, or divorced, while 17% are single. According to other recent studies, a surprisingly large portion of teachers (43%) do not have children, although this is most likely true for the youngest educators. Only 10% of the teachers had three or more children.[19]

Chapter Three

Geographic Distribution

According to studies in the 1970s, almost 30% of the teachers surveyed were teaching in the same community in which they had lived since childhood. Such variables as the age of the teacher, the region of the country, or the size of the school system were not found to change the findings to any significant degree. Conversations with job-placement officials in recent years support the belief that teachers like to stay in familiar territory. An estimated 80% of teacher-education graduates will find their first positions in the state in which they finish college.[20]

There are several reasons why teachers may identify with the communities where they teach. What may explain why 6 of 10 teachers live within the boundary of the district that employs them is that a number of systems require it. (Generally, the courts have upheld the right of governmental agencies—cities, states, and school districts—to impose this condition of employment.) The size of the district may be another factor. Teachers who are active in school programs may not want to commute long distances. Other teachers may feel that their district is the best in the region, and they want their children to attend it.

These statements do not mean that teachers are frozen into their districts. Nearly half of all teachers have taught in more than one school system; one in five has taught in another state. Teachers also tend to travel. In the 1976 studies, one in four indicated they had been on an educationally related trip within the previous 3 years.

PERSONAL PRIORITIES OF TEACHERS

These data just described reflect factors—sex, ethnic heritage, and social class—over which teachers have no control. This section focuses on selected preferences of teachers—organization affiliations, political involvement, academic pursuits, and sports and leisure activities. The general portrait painted of teachers' priorities should not obscure the individual exceptions that may exist between individual teachers, elementary and secondary teachers, as well as differences among educators in various subject fields.

Social and Professional Organizations

The periodic surveys by the National Education Association of its membership show that teachers belong to a variety of social organizations. The largest percentage (over 70%) belong to a church or synagogue. Slightly over 60% are members of a parent-teacher association. Under 20% belong to women's groups, hobby clubs, veterans groups, or civil liberties organizations. The percentage of teachers belonging to those organizations declined during the 1960s and 1970s, especially among younger teachers.[21]

In the 1972 survey, when asked how active they were in the organizations they joined, 15% of the teachers stated they gave three or more hours per week for group activities. The mean number of hours per week has, however, decreased from two to one.

Eight of 10 teachers were found to be active in one or more organizations. Thirty-six percent of all secondary teachers also held membership in some subject-matter or professional organization. (See Chapter 5.)

Political Affiliations and Beliefs

For many years, because of community expectations, individual and organized teachers maintained a low profile in political affairs. When the NEA surveyed teachers in 1961, only half felt it was proper for teachers to work actively in state or national elections on their own time; one-third opposed and 16% were uncertain. In 1966, 60% of teachers reported they felt restrained from publicly taking sides on political issues outside the classroom. Indeed, most teachers limited their political activity to the privacy of the voting booth—89% voted in 1964, but fewer than 12% contributed money to a political party and fewer than 9% worked for a political party.[22]

Between 1961 and 1971, formal membership in political party organizations dropped drastically from 31% to 13%. By 1980, however, another study revealed that almost two-thirds (64%) of the teachers surveyed classified themselves as a Democrat (40%) or a Republican (24%). Exactly 35% specified they were not affiliated with any political party, while .3% were members of yet another party. Approximately 80% indicated they had voted in the 1972 presidential election and over 70% voted in local elections. (That compares with 63% of the general population above 18 that voted in the 1976 presidential election.)[23]

In the 1971 study, respondents were asked to indicate whether they were liberal, tend to be liberal, tend to be conservative, or are conservative. More than 60% of the teachers rated themselves as being conservative or tending to be conservative. The results of that survey seem supported by another study that was conducted in five rural Pennsylvania counties and Pittsburgh. Researcher Paul Shaw concluded that among the teachers surveyed there was an almost dogmatic commitment to democratic values and the status quo of society.[24]

To what extent do teachers hold political office? Until recent years, the answer would have been, "Not much." In some states, laws required that certain elected offices be held full time, and teachers often felt they could not take a leave of absence from their jobs. In some circumstances,

school districts refused to retain a job for a teacher who wished to take a leave of absence to serve in a political office. To this day, some states prohibit teachers from membership on school boards in the district where they teach because of presumed conflict of interest. In 1975 the National Council of State Education Associations reported that more than 400 educators were serving as legislators. Approximately 2% of the teachers serve in local elected offices.[25]

Intellectual Activities

Because they are college graduates, teachers are above the norm of formal education completed when compared with the general population. In high school, they are among the top 25% of their classes academically. Most studies show that compared with their college classmates, they are ranked about average. Some studies suggest, however, that they are above average at campuses that require a higher grade point average to get into teacher education. Timothy Weaver claims that teacher education students are declining in their rank on standardized tests. In 1970, the high school students planning to become teachers tested in the top one-third of all students on tests like the SAT. Six years later they were found to be in the bottom one-third.[26]

On several different instruments comparing students from various career options, education majors were usually ahead of students in office-clerical and vocational-technical fields. One reason why graduate students in education do not have as high a grade point as do students in other graduate areas is that the number of graduate students in education is much larger than in other disciplines. Other graduate programs are highly selective and may take only the top 3% to 5% of those applying. Because many states require that teachers engage in graduate study to keep

Chapter Three

their certification, not all teachers seeking advanced training are top students. But to conclude that education students are poor graduate students is an unfair generalization.

The fact that teachers persist in graduate school and obtain degrees beyond the bachelor's level, as Table 3–2 reveals, attests to their interest in further education. Not to be forgotten, of course, is the fact that advanced academic work brings increased salaries (see Chapter 5). Other factors also explain teachers' interest in educational attainments: states are upgrading their certification requirements; opportunities in formal education are more readily available (extension courses are offered in more fields and locations). We should note, finally, that Table 3–2 does not reveal how many teachers have taken graduate credits beyond the bachelor's and master's degree levels, which are not counted as part of a degree program.

Several studies of teachers' reading habits show that, besides their reading for formal courses, educators are avid newspaper readers. Many use current events to enhance classroom discussions and provide illustrations for bulletin boards. While they read all segments of the paper, including the editorial pages, teachers indicate that their favorite columns are "Dear Abby" and "Ann Landers."

When polled about their magazine selections, *Reader's Digest* was cited as the leading choice of teachers. *Time* and *Newsweek* were other favorites. What may be of greater significance is that teachers statistically were not attracted to literary magazines such as *Saturday Review* or *Atlantic Monthly*, nor did many subscribe to journals in their teaching fields. The studies did not analyze why teachers did not select such journals. It could be lack of time, lack of interest, or the need to minimize expenses. However, a study published in 1980 noted that teachers spend as much time each week reading as they do watching television (8.6 hours).[27]

Leisure Activities

When teachers are not involved with school work or engaged in social and political activities or study, what do they do? The few existing studies (most are from the 1960s) have concluded that teachers mirror the general public in that they engage in sedentary hobbies. While they like sports, they are more likely to be spectators than participants.[28]

Table 3–2.
Percentage of teachers with academic degrees

Highest degree held	Total	Teaching level			Male	Female
		Elem.	Jr. high	Sr. high		
No degree	.3	.1	.0	.7	1.1	.3
Bachelor's degree	54.0	60.5	52.9	45.1	40.1	57.2
Master's degree	40.4	35.2	41.2	47.3	58.9*	42.4*
Education specialist (or 6-year degree)	4.6	3.9	5.3	5.8		
Doctor's degree	.6	.2	.6	1.1		

*Includes education specialist (or 6-year degree) and doctor's degree because additional breakdown by gender not available for these categories.

Source: National Education Association, *Research Memo, Nationwide Teacher Opinion Poll, 1979* (Washington, D.C.: NEA, 1979), p. 9. © 1979 by the NEA. All rights reserved. Data are based upon a sample survey of public school teachers. Because of rounding, percentages may not equal 100.0.

Myron Brenton has summarized the leisure preferences of teachers: "watching television, visiting people, reading, writing correspondence, attending religious services, dining out, going to parties, listening to records (semiclassical, musical comedy, and folk), and going to the movies . . . but only about one-fourth of the teachers attend a movie theatre as often as once or twice a month."[29]

Of teachers who are physically active, most (about 4 of 10) prefer walking or hiking. With increased interest in jogging, one wonders to what extent an updated study would replace these two pastimes or the more strenuous sports such as tennis or swimming. An older study reported 3 of 10 teachers liked to bowl, fish, or camp. We may project that such a figure is now low. Despite increased activity, it is likely that teachers, as a group, are in rather poor physical shape—like most American adults. David Aspy has reached that conclusion, and he is concerned because he has found a correlation between teaching effectiveness and physical condition.[30]

We may conjecture that school districts increasingly will be concerned about teachers' leisure-time activities. As declining enrollments force schools to combine teaching and extracurricular responsibilities, teachers who are interested in a variety of hobbies and active in sports may be more employable. The passage of Title IX, which mandated the discontinuance of sex discrimination in schools, has meant an increase in the number of athletic teams for women.

TEACHERS: ROOKIES AND VETERANS

To better understand who is going into teaching, we first looked at the background of those, historically and currently, who chose teaching. Then we examined some of the variables about teachers' interests and habits. These two sections helped us focus on the basic question: Are the best candidates going into teaching? If we assume now, based on the evidence, that an above-average, if not superior, pool of potential teachers is going into the profession, we need to ask: What factors keep them in teaching and what factors cause them to leave teaching?

Teacher Turnover

Earlier, we learned that 66% of teachers today have between 5 and 19 years of experience while another 20% have over 20 years in the classroom. Thus there is some stability in the teaching profession, but additional evidence points to a fairly high turnover among those entering the field. For example, an Oregon study found that only 33% of teachers who began teaching in 1962 remained beyond 4 years. However, several studies in St. Louis found that the range of those who did remain 4 or more years was from 44% to 84%.[31]

Nationally, a 1963 study found that slightly over 10% of those teaching that year would not return the following year. More recent data suggests that the dropout rate for teachers has declined to 6% to 8%. State departments of education in Delaware, Illinois, and Michigan report reductions in teacher turnover rates during the 1970s (between 10% and 12% in 1973–74 versus 7.5%–9.5% in 1977–78). The NEA estimates that almost 6% of the teachers employed in the 1978–79 school year were in positions vacated by teachers who did not return.[32]

Obviously, a number of factors explain the turnover of teachers—retirements, disabilities, death, movement of spouse, pregnancy, dismissals, and personal reasons. Personal reasons would include such categories as inability to get along with students, low pay, and poor working conditions. In the remaining sections we will look at factors that provide job satisfaction and those that produce teacher burnout.

Chapter Three

Job Satisfaction

Both the popular press and professional journals often convey the impression that teachers are unhappy with their careers. At least two studies, however, report that over 80% of the respondents indicated that they usually or always liked their work. Even the 1980 NEA survey of teachers, which emphasizes the teachers' dissatisfaction, noted that approximately 65% were satisfied with their jobs. The factors that seemed to have the most negative effect on teachers were the public's attitudes toward the schools, the media's treatment of education, student attitudes toward learning, and salary.[33]

What gives teachers a sense of satisfaction and accomplishment? Sociologist Dan Lortie found that, more than any other factor, teachers base their estimations of professional success or failure on what happens in the classroom.[34] When rating their feelings about school, teachers are more interested in instructor-student inter-

actions than with general school activities. Although there are many opportunities for teachers to work together, most of them want to use their personal interactions with students as the chief element in the evaluation of their success as a teacher.

The school system in America still largely operates in egg-crate fashion, with a single teacher responsible for a specific group of students. This isolation has both positive and negative features. Teachers usually do not like to give up their students to other activities. While they realize they may benefit from other teachers helping them, and sometimes request other teachers to evaluate their performance, most educators prefer to work alone. Apparently, being alone is seen as a way they can assess more easily the impact they have on the lives of their students.[35]

It is instructive to learn what teachers identify as a "good day." A good day occurs when the teacher is eager to go, feeling enthusiastic and possessing a lot of energy. During the day the teacher senses

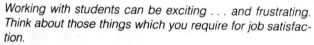

Working with students can be exciting . . . and frustrating. Think about those things which you require for job satisfaction.

he or she is reaching the students. The unit of work planned and assigned is completed with much student interest. The teacher finishes the day perceiving accomplishment. Lortie indicates that teachers in his study judged student participation during a "good day" by the following behaviors: they respond and cooperate, they behave, and they demonstrate positive feelings.[36]

Teachers recognize that good days will be interspersed with a few bad days and many average days. Eaton H. Conant (1974) prepared this description of a typical teaching day for an elementary teacher:

> Teachers spend only 30 percent of their time in activities that are even remotely related to academic instruction and learning—100 minutes out of the five-and-a-half-hour school day. Of the 100 minutes, an average of 75 are devoted to language arts, 18 minutes to numbers/math, and no more than 1 or 2 minutes daily to any other curriculum area, such as science or art. And less than an hour—an average of 59 minutes a day—is spent in individual or small-group teaching, an average of about 2 minutes per child in a class of 25.
>
> "Routine" activities, such as clerical work, housekeeping, child control, and other non-professional work, on the other hand, consume an average of 40 percent of the day. Another 10 percent of the day is accounted for by "non-learning" tasks, such as making announcements, participating in ceremonies, enforcing discipline, and the like. The remainder of the day is taken up with class planning, student evaluation, administrative work, "relaxation," and out-of-class free time.
>
> . . . Time recorded for the "relaxation" or free-time categories was so small that it left only bare traces in our records. But teachers are handed a mixed bundle of professional and non-professional tasks to perform, and the non-professional activities tend to crowd out the opportunities for teaching.[37]

You may wonder whether secondary teachers experience the same general division of responsibilities to oversee during the course of a day. No comparable study exists, as far as we could determine, although such studies as John Goodlad has conducted, suggest that the general relationship between academic instruction and nonacademic tasks is similar.[38]

There is obvious dissonance between this description of a typical good day and what often happens, perhaps explaining why teachers voice frustration about their vocation. Nevertheless, 88% of the 10,000 respondents to a poll by *Instructor* reported that they would be teachers if they had it to do over again. A National Education Association study finding indicated that there are different degrees of satisfaction among teachers at the elementary, junior high, and senior high levels. As a group, the junior high teachers are least satisfied with their pupils and jobs. The married woman who is a veteran of elementary teaching seems to be the most satisfied with the classroom.[39]

Two specific complaints by teachers surface in surveys. The first relates to the lack of respect they feel students show toward their classmates and the teachers. In interviews with one of the authors of this book, one teacher commented, "Even the first graders refuse to believe they have to follow rules. Some of them start yelling 'due process' whenever they are disciplined." The other concern of teachers is a belief that students want too much to be entertained. These complaints are blamed partly on the influence of television. It is probably no coincidence that the National Parent Teacher Association began a major campaign in 1977 to ask parents to look at the impact of that media.[40]

In Lortie's study of 94 teachers, about half mentioned that clerical duties, interruptions, and time pressures constituted severe problems. About the same num-

Chapter Three

"No, Miss Barbara -- that's not how they taught us to do it on 'Sesame Street'."

ber of teachers mentioned troublesome students as a major concern. Fewer teachers mentioned "administrative problems" as an issue. (The term, in this study, referred to problems the teacher had in organizing the classroom as well as relations with school officials.) Relatively few teachers complained about large classes, grading papers, income, and the lack of prestige, or status, in teaching.[41]

Teacher Burnout

The data concerning teachers make clear that teachers, like other members of the service professions—counselors, social workers, doctors and nurses—experience many moments of great exhilaration as well as times of great exhaustion and frustration. The stress of teaching, researchers are saying, has caused educators in recent years to experience unusually high levels of mental fatigue, anxiety, depression, anger, and physical ailments such as high blood pressure and insomnia, producing "burnout."

The teacher organizations (National Education Association and the American Federation of Teachers) are alarmed by the number of teachers who are dropping out and the problems of those staying in the classroom. In a survey conducted by the New York State United Teachers organization, the 10 most stressful situations for teachers were, ranked in order: managing disruptive children; lack of administrative support; maintaining self-control when angry; overcrowded classrooms; opening week of school; disagreeing with a supervisor; dealing with community racial issues; school strikes; being the target of verbal abuse by students; and theft and destruction of teacher property. Further, the study revealed that teachers under the greatest stress, regardless of the work setting, were in the 31–40 age group.[42]

To cope with stress, school districts around the country have tried numerous strategies, for example, rotating teachers' assignments. Various teacher associations have sponsored workshops to warn their members of burnout symptoms. Districts such as Chicago and Tacoma, Washington, have begun self-help programs and therapy groups for teachers. It is likely that teacher organizations will include this topic in future contract negotiations.

Violence in the School. A recurrent theme in interviews with burned-out teachers is that schools have become places of violence. Are they? Even if they are, is the violence of today really different from violence of years past? Is violence occurring in certain types of schools or against certain types of teachers? Most of these questions are hard to answer. Extreme care must be taken in conclusions about violence and vandalism in the schools.

The first question is: Are schools places where violent acts against persons and property occur? The answer, unfortunately, is yes. Over 200,000 persons were assaulted in schools in 1977, a phenomenon most likely to occur in junior high schools, and as prevalent in rural and suburban schools as in urban ones. In that same year, there were 100 murders, 12,000 armed robberies, 250,000 burglaries, and one-half billion dollars in damage from vandalism. Some districts now spend as much for repair of damage from vandalism as they do for the purchase of instructional materials.[43]

Such violence must be discouraging to teachers and to taxpayers. The only good news here is that the incidence of violence appears to have peaked. Concerned teachers avoid the temptation to blame the violence entirely on nonschool factors—television, lack of parental values, rock music, or whatever—and admit that some of the antagonism violently expressed by students may be caused by the rigidity of school curricula, lack of teacher empathy, and rarely, by the provocation of some modern-day Ichabod Cranes.

ACTIVITY 3–3
Visit a School

Arrange a visit to a local elementary or secondary school. Besides observing and recording your reactions to it, plan discussions with teachers and students and ascertain their attitudes about the school. Consider the following questions:

1. What is the condition of the buildings and grounds? Is the design modern, traditional, nondescript? Is there anything unusual or distinctive in appearance? Are there signs of vandalism?
2. As you enter the building, what meets your eye? Is it a display board, a portrait, a trophy case? Do you notice particular odors?
3. As you walk the halls, what do you see? Are they clean or cluttered? Are student displays visible or absent? Do students march in lines or do they move freely?
4. Can you hear many noises? Describe them.
5. What is the size of the school (student enrollment and faculty)?
   a. Do the teachers work alone, have aides, or team-teach? What is the average class size?
   b. Do the classrooms vary much (e.g., in seat arrangements, equipment)?
6. What are the students' attitudes toward school?
7. What are the teachers' attitudes toward school?

SUMMARY

William James, American philosopher and psychologist, once remarked that the nation expected too much of its teachers. There should be no greater number of geniuses among teachers, he reasoned, than among any other group in the country. James' position is relevant to the issues raised in Chapter 3. Are we recruiting and retaining the best candidates as teachers? Would you want to work with today's teachers?

Are the motivations of those going into teaching of the highest quality? Some choose teaching as a career to fill their psychological needs. Some teachers have been strongly influenced by a parent, friend, or teacher to choose education as their life's work. For still others, teaching is a vocational choice based on their interest in young people and/or their commitment to education as a field of service. Others weigh material rewards and job benefits more heavily than humanitarian concerns in their decision to teach.

The section on teacher background posed cautious generalizations about the socioeconomic aspects of teachers today. The key point was that teaching has been and continues to be a middle-class occupation that offers relatively modest pay but some prestige. Although certain variables about teachers' background are in flux (e.g., the average age of teachers), others—particularly the percentage of women in teaching and the number of minority group members who teach—seem to be stabilizing.

You may have been surprised by the data relative to the personal priorities of teachers, if not by information about their backgrounds. Studies show that they are involved in a variety of social clubs, have a conservative bent in political matters, tend to be about average in academic performance compared to other college students, and are like typical Americans in preferring sedentary leisure activities. They are avid readers of newspapers, but not of professional journals. Do these attributes strike you as consistent with the expectations society holds for good teachers?

Finally, Chapter 3 examined evidence about new and experienced teachers, with a focus on what factors related to feelings of success on the job. Although we learned that the teacher turnover percentage is dropping, and some studies show that teachers are happy with their career choices, an alarming number are dissatisfied with current work conditions. Public attitudes about the school, lack of student discipline, and violence have promoted teacher burnout.

As you consider the generalizations drawn in this chapter and in Part 1, remember that there is still a broad spectrum of personality types that have been successful teachers. The American system of education has been flexible enough to allow individual differences. You may conclude now that you fall within the profile sketched here of most teachers, and thus feel more comfortable. Perhaps you realize now that you are outside the mainstream. Do not, in either case, rush into a hasty decision about teaching as a career.

NOTES

1. A summary of studies in this area is found in Allan C. Ornstein, *Education and Social Inquiry* (Itasca, Ill.: Peacock, 1978), pp. 216–18.

2. George G. Stern et al., "Two Scales for the Assessment of Unconscious Motivations for Teaching," *Educational and Psychological Measurement* 21, no. 1 (Spring 1960): 9–27; Ann G. Olmsted et al., "Stances Teachers Take: A Basis for Selective Admission," *Phi Delta Kappan* 55, no. 5 (January 1974): 330–34 describes seven major personality types that enter the classroom; Mary Lynn Crow, "Recognizing the Authoritarian Personality Syndrome in Educators," *Phi Delta Kappan* 57, no. 1 (September 1975): 40–44.

3. National Education Association, *Status of the American Public School Teacher, 1970–71*, Research Report 1972–R3 (Washington, D.C.: National Education Association, 1972), p. 51; R. B. LeMon, "Reach Out, Listen, and Touch Someone," *School and Community* 62, no. 4 (December 1975): 4, suggests some similar reasons teachers mention, and adds certain philosophical and spiritual values teachers profess.

4. Clarence Fielstra, "Analysis of Factors Influencing the Decision to Become a Teacher," *Journal of Educational Research* 48, no. 9 (May 1955): 695–67. He notes that male teachers are twice as likely as female teachers to indicate that the person who most influenced them to teach was an educator rather than a parent.

5. Dan C. Lortie, *Schoolteacher: A Sociological Study* (Chicago: University of Chicago Press, 1975), p. 29.

6. John Calam, "A Letter from Quesnel: The Teacher in History, and Other Fables," *History of Education Quarterly* 15, no. 2 (Summer 1975): 131–46.

7. See Christopher Jencks et al., *Who Gets Ahead?* (New York: Basic Books, 1979).

8. Ellen Hogan Steele, "A Teacher's View," *Phi Delta Kappan* 57, no. 9 (May 1976): 590–92; Wilbur B. Brookover, "Teachers and the Stratification of American Society," *Harvard Educational Review* 23, no. 4 (Fall 1953): 257–67.

9. For a summary of historic studies about social class and teaching, see Robert J. Havighurst and Daniel U. Levine, *Society and Education*, 5th ed. (Boston: Allyn and Bacon, 1979), pp. 513–16.

10. Alma S. Wittlin, "The Teacher," *Daedalus*, Fall 1963: 745–63, especially 750.

11. Lortie, *Schoolteacher*, pp. 7, 12; Willard S. Elsbree, *The American Teacher* (New York: American Book Co., 1939).

12. Havighurst and Levine, *Society and Education*, pp. 514–18; Lortie, *Schoolteacher*, p. 262.

13. David B. Tyack, *The One Best System: A History of American Urban Education* (Cambridge: Harvard University Press, 1974), p. 233.

14. National Education Association, *Research Memo, Nationwide Teacher Opinion Poll, 1980* (Washington,

D.C.: National Education Association, 1980), p. 3. In its annual reports, *The Condition of Education*, the National Center for Education Statistics periodically gives information about the racial and ethnic background of teachers. Similarly, the Office of Civil Rights provides information on the number of minority teachers.

15. Meyer Weinberg, *A Chance to Learn: A History of Race and Education in the United States* (Cambridge: Harvard University Press, 1977), pp. 178–229; Margaret Connell Szasz, *Education and the American Indian: The Road to Self-Determination Since 1928* (Albuquerque: University of New Mexico Press, 1977).

16. Henry Allen Bullock, *A History of Negro Education in the South: From 1619 to the Present* (Cambridge: Harvard University Press, 1967); John U. Ogbu, *Minority Education and Caste: The American System in Cross-Cultural Perspective* (New York: Academic Press, 1978), pp. 154–55.

17. National Education Association, *Status of the American Public School Teacher, 1975–76* (Washington, D.C.: National Education Association, 1977), p. 49; also, from the NEA, *Highlights of Status of Public School Teachers* (Washington, D.C.: NEA, 1976), pp. 1–3; NEA, *Research Memo, 1980*, pp. 2–3.

18. NEA, *Research Memo, 1980*, p. 3.

19. National Education Association, *Research Memo, Nationwide Teacher Opinion Poll, 1979* (Washington, D.C.: National Education Association, 1979), p. 10.

20. NEA, *Status of the American Public School Teacher, 1975–76*, p. 14.

21. Ibid.

22. Ibid., pp. 1–10. Also see National Education Association, *NEA Research Information on the Status of Teachers, 1973* (Washington, D.C.: National Education Association, 1973), Special Memo I-3.

23. NEA, *Status of Teachers, 1973*; National Education Association, *What Teachers Think: A Summary of Teacher Opinion Poll Findings, 1960–65* (Washington, D.C.: National Education Association, 1965), pp. 50–51; NEA, *Research Memo, 1980*, p. 3.

24. Paul C. Shaw, "Teachers' Political Attitudes," *Urban Education* 10, no. 4 (January 1976): 366–78. The NEA study was conducted in 1970 and 1971, reported in *Today's Education* 61, no. 5 (May 1972): 14–17.

25. *Educators Serving as State Legislators* (Washington, D.C.: National Council of State Education Associations, 1975), p. 79: NEA, *Status of Teachers, 1975–76*, pp. 1–3.

26. W. Timothy Weaver, "In Search of Quality: The Need for Talent in Teaching," *Phi Delta Kappan* 61, no. 1 (September 1979): 30.

27. Myron Brenton, *What's Happened to Teacher?* (New York: Coward-McCann, 1970), p. 34, note 4. See also *Teaching* 97, no. 7 (April, 1980): 30 and Thomas W. George, "Teachers Tend to Ignore Professional Journals," *Phi Delta Kappan*, 61, no. 1 (September 1979): 69–70.

28. Research Division, National Education Association, *Reading and Recreational Interests of Classroom Teachers* (Washington, D.C.: National Education Association, 1967), pp. 7–13; Perry London and Donald Larson, "Teachers' Use of Leisure," *Teachers College Record* 65, no. 6 (March, 1964): 538–45.

29. Brenton, *What's Happened to Teacher?*, p. 31

30. Correspondence with David Aspy, Professor at Catholic University, Washington, D.C. Results of his research to appear in forthcoming publication, *Physical Health and Education*.

31. Jonathan H. Mark and Barry D. Anderson, "Teacher Survival Rates—A Current Look," *American Educational Research Journal* 15, no. 3 (Summer 1978): 379–83.

32. National Education Association, *Research Memo, Teacher Supply and Demand, 1977* (Washington, D.C.: National Education Association, 1978), p. 3; NEA, *Research Memo, Teacher Supply and Demand in Public Schools, 1979* (Washington, D.C.: National Education Association, 1980), p. 8.

33. A survey by the American Academy of Family Physicians, reported in *Teaching* 97, no. 7 (April 1980): 30; NEA, *Research Memo, 1980*, p. 4.

34. Lortie, *Schoolteacher*, especially pp. 82–108.

35. Ann Lieberman and Lynne Miller, "The Social Realities of Teaching," *Teachers College Record* 80, no. 1 (September 1978): 54–68.

36. Lortie, *Schoolteacher*, p. 172.

37. Eaton H. Conant, "What Do Teachers Do All Day?" *SR/World*, 1 June 1974, p. 55. Copyright © 1974 by Saturday Review. All rights reserved. Reprinted by permission.

38. M. Frances Klein, Kenneth A. Tye, and Joyce E. Wright, "A Study of Schools: Curriculum," *Phi Delta Kappan* 61, no. 4 (December 1979): 247. John Goodlad's assistants report that at every level of schooling, observers found that instruction occupies about 70% of the class time, approximately 15% is devoted to class routines, and a range of 4 to 12% of the time is spent with discipline situations.

39. National Education Association, *Status of American Public School Teachers, 1969* (Washington, D.C.: National Education Association, 1969). A more recent survey pointed out that those individuals who had made a career change late in life (coming into teaching from some other field) were among the most content teachers.

40. National PTA Television Commission, "Violence on TV: The Effects of Television on Children and Youth," a pamphlet available from the National Congress of Parents and Teachers, Chicago, Ill., copyright 1977. For a general perspective, see Kate Moody, "The Research on TV: A Disturbing Picture," *New York Times*, 20 April 1980, Section 15, p. 17.

41. Lortie, *Schoolteacher*, p. 176.

42. "Teacher Burnout: a Growing Hazard," *New York Times*, 7 January 1979; Dennis Sparks, "Teacher's Center," *Education Today* 68, no. 4 (November/ December 1979): 37–39.

43. James M. McPartland, *Violence in Schools: Perspectives, Programs, and Positions* (Lexington, Mass.: Lexington Books, 1977); Seymour D. Vestermark, Jr., *Controlling Crime in the School* (West Nyack, N.Y.: Parker Publishing Co., 1978).

FOR FURTHER STUDY

Balassi, Sylvester J. *Focus on Teaching*. New York: Odyssey Press, 1968.

Berger, Michael. *Violence in the Schools: Causes and Remedies*. Bloomington, Ind.: Phi Delta Kappa Educational Foundation, 1974.

Gelmas, Paul J. *So You Want to Be a Teacher?* New York: Harper & Row, 1965.

Jackson, Philip W. *Life in Classrooms*. New York: Holt, Rinehart and Winston, 1968.

McPherson, Gertrude H. *Small Town Teacher*. Cambridge: Harvard University Press, 1972.

Rothman, Esther P. *Troubled Teachers*. New York: David McKay Co., 1977.

Schlechty, Phillip. *Teaching and Social Behavior*. Boston: Allyn and Bacon, 1976. Especially Chapter 12, "Teacher Characteristics," pp. 235–51.

Smallwood, James. *And Gladly Teach: Reminiscenses of Teachers from Frontier Dugout to Modern Module*. Norman: University of Oklahoma Press, 1976.

Part 1
Self-Assessment

Date _____

To judge your changing attitudes about a teaching career, the school, and education in general, we suggest you respond to these self-assessment questions as soon as possible, and whenever you complete the additional parts of the book, compare your answers to the same questions.

We realize that some of the items under "Philosophy of Education Statement" and "The School as a Social Institution" will not be discussed in each part. Respond to only those items which are related to that part.

1.0 Decision on Teaching as a Career

1.1 My position regarding teaching as a career *today* is:
(Be as specific as you can, i.e., what type of career you have in mind, what grade level, the type of student you wish to work with, what subject areas, and communities you would most enjoy).

2.0 Philosophy of Education Statement

2.1 Goals of education:
(Questions to be considered: What are the purposes of schooling? How can you tell that a person is educated? Is everyone entitled to formal education?)

2.2 The curriculum:
(Is there a basic curriculum, i.e., a core of courses that everyone should have? If you answer that everyone should have the basics, or the three Rs, what do you really mean? For example, how much math—algebra, calculus—is essential? What about the arts, humanities, physical education?)

2.3 The role of the teacher:
(What is your general impression of the individuals who teach today? What responsibilities should teachers have today?)

2.4 Perceptions of learning:
(How do individuals learn best? How should the learning environment be structured—room design, media to be used, class size?)

2.5 Educational policies and procedures:
(How do you feel about the decision-making process in schooling? Who should control the school—local, state or federal government? Do you have strong feelings about such matters as grading and discipline?)

3.0 The School as a Social Institution

3.1 If you had to use just one word to describe the school, it would be _____because:

3.2 The following list contains just some of the social interactions found in schools. Comment briefly on three of them: student-student; teacher-students; teacher-teacher; teacher-administrator; administrator-school board; school-community.

4.0 Information Gained

4.1 What specific information or concept(s) mentioned in Part 1 did you personally find most significant or interesting?

4.2 What information did you find of least interest?

5.0 Reflection on an Educational Issue

(Select *one* of the three issues below, and outline your position on it. Before the course ends, reread your answer, and note any modifications.)
5.1 (Chapter 1) Am I intellectually and emotionally suited to be a teacher?

5.2 (Chapter 2) Are current community expectations for teachers realistic?

5.3 (Chapter 3) Are the best teachers being hired and retained today?

Part 2
Teaching as a Career

Beginning with a challenge to assess yourself and your career goals, Part I then described the types of individuals who have become teachers. Part I focused on the personal aspect of teaching, with some attention to the expectations society has for its educators.

In contrast, Part 2 stresses what is required of tomorrow's teachers—the social demands of the career, as well as its rewards. Chapter 4 discusses education of and certification requirements for prospective teachers and employment opportunities. Chapter 5 focuses on the teacher as a person likely to be involved in professional organizations and issues. In Chapter 6, the educator's major responsibility, effective teaching, is analyzed. Part 2 concludes with an examination of assessment techniques that teachers and regional groups are using to evaluate student performance.

CAREER PREPARATION AND EMPLOYMENT OPPORTUNITIES

The institution that grants you a degree in education does not certify you to be a teacher; a state agency does. The interesting and complex array of teacher education programs will be discussed briefly. The second segment of Chapter 4 will explore facets of certification, explaining both the process of certification and the types of requirements you must meet to be a teacher.

Another portion of the chapter analyzes the probable teacher supply and demand in the early 1980s. Are some subject matter areas more likely to provide better job opportunities than others? If you want to teach, is there additional training, besides your major, that will enhance your chances of getting a job? As part of the employment profile, education-related positions outside schools also will be examined.

THE TEACHING PROFESSION

Increasingly, teachers are joining organizations that they believe will improve the educational environment for themselves and their students. As a future educator, you need to learn of these associations, their histories, goals, and current strategies. Chapter 5 describes their activities, focusing on collective bargaining, the increasing number of teacher strikes, and their involvement in political affairs. In addition, the chapter highlights some of the major concerns facing teacher organizations today: teacher salary and working conditions, tenure, legal rights, and professional development.

Part Two

EFFECTIVE TEACHING

The school environment changes constantly, and conscientious teachers eagerly seek the right combination of instructional methods to aid pupils in developing their skills and knowledge. When we asked the advice of experienced teachers on what to tell prospective educators about teaching, they suggested we emphasize first that students are individuals who learn in many different ways. The chapter begins with a brief discussion of traditional perspectives on student learning, and how it has been refined in the last 100 years.

The second section of Chapter 6 highlights some of the major battles regarding the most effective instructional techniques and educational variables. Researchers disagree about the impact of class size, room decor, and teacher attitudes toward students on student performance. What can teachers do to motivate students and reduce disciplinary problems?

A perennial question of teachers, administrators, school boards, and the public is: What is effective teaching? A related question is: What criteria should be used in evaluating teaching performance? The final segment of the chapter discusses the many ways teachers can be evaluated.

ASSESSMENT OF LEARNING

Questions about effective teaching methods and the performance of individual teachers are related ultimately to the basic question: Has student performance been altered in any significant way? In light of such factors as the rapidly escalating costs of education and declining test scores, consumers of schooling (students and their parents especially) want proof that educational systems are offering meaningful programs. The chapter reviews assessment procedures—from teacher-made tests to grading systems to national evaluations of student work and abilities. Because of the controversies surrounding standardized achievement and aptitude tests and minimum competency examinations, those topics will be covered in more depth.

ISSUES OF PART 2

When you have completed Part 2, you should have a good idea of what it takes to be a teacher today, from the requirements you must meet to the types of decisions that have to be made daily in the classroom. You should also have a more specific idea of employment opportunities in your areas of interest.

By the end of Part 2, you should have informed opinions on the following issues:

1. Who should set the standards for teacher certification requirements?

2. Is there a teacher surplus?

3. What role should teachers have in determining salaries, working conditions, and educational policy?

4. What criteria should be used in determining effective teaching performance?

5. Are national assessment evaluations or standardized tests necessary and/or valuable?

4

Career Preparation and Employment Opportunities

For as a society makes up its mind about the education of its teachers, it is really undertaking to define its own future.

Lawrence A. Cremin

Teacher education provokes debate. For those who believe teaching is a talent that one either has or doesn't have, teacher training programs seem a waste of time, or worse, a deliberate societal device to weed out creative educators. For those who hold that teaching is more a science than an art, teacher training is vital.

How do the states regulate the quality of teacher preparation programs? Who should control teacher preparation? Are teacher education programs providing adequate job skills? If not, can the programs

be improved under the existing organizational framework, or is it necessary to shift the decision-making powers to other groups such as teacher organizations or federal agencies? Other questions can be raised about the process and criteria used to certify teachers.

There may be less debate about the second major topic of the chapter—supply and demand of teachers. Whether there is a teacher surplus is not an easily answered question, as the data show. Because employment opportunities in nonschool positions appear to be rising, these careers will be discussed in some detail. Finally, there is a description of the procedures that teachers may use in job searching. You may find this beneficial even in getting a summer job.

After you have read Chapter 4, you

should be able to (1) describe three major components in teacher education, (2) list the basic elements in the certification process, (3) determine the employment possibilities in your content area or teaching field, and (4) identify three employment areas outside the classroom for individuals with teaching certificates.

APPROACHES TO TEACHER EDUCATION

How many individuals have been (or are being) trained to teach? One writer estimates "that from the end of the Civil War until Pearl Harbor, at least 50 percent of all persons completing two years or more of college were destined to teach in school or college."[1] Between 1941 and 1957, the percentage had dropped to 33%. Today, between 15% and 20% of those students in two-year and four-year institutions of higher education are in teacher education programs.

There are usually three major components in teacher education programs. The first is a general education requirement, a block of courses which is still called the "liberal arts core" on some campuses. It is usually a distribution of humanities, natural science, and social science courses. The second component of teacher education programs is the major or area of specialization. While this is largely content-oriented, it sometimes includes special methodology courses for teaching subject matter in the major. The third component of teacher education programs is the professional or education course sequence.

The balance, or rather imbalance, among the three elements has produced heated debates. Critics such as James Conant and James Koerner felt that there were too many education courses and not enough subject-matter courses or general education options.[2] In light of such criticism, liberal arts and subject-matter courses in-creased in recent years, but the pendulum is swinging again in favor of more field experiences and technical expertise.

Because the education component receives the most criticism, it is important to understand what it contains. Haberman and Stinnett provide a helpful review of the predominant emphases.[3] Most programs begin with or include one or two courses in foundations of education, to provide teacher candidates with knowledge about the *social setting* of the school. Prospective teachers are alerted to the ways in which cultures, past and present, have asked schools to meet society's goals. Such courses may stress the history and philosophy of education, or analyze sociological trends.

Either directly or indirectly, teacher education programs indicate *ethical* approaches a teacher should follow in the classroom. Some programs encourage teachers to be democratic, while others stress that teachers need to be authority figures. Many schools promote the work ethic. Recently, there has been much discussion about preparing future educators to incorporate *affective* goals (e.g., helping students to build good self-concepts) as well as *cognitive* goals in the classroom. The popularity of values clarification and moral-development activities in schools may lead to more discussion of values in teacher-education courses.

How students learn is discussed in several teaching courses. On many campuses, a course in developmental psychology is required, covering the *characteristics of learners* and *learning theories*. Methods courses may treat learning theories as well as techniques for teaching students how to *think conceptually*.

Most programs of teacher education provide a cluster of courses on *teaching methodology, technology*, and *curriculum*. The goals of these courses include improving teaching skills, analyzing curricu-

FRANKLY SPEAKING .... by phil frank

Courtesy of College Media Services, Berkeley, California.

lum, designing behavioral objectives, and preparing daily and unit lesson plans. The emphasis in these courses is upon day-to-day classroom techniques. Operating media equipment and presenting mini-lessons for peers are frequently stressed in such courses.

The capstone of the teacher-education professional courses is *student teaching*. Usually, it is the final course and is roughly analogous to the medical student's internship. Frequently, student teaching is mentioned by education graduates as the most meaningful course in their program. That is to be expected. Although the total education package is often viewed as a major part of a student's program, in fact all education courses, including student teaching, typically represent only 20% or 25% of the total credits.

Variations in Teacher-Education Programs

Although teacher-education programs have similar requirements, they also display a range of organizational patterns. The 4-year format is the most common. Students con-

centrate upon their general education courses during the first 2 years. In the sophomore and junior years, professional and specialization courses are introduced. Under the 5-year plan, students focus on their majors and general education requirements during the first 4 years, with the fifth year devoted to professional courses.

The 4-year plan enables students to learn quickly whether a career in education is appropriate for them. Another advantage is that they can blend what they are learning in their subject-matter courses with their education courses. The chief advantage of the 5-year plan is that a more thorough general background and major can be developed.

Performance-Based Teacher Education (PBTE) or Competency-Based Teacher Education (CBTE) is a recent development.[4] A PBTE program divides teaching skills into discrete, specific behaviors that can be observed and measured objectively. Such a program does not usually or necessarily eliminate courses, but frequently reorganizes them into modules or units which may have self-paced instructional kits. When students feel ready to be tested on the new knowledge or skill acquired, they arrange to demonstrate their mastery to the instructor.

You may realize now that the design of teacher-education programs is far from simple. While there may be numerous similarities, these approaches reflect differing points of view about the roles and responsibilities of teachers. There always have been, and will continue to be, debates among special interest groups, subject-matter specialists, and teacher organizations about the structure of teacher-education programs.

Trends in Teacher Education

The availability of federal and state funds, the power of various pressure groups, and the priorities of local institutions change

Chapter Four

the shape of teacher education from year to year. Although it is therefore difficult to predict general trends in teacher education, at least three appear strong enough to continue in the 1980s: increasing contact of teacher candidates with schools prior to student teaching; the expansion of student teaching; and the addition of interpersonal and intergroup training in communication skills.

A number of factors explain why teacher-education programs demand that students spend more time working in schools prior to student teaching. Future teachers want to learn early whether teaching is a viable career choice; teacher organizations wish to make a greater impact on future educators; administrators in the schools welcome extra help; accreditation groups such as the National Council for the Accreditation of Teacher Education (NCATE) want to upgrade the internship aspect of the profession; and state legislators exert pressure to improve programs.[5]

A number of colleges now provide opportunities for their students to work as teacher aides while they are enrolled in their first education course. Aides may assist reading groups, provide individual attention to students, prepare bulletin boards, correct exams, and work with individuals and groups on research projects.[6]

All groups that support the professionalization of teaching are advocates of a rigorous and extended student teaching experience, as are state departments of education. Ultimately, each state sets its own requirements. The minimum in most states is specified either as semester units of credit or as a time allotment (the number of hours or weeks). While a half-semester is common, some states mandate a full semester of student teaching. The general trend has been to increase from a minimum of 6 weeks to 16 weeks. A proposal to convert student teaching into an internship of one year has gained national attention.[7]

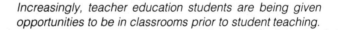

Increasingly, teacher education students are being given opportunities to be in classrooms prior to student teaching.

Officials in higher education are concerned that high school graduates are entering colleges with deficiences in writing and conceptual-thinking skills. Some likely trends are more requirements in mathematics and English composition. For those students going into teacher education, oral communication skills may also be stressed.

More than 30 states have passed legislation requiring that teacher-education programs contain some form of human relations training. Most of the programs include two aspects. The first teaches students listening skills, procedures for conflict resolution, techniques of constructive criticism, and awareness of their biases. The second area is multicultural education. Students are expected to learn about the life-styles and contributions of various racial and ethnic groups. Increasingly, multicultural education is envisioned as a goal of the total teacher-education curriculum, not just material to be concentrated in one or two courses.[8]

THE CERTIFICATION PROCESS

Teacher candidates must not only pass their college's requirements but also be certified by the state in which they plan to teach. Just what does *being certified* mean? What criteria are used? How is a certificate obtained? Will a certificate be valid in other states? Not only is this information personally useful, but the process of certification is another facet of the issue of who controls teacher education.

What Is Certification?

Certification can be defined as "a process of legal sanction authorizing the holder of a credential to perform specific services in the public schools of the state."[9] A certificate is, in essence, a license to teach. The license indicates what level and broad areas you may teach, such as elementary education, K-12 physical education, or art.

These teaching areas are sometimes referred to as *endorsements* or *endorsement areas*. A certificate may also state that you are qualified to teach in more specialized areas, e.g., driver's education or coaching. Also, if you are a secondary teacher, your endorsement might be social studies, but your *approval areas* could include world history, political science, economics, and geography. (Each state may have different terminology concerning certification provisions.)

Another important term is *approved program,* the approach to certification adopted in 18 states. Each institution in those states submits what it considers an acceptable course of study for each area in which it prepares teachers. Of course, the state provides some minimum criteria for the programs. The minimum criteria are usually proposed by advisory committees whose members reflect such groups as teacher organizations, administrators, school boards, and teacher educators. Also, the directors of the states' certification departments share information with each other.

The responsibility for certifying teachers belongs to an agency or division of the state department of education. The title of the agency varies from state to state. This bureau is under the jurisdiction of the chief state school officer and, of course, is subject to the rules established by the state board of education and the legislature (see Chapter 9).

Who Is Certified?

If you want to be a public school teacher or administrator in any state in the nation, you must be certified. Not only does this apply to kindergarten through 12th grade teachers, it encompasses other areas as well. Counselors, librarians, remedial reading specialists, and learning disabilities teachers are likely to need certification in most states. Junior-college instructors increasingly are being required to have a certificate.[10]

Those who plan to teach in nonpublic schools and vocational training programs may find that they need certificates also. In some states, anyone teaching children who are in the age ranges of compulsory attendance must have a valid teacher's certificate, regardless of the type of school.

The general trend in education is to have more certification fields. In part, the movement is due to the development of new fields of knowledge. Often, an emerging field of expertise wishes certification; those in the area want others to recognize that they have a legitimate body of knowledge and skills requiring specialized training. The school psychologist is one example of a relatively new field of certification. Even in such nonteaching positions as attendance officers, school social workers, and school bus drivers, some states require certification.[11]

What Are the Criteria for Certification?

All states now require a bachelor's degree to teach at the elementary or secondary level. Among the general requirements for certification in many states are that the teacher be recommended by the college or employer (44 states); a minimum age, ranging from 17 to 20 (33 states); United States citizenship (25); an oath of loyalty or allegiance (13); and a general health certificate (18).[12]

National or local examinations may be part of the screening process for teachers and are sometimes used for certification per se. In Mississippi, North Carolina, and South Carolina, the National Teachers Examination is a prerequisite to certification. In Florida and several other states, prospective educators must obtain a certain score before they can be considered eligible for a contract. Some cities, like Chicago, also use the National Teacher Examination, but others, including New York

City and Dallas, have developed their own examinations.[13]

In addition, 22 states test specific phases of teacher preparation. In teaching areas where a specific skill level is required, such as music, teachers may have to demonstrate that skill. Certain states require that teachers of foreign languages pass a test showing their writing proficiency in the language.

What Are the Steps in Being Certified?

For most applicants the certification procedure is simple. The student's main responsibility is to complete the prescribed course of study, i.e., the approved program, at the institution. It is also the individual's responsibility to make sure he or she has successfully completed any special requirements for endorsements and approval areas. Most colleges require students to register formally in the institution's teacher-education program sometime in the sophomore or junior year, so that their progress through the program can be monitored.

In the student's last school term, after it has been ascertained that all the requirements have been met, the certification officer at the institution files the student's name (and in some cases, record) with the appropriate state agency. An application fee may be required. The student receives the teaching certificate either with the diploma or four to six weeks later.

What Is Reciprocity?

Will the certificate you obtain in one state be good in another? Not necessarily, because all states do not have exchange, or *reciprocity* agreements. You should investigate whether the states where you are likely to work have reciprocity agreements with the state where you are studying.

The Interstate Agreement on Qualification of Educational Personnel and the Na-

An example of a state certification form.

4600-D4711-3/79

Form 2-73
Revised 11/78

State of Iowa
DEPARTMENT OF PUBLIC INSTRUCTION
Teacher Education and Certification Division
Grimes State Office Building
Des Moines, Iowa 50319

TEACHER APPROVAL STATEMENT

I. TO BE COMPLETED BY APPLICANT (Use Typewriter or Print)					
1. Applicant's Folder Number	2. Social Security Number	3. Date of Birth	Month	Day	Year
		XXXXXXXXXX			

4. Last Name	First Name	Middle Name	Maiden Name	Gender
				☐ Male ☐ Female

5. Street and Number or R.F.D.	City	State	Zip Code

II. *TO BE COMPLETED BY DESIGNATED RECOMMENDING OFFICIAL AT TEACHER EDUCATION INSTITUTION*

A. This person has completed an approved elementary teacher education program. If so indicated below, the person has completed an approved program for teaching the specific subject(s) or area(s) checked below in kindergarten and grades one through nine.

B. This person has completed an approved secondary teacher education program and an approved program for teaching the specific subject(s) or area(s) checked below in grades seven through twelve.

APPROVAL AREAS

1. AGRICULTURE
General . . . .(31) ☐
Vocational . . . .(32) ☐

2. ART . . . .(34) ☐

3. BUSINESS EDUCATION
Accounting . . . .(35) ☐
Business Law . . . .(36) ☐
Basic Business . . . .(37) ☐
Shorthand . . . .(38) ☐
Typewriting . . . .(39) ☐
Data Processing . . . .(100) ☐
Office Skills . . . .(101) ☐

4. DISTRIBUTIVE EDUCATION . . . .(40) ☐

5. DRIVER EDUCATION . . . .(41) ☐

6. ENGLISH . . . .(45) ☐

7. HEALTH. . . . .(102) ☐

8. HOMEMAKING
General. . . . .(50) ☐
Vocational . . . .(51) ☐

9. INDUSTRIAL ARTS. . . . .(53) ☐

10. JOURNALISM . . . .(47) ☐

11. LANGUAGES
French . . . .(54) ☐
German. . . . .(55) ☐
Latin . . . .(56) ☐
Russian . . . .(90) ☐
Spanish. . . . .(57) ☐

12. MATHEMATICS . . . .(58) ☐

13. MUSIC . . . .(60) ☐

14. OFFICE EDUCATION. . . . .(79) ☐

15. PHYSICAL EDUCATION . . . .(62) ☐

16. PSYCHOLOGY . . . .(87) ☐

17. READING . . . .(91) ☐

18. SCIENCE
Biology. . . . .(63) ☐
Chemistry . . . .(64) ☐
Earth Science . . . .(89) ☐
General Science . . . .(65) ☐
Physical Science. . . . .(88) ☐
Physics . . . .(66) ☐
Physiology . . . .(67) ☐
Science, all . . . .(68) ☐

19. SOCIAL SCIENCE
American Government . . . .(71) ☐
American History . . . .(72) ☐
Economics . . . .(69) ☐
Geography. . . . .(70) ☐
Sociology . . . .(74) ☐
World History . . . .(73) ☐
Social Studies, all . . . .(75) ☐

20. SPECIAL EDUCATION
Communication Handicapped. . . . .(85) ☐
Emotionally Maladjusted. . . . .(80) ☐
Hearing Handicapped. . . . .(82) ☐
Learning Disabilities . . . .(97) ☐
Mentally Handicapped . . . .(81) ☐
Physically Handicapped . . . .(84) ☐
Visually Handicapped . . . .(83) ☐

21. SPEECH . . . .(46) ☐

22. TEACHER-LIBRARIAN. . . . .(86) ☐

23. OTHER . . . .(78) ☐

☐ C. This person has completed two (2) semester hours in American history or American government.

☐ D. This person has completed an approved human relations program.

_____
Date and Seal

_____
Signature of designated recommending official

_____
Institution

tional Council for the Accreditation of Teacher Education (NCATE) each have 28 states honoring reciprocity. If you graduate from an NCATE-approved program, and choose to teach in a state which accepts NCATE standards, your preparation will be recognized in that state. Between the two systems of reciprocity, most states, except about 10, are covered.

ACTIVITY 4–1
Are You Up To Standard(s)?

Report in writing your findings on the following questions:

1. What are the state certification requirements in your teaching field?
2. What additional requirements will you have to meet in a second area of interest? (If you plan on coaching, or having an approval area, list its requirements.)
3. Is your institution's program NCATE-approved?
4. What are the certification requirements in one nonreciprocity state where you might like to teach?

Resource persons you might consult about this activity include your major adviser, the director of student teaching, the certification or placement officer, and a certification official in the state department of education. One particularly helpful resource is Elizabeth Woellner (ed.), *Requirements for Certification* (Chicago: University of Chicago, 1980).

EMPLOYMENT OPPORTUNITIES IN EDUCATION

Have you been told to go into special education or heard that there may be a shortage of teachers in the 1980s? Have you read that there are numerous jobs for former teachers in other lines of work? How do teachers enhance their chances of getting a teaching position or a post in an education-related field? These questions are all related to the second issue of the chapter: Is there a teacher surplus?

Before you read the remainder of the chapter, you may wish to do the following activity, which pinpoints some of the job characteristics found among teachers.

ACTIVITY 4–2
Matching Personal Interests and Job Characteristics

How important to you are each of the following characteristics and requirements for an occupation? Rate each on a three-point scale: 3 means very important for you; 2, moderately important; and 1, not important for your career.

1. _____college degree required;
2. _____helping people;
3. _____working with people—ability to get along with others;
4. _____working with ideas—using one's intellect to solve problems;
5. _____working with things—manual skills generally required;
6. _____able to see physical results of work—producing a tangible product;
7. _____working as part of a team—interacting with other employees in performing work;
8. _____work is closely supervised—supervisor controls job performance and work standards;
9. _____opportunity for self-expression—freedom to use one's own ideas;

10. _____working independently—initiative, self-discipline, and ability to organize required;

11. _____directing activities of others—having supervisory responsibilities;

12. _____overtime or additional work required beyond regular hours;

13. _____high level of responsibility and decision making;

14. _____motivating others—must be able to influence others;

15. _____generally confined to work area—physically located at one work setting;

16. _____exposed to weather conditions—working outside;

17. _____physical stamina required;

18. _____working with details;

19. _____competing with other people on the job for recognition and advancement;

20. _____repetitious work—performing same task on a continuing basis.

After you have completed your self-assessment, compare your results with the characteristics usually identified with teaching.

Items that generally characterize teaching occupations are numbers 1 to 4, 9 to 14, and, for elementary teachers, 20.

Do you have a high score on the items associated with teaching? Remember, all teaching positions are not the same. An industrial arts teacher, for example, works with things (item 5), and a physical education teacher may work outside (item 16). You may want to consider other occupations which are consistent with your personal preferences. See Don Dillon, "Toward Matching Personal and Job Characteristics," *Occupational Outlook Quarterly* 19, no. 1 (Spring 1975), a publication of the U.S. Department of Labor, Bureau of Labor Statistics.

Long hours used for preparing lessons and grading are a part of teaching.

Teacher Supply and Demand

It is simplest to treat the issue of teacher supply and demand as a debate on this question: Is there a teacher surplus? We begin with the affirmative, that there is a surplus, a position widely promoted by the media.

Is there a teacher surplus?
Yes, because

1. *There has been a drop in the number of students.* The usual explanation for the decline in teacher openings is the drop in student enrollments due to a declining birth rate. As Table 4–1 indicates, all but 10 states experienced enrollment declines from 1970 to 1978. Fourteen states had losses that were 6% or less, while 20 states had a reduced student enrollment that ranged from 6.1% to 13.9%. Five states and the District of Columbia had losses over 14%. (Figures for the state of Georgia were not available.)

Chapter Four

Table 4–1.
Total public elementary/secondary school enrollments

State	Fall 1970 (in thousands)	Fall 1978 (in thousands)	Percentage Change
Alabama	805	762	− 5.4
Alaska	80	91	+ 13.7
Arizona	440	510	+ 15.9
Arkansas	463	457	− 2.3
California	4,633	4,188	− 9.6
Colorado	550	558	+ 6.9
Connecticut	662	594	− 10.3
Delaware	133	111	− 16.6
Dist. of Columbia	146	114	− 22.0
Florida	1,428	1,514	+ 6.0
Georgia	1,099	NA	NA
Hawaii	181	171	− 5.6
Idaho	182	203	+ 11.5
Illinois	2,357	2,100	− 11.0
Indiana	1,231	1,113	− 9.6
Iowa	660	569	− 13.8
Kansas	512	434	− 15.3
Kentucky	717	693	− 3.4
Louisiana	842	817	− 3.0
Maine	245	240	− 2.1
Maryland	916	810	− 11.6
Massachusetts	1,168	1,081	− 7.5
Michigan	2,181	1,911	− 12.4
Minnesota	921	808	− 12.3
Mississippi	534	494	− 7.5
Missouri	1,039	900	− 13.4
Montana	177	164	− 7.4
Nebraska	329	298	− 9.5
Nevada	128	146	+ 14.0
New Hampshire	159	172	+ 8.1
New Jersey	1,482	1,337	− 9.8
New Mexico	281	279	− 1.0
New York	3,477	3,094	− 11.1
North Carolina	1,192	1,163	− 2.4
North Dakota	147	122	− 17.1
Ohio	2,426	2,102	− 13.4
Oklahoma	627	589	− 6.1
Oregon	480	471	− 1.9
Pennsylvania	2,364	2,047	− 13.4
Rhode Island	188	161	− 14.4
South Carolina	638	625	− 2.0
South Dakota	166	138	− 16.9
Tennessee	900	872	− 3.0
Texas	2,840	2,867	+ 1.0
Utah	304	325	+ 6.9
Vermont	103	101	− 2.0

Table 4–1. (*continued*)

Virginia	1,079	1,055	−· 2.3
Washington	818	769	− 6.0
West Virginia	400	396	− 1.0
Wisconsin	994	886	−10.9
Wyoming	87	94	+ 8.0

Source: Modified from National Center for Education Statistics, *The Condition of Education, 1980* (Washington, D.C.: Government Printing Office, 1980), p. 58.

2. *Schools are forced to cut back due to financial constraints.* A second potent force reducing the number of teacher openings is inflation. Since teacher salaries constitute the largest single item in a district's budget, teacher positions are usually cut when large sums of money must be saved.

Closely related to inflation is the state of the nation's economy. If the economy is booming, many college graduates with teaching certificates will find employment in business. However, when the economy is stagnant and industry lays people off, the pool of teachers increases. Similarly, in tight economic times, teachers who are unhappy with their positions are less likely to resign.

Another economic factor affecting teacher openings is the decrease in funding of programs. Federal revenue especially has been cut from a variety of programs—for remedial instruction, for the handicapped, for the talented and gifted. Some argue that the successful efforts by teacher organizations to raise salaries ultimately result in fewer positions as districts attempt to economize.

3. *Too many teacher candidates are being prepared.* The number of teachers in America has increased dramatically since the baby boom following World War II. In 1950 there were fewer than 1 million elementary and secondary teachers in public schools; in 1977 there were 2.2 million. Now that the birth rate has declined sharply, the nation does not need the same number of teachers. In 1969 there were

78,000 new positions in education; in 1971 it dropped to 19,000; in 1979 the number of prospective teachers seeking classroom positions (133,500 persons) exceeded by 58,750 the number of positions actually open to them (74,750).[14]

Those who argue that there is a teacher surplus and oversupply of teachers, will concede that the number of individuals preparing to teach has declined sharply. Since 1972 the number of students completing a teacher education program has decreased each year. Figure 4–1 details the relationship of job openings and the number of new graduates in teacher education. As indicated, the supply of new teacher graduates is expected to more than fill the total demand for additional classroom teachers, at least until the mid-1980s.

Many sources will argue that these factors combined paint a grim picture for those contemplating a future as a teacher. The Bureau of Labor Statistics' outlook for careers in the professional-technical area estimated that by 1990 there will be a 3% decline in teaching jobs, although it acknowledged that in the years to come there will be a growing surplus at the secondary level and a shortage at the elementary level.[15] The competition for the available positions will be fierce.

Is there a teacher surplus?
No, because

1. *Teacher-pupil ratios are too high.* A favorite argument of teacher organizations

Figure 4–1.
Estimates of new teacher supply and additional teacher demand

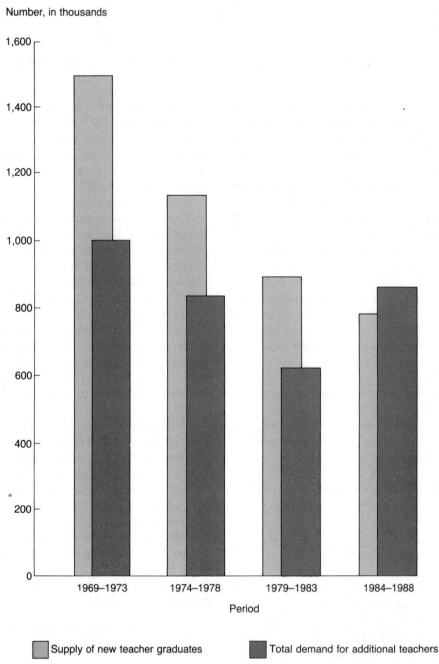

Number, in thousands

Supply of new teacher graduates

Total demand for additional teachers

Source: National Center for Education Statistics, *The Condition of Education, 1980* (Washington, D.C.: U.S. Government Printing Office, 1980), p. 73.

is that most classes, especially in inner-city schools, are too large.[16] Furthermore, when the schools add to their inadequate staffs not only more regular classroom teachers, but specialists such as librarians, remedial reading experts, and speech therapists, to name a few, the surplus vanishes.

You may wonder what teacher-pupil ratios are. It was estimated that in 1980 there was one teacher for every 17 students in public secondary schools and a 1:21 ratio at the public elementary level. (The teacher-pupil ratio is not identical with average class size, due to the number of specialists that are included.) As Figure 4–2 indi-

Cartoon by Randy Glasbergen, in *Phi Delta Kappan*, February 1980, p. 405. Used with permission of the artist.

"Any new applications for that teaching position, Mrs. Brown?"

Figure 4–2
Student-teacher ratios in elementary/secondary public and nonpublic schools

Student-Teacher Ratios

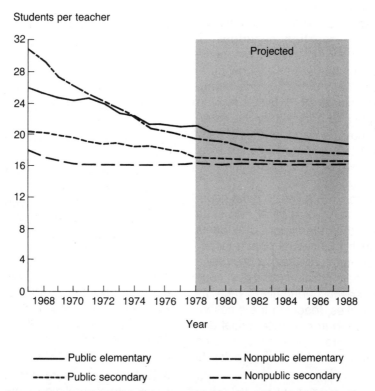

Source: National Center for Education Statistics, *The Condition of Education, 1980* (Washington, D.C.: U.S. Government Printing Office, 1980), p. 71.

cates, the teacher-pupil ratio has been declining since the late 1960s. The number of public elementary school teachers is expected to rise in the mid-1980s, while the number projected for public secondary school teachers declines and for nonpublic school teachers remains constant.

2. *Shortages exist in certain parts of the country and in certain fields.* While it is true, as Figure 4–1 shows, that the majority of states have suffered declines in enrollment, 10 states had increases. The same data reveals that almost 50% of the states had only a modest loss. In some states there is even talk of small baby booms.

More significantly, there are certain subject fields that are now in critical need of teachers, and other disciplines are beginning to experience growing numbers of vacancies. Critical shortages of teachers exist in agricultural education and industrial arts. Mathematics and the physical sciences show mounting shortages of teachers. To a lesser extent, vacancies are appearing in the natural sciences, distributive education, and music. One expert, who annually since 1976 has surveyed teacher supply and demand for the Association for School, College, and University Staffing, states that teacher surpluses exist in only one or two of the approximately 40 different preparation areas.[17]

Special education is a field in great need. Due to the passage of federal and state laws requiring that handicapped students be given equal educational opportunities, school districts throughout the country have been adding new positions in the various branches of special education, such as learning disabilities, teaching the emotionally disturbed, and in multicategorical disabilities. New programs in a variety of fields may spawn the need for more specialists in the future.

3. *Schools have a variety of special (often part-time) positions.* A perennial problem

of schools is finding the teachers who fit their particular needs. Districts often seek teachers who, besides being good classroom instructors, can coach sports, sponsor clubs, direct plays, and advise students working on the school paper or yearbook. It is not uncommon today to see rural schools dropping activities and occasionally courses because they could not find teachers with the combination of interests they desired. The smallest school districts, studies reveal, must ask staff members to do a variety of duties. The smallest districts, proportionately, will have more openings than large districts due to high turnover resulting from lower salaries and remoteness of locale. Thus, your first teaching job may be in a small district.[18]

In summary, despite the general perception that there is a teacher surplus, there is evidence that openings are available. Those who are sincere about teaching, who will train in several areas, and who will be geographically mobile will probably have the best employment opportunities.

Is there a teacher surplus? You must weigh the evidence very carefully. Get the latest information possible, as swings in individual subject-matter fields can fluctuate in a matter of years. Estimates from various agencies vary considerably depending upon the techniques they used in gathering data. The point is that the answer to the question of a teacher surplus is complex. We urge you to consider these possibilities:

● Base your decision about teaching as a career primarily upon your desire to work with youth and your interest in your specialty. You should not select a career only or primarily because it offers a good chance of employment.

● Because of tenure and seniority provisions, when enrollments and employment decline, the older, more experienced teachers will be retained. How will you feel about working with a staff that is likely to be older than you?[19]

• Affirmative Action requirements may mean that school districts will hire proportionately more members of minority groups.

• Teachers will use the collective bargaining process more militantly to guarantee teaching positions, job security, and favorable working conditions. Increasingly, one provision in contract negotiations is maximum class size; smaller classes mean more jobs.

• Where there are more teachers than openings, schools can hire more selectively, resulting in the use of more structured interviews and videotape demonstrations of teaching by applicants. Employment may become more political in that knowing someone in the system may secure a job.

• The openings in various fields will fluctuate. To ensure a position, many experienced teachers will retrain, becoming certified in new areas. Prospective teachers will be well advised to prepare in two or three areas.

• Even a tenured teacher will be less certain of a position from year to year. Districts in a financial bind will notify a number of teachers in February or March (when state laws mandate that teachers must be informed about the following year's contract) that there will be a reduction in force, and that they are being laid off. If the districts' financial situation improves, they would hire back some or all of those teachers. Would you want to work under such conditions, even if you knew in advance that you were likely to get rehired?

Other Educational Openings

Information in the previous section may cause you to think twice about a career in the classroom. You might consider working in a nonschool setting, if you still believe that you want to teach.

According to experts such as Ralph Tyler, there is strong evidence that a number of opportunities for educators will emerge in a variety of occupations and support services. In 1900 approximately 75% of the jobs in America produced goods and were traditionally learned through family training or an apprenticeship program. By 1975 some 65% of the occupations in the country were service-related, most requiring training outside the family. Despite occasional setbacks in the economy, Tyler predicts that American society will continue to demand such services from agencies and firms. They will have to hire persons to train their service personnel.[20]

Adult education programs are also booming. It is estimated that adults spend 800 hours a year learning activities—in interest classes, by correspondence, and through individual reading and research. The increase in the use of free time for educational pursuits has spurred programs in the leisure studies area.[21]

Educational Agencies and Service Groups. Among firms employing teachers are designers and manufacturers of educational equipment, local and state councils of higher education, teachers' organizations, foundations, research firms, publishing houses, museums, national associations of universities and colleges, day-care centers, and television studios. Specifically, you might be hired as a consultant to advise classroom teachers, a salesperson to demonstrate educational products, an editor of textbook material, a director of programming or education for a museum, or a recreational leader.[22]

Service organizations such as the YMCA, YWCA, YMHA, and YWHA, churches and synagogues, as well as scouting and 4-H clubs, have extensive educational programs and need teachers and youth advisers. Various private and public welfare agencies, social work firms, and rehabilitation programs often need individuals with a teacher-education background.

Adult Education Opportunities. Community colleges, local school districts, regional education agencies, libraries, and state departments of education offer programs for adults. The programs include adult basic education, the teaching of English as a second language (TESL), citizenship classes for foreign-born, art history, psychology, hobbies for leisure, and book discussion groups. Colleges and universities are hiring conference directors, continuing education coordinators and instructors, retirement counselors, and researchers for gerontology projects.

If you choose to enter this field, you should have some knowledge of adult learning styles, which are different than those of children. Most adult programs are nongraded and run informally. If you prefer a less structured environment than a typical K-12 classroom, adult education might be for you.

Governmental Agencies. Governmental agencies from the local to the federal level are among the largest employers of college graduates. One of every six employees in the country works in a government post, and one-third of these are in education.[23] Government jobs are available in public works, health and hospitals, urban renewal offices, beautification departments, reform schools and prisons, Bureau of Indian Affairs' schools, and parks. In Washington, the Department of Education's many divisions hire education personnel; in the states, the departments of education are staffed by numerous individuals who have been teachers.

Specific examples of positions in governmental agencies include instructors in the children's wards of hospitals; music or art therapists in rehabilitation centers

or rest homes; and evaluators of grant proposals submitted to government agencies. These agencies may also hire school psychologists, attendance (truant) officers, guidance counselors, speech therapists, and social workers who counsel families with school-related problems.

Business and Industry. Larger businesses and industries employ teachers in their staff training programs and consumer services departments. Communication skills are especially helpful, for example, in developing the report- and letter-writing abilities of staff members. Factories have found that industrial arts teachers can explain procedures effectively to workers on the assembly line.

Firms such as insurance companies and automobile dealerships also like to hire persons with teaching credentials or experience, because the companies have learned such individuals usually relate well to people. Teachers tend to be interested in a variety of topics and can be effective in selling a wide range of products.

Nonpublic Teaching and Overseas Opportunities. The data presented in this chapter has referred almost exclusively to the public schools. You might consider employment as a teacher in a private, independent, or parochial school. Approximately 247,000 teachers are employed by nonpublic schools. (See Chapters 10 and 15 for further discussions of these types of schools.)

If you enjoy traveling, you might be interested in employment abroad. Teaching opportunities exist in other countries, sometimes through the schools for military personnel abroad, the Peace Corps, or in schools established by Americans living overseas.[24] In addition, there are jobs with international corporations and government agencies in such capacities.

To work overseas, you must be tolerant of diverse cultural customs, flexible in or-

Skilled teachers work abroad with the Peace Corps. Clockwise, top left: _Joan_ (special education) shows a blind Thai student how to use a dictaphone. _Jeri_ (secondary education) teaches English in the Philippines. _Sandy_ (B.A., Spanish) emphasizes self-awareness in her preschool class in Honduras. _Marge_ (home economics) shows islanders in the Solomons how to build a cooker from biscuit tin. _Phil_ (industrial technology) teaches shop and Spanish in the West Indies.

ganizing alternate approaches to instruction, and emotionally stable. Before you accept a post abroad, examine the terms of the contract, the necessary skills (especially language), and living conditions.

Regardless of the job opportunity, whether in public school or nonclassroom, carefully weigh the importance of such factors as size of community, salary, hours, job responsibility, security, and reputation of the employer. Make sure it is a position you really want.

Applying for an Educational Position

If you pursue a career in education, you know there will be a lot of competition for jobs. What can you do to be a successful candidate?

The following suggestions should help. If you are just beginning your professional courses, however, some may be premature. Nevertheless, they may be useful in applying for part-time positions and in helping you evaluate your commitment to education.

Volunteer and Work Experiences. Future employers will be interested in the types of experiences you had through your high school and college years. Were you a cadet teacher or did you tutor? Did you volunteer to be a Sunday school teacher or a youth club adviser? Have you been a camp counselor or scout troop leader?

Similarly, to what groups have you belonged? Will your resume show that you were active in a variety of plays, sports, and interest clubs? Interviewers look for those individuals who have been active socially. Recall all the positions you have held, or consider those you might hold between now and graduation. Were or are they people-oriented? Will they provide you chances to work with the age group you would like to teach?

Keep a record of your leadership roles or significant responsibilities. Ask your su-

pervisors for a recommendation including a statement of your performance for inclusion in a future placement file.

Contact Your Placement Office. Most campuses have a placement office to help students and alumni make job contacts. On larger campuses there will be several, and you may be eligible to enroll in more than one. Visit the placement office early in your college career to learn about its services, which may include career counseling. Late in your junior year, or certainly early in your senior year, you will want to register and establish a placement file, since it takes time to fill out forms and gather reference letters.

As part of their service, some placement offices notify you of openings in your field and related areas of work. The placement office will send, usually for a fee, sets of your credentials to prospective employers. Some offices have one fee that entitles you to a specific number of credential sets; others charge for each set mailed.

Prepare Your Professional File. Your professional file includes records of your college performance, personal information, and several letters of recommendation. In many respects, the letter of recommendation (in some cases, an evaluation form) from the teacher under whom student teaching is done, is most important. Similarly, a recommendation from the professor who supervised student teaching is very important. If at all possible, have the principal observe your student teaching and write a letter of recommendation. Employers or other persons who would have insight into your ability to teach could be asked to submit reference letters. Usually, three to five letters are included in a file.

Applying for a Position. The following advice can be used, with some modifications, for part-time positions as well as full-time teaching positions. Once you have identified a possible opening, look at the requirements carefully. If you qualify, then:

1. *Send a typed letter of application.* Use standard business form, quality paper, and a good ribbon. Be concise, stating the position for which you are applying, the pertinent facts about yourself, and the reasons you think you are suited for the position. Indicate where or how you learned of the opening. Address your letter to the hiring official by name, if known. Be sure to proofread your letter. Typographical errors and poor grammar will doom your application to the wastebasket. Remember, this is your first contact with the employer; don't make it your last.

2. *Include a resume.* An attractive one-page resume will be an asset. For the hiring official who must scan many letters of inquiry, the resume provides data which may earn you a second look. Expanding upon the basic information in your letter, the resume notes your accomplishments and honors, volunteer and work experi-

ences, school activities, and hobbies. Definitely include where your placement file can be obtained and your telephone number. You might include a short statement of your educational philosophy.

3. *Send your placement file.* Arrange to send your credentials to those districts in which you are very interested. When hiring officials have to order the files, it is an extra burden on them which you can eliminate. However, some placement offices will not send files unless requested to do so by employing organizations. Furthermore, costs may limit the number of folders you can afford to send.

4. *Arrange to visit.* If you get some positive response from a personnel office, arrange to visit if you are within a reasonable travel distance. A visit is an informal way to see the facilities and perhaps meet some of the teachers. Be sure to inform the personnel office that you are coming and, if possible, make an appointment for an interview.

Interviewing for a job gives you a chance to express your personal priorities as well as your philosophy of education.

5. *Schedule an interview.* In a tight job market, you may need to send out 10 or more applications before you have an interview. When your first steps are successful and you are invited to interview, how can you prepare to meet the hiring official?

a Learn something about the community and its education situation; it will be advantageous to both you and the school to know each other.

b. Remember that an interview is a two-way conversation. Anticipate the types of questions that will be asked. Consider taking samples of your lesson plans. Most interviewers will be willing to answer your questions about the district (and consider them as a sign that you are really interested).[25]

c. Be at ease in the interview.

d. Be clear about your educational philosophy. Share your point of view honestly; don't try to give the answer you think is expected.

ACTIVITY 4—3
Should I Become an Educator?

Respond briefly to the following questions. Then summarize your position on each of the topics.

Compensation

1. Am I satisfied to have only a moderate income for the rest of my life?
2. Am I willing to spend time after school and during evenings with student clubs and activities or correcting papers?
3. Am I willing to work sometimes during the summer (without pay) to develop courses?

Job Security

4. Is the protection of tenure for job security important to me?
5. Am I willing to get involved in negotiations with the school board for salaries, working conditions, and benefits?
6. Can I live with the subtle pressures to be a model of appropriate behavior for the community?

Job Availability

7. In what kinds of communities would I be willing to live?
8. Am I open to change, willing to try jobs with many unknowns?
9. Am I willing to take new and different assignments, once on the job? Must job descriptions always be clearly defined for me?

Professional Standards

10. Do I like to read and do research?
11. Do I really enjoy working with youth? Am I patient?
12. Do I have a good self-concept and self-confidence?

Career Preparation and Employment Opportunities

Opportunities for Advancement

13. Am I willing to take courses at my own expense to improve my knowledge and skills?

14. Am I willing to have limited advancement unless I leave the classroom and become an administrator?

Responsibilities on the Job

15. Do I get paperwork done even if I don't like to do it?

16. Am I willing to explain to the community what the school is trying to do?

17. Am I willing to listen to criticism about what the school is trying to do?

18. Do I try to get along and support co-workers even if I don't like them personally?

19. Do I want to be a model of good behavior in the classroom? Am I a perfectionist with students?

Source: Karen Willis, teacher, Lake City, Iowa

SUMMARY

In an introduction to a book highly critical of teacher education and teachers, Sterling M. McMurrin wrote, "However important other factors may be, and whatever else may be done to effect improvement, the quality of education in this nation will never be better than the intellectual caliber of our teachers and the education they themselves received in colleges and universities."[26] Now that you have finished

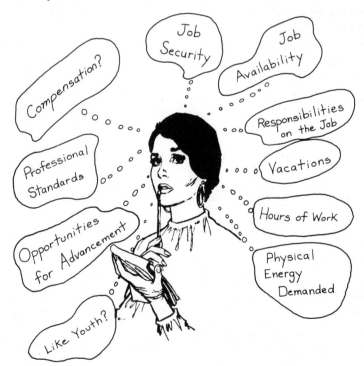

Chapter Four

the chapter, you should be able to state some reasons why you agree or disagree with that statement.

As you learned, while there are similarities in teacher education programs, there are numerous organizational patterns for preparing future teachers. A new approach, CBTE, attempts to place greater stress upon specific competencies gained rather than the completion of a series of courses.

There are disputes over what constitutes the best way to organize teacher education, which in turn influence the certification programs in various states. As the section on the employment outlook noted, the job market for teachers is in flux today, and we hope you become more sensitive to the many variables that influence teacher supply and demand. Because of the projected growth of educational opportunities outside the classroom, you should investigate them. We would like to predict that everyone who finishes a teacher-education program could find a job as an educator, but even some of the best graduates did not get hired in recent years. Our suggestions, we hope, may enhance your chances when you apply for a job.

NOTES

1. John E. King, foreword to M. L. Cushman, *The Governance of Teacher Education* (Berkeley, Calif.: McCutchan Publishing Co., 1977).

2. Merle Borrowman, *The Liberal and Technical in Teacher Education* (Westport, Conn.: Greenwood Press, 1956, 1977 edition); James B. Conant, *The Education of American Teachers* (New York: McGraw-Hill, 1963); James D. Koerner, *The Miseducation of American Teachers* (Boston: Houghton-Mifflin, 1963).

3. Martin Haberman and T. M. Stinnett, *Teacher Education and the New Profession of Teaching* (Berkeley, Calif.: McCutchan Publishing, 1973), pp. 77–85.

4. W. Robert Houston, *Competency-based Teacher Education* (Chicago: Science Research Associates, 1972); James M. Cooper et al., *Competency-Based Teacher Education* (Berkeley, Calif.: McCutchan Publishing, 1973); Hazel W. Hertzberg, "Competency Based Teacher Education," *Teachers College Record* 78, no. 1 (September 1976): 1–21.

5. James Mackey, Allen Glen, and Darrell Lewis, "The Effectiveness of Teacher Education," *Peabody Journal of Education* 54, no. 4 (July 1977): 231–38.

6. John McNamara, *An Effective Program for Teacher-Aide Training* (West Nyack, N.Y.: Parker Publishing, 1972); Alan Gartner, Frank Riessman, Vivian C. Jackson, eds., *Paraprofessionals Today, Volume I: Education* (New York: Human Sciences Press, 1977).

7. "Have License, Will Teach," *Teacher* 94, no. 3 (November 1976): 129.

8. Harold Harty and James A. Mahan, "Student Teachers' Expressed Orientations toward Education While Preparing to Teach Minority and Mainstream Ethnic Groups," *The Journal of Experimental Education* 46, no. 1 (Fall 1977): 34–40; William A. Hunter, ed., *Multicultural Education through Competency-Based Teacher Education* (Washington, D.C.: American Association of Colleges for Teacher Education, 1974).

9. Lucien Kinney, *Certification in Education* (Englewood Cliffs, N.J.: Prentice-Hall, 1964), p. 3.

10. Karl Massanari, in T. M. Stinnett, *The Unfinished Business of the Teaching Profession* (Bloomington, Ind.: Phi Delta Kappa, 1971), p. 85; T. M. Stinnett, *Professional Problems of Teachers*, 3rd ed. (New York: Macmillan, 1968), pp. 436–37.

11. Kinney, *Certification*, p. 17; Christopher Lucas, "The Foundations of Education Component in State Regulations Governing Teacher Preparation and Initial Certification," *Educational Studies* 10, no. 1 (Spring 1979): 1–29.

12. T. M. Stinnett, *A Manual on Standards Affecting School Personnel in the United States* (Washington, D.C.: National Education Association, 1974), p. 24.

13. The National Teacher Examination program is a part of Educational Testing Service, located in Princeton, N.J.; Richard Mitchell, "Testing the Teachers: The Dallas Experiment," *The Atlantic Monthly* 242, no. 6 (December 1978): 66–70.

14. National Education Association, *Teacher Supply and Demand in Public Schools, 1977* (Washington, D.C.: National Education Association, 1978); National Center for Education Statistics, *The Condition of Education, 1977* (Washington, D.C.: U.S. Government Printing Office, 1977), p. 104; Herold Regier, *Too Many Teachers: Fact or Fiction?* (Bloomington, Ind.: Phi Delta Kappa, 1972), pp. 19–21; National Education Association, *Research Memo, Teacher Supply and Demand in Public Schools, 1979* (Washington, D.C.: National Education Association, 1980), p. 1.

15. Bureau of Labor Statistics reported in *Newsday*, 27 April 1980; Jeremy Main, "The Right Stuff for Careers in the '80s," *Money* 9, no. 5 (May 1980), pp. 68–76. Using data from the Bureau of Labor Statistics, *Money* predicted which careers will be best and worst in the 1980s. To determine best and worst, four factors were used: estimated growth in jobs to 1990, prospects for job seekers, starting salary, and mid-career salary.

16. NEA, *Teacher Supply and Demand, 1979*, pp. 7, 8, and 13; M.M. Chambers, "No Teacher Surplus,"

Phi Delta Kappan 52, no. 2 (October 1970): 118–19.

17. James N. Akin, "Teacher Supply and Demand: A Recent Survey," *A Job Search Handbook for Educators* (Madison, Wisc.: Association for School, College and University Staffing, 1980), pp. 4–5.

18. Arni T. Dunathan, "Midwest Schools Face Shortages of Good Teachers," *Phi Delta Kappan* 61, no. 2 (October 1979): 121–23.

19. Susan Abramowitz et al., "Declining Enrollments: The Effects on States and Districts," *National Institute for Education Report*, April 1977; Thomas Calhoun, "Throwaway Teachers," *Educational Leadership* 32, no. 5 (February 1975): 310–15; David L. Martin, "RIF: Out of a Job, Out of Teaching," *Learning* 5, no. 8 (April 1977): 22–28; Robert W. Herman, "Now Inevitable: A Substantial and Lengthy Teacher Shortage," *Phi Delta Kappan* 59, no. 10 (June 1978): 693.

20. Ralph Tyler, lecture at Iowa State University, 15 February 1978.

21. Rogert Hiemstra, *Life-long Learning* (Lincoln, Neb.: University of Nebraska Press, 1976); Donald D. Henkel and Geoffrey C. Godbey, *Parks, Recreation, and Leisure Services Employment in the Public Sector: Status and Trends* (Arlington, Va.: National Recreation and Parks Association, 1977).

22. Dorothy Koch Bestor, "Career Alternatives for Educators," *A Job Search Handbook for Educators*, pp. 28–34; Bill McKee, *New Careers for Teachers* (Chicago: Contemporary Books, 1972); Ben Greco, *How to Get the Job That's Right for You* (Homewood, Ill.: Dow-Jones-Irwin, Inc., 1976).

23. E. K. Coughlin, "Job Prospects Improve for New College Graduates, Three Studies Show," *The Chronicle of Higher Education* 15 (December 1977): 7.

24. Priscilla A. Scotlan, "Overseas Employment for Educators," *A Job Search Handbook for Educators*, pp. 26–27; Harold A. Dilts, *Teachers' Guide to Teaching Positions in Foreign Countries* (Ames, Iowa: Carter Press, 1979); Eric Kocher, *International Jobs: Where They Are; How to Get Them* (Reading: Addison-Wesley Publishing Co., 1979).

25. Jenny King Johansen and Peter Madden, "Getting That First Teaching Job," *Learning* 5, no. 7 (March 1977): 14, 16, 18; Eugene Williams, "Assessing Teacher Competencies with the Audiovisual Portfolio," *Educational Leadership* 37, no. 3 (December 1979): 246–47.

26. Sterling M. McMurrin, introduction to James Koerner, *The Miseducation of American Teachers*, p. xii.

FOR FURTHER STUDY

American Association of Colleges for Teacher Education, Bicentennial Commission on Education for the Profession of Teaching. *Educating a Profession*. Washington, D.C.: American Association of Colleges for Teacher Education, 1976.

Bestor, Dorothy Koch. *Aside From Teaching English, What in the World Can You Do?* Seattle: University of Washington Press, 1979.

Combs, Arthur. *The Professional Education of Teachers*. 2nd ed. Boston: Allyn and Bacon, 1974.

Cushman, M. L. *The Governance of Teacher Education*. Berkeley, Calif.: McCutchan, 1977.

Ellner, Carolyn L. *Schoolmaking: An Alternative in Teacher Education*. Lexington, Mass.: Lexington Books, 1977.

Miller, Anne. *Finding Career Alternatives for Teachers*. New York: Apple Publishing Co., 1979.

Miller, Jean M., and Dickson, Georgianna M. *When Apples Ain't Enough*. Sacramento: Jalmar Press, 1980.

Parnell, Dave. *The Case for Competency-Based Education*. Bloomington, Ind.: Phi Delta Kappa Educational Foundation, 1978.

Pollack, Sandy. *Alternative Careers for Teachers*. Cambridge: Harvard Common Press, 1979.

Ryan, Kevin, ed. *Teacher Education*. The 74th Yearbook of the National Society for the Study of Education, Part II. Chicago: National Society for the Study of Education, 1975.

5

The Teaching Profession

With the passage of time, the unionization of salaried professionals, once regarded as a threat to professional status, has become respectable.

Theodore Caplow

Classroom teachers have organized themselves and are seeking guarantees that they will not only be listened to on matters concerning school policy but that they shall be given an active part in determining policy.

Alan Rosenthal

The teaching profession has come of age. Over a decade ago, Alan Rosenthal concluded that the "teachers movement" was gaining strength and that militancy had "begun to alter educational power relationships."[1] Today over 90% of American public school teachers are members of local associations or unions affiliated with the National Education Association (NEA) or the American Federation of Teachers (AFT).

Some of the most important changes in conditions affecting teaching in recent decades are the result of the growing influence and power of professional teacher organizations. Through lobbying, collective bargaining, strikes, and other forms of political action, organized teachers have affected their profession and American education. Critics have argued that unions and strikes are unprofessional, that they have not significantly improved the salaries and status of teachers, and that unionization has had negative effects on the quality of education.

The pervasive issue throughout this chapter is what role teachers should have in determining their salaries, their working conditions, and educational policy. How should their influence be exerted? What is the appropriate role of teacher organizations? (Chapter 9 will focus on the roles and responsibilities of administrators and boards of education.)

We will examine first the development of teacher organizations, the changes they have undergone in recent decades, and the emergence of collective negotiations, strikes, and political action. A number of professional concerns will be discussed, including salaries, fringe benefits, working conditions, tenure, professional development, and teacher rights.

After you have completed Chapter 5, you should be able to (1) compare and contrast the historical development and strategies of the NEA and AFT, (2) describe the process of collective bargaining, and (3) summarize four areas of professional concern for teacher organizations.

PROFESSIONAL ORGANIZATIONS

Teaching is usually regarded as a profession since it requires considerable formal education, specialized knowledge, and intellectual skills. Although teachers receive lower salaries and status than many, all professionals render services for fees or salaries rather than commercial profit. The primary commitment of professionals is to their clients and colleagues. Professionals generally exert considerable autonomy in making decisions and judgments. Indeed, the process of professionalization focuses on "efforts of a vocation to gain full control over its work." Every profession has an association primarily devoted to enhancing the status of the profession.[2] You've already read in Chapter 4 about the efforts of teacher groups to influence teacher education and certification.

An organization also provides "a sense of group identity" and a "source of ideas" for the conduct of work.[3] Teachers are joiners and most belong to more than one professional organization. Most numerous are the several thousand associations of teachers in local districts. The *Education Directory* lists over a thousand different organizations. College students can join clubs for future teachers (the Student NEA), and may be elected to education honor societies (Kappa Delta Pi, Phi Delta Kappa, and Pi Lambda Theta) that also include teachers. The Association for Childhood Education International, Music Educators National Conference, and the National Council of Teachers of Mathematics are among the specialized interest groups found in virtually every teaching field. Some of these societies also have local or state organizations and student memberships at reduced rates.

The oldest and largest comprehensive teacher organization is the National Education Association, which has nearly one and three-quarter million members. Membership in the rival American Federation of Teachers is over a half million. Some local teacher organizations are not affiliated with either the NEA or AFT, and a small percentage of teachers belong to both the NEA and AFT, either under local mergers or through individual memberships.

Development of Teacher Organizations

Teachers first organized in 1794 when 15 schoolmasters met to form the short-lived Society of Associated Teachers of New York City. Other local and county organizations followed and, beginning in the 1840s, teachers formed state associations.

National Education Association. In 1857, the presidents of 10 of these state organizations invited "practical teachers" to form a National Teachers' Association. Forty-three men signed the constitution and heard an address urging them to make teaching a profession by setting standards and judging qualifications of candidates.

The organization grew slowly in its first half century. In 1870 it became the National Educational Association, having expanded to include existing organizations of normal schools, school superintendents, and colleges. Most members and virtually all the leaders were school administrators and college professors rather than classroom teachers. For many years the NEA's main activity was its annual meeting. Its effort to establish a profession was mainly rhetoric, and it paid little attention to teacher welfare and salaries. In the 1920s, the NEA created publishing and research divisions, which demonstrated its basic commitment to public information and education.[4]

Membership grew steadily after World War I as a result of recruiting drives and expanding school enrollments in the postwar periods. (See Table 5–1.) Although over 90% of public school teachers belonged to NEA-affiliated state associations in 1960, fewer than half held individual membership in the National Educational Association. In the 1970s the NEA instituted a unified membership plan requiring members of a local, state, or the national association to join all three.

As membership grew, the organization changed. A representative assembly was instituted in 1920, and over the years new educational groups affiliated and others became independent. After cooperating for many decades, the predominantly black American Teachers Association merged with the NEA in 1966. Segregated NEA state associations in the South also began to merge.

Since education in America is primarily a state responsibility and significant federal involvement is relatively recent, it is not surprising that for many years the NEA has been strongest at the state level. Names of state organizations vary, but usually include the word "association," for example, the Michigan Education Association,

California Teachers Association, and Georgia Association of Educators.

A major activity of NEA state organizations has been to work closely with the state education department and lobby the legislature. Teacher organizations thus have sought increased state aid to education and laws to improve working conditions of teachers, ranging from the establishment and improvement of retirement plans and tenure laws to minimum salaries and sick leave. State associations also hold conventions, publish journals for their members, and provide research and field services (e.g., regional salary studies).

Table 5–1.

Membership in national teacher organizations

Year	NEA	AFT
1857	43	—
1870	170	—
1880	354	—
1890	5,474	—
1900	2,332	—
1910	6,909	—
1920	52,850	9,808
1930	172,354	6,872
1940	203,429	29,907
1950	453,797	41,415
1960	713,994	59,181
1970	1,100,155	205,323
1980	1,680,566	551,359

Source: Data from *NEA Handbook, 1979–80*, p. 143; letter from William S. Graybeal, NEA Research, 25 June 1980; *AFT Officers' Reports to the AFT Convention*, various years.

Local teacher associations were traditionally weak and generally ineffectual before the 1960s. Many were primarily social groups. An NEA study in 1959 indicated that nearly two-thirds of local associations had annual dues of less than $4, only one-fourth had a representative attending board of education meetings regularly, and fewer than 15% had three or more written communications to or from school authorities in the preceding year.[5]

Chapter Five

NEA's symbol combines "the legacy of the past (π for *paiδεια* [paideia], the ancient Greek word for education) with new direction for the future (➤)." The spherical triangle represents the "mutually supportive programs of local, state, and national education associations to advance education."

Besides the local and state affiliates, the NEA in the early 1960s had over 30 departments or affiliated groups, including specialized organizations for teachers of each subject area, administrators, supervisors, and retired teachers. Although the Classroom Teachers was numerically the largest NEA department, representing about 85% of the members, national leadership through the 1950s was primarily in the hands of school administrators and the full-time staff executives.

The NEA and its affiliates have made substantial contributions to American education. For many decades it emphasized professional development, research, curriculum improvement, and educational policy. As the dominant organization in public education, it included a broad spectrum of professional educators and influenced education at all levels. Significant changes occurred in the 1960s as a result of increasing competition with the rival AFT.

American Federation of Teachers. Women elementary teachers organized the first teachers' union in this country in 1897. This Chicago Teachers Federation later joined two other Chicago unions representing men teachers and women high school teachers to call for the establishment of a national organization affiliated with the American Federation of Labor. The three Chicago unions and locals ranging from

Oklahoma to New York City formed the American Federation of Teachers in 1916. The original AFT constitution set forth its objectives:

1. To bring associations of teachers into relations of mutual assistance and cooperation.

2. To obtain for them all the rights to which they are entitled.

3. To raise the standards of the teaching profession by securing the conditions essential to the best professional service.[6]

Some AFT members originally hoped to affiliate with the NEA, but the NEA viewed the ties with organized labor as a deterrent to professional status for teachers and embarked on an anti-union campaign. Furthermore, some boards of education dismissed teachers for union membership. While the NEA was growing in the 1920s, the AFT barely survived as membership declined and many locals dissolved. Membership increased during the 1930s, but growth was slower in the next two decades. (See Table 5–1.) By 1959 AFT membership was 55,000, representing less than 4% of the nation's teachers, but concentrated in large cities with a strong labor movement.[7]

AFT strength has been in its locals; historically the national organization was weak and state branches were nonexistent for many years. Teacher organizations embarked on a new era of militancy in the 1960s, with intense competition between the AFT and NEA transforming both groups.

Growing Militancy

The NEA and AFT represented two distinct approaches and philosophies through the early 1960s, when the contrast between the two organizations was substantial. As a professional association, the NEA sought to represent all professional educators, including principals and superintendents as well as teachers. The underlying assumption was that there should be a harmony of interests and cooperation to advance education and the profession.

As the nucleus of the education establishment, the NEA was criticized in the 1960s for being conservative and complacent. The AFT charged that the NEA was a "company union" because of the dominance of administrators. In the 1950s, no classroom teachers served on the NEA Board of Trustees or Executive Committee. Local superintendents sometimes pressured teachers to join the state associations. Local associations often included principals and other administrators who sometimes dominated the meetings.

The NEA was most critical of the AFT's affiliation with organized labor. Although the AFT claimed to be a "union of professionals," the NEA felt that unionism with its blue-collar associations was detrimental to efforts to establish teaching as a profession. The union orientation led the AFT to presume both an adversary relationship between teachers and administrators and an inherent conflict of interests. Hence, locals generally restricted membership to teachers and educators in nonsupervisory positions. The AFT emphasized improvement in salary and working conditions and advocated collective bargaining. Strident and militant, the AFT was more likely to advocate strikes.[8]

The AFT symbol represents teacher power. The hands holding the AFT sign indicate that the grass roots members are the backbone and real strength of the union.

Teacher organizations have undergone considerable changes in recent years. The AFT victory in a representational election in New York City in 1961 was a turning point. Since then the NEA and AFT have competed for members and influence, and both organizations have grown substantially in numbers and power. The advent of collective bargaining significantly changed the patterns of teacher organization in local districts. Teachers have become more militant and strikes more frequent. Changes in the internal order and philosophy of the national organizations have blurred many of the historical distinctions between the NEA and AFT.

Beginning in the 1960s, the NEA encountered pressure to change its policies as a result of AFT successes and, internally, from leaders of its own urban associations. As a result, "The NEA experienced a fundamental reorientation not only in its policies but also in its philosophy as a professional organization."[9] Most of the specialized affiliated and associated organizations became independent. The superintendents withdrew in 1973, and although some local and state associations permit administrative membership, relatively few administrators now join. Internal control of the NEA is now in the hands of classroom teachers.

The NEA became more aggressive and gradually moved to endorse collective bargaining and to support the right to strike. Emphasis increased on improving salaries and teacher welfare. Discarding its tradition of being above partisan politics while lobbying for education bills, the NEA now endorses and supports political candidates.

The NEA today is a large organization with its headquarters in Washington, D.C., an annual budget of over $60 million, a full-time professional staff of over 2,000, and some 1.7 million members. Increased dues finance additional services, and local associations are strengthened by regional

The NEA and AFT meet in national conventions annually to set future policies.

field representatives. (Combined dues for the national and state associations ranged from $70 to over $150 per member in the early 1980s.) Activities of the National Association include lobbying for federal legislation; research on teaching and education; publication of numerous reports, bulletins, and journals; legal aid to teachers involved in educational litigation; and various other efforts and activities to increase public support for teaching and education.[10]

As the NEA has become more militant, the AFT has broadened its scope. In response to NEA criticisms of narrow concern for salaries and working conditions, the AFT increased its professional activities to include research, publications, and conferences to improve education. The AFT now represents many principals and supervisors, who are organized in separate locals. The AFT also has actively sought to organize paraprofessionals or teacher aides, Catholic parochial school teachers, college teachers, and health professionals in hospitals. Under the strong presidency of Albert Shanker, the national AFT has as been strengthened in recent years.[11]

Large city unions are still the backbone of the AFT and state organizations are rather weak, except in New York where the AFT reaped the legacy of a short-lived 1972 NEA-AFT state merger.

The similarities today between the NEA and AFT are more striking than the differences. Both now engage in collective bargaining, strikes, and political action to improve teacher welfare, as well as various professional activities. Both seek a federal collective bargaining law for state and local employees, though they advocate different approaches. (The NEA prefers a separate law for public employees, while the AFT would like to see the National Labor Relations Act extended.) Some differences are internal. The NEA, for example, elects officers by secret ballot and guarantees representation for ethnic minorities, while the AFT has a roll-call vote and opposes quotas.[12]

Merger has been a perennial issue for the NEA and AFT in recent years. National merger talks broke down in 1974, and the NEA's experience with state mergers in Florida and New York led it to ban future local mergers. Though the substantive dif-

Albert Shanker

Born and raised in New York City, Shanker is a graduate of the University of Illinois and did graduate work in philosophy and mathematics at Columbia University. He taught for 7 years in New York City public schools. Since 1959 he has been involved full time in union activity, beginning as an organizer. In 1964 he was elected president of the United Federation of Teachers in New York City and firmly established his reputation as a talented and shrewd strategist. Shanker was elected president of the American Federation of Teachers in 1974. He retains his position as head of the largest local teachers' union in the country, is vice-president of the New York State AFL-CIO, and is active in other aspects of the labor movement as well. Realistic and pragmatic, Shanker is one of the most powerful individuals in American education.

ferences between the NEA and AFT are now less than in the 1950s, merging would be difficult in the immediate future.[13]

The AFT's affiliation with the AFL-CIO is still a stumbling block for the NEA, despite the latter's political cooperation with a public employees' union affiliated with the AFL-CIO. The AFT fears being swallowed in a merger with the much larger NEA. Leaders are rivals and have vested interests in their own organizations. Representational elections are costly for both, however, and some type of accommodation or merger will probably occur eventually.

Teacher organizations are obviously here to stay. Future gains in membership, however, will be more modest than in the past. Most teachers are now affiliated with one of the national organizations, and the number of teachers is not increasing as rapidly because of declining enrollments. The NEA and AFT will probably continue their power struggle to represent teachers. Per-

haps more important to both organizations than merger will be their success in collective bargaining and political action.

Collective Bargaining

The role of teachers in educational decision making has been transformed in recent years by collective bargaining and written contracts. Traditionally, boards of education determined teacher salaries and working conditions, subject to any state-mandated minimums. Teacher organizations might submit salary requests or proposals, but boards were under no legal obligation even to discuss these with the teachers. In 1959, Wisconsin became the first state to guarantee public employees the right to organize and negotiate. Only a few school districts in the entire country then had negotiated written agreements with their teachers.[14]

Events in New York City in 1960–62 were a major catalyst for the expansion of collective bargaining. After teachers supported collective bargaining by a 3-to-1 referendum and two 1-day district-wide strikes, the local AFT union successfully negotiated a 40-page contract with the New York City Board of Education. Meanwhile, the NEA began to shift its policy to support "professional negotiations," and President John F. Kennedy extended collective bargaining rights to federal employees. These developments stimulated organization and collective bargaining among teachers and other government employees.[15]

With the changing attitudes of teachers and their organizations toward collective bargaining, more states adopted legislation mandating or permitting bargaining by public employees. Over two-thirds of the states now have public employee or teacher collective bargaining legislation. In states without such legislation (mostly in the South), local boards of education may agree to negotiate with teacher representatives even though not so required by

law.[16] The overwhelming majority of American teachers are now covered by negotiated contracts.

The state laws establish guidelines for negotiations and set up machinery to administer the law, although specific provisions vary. Some are very comprehensive whereas others provide limited rights for teachers. Most include some arrangement for union security (e.g., payroll deduction of dues), about half permit binding arbitration, and a few states allow teachers the right to strike.

Under collective bargaining, one organization has the exclusive right to represent everyone in the bargaining unit. The AFT and NEA have competed in some districts for the right to represent teachers. In such situations, a representational election is held and the organization favored by the majority represents all teachers—whether members or nonmembers—in the bargaining unit.

Collective bargaining is a "process

The end product of hours of negotiations—a signed contract.

whereby a representative of the employees and their employer jointly determine their conditions of employment."[17] Both sides are expected to bargain in good faith, making offers and counteroffers, to achieve a mutually acceptable written agreement on terms and conditions of employment. Under collective bargaining, policymaking in education becomes a shared responsibility of employer and employee rather than a responsibility of the board of education alone.

Bargaining is usually conducted by negotiation committees selected by each side. Officers of the teachers' organization or a specially selected negotiation team bargain for the teachers; central office administrators often represent the board of education. The teachers may have a consultant and assistance from a field office of the NEA or AFT. Increasingly, each side hires a lawyer or negotiations expert to be their chief negotiator at the bargaining table.

Since it is usually anticipated that negotiations will take considerable time, meetings generally begin several months before the expiration of a contract. The teachers submit their proposals, or both sides may exchange proposals. Typically, each side initially asks for more than it expects to achieve. Individual items will be discussed, counterproposals offered, and compromises may be reached. Many sessions are usually necessary, and if agreement is not forthcoming, an impasse may be declared and fact-finding or mediation requested. (State laws provide guidelines for procedures resolving impasse situations.) Eventually, although sometimes only after round-the-clock bargaining, an agreement is reached by the negotiators. Members of the teachers' organization and the board of education then vote on ratification of the contract. Although strikes receive much publicity, they are the exception; most agreements are reached

through the regular collective bargaining process.

Collective bargaining agreements are usually lengthy documents, especially in districts where contracts have been negotiated for a number of years. (Contracts cover specified time periods, often two or three years.) Each contract is unique, but among the items usually included are recognition of the teachers' organization, grievance procedures, salary schedules (including salary supplements for coaching and extracurricular activities), working conditions (e.g., duration of school day, teaching load, and maximum class size) paid absences and leaves (e.g., for personal and family illness), insurance benefits, job security provisions (e.g., transfer and reduction-in-force procedures), and rights of the teachers' organization (including payroll dues deduction and released time for officers).

Trends and Issues in Negotiations. Teacher organizations are often forbidden from negotiating in a number of critical areas because state laws recognize the responsibility of elected school boards to set school policy. State laws may specify certain items that must be negotiated, e.g., salary and other terms and conditions of employment.

Teacher organizations, traditionally concerned with improving education, have exerted their influence on educational policy issues in the name of professionalism. Some boards and administrators have resisted this trend in the name of managerial rights and public control of education. Many educational policies inevitably affect working conditions and professional issues. Similarly, working conditions may affect educational policy and managerial rights, so it is difficult to draw a firm line between competing prerogatives.

The trend has been for negotiated contracts to become "stronger and broader as the bargaining relationship matures."[18] Thus, some contracts include provisions on instructional policy committees, number of teacher aides, substitute teachers, textbook selection, student discipline and grading procedures, teacher transfers, and participation in hiring and promotion decisions (for teachers, principals, and district-wide administrators, including the superintendent).

One recent study concluded that collective bargaining has limited the "flexibility of school boards in making budgetary decisions" and "made the principal's job more difficult." The effect on classrooms and the quality of education is more difficult to determine. Teacher morale has been improved, and teachers sometimes gain more autonomy.[19] Teacher organizations have increased their influence over educational policy in schools and districts through collective bargaining. Some critics charge that they have become too powerful.

In an era of declining enrollments, teacher surpluses, and limited teacher turnover, job security has been a major issue in negotiations in many school districts. State education laws may specify procedures for reductions in the teaching force, as do many contracts. (Generally, reverse seniority governs within tenure or certification areas.) A job-security clause in a local agreement might provide a paid sabbatical for retraining tenured teachers who would otherwise be no longer employed. Sometimes bargaining efforts to reduce class size may be a tactic to protect job security by maintaining the number of positions when enrollments drop. Job security provisions can be expensive, and boards of education generally oppose them.

The "agency fee" or "financial responsibility" clauses in contracts are sometimes an issue, not only in negotiating with the board, but also among teachers. An agency fee requires teachers who do not join the union or association representing the majority in the bargaining unit to pay a "fair share" fee to the organization, often equivalent to the amount of dues. (Some states have right-to-work laws which prohibit these arrangements.)

In some states and districts, third parties representing the public participate in educational negotiations. These "trilateral practices" may range from naming a citizens' advisory committee, to making bargaining proposals public, to having observers present at the negotiating sessions.[20]

Both the NEA and AFT are seeking a federal law guaranteeing state and local public employees the right to organize and bargain collectively. They also continue their efforts to amend and improve existing state legislation and to secure collective bargaining laws in the states without them. Some observers predict the development of regional bargaining as state financing of education increases. Laws, policies, and practices are still emerging in collective bargaining for teachers, and changes can be expected. With more experience and new mechanisms for settling collective bargaining disputes peacefully, strikes will probably lessen.

Strikes. Among the most notable changes in recent years are the increases in the number and length of strikes by teachers. Strikes are not a totally new phenomenon, however. There were 86 work stoppages by public school teachers in the 1940s and 1950s. Many factors contributed to the growing militancy of teachers in the 1960s and 1970s. The competition between the NEA and AFT and the new laws and practices regarding collective bargaining were mentioned earlier. The social activism of the civil rights movement made new forms of social protest more acceptable, while consolidation of districts and growth in enrollments created larger bureaucratic structures in schools and a feeling of alienation among teachers. Low salaries and poor morale, more upwardly mobile males, better educated young teachers, and growing professionalization also contributed to the militancy.[21]

Although the AFT had a reputation of being militant and willing to strike, it was not until 1964 that the AFT officially recognized the "right of locals to strike under certain circumstances." Teachers' attitudes toward strikes changed. In 1965, 53% indicated support for strikes by public school teachers; by 1973, support had grown to 74%. Reflecting this shift and stimulated externally by the AFT unions and internally by its own urban members, the NEA became more militant. In the 1960s, the NEA moved from professional sanctions (blacklisting a state or district to pressure the legislature or school board) to threats of mass resignations or refusals to renew contracts. Other strategies included not performing extracurricular duties and taking so-called professional holidays. The NEA finally officially supported strikes in the late 1960s.[22]

Teacher strikes still are controversial. Some teachers and many citizens feel that they are unprofessional. Many states have laws prohibiting them, but despite injunctions and penalties, the laws and courts have not prevented teacher strikes. Their numbers began to increase dramatically in the mid-1960s. (See Table 5–2.) The 1979–80 school year set a record with 235 teacher strikes. Eighty-six percent were by groups affiliated with the NEA. Many of the AFT strikes were in large-city districts and hence often involved many more teachers.[23]

Table 5–2.

Strikes by teachers: calendar years 1959 to 1979

Year	Number of strikes	Teachers involved	Days idle during year
1959	2	210	670
1960	3	5,490	5,490
1961	1	20	20
1962	1	20,000	20,000
1963	2	2,200	2,590
1964	9	14,400	30,600
1965	5	1,720	7,880
1966	30	37,300	58,500
1967	76	92,400	969,300
1968	88	145,000	2,180,000
1969	183	105,000	412,000
1970	152	94,800	935,600
1971	135	64,600	713,000
1972	87	33,900	207,300
1973	117	51,400	620,700
1974	133	60,100	538,100
1975	218	182,300	1,419,800
1976	138	65,100	713,500
1977	111	54,500	603,200
1978	125	50,100	554,500
1979	180	58,600	835,900

Source: National Center for Education Statistics, *The Condition of Education, 1978* (Washington, D.C.: U.S. Government Printing Office, 1978), p. 182; Bureau of Labor Statistics [BLS], *Analysis of Work Stoppages, 1977,* Bulletin 2032, U.S. Department of Labor, BLS, September 1979, p. 39; BLS *Analysis of Work Stoppages, 1978,* Bulletin 2066, June 1980, pp. 38–39; and (for 1979) unpublished figures from BLS. The data are for a calendar year rather than school year.

Not only was the number of strikes up from two or three a year in the 1950s, but they tended to be longer—averaging about 10 days in the 1970s, compared to 1 or 2

Grin and Bear It by Lichty & Wagner © Field Enterprises, Inc. Courtesy of Field Newspaper Syndicate.

"Your point about the rights of teachers to strike is well taken, Otis, but it's beginning to sound like you WANT us to strike!"

days through the early 1960s. In 1979, San Francisco teachers were on strike for 7 weeks, and Cleveland teachers for 11 weeks.

Salaries are generally the main issue in strikes. Work load, class size, job security, teacher evaluation, discipline, union rights, and maintenance of gains also are frequently the issues.

Although strikes make the headlines, thousands of agreements are concluded through the regular processes of collective bargaining, and most teachers have not gone on strike. Traditionally, the strike has been a union's last resort or ultimate weapon. In a few states, including Hawaii, Montana, Oregon, Pennsylvania, Vermont, and Wisconsin, strikes by public school teachers are legal. Most states that prohibit teachers from striking provide in their collective bargaining legislation alternative means of resolving disputes. These may include fact-finding, mediation, and binding arbitration.

If procedures reach an impasse, however, teachers sometimes strike despite the legal prohibition. Injunctions may be sought and penalties imposed on the union and individual strikers. Penalties are often specified in the legislation and, of course, vary. Union officials and teachers may be sent to jail for an illegal strike, and the teacher organization may be fined and lose its dues-deduction privileges. Under New York law teachers lose two days' pay for every day on strike. In some districts teachers have been fired for striking.

Emotions are strong during a strike, and name-calling, harassment, and incidents of petty vandalism against nonstrikers are not uncommon. Peer pressures to support the majority are intense. When there is not 100% support, strikes may be very divisive among teachers. In some schools for many years after a strike, teachers who picketed do not speak to the teachers who crossed the lines and taught during the strike. Teachers who substitute during

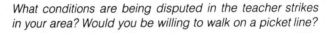

What conditions are being disputed in the teacher strikes in your area? Would you be willing to walk on a picket line?

a strike may find themselves ostracized or blacklisted as "scabs" by teachers who supported it.

Should teachers strike? Are strikes unprofessional? Should teacher strikes be legalized? Under what conditions, if any, is a strike justified? What penalties should be imposed for striking? What other tools do teachers have for achieving their goals?

What peaceful means can be used to resolve disputes between teachers and boards of education? These questions confront the teaching profession and our society as collective bargaining in the public sector matures and evolves. What are your views on these issues as a citizen and future teacher?

ACTIVITY 5–1
Teacher Strike

Your school board is facing financial problems and offers no salary increase to the teachers. Inflation has increased the cost of living. Your teacher organization is having a meeting to take a strike vote. Where do you stand? How do you feel about teachers striking? What additional information would you want? If you vote in the minority on a decision to strike, what do you do during the strike? Support the majority decision? Cross the picket line to teach? What are the likely consequences of your action, whichever you choose?

Investigate the law in your state regarding teacher strikes. Are there penalties and risks for teachers who strike? You might contact officials of local teacher organizations, regional offices of the NEA or AFT, or do research in the library on the law and recent teacher strikes. You can present your findings and the reasons for your position in an oral or written report, or your instructor may want to devote class time to a role-playing situation.

Political Action

For many years, in line with a prevailing belief that schools should stay out of politics and politics out of education, organized teachers maintained a low profile in political affairs. Nonetheless, teacher organizations have a long record of involvement in educational politics. The NEA for many years has actively lobbied for federal aid to education and other legislation. The state teachers' associations, often working closely with state organizations of school boards, superintendents, and PTAs, have influenced educational legislation in the states.[24] Moreover, collective bargaining is itself a form of political action.

Teacher organizations greatly increased their political activities and expanded in the 1970s into partisan political campaigns. Both the NEA and AFT now endorse candidates and contribute millions of dollars to political campaign funds—the NEA through its Political Action Committee (NEA-PAC), and the AFT through its Committee on Public Education (COPE). Many individual teachers work to elect candidates whom their organizations endorse. More teachers are running for political office themselves, serving in state legislatures and on local school boards.[25]

The teacher organizations regularly issue what the NEA calls a "Legislative Report Card," which indicates how state or federal public officials voted on education bills and other issues of concern to teachers. Moreover, the AFT's alliance with state labor councils and the AFL-CIO, and the NEA's alliance with public employee unions in the Coalition of American Public Employees, have increased their political power at the state and national levels. Organized teachers have become more influential and powerful as a result of their increased political activities in recent years.

PROFESSIONAL CONCERNS

Individual teachers and their local, state, and national organizations have many professional concerns. Teachers individually and through their organizations have sought to improve education and the status of the teaching profession. As we have seen, state associations for many years have sought and achieved legislation to improve salaries and working conditions. Local teacher organizations increasingly are using collective bargaining to enhance teacher welfare and teaching conditions. Among the most important professional concerns are salaries, fringe benefits, working conditions, tenure, professional development, and teacher rights.

Salaries

Historically, teaching has been a field where salaries are relatively low. Teacher salaries have increased in recent years, but not always in step with inflation. Beginning salaries for teachers are lower than those received by most other college graduates. According to recent government statistics, for example, engineers, computer specialists, accountants, sales people, registered nurses, and managers received several thousand dollars higher average starting salaries than teachers.[26]

Moreover, maximum salaries in teaching are also considerably lower than in many other occupations. Some teachers increase their income by assuming additional responsibilities for extra pay, such as coaching or teaching summer school. Many moonlight in second jobs. Others seek advancement by leaving the classroom and becoming administrators; superintendents,

principals, and supervisors receive substantially higher salaries than teachers.

Salary is usually the major issue in negotiations. Salaries differ from district to district, and average salaries vary considerably among the states. In 1978–79, the average salary of teachers was $15,040. Teachers in Arkansas averaged $11,126, and those in Alaska $24,150. Salaries generally are highest in the Far West and lowest in the South. The average beginning salary was $10,138 and the average maximum salary, $20,234.[27]

Today most districts have a single salary schedule for all classroom teachers. Guidance counselors, department chairpersons, and some specialists may be on different salary schedules or on an index tied to the teachers' salary schedule. Historically, teachers bargained individually for salaries, or salary schedules were differentiated on the basis of sex, race, marital status, or level of teaching. For example, high school teachers usually received more than elementary teachers and men more than women.

Salaries of teachers are usually based on years of teaching experience and graduate credits. Table 5–3 is a sample salary schedule. Salary schedules differ in dollar amounts as well as the number of steps to reach maximum salary and the amounts between steps and classes. Beginning teachers with a B.A. or B.S. degree start at the minimum (step 1, class 1). Usually teachers advance each year to the next step until they reach the top step or maximum. Some districts provide supermaximum or longevity steps (e.g., in Table 5–3, at 20, 25, and 30 years). Teachers completing graduate credits or degrees (or receiving in-service credits) may also move horizontally along the salary schedule to a new salary class. Teachers moving to another district generally will receive credit for their prior teaching experience and be placed on an appropriate step. Many districts, however, limit the number

Table 5–3.
Teachers' salary schedule

Step	Class 1 BA	Class 2 BA+30	Class 3 BA+45	Class 4 MA	Class 5 BA+60	Class 6 MA+15	Class 7 BA+75	Class 8 MA+30	Class 9 BA+90	Class 10 MA+45	Class 11 MA+60	Class 12 Doctorate
1	12,834	14,013	14,667	14,759	15,257	15,309	15,847	15,859	16,370	16,422	16,986	17,640
2	13,397	14,701	15,348	15,467	15,944	16,016	16,528	16,580	17,058	17,142	17,706	18,348
3	13,960	15,389	16,029	16,174	16,631	16,723	17,207	17,300	17,745	17,863	18,426	19,054
4	14,525	16,076	16,711	16,881	17,319	17,431	17,889	18,020	18,433	18,583	19,147	19,762
5	15,086	16,770	17,392	17,589	18,008	18,139	18,570	18,740	19,121	19,302	19,867	20,469
6	15,650	17,464	18,073	18,295	18,694	18,845	19,258	19,461	19,807	20,024	20,587	21,184
7	16,212	18,159	18,754	19,003	19,382	19,558	19,945	20,180	20,496	20,744	21,308	21,896
8	16,776	18,852	19,434	19,710	20,069	20,272	20,633	20,901	21,184	21,463	22,028	22,610
9	17,339	19,546	20,123	20,417	20,756	20,987	21,320	21,622	21,870	22,184	22,748	23,325
10	17,903	20,240	20,809	21,130	21,445	21,699	22,007	22,341	22,558	22,905	23,469	24,038
11	18,459	20,933	21,497	21,852	22,139	22,414	22,695	23,069	23,246	23,632	24,194	24,752
12	19,014	21,687	22,316	22,617	22,880	23,271	23,429	23,848	24,070	24,411	25,067	25,628
13	19,558	22,316	22,897	23,344	23,475	23,868	24,070	24,477	24,659	25,078	25,682	26,257
14	20,012	22,897	23,481	23,953	24,070	24,497	24,659	25,112	25,249	25,695	26,304	26,885
15	20,431	23,481	24,070	24,562	24,627	25,124	25,249	25,701	25,832	26,317	26,925	27,489
16	20,862	24,163	24,724	25,243	25,276	25,820	25,931	26,389	26,480	27,043	27,606	28,182
20				25,743		26,320		26,889		27,543	28,106	28,682
25				26,243		26,820		27,389		28,043	28,606	29,182
30				26,743		27,320		27,889		28,543	29,106	29,682

of years of credit they will grant for prior teaching experience.

Some districts use an index salary schedule, specifying increments as percentages of a base salary. For example, step 2 in the B.A. class might be 104% of base; B.A. step 3, 109% of base; and M.A. step 1, 115% of base.

Merit Pay. Some districts have enacted varying forms of merit pay to reward superior teachers. Most teachers and both the NEA and AFT are strongly opposed to merit pay because of the difficulties in evaluating teachers fairly. Although the concept is popular with many citizens and board members, the problems in implementing a fair program have led many districts to abandon merit plans.

True merit pay systems are rare. Only 4% of districts had merit pay plans in the late 1970s. With the extension of collective bargaining agreements, the percentage has probably declined further.[28]

ACTIVITY 5–2
Investigate Local Teacher Salaries

Obtain copies of several current teachers' salary schedules, for example, from your hometown, a local district, or a district where you would like to teach. (You may want to exchange copies with other students.) Analyze and compare the minimum and maximum salaries, number of steps, the amounts of increments, and special features. Which do you think is the best schedule? For additional comparisons, try to locate a recent study of teacher salaries (e.g., NEA's *Salary Schedules*, AFT's *Survey of Teacher Salaries*, or a regional analysis).

Chapter Five

This cartoon is from the 1920s, but the message is still true today.

THE PUBLIC PAYROLL

Reprinted by permission of J.N. "Ding" Darling Foundation, Inc., Des Moines, Iowa.

Differentiated Staffing. Under differentiated staffing, teachers may specialize in areas of individual strength and advance along a career ladder while remaining within the classroom. Most proposals for differentiated staffing envision a hierarchy, for example, a master teacher, associate teachers, beginning teachers, and teacher interns, as well as teacher assistants. Community consultants, staff specialists, instruction assistants, and clerical aides may also be utilized. Differentiated staffing is a form of team teaching. Moreover, since teachers at different ranks with varying responsibilities generally receive different salaries, it may be a means of providing merit pay.

Although differentiated staffing has been much discussed, implementation usually has been limited to the use of paraprofessionals and teacher aides who are paid much less than teachers and usually have fewer qualifications. Some economy-minded districts use teacher aides to increase class size and to replace professional, certified teachers. Hence, the NEA urges that local associations be involved in planning and implementing differentiated staffing and that certified teachers define the responsibilities of paraprofessionals. Some negotiated contracts provide a minimum number of aides per classroom. In New York City, paraprofessionals affiliated with the AFT successfully bargained with the Board of Education for assistance for college study. Many thus have become regular teachers.

Fringe Benefits

Teachers receive salary supplements in the form of fringe benefits—paid leaves, insurance coverage, and various other services. The district's cost to provide fringe benefits is usually several thousand dollars per teacher. Some benefits, such as retirement, are mandated by state law. Specific provisions vary a great deal.

Virtually all districts provide some form of paid sick leave, though the number of days per year and the extent to which sick leave may be accumulated vary from district to district. Usually from 10 to 19 days a year are permitted, and the trend is to permit accumulation or carry-over of unused sick-leave days.

Most districts provide a few additional days for personal leave, but about a third charge these days to sick leave. Personal leave may be granted for illness or death in the immediate family, religious holidays, or family responsibilities. Specific policies

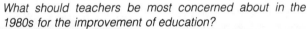

What should teachers be most concerned about in the 1980s for the improvement of education?

Chapter Five

vary, of course, and in some districts, the cost of a substitute is deducted from the teacher's salary.[29]

Unpaid leaves of absence for a year or two may be granted for such purposes as study, exchange teaching, Peace Corps service, election and service in political office, services for a teachers' organization, military service, and maternity or child care. A leave of absence ensures the teacher a position upon return without loss of salary status and seniority rights.

Most districts provide group health insurance coverage which may include hospitalization, medical-surgical, major medical, dental, and other health services. The specific coverage and the extent to which the district pays the cost, especially for dependents, vary greatly.

Other types of insurance that may be provided are life insurance, professional liability insurance, legal insurance, and disability insurance (income protection). Teachers often are covered by workmen's compensation and social security.

All states have teacher retirement systems, and a few large cities have their own systems. Many are contributory systems, in which the teacher and district (or state) each contribute, for example, 5% of salary. Teachers who move to another state may be able to purchase retirement credit for their out-of-state experience. The minimum age for retirement ranges from 55 to 65, and the required minimum number of years of teaching varies greatly. About one-third of districts provide severance pay, usually calculating credit for accumulated unused sick days. Some districts offer other incentives to encourage highly paid teachers to retire when first eligible. Tax-deferred annuities (as well as social security) may also be available to supplement retirement income.

Working Conditions

Conditions for teaching vary tremendously.

Some are determined by state laws, negotiated in local agreements, or established in district policies. Others may be affected by the size of the school or district and the nature of the community (e.g., its financial resources and interest in education). Provisions on working conditions in bargaining agreements may include teaching load, maximum class size, number of teaching periods, maximum number of students, length of school day and school year, unassigned periods of preparation time, teaching assignments, duty-free lunch period, instructional equipment and materials, specialists, relief from nonteaching duties, teacher aides, teachers' work area, faculty lounge, rest rooms, parking space, number and duration of after-school meetings, and evaluation procedures (e.g., written reports, teacher's right to respond, and access to personnel file). Most contracts probably do not include all of these items, but they indicate the scope.

Tenure

Most states have laws providing that after evaluation during a probationary period (usually two to three years), teachers can receive tenure or security of employment. Tenure usually applies only within the district. Sometimes transfer to another tenure area within a district (e.g., from elementary to high school teacher) requires a new probationary period. Tenure does not guarantee teachers jobs if positions are eliminated because of financial emergencies, a decline in enrollment, or a decision to drop certain subjects. Tenure assures teachers that they will not be dismissed for espousing unpopular views or for arbitrary or capricious reasons.

Tenured teachers may be dismissed for incompetence, but they are assured due process. Among the reasons specified in state statutes for dismissal of tenured teachers are immorality, insubordination, neglect of duty, inefficiency, mental incapacity, unprofessional conduct, and "good and just cause." Tenure laws enumerate the procedures for dismissal of tenured teachers. They must receive a written notice specifying charges, and they have the right to a hearing and appeal.

In some states, tenure applies only in large city districts, or very small districts are exempt from tenure laws. In the absence of tenure, teachers will have individual annual, continuing, or long-term contracts for a definite number of years (e.g., 3 to 5 years). These provide less protection for teachers, but usually sufficient notice must be given if a contract is not being renewed. In unusual situations, teachers may be suspended or dismissed during a school year.[30]

Tenure has been criticized on grounds that it protects incompetent teachers or encourages teachers to be lax about their professional responsibilities. Periodically there are efforts to abolish tenure or to make it renewable every five years. Meanwhile, some states have enacted fair dismissal laws and court decisions have begun to extend certain due-process rights to non-tenured teachers whose contracts are not renewed. These trends provide greater protection to all teachers.

Professional Development

Virtually all school districts have provided or encouraged formal and informal in-service teacher education or staff development. Typical practices include district-run in-service workshops; superintendent's conference days; professional libraries; tuition reimbursement and salary increments for advanced study; unpaid leaves of absence or paid sabbaticals for study or travel; and released time and travel expenses for school visitations and professional conferences. Certification and tenure laws sometimes specify professional development standards which must be maintained.

Organized teachers have sought a greater role in professional development as part of the larger effort of the profession to assume responsibility for teacher education. Teacher organizations may offer in-service courses, publish curriculum and resource guides, and organize professional conferences for teachers. Beginning in the late 1970s, a number of local NEA and AFT groups received federal funds to operate teacher centers for professional development renewal.[31]

Teacher Rights

The NEA and AFT have financed many lawsuits to protect the rights of their members and the teaching profession. As the U.S. Supreme Court stated in the landmark *Tinker* case, "It can hardly be argued that either students or teachers shed their constitutional rights to freedom of speech or expression at the schoolhouse gate."[32] Academic freedom and freedom of speech in the classroom, however, are not absolute rights. The courts generally have balanced individual rights with society's interest in maintaining school discipline. Relevant controversial issues may be discussed in the classroom, and teachers can assign books or articles containing offensive language. But the courts have upheld the dismissal of a teacher for making "unbecoming and unnecessary risqué remarks . . . of an immoral nature."[33]

Louis Fischer and David Schimmel summarize the status of academic freedom in public school classrooms:

> As a general rule, the teacher's use of controversial material or language will be protected by the First Amendment unless it can be shown that it is irrelevant to her teaching objective, inappropriate to the age and maturity of her students, or disruptive of school discipline.

But they also warn that despite the laws and court decisions, "A sizable gap exists between what the law is and what communities practice. It would be both naive and misleading to suggest that teachers have as much freedom of expression in practice as the courts allow them."[34]

A teacher's freedom of speech and association outside the classroom are also protected by the First Amendment. Teachers cannot legally be dismissed for advocating unpopular views, e.g., on foreign policy, abortion, or politics. Many cases in the 1950s successfully challenged loyalty oaths that required teachers to disclaim membership in subversive organizations. The courts, however, have sustained laws requiring public employees to uphold the U.S. Constitution. The First Amendment generally also protects a teacher who publicly criticizes school officials and policies. The courts have indicated limits to this right if confidentiality is breached, grievance procedures ignored, or relationships with a superior impaired.[35]

Courts have ruled that the First Amendment protects teachers who are members of controversial organizations such as the Nazi Party or Ku Klux Klan. But in this area, too, there is often a gap between law and practice. Even less radical groups may be suspect. Indeed, in conservative communities, administrators may oppose militant teacher unions. "A variety of subtle means," Fischer and Schimmel caution, may be "used to discourage teacher participation in such organizations, such as less favorable evaluation reports, transfer to less desirable teaching situations, and assignment to more difficult classes."[36] Moreover, the right to join a teacher organization does not include the right to strike where teacher strikes are illegal. The Supreme Court has upheld a board that dismissed striking teachers, but this power rarely has been invoked by districts.[37]

Historically, teachers have been expected to be models of exemplary behavior in their private lives (see Chapter 2). Teachers who violate community standards of conduct—homosexuals, unwed mothers, trans-sexuals—may find themselves dismissed. The courts in recent years, however, have generally protected the private lives of teachers. Beyond the limits of court protection are public immoral or illegal conduct, sexual relations with a student, and behavior that negatively affects teaching. The courts have upheld school districts that dismissed teachers convicted on marijuana charges.

The Supreme Court has ruled that school districts cannot arbitrarily require pregnant teachers to take a mandatory leave in the fourth or fifth month of pregnancy, and federal regulations now prohibit any arbitrary requirement of leave for pregnancy. Reasonable residency requirements for public employees have been supported. The Supreme Court also has upheld the use of corporal punishment to discipline students.[38]

Many court decisions have upheld the due-process rights of teachers who have been dismissed or who have not been granted tenure. These are important protections. Other court cases have involved teachers' grooming and dress. The courts protected beards as symbolic speech and generally upheld dress codes. Many schools, however, have relaxed their regulations on dress.

The law on teacher rights is still evolving, and in some areas there are conflicting decisions by district courts or different interpretations of Supreme Court decisions. As mentioned earlier, there is often a gap between legal rights and actual practice. Some teachers have been dismissed for reasons that are clearly illegal, but court challenges are not always feasible. Unless they wish to risk dismissal, teachers on probationary status may be well-advised to be cautious and not rock the boat. All teachers should be aware of their legal rights, however, and realize that the teacher organizations will assist them if they are treated unjustly by their school districts.

The NEA's DuShane Emergency Fund and the National Teachers Assistance Fund, as well as the American Civil Liberties Union, have been especially active.

SUMMARY

Teacher organizations have grown and substantially changed in recent decades. The NEA and AFT ideologically represent what one commentator describes as a "kind of two party system in education" competing for the "allegiance and dues of teachers."[39] This competition has contributed to the growing militancy of teachers who have resorted more frequently to strikes. Educational power relationships have changed further through the quiet revolution of collective bargaining in local districts. As one observer noted, "The impact of collective bargaining and negotiations on the governance and operations of educational institutions has been greater than that of any other single force in the last decade."[40] More visible has been the growing involvement in partisan politics. Campaign contributions and teacher volunteers have increased the political clout of teachers in elections and legislatures.

For many years, teacher organizations have striven to improve salaries and working conditions and to protect teachers' legal rights. Increasingly they turn their attention to other professional concerns and educational policy, seeking a greater role in decision making. Organized teachers still strive for the goal of their predecessors who founded the National Teachers Association in 1857: "To elevate the character and advance the interest of the profession of teaching and to promote the cause of popular education in the United States."[41]

How do *you* feel about teachers engaging in collective bargaining, strikes, and political activities? What do you think is the proper role of teachers and their organizations in determining educational policy in schools and districts or at the state and national levels? Even as war is too important to be left to the generals, is education too important to be left to the educators? Which educators should influence what decisions? Are teachers exercising appropriate professional prerogatives or playing power politics? We'll look at other aspects of the governance of education, including the roles of the public, its elected representatives, and educational administrators in Chapter 9.

NOTES

1. Alan Rosenthal, *Pedagogues and Power: Teacher Groups in School Politics* (Syracuse, N.Y.: Syracuse University Press, 1969), p. 185.

2. Myron Lieberman, *Education as a Profession* (Englewood Cliffs, N.J.: Prentice-Hall, 1956), pp. 1–6; Ronald D. Corwin, *A Sociology of Education* (New York: Appleton-Century-Crofts, 1965), pp. 217–64; and Robert J. Havighurst and Daniel U. Levine, *Society and Education*, 5th ed. (Boston: Allyn and Bacon, 1979), pp. 560–61.

3. Donald A. Myers, *Teacher Power: Professionalization and Collective Bargaining* (Lexington, Mass.: D.C. Heath, 1973), p. 28.

4. Edgar B. Wesley, *NEA: The First Hundred Years: The Building of the Teaching Profession* (New York: Harper & Brothers, 1957), pp. 20–23, 44, 55, 334–37. The present name, National Education Association, was adopted in 1906.

5. Myron Lieberman and Michael H. Moskow, *Collective Negotiations for Teachers* (New York: Rand McNally, 1966), p. 56.

6. Commission on Educational Reconstruction, *Organizing the Teaching Profession* (Glencoe, Ill.: The Free Press, 1955), pp. 24–29.

7. Lieberman and Moskow, *Collective Negotiations*, p. 302; and Marshall O. Donley, Jr., *Power to the Teacher: How America's Teachers Became Militant* (Bloomington, Ind.: Indiana University Press, 1976), p. 44.

8. For comparisons of the NEA and AFT in the 1950s and 1960s, see Lieberman, *Education as a Profession*, pp. 257–333; Robert E. Doherty and Walter E. Oberer, *Teachers, School Boards, and Collective Bargaining: A Changing of the Guard* (Cornell, N.Y.: New York State School of Industrial and Labor Relations, Cornell University, 1967), pp. 22–44; James D. Koerner, *Who Controls American Education?* (Boston: Beacon Press, 1968), pp. 26–45; and T. M. Stinnett, *Turmoil*

Chapter Five

in Teaching: A History of the Organizational Struggle for America's Teachers (New York: Macmillan, 1968), pp. 87–224.

9. Lorraine M. McDonnell, "The Internal Politics of the NEA," *Phi Delta Kappan* 58, no. 2 (October 1976): 185. See also Donley, *Power to the Teacher.*

10. *NEA Handbook, 1979–80* (Washington, D.C.: NEA, 1979).

11. Bernard Bard, "Albert Shanker: A Portrait in Power," *Phi Delta Kappan* 56, no. 7 (March 1975): 466–72.

12. Marshall O. Donley, Jr., *The Future of Teacher Power in America* (Bloomington, Ind.: Phi Delta Kappa, 1977), p. 30; and Stanley M. Elam, "Teachers in Politics and the Merger Issue," *Phi Delta Kappan* 58, no. 2 (October 1976): 154.

13. Kenneth P. Lubetsky, "Will the NEA and the AFT Ever Merge?" *Educational Forum* 41, no. 3 (March 1977): 309–16.

14. Michael H. Moskow and Robert E. Doherty, "United States," *Teacher Unions and Associations: A Comparative Study*, ed. Albert A. Blum (Urbana: University of Illinois Press, 1969), pp. 305–6.

15. Lieberman and Moskow, *Collective Negotiations*, pp. 35–54. By the mid-1970s the NEA espoused collective bargaining; the terms are now used interchangeably.

16. "State-by-State Roundup of Collective Bargaining Laws," *Phi Delta Kappan* 60, no. 6 (February 1979): 472–73. Only in Virginia, as a result of a state court decision, are collective bargaining agreements with government agencies forbidden.

17. Lieberman and Moskow, *Collective Negotiations*, p. 418.

18. Lorraine McDonnell and Anthony Pascal, *Organized Teachers in American Schools* (Santa Monica, Calif: Rand Corp., 1979), p. 83.

19. Ibid., p. 75.

20. John Ralph Pisapia, "Trilateral Practices and the Public Sector Bargaining Model," *Phi Delta Kappan* 60, no. 6 (February 1979): 424–27; and Douglas E. Mitchell, "The Impact of Collective Bargaining on Public and Client Interests in Education," *Teachers College Record* 40, no. 4 (May 1979): 695–717.

21. Lieberman and Moskow, *Collective Negotiations*, pp. 90–91; James Cass and Max Birnbaum, "What Makes Teachers Militant," *Saturday Review* 51 (20 January 1968): 54–56; Ronald C. Corwin, "The New Teaching Profession," *Teacher Education*, ed. Kevin Ryan. 74th Yearbook of the National Society for the Study of Education. (Chicago: NSSE, 1975), pp. 230–64; and Donley, *Power to the Teacher*, pp. 191–202.

22. Lieberman and Moskow, *Collective Negotiations*, p. 292; Donley, *Power to the Teacher*, pp. 80–126; and correspondence from William S. Graybeal, NEA Research, 22 April 1980.

23. *American Teacher* 65, no. 1 (September 1980): 8.

24. See, for example, Nicholas A. Masters, Robert H. Salisbury, and Thomas H. Eliot, *State Politics and Public Schools* (New York: Knopf, 1964).

25. James Browne, "Power Politics for Teachers, Modern Style," *Phi Delta Kappan* 58, no. 21 (October 1976): 158–64.

26. National Center for Education Statistics, *The Condition of Education, 1979* (Washington, D.C.: U.S. Government Printing Office, 1979), pp. 86–87.

27. *Financial Status of the Public Schools, 1979*, NEA Research Memo, (Washington, D.C.: NEA, 1979), p. 37; and *Salary Schedules, 1978–79*, NEA Research Memo, (Washington, D.C.: NEA, 1979), p. 5.

28. Educational Research Service [ERS], *Merit Pay for Teachers* (Arlington, Va.: ERS, 1979), p. 35.

29. ERS, *Fringe Benefits for Teachers, 1975–76*, (Arlington, Va.: ERS, 1976), pp. 11–13.

30. NEA, *Teacher Tenure and Contracts, A Summary of State Statutes*, Research Report 1972-R11 (Washington, D.C.: NEA, 1972).

31. See Maurice Leiter and Myrna Cooper, "How Teacher Unionists View In-Service Education," *Teachers College Record* 80, no. 1 (September 1978): 107–26, and other articles in this issue devoted to staff development.

32. Quoted in Louis Fischer and David Schimmel, *The Civil Rights of Teachers* (New York: Harper & Row, 1973), p. 191.

33. Ibid., p. 41.

34. Ibid., pp. 149–50.

35. Ibid., pp. 14–27.

36. Ibid., p. 155.

37. Thomas J. Flygare, "Supreme Court Upholds [Wisconsin] Board's Right to Fire Striking Teachers," *Phi Delta Kappan* 58, no. 2 (October 1976): 206–7.

38. Perry A. Zirkel, ed., *A Digest of Supreme Court Decisions Affecting Education* (Bloomington, Inc.: Phi Delta Kappa, 1978), pp. 45–46, 66, 98–99; and Tobyann Boonin, "The Benighted Status of U.S. School Corporal Punishment Practice," *Phi Delta Kappan* 60, no. 5 (January 1979): 395–96.

39. Koerner, *Who Controls American Education?*, p. 29.

40. Steven M. Goldschmidt, "Collective Bargaining," *Yearbook of School Law, 1976*, ed. Philip K. Piele (Topeka, Kansas: National Organization on Legal Problems of Education, 1976), p. 215.

41. Wesley, *NEA: The First Hundred Years*, p. 23.

FOR FURTHER STUDY

Corwin, Ronald G. *Militant Professionalism*. New York: Appleton-Century-Crofts, 1970.

Cresswell, Anthony M., et al. *Teachers, Unions, & Collective Bargaining in Public Education*. Berkeley, Calif.: McCutchan, 1980.

Dorros, Sidney. *Teaching as a Profession*. Columbus, Ohio: Charles E. Merrill Publishing Co., 1968.

Flygare, Thomas. *Collective Bargaining in the Public Schools*. Bloomington, Ind.: Phi Delta Kappa Educational Foundation, 1977.

Perry, Charles R., and Wildman, Wesley A. *The Impact of Negotiations in Public Education*. Worthington, Ohio: Charles A. Jones Publishing Co., 1970.

Rubin, David. *The Rights of Teachers: The Basic ACLU Guide to a Teacher's Constitutional Rights*. New York: Discus/Avon, 1972.

Stinnett, T.M. *Professional Problems of Teachers*. 3rd ed. New York: Macmillan, 1968.

Walter, Robert L. *The Teacher and Collective Bargaining*. Lincoln, Neb.: Professional Educators Publications, 1975.

6

Effective Teaching

My heart is singing for joy this morning. A miracle has happened! The light of understanding has shone upon my little pupil's mind, and behold, all things are changed.

Annie Sullivan, 1887

Education is too significant and dynamic an enterprise to be left to mere technicians; and we might as well begin now the prodigious task of preparing men and women who understand not only the substance of what they are teaching but also the theories behind the particular strategies they employ to convey that substance.

Lawrence A. Cremin, 1965

A common thread running through the previous chapters is that teachers exert a lot of influence on students' lives. Teaching,

as Chapters 4 and 5 noted, requires special training and is enhanced when educators work together. Reading this you may wonder even more about the specific kinds of skills it takes to become an effective teacher, whose words and actions proclaim to students, "I am glad I'm here because you're here, and before today's class ends you'll be glad you're here, too."

It is understandable if you are apprehensive about being responsible for a class of 25 to 35 students. To be effective, you not only must know your subject matter well, you must organize and present it in an appealing manner. You must become an expert in reading the individual needs of your students, learning when it is best to talk and when it is best to listen, so that there are vibrant exchanges of opinion with a minimum of discipline problems.

To understand the techniques of effective teaching, we must first appreciate how learners learn. Therefore, the first section of the chapter briefly examines some of the major perspectives that describe the learning phenomenon. Behaviorism and cognitivism, the two dominant theories of learning, are highlighted.

The second section of the chapter focuses on classroom interactions, especially those over which the teacher has some control. Teacher behaviors toward students (self-fulfilling prophecy and body language) and environmental factors (class size and room decor) are examples. Motivation and discipline, perennial concerns of teachers, also will be discussed.

How will you know whether you have been successful in the classroom? The final section of Chapter 6 describes the methods that are employed now to evaluate teachers. It also discusses why such factors as the teacher's ability to manage the classroom, the performance of students on standardized tests, the evaluations of students and parents, and the teacher's personality are or are not good indicators of teacher performance.

Such topics crystalize the main issue of the chapter: What is effective teaching? There are related issues: To what extent should teacher performance in the classroom be monitored? What criteria should be used to determine the effectiveness of teaching?

After you have read Chapter 6, you should be able to (1) summarize the major features of behaviorism, cognitivism, and humanistic psychology; (2) list instructional practices that appear most effective in increasing student performance in the classroom; and (3) state the chief methods of the evaluation of teacher performance.

PERSPECTIVES ON LEARNING

What is learning? How does it happen? Why can it be so easy some times and so difficult at others? Why will certain teaching methods excite some pupils and bore others? Do we use different learning processes when we memorize facts, gain motor skills, solve problems, or seek comprehension?

For centuries philosophers have grappled with these complex questions. More recently psychologists developed learning theories based on experiments with animals and clinical and classroom observations of students. Today it is recognized that there is no grand theory that can satisfactorily explain all types of learning; also, most teachers employ a variety of strategies that reflect aspects of several theories of education. Therefore, this segment is called perspectives on learning, an examination of the explanations of *how* individuals learn. (Later chapters explore *what* students ought to learn.)

Lest you assume that a discussion of learning perspectives is just for psychologists and professors of education, remember that all teachers have operational learning theories. It will be implicit in whatever you do in the classroom.[1] Will you trust students to be alone, or will you insist on constant supervision? To what extent will you plan lessons based on students' interests, as opposed to the textbook's arrangement? And what do you believe are the best ways to acquire, retain, and transfer knowledge? How you answer these questions day to day will reveal your learning theory or perspective.

What Is Learning?

Because we have done it for so long and because it seems so natural, we give little thought to what learning is and how complex are its many facets. Let's focus our attention briefly on learning in general, and then reflect on how learning was treated in schools for many centuries.

Learning has been defined as "a change in human disposition or capability which persists over a period of time and which is not simply ascribable to processes of growth."[2] This definition, by Robert M. Gagné, emphasizes that learning requires a change in behavior, it is not to be confused with whatever happens "naturally," and it cannot be a momentary change.

Gagné continues, noting that humans have developed five major categories of learning capabilities—three cognitive, one motor, and one affective. We are able, cognitively, to react to and influence our environment because of our basic ability to learn intelligently. We learn how to read numbers, signs, commands, and warnings. Moreover, we learn how to process information and repeat facts (information processing). Eventually we devise cognitive strategies, developing methods of problem solving and recalling particular events and details in books. Humans are able to take numerous bits of cognitive knowledge and use them to develop certain motor skills—driving a car, running a drill press, climbing an obstacle course. Finally, humans learn attitudes based on previously gained information and experiences.

How does learning take place? What techniques employed in teaching and learning are most effective in helping the learner remember? Gagné lists eight levels of learning, each given here with an example:

1. *signal learning:* the teacher may clap his or her hands to get attention, or the school may institute a bell system;

2. *stimulus-response* (or *operant learning*): the teacher's tone of voice indicates approval or disapproval, resulting in reinforcement of or change in students' behavior;

3. *chaining (motor):* the teacher instructs students in the proper sequencing of school events, i.e., how to enter the classroom, how to use the computer, how to sign up for the junior high band;

4. *verbal association:* the teacher shows students how to put words together that have meaning (a verse of poetry, a business letter, letters in the alphabet);

5. *multiple discrimination:* the teacher instructs students in differences and similarities between objects, such as geometric designs;

6. *concept learning:* the teacher aids learners in placing objects in a class or category and then responding to them (select all the green objects; name the events leading to the Civil War);

7. *principle learning:* the teacher assists the students in linking concepts to form a principle, e.g., for every action there is a reaction;

8. *problem-solving:* the teacher shows students how to apply principles to novel situations.

Obviously, these eight steps form a hierarchy of learning strategies. Teachers must decide when to employ them, consistent with knowledge of educational and developmental capabilities of students of various age levels.

What you just read in the previous paragraph you may assume is common sense. Remember, though, that proof of differences in learning abilities and stages of development is a phenomenon of the twentieth century. For many centuries it was assumed that all individuals, regardless of age, learned in the same way. In other words, children were considered miniature adults who reasoned just as their parents and elders did.

One of the earliest perspectives of learning familiar to American education has its origins in Greek culture, particularly in the writings of Plato and Aristotle. The unique characteristic of human beings, they believed, was rational thought. The mind could best be trained to reason through increasingly difficult intellectual endeavors. The subjects best suited for strengthening the

Chapter Six

"mind substance" were thought to be mathematics and philosophy. Socrates, Plato's mentor, had developed a questioning technique used in philosophy, particularly, that continually forces the students to justify their points of view.

In time, the curriculum that was supposed to provide the best training of the mind was grammar, rhetoric, logic, arithmetic, and geometry. Teachers resorted to drill work to increase memory skills and were not especially concerned whether students were really interested in the subjects. (In fact, it was argued that self-discipline was gained from studying an uninteresting topic).

This perspective on learning, which came to be called mental discipline, was very popular in this country in the colonial period and was predominant well past the Civil War. While its popularity has certainly diminished today, the belief that the mind can be trained is reflected in proposals by back-to-basics advocates.

A variety of factors in the late 1800s, including the development of psychology as a separate field of study, brought heated debates on the nature of learning. Two main schools of thought developed prior to World War II, plus many subtheories. The two dominant theories of learning are usually called behaviorism and cognitivism.[3] In the 1950s and 1960s a third perspective on learning—humanistic psychology— emerged.

Behaviorists assert that learning is the result of a connection or association made between a stimulus (sense impression) and a response. Pets responding to calls by their masters, infants showing off at a signal from their parents, or students reciting multiplication tables are examples of association learning. Cognitive theorists, on the other hand, see learning as a reorganization of a number of perceptions. They argue that most learning experiences cannot be described as small stimulus and response steps: a fifth grader suddenly grasps the concept that multiplication is successive addition; or a high school student discovers that there are parallels between two writers.

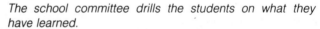

The school committee drills the students on what they have learned.

Behaviorism

When psychology emerged in the late 1800s, its leaders came under the influence of research in physiology, much of which centered on experiments with animals. Wanting to build a defensible scientific field, psychologists came to hold the position that the only proper data psychologists could use for study were observable behaviors in their subjects—animals or human.

One of the leading psychologists in the early twentieth century was Edward L. Thorndike, whose first experiments were in animal psychology. Cats in a box had to depress a pedal or pull a loop to escape, after which they would find food outside the cage. Thorndike believed his experiments demonstrated conclusively that animals solved their problems in a mechanical way; that is, a number of responses would be tried, with successful strategies increasing and unsuccessful responses decreasing. Just as animals learn through a trial-and-error process, Thorndike extrapolated, so do humans.[4]

Thorndike conducted experiments with human learning as well. In one experiment, for example, he sought to discover whether the study of Latin made reasoning in other fields any easier (a fundamental principle of the mental discipline perspective already discussed). Thorndike concluded that the study of Latin did not improve general intelligence more than did the study of other subjects.

Thorndike was very influential in American education, in part because he taught at one of the leading educational institutions of the time, Teachers College, Columbia University. Also, his findings were welcomed by progressive educators (see Chapter 8) who believed that students learn more when education is interesting. Based on their interpretation of Thorndike's work, as well as other educators' philosophies,

the progressives asked teachers to emphasize learning experiences rather than lecturing. For example, they thought students learned history better if they were writing plays about the medieval world rather than hearing the teacher talk about it. Moreover, they believed that the more senses students used in learning, the more effective it would be. In short, learning takes places most effectively through experiences. Nowhere was this better demonstrated than in the laboratory school in Chicago, founded by John and Alice Dewey.[5]

Thorndike's importance is that he convinced educators that the learning process is mechanical rather than insightful. Conditioning is more important than the use of reason, in terms of what is learned and how learning occurs. Thorndike developed three laws of learning as a result of his research—the laws of effect, readiness, and exercise.

The latter two, discussed first, grow from the first. The concept of readiness indicates that "when one is ready to act in a certain way, to do so is satisfying; not to do so is annoying." John Dewey put this in other terms: learning is more likely to take place when there is a "felt need." The law of exercise (or of use and disuse) is that "repeated response to some situation makes repetition easier; disuse makes repetition more difficult." The cliché "practice makes perfect" is somewhat analogous.[6]

The law of effect, which John B. Watson of Johns Hopkins University later publicized into the main theory of behaviorism, had two parts. Thorndike said that if a stimulus was followed by a response and then by a "satisfying state of affairs," the association or connection between the stimulus and response would increase in strength. But, said Thorndike, if a stimulus was followed by a response and then "an annoying state of affairs," the connection would be weakened. The law of effect, behaviorists posited, reveals that learning is automatic, done apart from reason or insight.

The pioneering work of Thorndike was extended by B.F. Skinner, who in 1938 published *The Behavior of Organisms*, a description of his experiments with rats. Skinner had designed a chamber for the rats, in which they pressed a bar to obtain food. Skinner explored methods of *operant conditions*, i.e., what movements the rats used that clearly revealed that they were manipulating or operating their environment. Skinner found that the critical elements in conditioning were the use and timing of rewards. Rewards (food) given at regular intervals did not teach them to press the bar at a faster rate; in fact, it disoriented the rats. Reinforcement had to come as soon as possible after the rats pressed the bar.[7]

Skinner's research had educational implications, as had Thorndike's. The teacher who would change a student's classroom performance must—

1. define the desired behavior as specifically as possible;

2. develop a procedure for recording the behavior and counting its frequency;

3. identify a reinforcer (according to Skinner, depriving a human of something is not a particularly good reinforcer: tangible rewards are better, and in many cases, increased teacher attention to the desired behavior may be adequate);

4. make the behavior necessary for obtaining the reinforcer.

Related points are also found in Skinner's work: the reinforcer should be given as quickly as possible; the student should be as active as possible in the process (not just a passive spectator who is being manipulated); the steps in the learning process are to be as gradual as possible; and teachers should remember that students learn at different rates.

Teachers today practice many forms of behaviorism. Some reward students with gold stars and candy while others use verbal praise or good grades to reinforce acceptable student behaviors. Teachers may develop units about complex topics that are broken down into smaller components and developed sequentially. Much of the curriculum that is labeled programmed instruction, whether it is a teacher-made self-paced kit or a computer-assisted lesson, is built upon the principles developed by Thorndike and Skinner. You may have used a reading book that had a column on either the inside or outside margin which you kept covered until, at several points in the text, you had to check an answer in the column. You were being reinforced, according to the behaviorists' perspective on how learning ought to occur.

Cognitivism

As you learned earlier, not everyone accepted the behaviorist point of view regarding education. In the 1920s the *Gestalt*, or field theory concept, was introduced in the United States.[8] Contrary to the behaviorists, who depicted individuals as respondents to minute events in the environment, this approach emphasizes that learning is just as likely to occur in other fashions. Individuals, they contend, are aware of their surroundings, and can grasp new patterns and gain new insights on very short notice. (This is sometimes called the *Aha!* principle.) Cognitivists also criticized the behaviorists for drawing too many conclusions from animal experiments and for making too many inferences based on the observations of minor motor-skill developments.

A central feature of this learning perspective is that teaching should emphasize the processes and concepts that are characteristic of the inquiry methods used in various disciplines. One of the key points

Reprinted, with permission, from *Programmed Reading*, Book 1, 3rd ed., Cynthia Dee Buchanan, Sullivan Associates, Copyright 1973, Behavioral Research Laboratories, distributed through Webster Division of McGraw-Hill Book Company, p. 4.

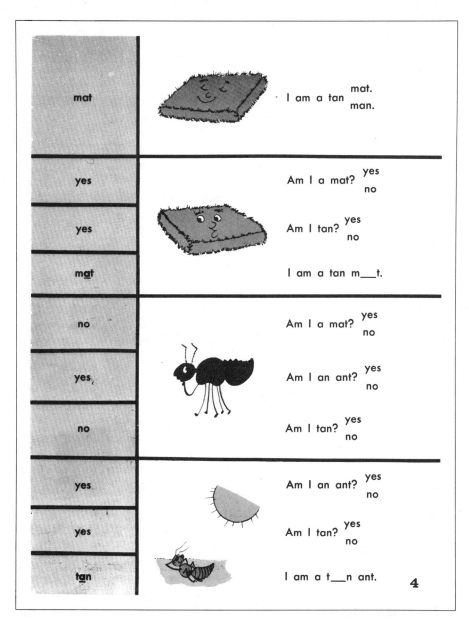

developed by Jerome Bruner and others is that students, to keep up with today's knowledge explosion, must learn how to conceptualize, and conceptualization differs among various fields of study. Hence their approach is sometimes called the "structure of the disciplines" perspective (see Chapter 12).[9] Cognitivists emphasize the importance of both structure and meaning in the learning process. They see learning as more than a collection of isolated facts, and thus they encourage teachers to allow students to discover knowledge on their own in a way that is meaningful to the child at the time.

In *The Process of Education*, Bruner proposes that "any subject can be taught effectively in some intellectually honest form to any child at any stage of development." Bruner accepts the premise that learning for humans goes from the simple to the complex, that learning has a sequential nature, that students can be taught to become more logical. The combination of an increasingly complex curriculum and an interweaving of disciplines has also earned the description of this perspective as "the spiral curriculum."

Bruner's conceptions about learning, which were further explained in *Toward a Theory of Instruction* (1966), are largely based on the research of Jean Piaget, a Swiss developmental psychologist. Piaget is considered the premier cognitivist theoretician.[10] He maintains that there are four stages of cognitive growth through childhood—the sensory-motor stage, which lasts from birth to about 2 years; the pre-operational or representational stage (2 to 6), the stage of concrete operations (7 to 11), and the stage of formal operations (12 to 15).

To understand the demarcations between stages, several examples may help. The first-stage child can only begin to grasp that objects can exist when they are not seen: when a screen is placed in front of an object, the object, to most first-stage children, is "gone." Stage 2 children are prone to accept magical explanations to explain their world. God "pushes" the sun from the sky at night. It is difficult for children in Stage 2 to understand how persons can have multiple roles. Can mother and father also be doctors? No, most Stage 2 children would say. Stage 3 students begin to make sense of such concepts as "volume," "number," and "length." In one experiment, two rows of corks, nine per row, are placed on a table. When asked if there are equal numbers of corks in the rows, 7-year-olds will answer "yes." When one row is changed to be either longer or shorter than the other, without changing the number of corks, the 7-year-olds will know that the rows still contain the same number of corks. However, 5- and 6-year-olds are likely to say that the longer row has more corks than the shorter row.

Piaget noted that Americans frequently ask whether there is any way to accelerate the stages. Can the concrete operational stage be reduced from ages 7 to 11 to ages 6 to 10? While he acknowledges that some acceleration may be possible, and some recognition be made of the individual maturation of students, Piaget suggests that the stages are firm.

Some have questioned the relation of Piaget's findings to areas other than cognitive skills. Do individuals also go through stages in the development of their attitudes, emotions, and values? Lawrence Kohlberg, Harvard University, is the foremost proponent of the concept that, indeed, there are stages of moral development. (See the discussion on this topic in Chapter 11.)

In summary, what are the implications of cognitivism for the classroom? For one, the current emphasis in some school subjects on teaching skills for problem solving and decision making is a reflection of the influence of cognitivism. "Inquiry" or "discovery learning" is a method that begins with teachers having students look at information (books, skeletons of animals, primary source materials), without having first heard the teachers' comments or point of view. Rather than being spoon-fed the answers, students analyze the data. Their skills in comparing, contrasting, generalizing, and postulating are enhanced. This approach to teaching is being tried not only in subjects such as mathematics and the sciences, but also in the humanities. By evaluating data, it is felt that students will be able to become more rational citizens.

Humanistic Psychology

The concern of the cognitivists for meaning and discovery in the learning process has helped focus attention on the feelings and attitudes of the child as he or she learns. This concern with the attitudinal dimensions of personality as they relate to learning has received increased attention since the 1950s. Relying on the Gestalt principle and the emerging field of psychotherapy, humanistic psychologists argue that more attention must be paid to the total person. School performance, they believe, is closely related to such factors as self-concept and personal value systems.

From this perspective, teachers, as well as therapists and school counselors, should not dictate to students what is right for them. The learners must determine what their personal goals are and how they feel about schooling. The teacher's basic premise, according to Carl Rogers, a therapist who developed a client-centered or nondirective approach to counseling, should be that humans are organisms who want a harmonious relationship with their environment. To facilitate learning, the individuals in the classroom must be trusted and allowed to set as many of their instructional goals as possible. Rogers believes that an educational environment which provides the maximum freedom to learn will, despite mistakes by students due to their immaturity, be the most productive one, and will help students achieve the major goal of education, which is individual fulfillment, not knowledge per se. Specifically, such devices as grades and detention penalties ought to be abolished because they prevent honest communication between teachers and students.[11]

A slightly different perspective by another humanistic psychologist, Abraham Maslow, has received attention in schools in the last two decades. Maslow believes that humans have a hierarchy of needs—physiological, safety, love and belonging, esteem, self-actualization, desire to know and understand, and aesthetic. The implication of Maslow's perspective, developed further by William Glasser in *Schools Without Failure*, is that individuals, if they are healthy, want to be successful ("self-actualized" in Maslow's terms). To be successful, students must experience reaching goals that they have set, and it is the function of the teacher to help students develop goals which are both constructive (to meet the students' needs) and reasonable (if they are unrealistic, the students will fail).[12] In contrast to Rogers' point of view, this humanistic psychology perspective advocates teachers structuring the learning environment for students.

ACTIVITY 6–1
Applying Learning Theories

As you have just read, learning theories have educational implications. Certain teaching methods and school policies are adopted because instructors believe they are effective.

Using one of the sources cited in the text or in the "For Further Study" section, read about one of the perspectives just described or about the point of view of a specific individual discussed in this section. Then list five educational implications of that perspective or five educational practices advocated by the individual you studied. (Since some practices were mentioned already, use illustrations that have not appeared here.)

For example, does your source favor teachers using letters grades (A to F) to motivate

Chapter Six

achievement, or believe that certain subjects should be studied by all students, or condone spanking students for misconduct or using popular magazines (sports, teen periodicals) to teach reading?

Source: Karen Willis, teacher, Lake City, Iowa.

Cartoon by Bardulf Ueland in *Phi Delta Kappan* 65, no. 9 (May 1973): 604.

"I just love psychology. It's opened my eyes to a whole new and exciting world of incomprehensible mumbo-jumbo."

IMPROVING CLASSROOM INTERACTIONS

The first section emphasized the major perspectives on *how* children learn and noted some specific educational implications. Are there specific environmental factors and teacher behaviors in the classroom that are likely to improve student learning? Research studies indicate there are, as well as factors that diminish learning. In this section we consider several, beginning with physical conditions in the classroom. Next, we'll review studies that show how teachers' attitudes, body language, and movement throughout the room affect students. Finally, we'll discuss studies that treat the perennial concerns of teachers—how to motivate student performance and how to minimize discipline problems.

The Classroom Environment

Educators have long stressed the importance of the personal interactions of teachers and students in the learning process, but they have slighted the significance of the classroom setting. A general assumption is that instruction will be better in a modern, well-equipped school than in an old, poorly furnished facility. Similarly, many assume that the more money a district spends per pupil, the better students will perform academically because of such factors as more recent books, more well-prepared teachers, and smaller classes. An extensive study done in the 1960s became quite controversial when it challenged some of these common assumptions. The Coleman study and the Jencks report, which reviewed the Coleman data, both concluded that it would be beneficial to make schools decent places to be physically but doubted that such factors as the age of the building, equipment in the rooms, and the numbers of books in the school library make significant differences in student performance.[13] What factors do make a difference in student achievement?

Class Size. As mentioned in Chapter 5, one of the emerging bargaining issues for teacher organizations is the size of classes. Teachers argue that it is harder to teach a large class than a small class. Is it or isn't it? Do students necessarily achieve more in a smaller class?

Most studies prior to World War II concluded that there is little difference between large or small classes in cognitive student achievement when measured by standardized tests.[14] In other words, a class of 20 students is likely to differ little in cognitive performance from a class of 30.

What is not revealed by such tests, however, are the affective changes in students; that is, how they feel about school, and how they have changed their values. More recent studies suggest that students in smaller classes perceive their environment to be friendlier and more conducive to learning.[15]

Furthermore, such surveys do not reveal what happens to teacher performance. There is some indication that teachers in larger classes are under more stress than those in smaller classes. It is argued that large classes limit teachers' options in attempting to individualize, in using a variety of instructional methods, and in giving essay examinations.

According to recent research, one reason that the studies prior to World War II showed little relationship between class size and achievement was because of their design. Relatively few studies dealt with classes of fewer than 15. Figure 6–1 summarizes data from over 100 studies on class size. Glass concluded that the average pupil achievement increases as class size decreases. The typical achievement of students in classes of 15 or fewer is several percentiles above that of pupils in classes of 25 and 30. Moreover, other studies suggest that class size has an impact upon the amount of student participation, how well the teacher knows each student, and the amount of creativity that students exhibit.[16]

Two other points should be noted about class size. First, the increase in classroom performance, as class size drops, is gradual. It can be argued that the relative gain in reducing the size of the class from 25 to 22 or from 30 to 27 will make so little difference that it will not be worth the cost. Second, the issue of class size, as the first point suggests, is related to the financial decisions each district must make. What school system can afford to have most classes in the range of 10 to 15 students? If the district wishes to have some classes at that size, other classes will have to be 30 to 40. Who determines teaching loads and student placements under those conditions?

Classroom Decor. Another influence upon student learning, research studies show, is the decor of the classroom, although again there is some disagreement about the degree of impact.[17] Psychologists tell

Figure 6–1.

Relationship between achievement and class size

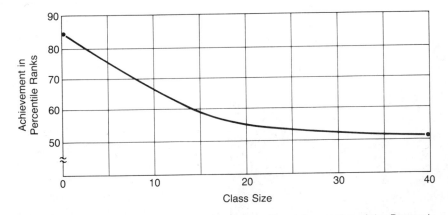

From Gene Glass et al., "Class Size and Learning—New Interpretation of the Research Literature," *Today's Education* 62, no. 2 (April–May 1979): 44.

Chapter Six

us that various shades of red or yellow make us more hungry, blues and greens tend to pacify us, and browns and yellows have the effect of making us feel warmer. The few studies on the effect of placing fish tanks, gerbil cages, and green plants in elementary class rooms conclude that they enhance the attitudes of students about being in the classroom. There is some indication that teachers' efforts to display students' art work, papers, and projects also has a positive effect on the feelings of students about school.

Teacher Expectations and Behaviors

Much attention in recent years has been focused on the ways teacher expectations and behaviors can alter student self-concepts and performance levels. To a large extent, research focuses on the teachers' self-fulfilling prophecies. Because these prophecies are as much nonverbal as verbal, it is important to examine that aspect as well.

Self-fulfilling Prophecy. In educational terms, a self-fulfilling prophecy is a teach-

How important are "active" bulletin boards and use of objects to effective instruction?

er's expectation about a student that influences how the student performs in class. Over 200 studies support the hypothesis that how teachers feel about students will usually provide an accurate forecast of the students' classroom achievement.

Extensive research on the self-fulfilling prophecy in education has been done by Robert Rosenthal.[18] In his first major school experiment, Rosenthal and his associates told teachers that some of their students, who had been selected randomly, were "late bloomers" intellectually. The students, it turned out, raised their achievement scores on standardized tests markedly. The students so identified not only did well, but their classmates also showed improved scores. (Some of the teachers in the school were told that they had no "bloomers" in their classes, and their classes did not improve as did the experimental classes.)

The teachers' expectations were conveyed by eye contact, tone of voice, and more frequent physical contact with the allegedly better students. In subsequent studies it has been learned that teachers give the so-called good students more questions to answer, and allow them more time to answer difficult questions. Better students are given more—not less—work than poorer students and often are graded more severely than the weaker performers. Some studies suggest that when students' actions are not consistent with the teacher's prophecies, the teacher will tend to ignore the new images (e.g., the teacher will assume that the poor student's accurate answer to the question was a lucky guess.)

Not all researchers have accepted Rosenthal's findings. They question the design of his experiments and doubt the validity of his pretest data. Some researchers who have attempted to replicate earlier self-fulfilling prophecy research find neither a negative nor positive correlation in achievement score changes, reading improvement, or self-concept scales. Others mention that there are other factors that influence the self-fulfilling prophecy, including race and social class, and that Rosenthal's studies do not sufficiently account for these measures.

The issue of self-fulfilling prophecies highlights a dilemma for teachers. Should the teacher learn as much about new students as possible? Or is it better to postpone reading the new students' permanent records? To read information on individual students may give the teacher a mind-set about which ones are the "bloomers" and which ones the troublemakers. Not to read the folders raises the possibility that the teacher fails to learn about the needs of certain students, so that they might be helped to get the school year off to a good start. As we shall see in Chapter 14, the self-fulfilling prophecy debate has particular ramifications for the education of minority and low-income students.

Body Language. Kinesics, the study of communication through body motion, is very important to educators. Approximately 75% of human interactions are nonverbal. Moreover, when there is a conflict between a verbal message and a nonverbal message, the viewer is much more likely to believe the nonverbal communication.[19]

Teachers convey their attitudes and expectations to students largely through eye contact and voice tone. Their postures, as well as their movement patterns throughout the room, indicate whether they really like to interact with their students. Generally, when a teacher folds his or her arms, it is a sign of disagreement with the point the student is making, or reluctance by the teacher to continue the discussion. Teachers and students may exhibit similar body language in discussion groups. When they put their fingertips together, perhaps resting them under their chins, as someone else talks, it is likely to mean, "I agree

with you." A tug at the ear or a clearing of the throat can mean, "I want to say something now, but I am somewhat reluctant." Arms open wide are usually associated with honest points of view. Finally, there is some evidence to suggest that students are more relaxed and believe the teacher is more concerned about them when the teacher walks frequently around the room. The observations of teacher movements, however, show most teachers remain in the front of the room, near their desks or chalkboards.

No single body sign (such as crossed arms) means the same thing every time it is used, and caution must be exercised in interpreting body language. The data from research studies indicate, however, that teachers are not very proficient at reading students' body language and are often unaware of their own signs.

Motivation and Discipline

Those who are conscientious about becoming effective teachers may be bewildered by the number of suggestions from other professionals about two of the most perplexing problems facing teachers—how to motivate and how to discipline students. Most instruction still is organized along three general patterns, and individual teachers will vary slightly from these broad types. The first format is the lecture. The second is teacher-pupil interaction, with teacher and students having input into class format and topics for discussion. There is more verbal interaction than the lecture, but it is clear that the teacher still controls the flow of discussion. The third form, seatwork, has students working independently, but not necessarily doing individualized assignments. In a survey that studied teacher use of these forms of instruction, it was found that individual teachers showed remarkable consistency in the proportion of time each allocated to the three types: 20% lecture; 33% seatwork; and 47% teacher-pupil interaction.[20] If we can assume then that most teachers use approximately the same format for teaching, why is it that some appear to have more success motivating students and fewer problems with disruptions?

Motivation. We begin by acknowledging that even the most effective teachers cannot motivate all students to perform at peak ability. We believe, however, that certain teacher behaviors are likely to enhance learning and simultaneously reduce the incidence of poor discipline. Following are five critical aspects of teaching:

1. *clarity* in explaining objectives so that students know exactly what is expected of them and how they are to achieve the objectives;

2. *variability* of approaches and pace;

3. *enthusiasm* about the subject matter, as expressed by teachers' vigor in asking and answering questions, and by their body language;

4. *task-orientation* in assignments that indicate to students a specific lesson objective, how students may achieve it, and what resources are available to them;

5. *congruence* between what is taught and what is tested on exams, so that students know what their tests will contain (in general terms) and thus demonstrating fundamental fairness that the teacher can invoke for other demands.[21]

To motivate students, teachers will find it beneficial to give their pupils numerous opportunities to display what they have learned, learning tasks of appropriate difficulty (neither too easy nor too difficult), chances to talk about their nonschool interests and projects, and alternate ways to display their abilities. Other generalizations that can be made about motivation include: successful experiences

provide more encouragement than assignments that end in failure; fear is a less powerful motivator than praise; and competition, particularly for grades, is no more successful than projects that demand cooperation.[22]

Discipline. There are few topics, if any, in education that are of more mutual interest to teachers and the general public than discipline, or more precisely, the lack of discipline. As the discussion in Chapter 11 will indicate, the lack of discipline in public schools has been perceived to be the chief problem of the schools in all but one year since the Gallup polls on education have been taken. For new teachers, the fear of being unable to control a class is probably the greatest concern they have.

How do we determine whether a class is under control? Formerly, the chief mark of well-disciplined class was quietness. Most teachers now believe some socializing is necessary. Many projects require student movement. Perhaps a better gauge of a productive classroom climate is the manner in which students respond to the teacher's questions and how well the instructor's directions and rules are followed. Other ways to measure a well-managed class may include how much time is spent on the tasks assigned and what percentage of class time is spent doing instructional tasks.

Because of the mixed results of various teacher strategies, it may be pertinent also to ask whether there are some teacher actions that rather clearly, according to research, do *not* work. The answer is "yes," there are some disciplinary tactics that appear minimally effectively—the use of threats, ridicule, repeated trips to the principal's office, and corporal punishment. Nonetheless, one study noted that 65% of the teachers in elementary schools and 55% of those in high schools favored the judicious use of corporal punishment.[23]

J.S. Kounin studied classroom management techniques of teachers in an attempt to distinguish successful managers. He found that once a class was out of control, or an individual discipline problem erupted, there was not a significant difference in the ability of teachers to cope with the problem. According to Kounin, the difference lies in the ability of the skilled teacher to avoid the occurrence of such problems. His research indicated that teachers skilled in classroom management were able to monitor their classrooms effectively and thus deal with behavior problems before they became major disruptions. Appropriately, Kounin terms this ability to monitor "with-it-ness" and concludes that the "with-it" teacher possesses the key to good classroom management.[24]

A number of articles on discipline reiterate earlier statements about motivation. There is a widespread consensus among educators, both administrators and teachers, that teachers must establish academic and behavioral guidelines at the beginning of the school year.

TEACHER PERFORMANCE EVALUATION

All teachers are evaluated. Regardless of how formal the system for evaluation is, what evidence is collected or analyzed, how often formal reports are written— teachers are evaluated and they are evaluated rather often. Students, parents, other teachers, administrators and supervisors, and even the public evaluate teachers. The question, then, is not whether teachers should be evaluated, since this cannot be avoided; rather the question is how systematic the evaluation should be in order to be the most effective.[25]

While we nod our heads in agreement, we may also think of several major problems that arise in the evaluation process. First, why and how are teachers being evaluated? Is it done primarily to diagnose teacher strengths and weaknesses for the purpose of improving performance, or is it done primarily to aid the administration in making decisions regarding retention or dismissal? Second, how accurately can we ascertain the particular impact of an individual teacher, considering the many variables in the learning process? It is estimated, for example, that no more than 10% of the gains made by students can be attributed to any one specific teacher.[26]

There is general agreement today that as the accountability movement forces educational systems to make more stringent teacher evaluations, the appraisal instruments must be valid, reliable, and discriminating.[27] Moreover, the instruments should be used primarily to improve teacher performance. If teachers believe evaluation is primarily an administrator's tool to determine dismissal, they will be less cooperative.

This section examines the development of the evaluation systems now being used. It raises the questions of who evaluates, for what reason, and what criteria are used in the process. The section ends with a brief description of trends in teacher performance evaluation.

Development of Evaluation Systems

In the late 1800s and early 1900s, the interest in scientific measurement of educational results gradually spread to include formal evaluation of teachers. By 1915, research was being conducted on the rating of teachers. Throughout the 1920s, the prime function of the instruments was philosophical. Teachers were checked to see whether their practices matched the theoretical ideas of William James, John Dewey, or Maria Montessori.[28]

From the 1930s through the 1940s, teacher evaluations emphasized certain personality traits that supposedly indicated

124

Chapter Six

An evaluation session for the teacher can be the occasion for professionalism at its best.

good teachers—trust, flexibility, warmth, a democratic style, a good self-concept, and a sense of humor. It is interesting to note that researchers have been unable to link any of these personality characteristics to effective teaching. Specific teacher behaviors seem to provide a more accurate indication of effectiveness and thus, by the 1950s, the emphasis in teacher evaluation moved to specific teacher behaviors in the classroom. How clearly were teachers stating their objectives? Were instructors giving students positive reinforcement? In the 1960s and 1970s, concern was voiced that evaluation efforts should take more account of pupil characteristics, institutional settings, and subject matter content, as well as teaching style and outcomes.[29]

What Criteria?

The two major approaches to teacher performance evaluation are *process evaluation*

(the assessment of the teacher's behavior in the classroom) and *product* or *outcome evaluation* (the assessment of changes in the student brought about by the educational process). Before choosing specific criteria for evaluation, a school system must decide whether one approach or a combination of the two approaches will be used.

In process evaluation, numerous research studies have attempted to determine which set of criteria reveal a good teacher. Some researchers using this approach have identified 30 valid behaviors in five general categories—productive teaching techniques, positive interpersonal relations, organized class management skills, intellectual stimulation, and desirable out-of-class behaviors.[30]

Thus we begin to see an emphasis on process evaluation emphasizing observable, measurable teacher behaviors such as frequency of one-to-one contact with students, use of positive feedback, and teacher use of structuring, organizing statements in the lesson. The more vague personality variables like warmth or outgoingness are not emphasized as much. It is obviously difficult to find the right set of criteria to measure all teachers, and it may well be true that "a good teacher is harder to define than to find."[31]

Product evaluation, like process evaluation, has had a difficult history. The first efforts using these criteria compared the achievement scores of one class with those of another. Since no two classes are alike, and since achievement test scores are more an indication of student ability than of classroom learning, this approach has come into disfavor.

Some researchers have attempted to compensate for class and individual differences by utilizing pre– and post–testing techniques. Differences in scores at the beginning and end of the year can be compared to see whether the teacher made any difference. Other forms of product evaluation have emerged. Widely used criteria in assessing teacher competency include the following: student ratings; self-ratings; administrator, supervisor, and peer evaluations; classroom environment checklists; systematic observations; personal attributes; and contract plans using student gains on performance tests.[32]

More specifically, what do the various evaluation forms attempt to measure? One aspect is classroom control. Good teachers are expected to exhibit good management practices in running their classes. Some districts prefer teachers who are popular with students. A factor that is weighed heavily by some evaluators is how compatible the teacher is with staff and community. Because they are relatively objective, some school systems prefer to look at the test performance scores of students.[33]

There are no easy choices among criteria to be used, but the following guidelines for implementing evaluation systems are generally accepted:

1. teachers and administrators both should be involved in and agree with the selection of criteria;

2. the range of criteria should adequately represent the roles of the teacher;

3. the criteria should be observable, measurable, and related to student learning;

4. allowance should be made for individual differences among teachers and students.

Who Evaluates?

In almost 90% of the school districts in the country, the primary evaluator is the principal. In some larger districts and schools, department chairpersons, vice-principals for instruction, and assistant superintendents may also have the task of appraising teachers. There are significant differences among principals at the elementary, junior high, and senior high levels in terms of what they desire in teachers. Elementary principals prefer warm, accepting, highly organized and creative teachers. Intermediate principals prefer teachers who are very organized, in control, warm, sociable, imaginative, and dynamic. Secondary principals favor teachers who are highly systematic, organized, and task oriented.[34]

The most common way for principals to evaluate their teachers is through classroom observations. Teachers may or may not know when observations will be made. Conferences with teachers preceding and following the observations can help to make teachers more effective. One criticism of this method of evaluation is that it may distort the teacher's performance. The instructor may become nervous or, with the cooperation of the students, put on the kind of show he or she believes the principal wants.

An emerging evaluation process is the principal-teacher contract system, sometimes called the "management-by-objectives" approach. Under such a system, the teacher meets with the principal several times a year. In their initial conference, they agree upon student and teacher goals for the year. Progress is checked during the year, and in the last conference, a general assessment is made about the successful completion of the teacher's and the students' goals. Observations remain a part of the system. Some of the desirable features of this system are that the teacher is able to set the terms of the evaluation in conjunction with the principal (hence, no hidden criteria), the emphasis is upon improvement of students and teacher, and a diversity of criteria are usually employed. One limitation of this approach is that it is very time-consuming.

In schools that have team teaching, another method of evaluation has been tried and appears to be gaining favor among faculties and administrations. All of the

Chapter Six

teachers, including the principal, rate each other. Each teacher must also rate himself or herself. In theory, ratings by peers provide the teachers with considerable feedback from their colleagues. Modest teachers may find that they consistently underrate their own talents and will be encouraged to learn what others think of their abilities. One disadvantage is that some staffs, fearful of hurting feelings, will turn the system into a mutual admiration society.

Ratings of teachers by students are the least popular form of evaluation, in the opinion of the educators. Teachers believe that students will praise the easy or popular teachers, or that young students do not have the maturity to judge good teaching. Conversely, advocates of greater student input argue that students are the consumers of education and have every right to be heard. Additionally, there is evidence that students consistently pick the same best teachers as do their elders when there have been comparative ratings.[35]

Because there are enough instances where evaluation has been closely tied to promotion, salary raises, and denial of tenure, teachers are somewhat suspicious of most systems of evaluation. But when they are convinced that the evaluation system is fair, that it is used primarily to improve their instruction, and that it works promptly, they are willing to support the system, regardless of which one it is.

Trends in Teacher Evaluation

For many teachers, the chief problem with evaluation systems is that they are implemented subjectively. As one teachers' organization has stated: "Existing methods of evaluation are subjective, punitively oriented, based on the opinion of supervisors who do not know more about teaching than they [teachers] do; are easily used in a discriminating way against the outspoken, the nonconformers, the union activists, the 'creative'. . . ."[36]

To counter such charges and allay such

Cartoon by Kaufman in Iowa Department of Public Instruction *Dispatch*, January 1974. Reprinted with permission of Masters Agency.

"Would you mind repeating that part between Good morning students and Class dismissed?"

fears, and in response to such trends as accountability and the need to reduce teacher staffs and be more selective in hiring new teachers, school systems have been trying a variety of new methods for teacher performance evaluation. The most significant shift is the greater involvement of teachers in the evaluation process. In part this is a result of the growing power of teacher organizations. While teachers welcome a greater voice, parents' organizations also wish to be heard, although they have not obtained the power in determining criteria that teacher associations have.

Among the innovations in evaluation procedures are video recorders and time-lapse cameras. In-service workshops and programs at regional teacher centers are developing more programs to instruct teachers on the strengths and weaknesses of their teaching styles.

Teacher evaluation is an ongoing, necessary task that is unlikely to satisfy all its participants. Increasingly, the individuality of the education system, the uniqueness of learners and teachers, and the requirements of the states will force changes in the system. It is interesting to speculate whether the trend toward districts creating individual evaluation instruments will eventually cause a backlash of sentiment for a federal model of evaluation.

ACTIVITY 6–2

A System for Evaluating Teachers

Design a system you think is appropriate in evaluating teachers.

1. Begin by describing the educational setting in which your system is to be used.
2. Indicate the persons who are to do the evaluating: administrators, peers, students, community representatives, and/or a self-report by the individual teacher.
3. Specify what type of evaluation it is to be: process, product, or some combination.
4. Describe the criteria you wish to use.
5. Describe the way(s) information would be gathered.
6. Would *you* be willing to be evaluated by this system? Why or why not?

SUMMARY

Whatever else effective teaching is, it is hardly accidental. As the opening portion of the chapter suggests, good teachers begin with a clear sense of purpose about their goals and are knowledgeable about the ways in which students learn. That is not to say that everyone has to be a cognitivist or a behavorist to be a successful teacher. Rather, it means that the best teachers can and do employ a variety of educational strategies effectively because they know what they are doing and why.

The difficulty of determining who are effective teachers is compounded by the many variables in the educational setting.

Teachers do have some control over the classroom setting (in terms of decor of the classroom), and that can make a difference in the students' attitudes about learning. Individually, teachers have less to say in determining class size, although small class size enhances the chances for learning. There is debate among educational researchers about the significance of various teaching styles, although most conclude that teachers can make a difference in the motivation and discipline of students.

All of these points are related to a second issue of the chapter: How should teacher performance be assessed? Those who are responsible for evaluation should reach a basic decision about the type of approach the school system is to use—a process or product instrument, or combination of the two types. Careful attention must be given to those who are doing the evaluation and the criteria they are using.

Considering the huge investment of money in schools and the amount of time students prepare for their futures, it is incumbent upon society to determine whether the most effective teachers are educating the young. Do you believe that current assessment techniques are fair to both the teachers and the consumers of education?

NOTES

1. Gordon W. Allport, *Pattern and Growth in Personality* (New York: Holt, Rinehart and Winston, 1961), p. 84.

2. Robert M. Gagné, *The Conditions of Learning*, 3rd ed. (New York: Holt, Rinehart and Winston, 1977), p. 3. Gagné's eight steps of learning are described on pp. 79–159.

3. Frederick J. McDonald, "The Influence of Learning Theories on Education (1900–1950)," in *Theories of Learning and Instruction*, ed. Ernest R. Hilgard, Sixty-third Yearbook of the National Society for the Study of Education, Part I (Chicago: University of Chicago Press, 1964), pp. 1–26; Robert E. Mason, *Contemporary Educational Theory* (New York: David McKay, 1972).

4. Edward L. Thorndike, *The Fundamentals of Learning* (New York: Teachers College, Columbia University, 1932).

5. Katherine Camp Mayhew and Anna Camp Edwards, *The Dewey School: The Laboratory School of the University of Chicago, 1896–1903*, (1936; reprinted, New York: Atherton Press, 1966).

6. Gary S. Belkin and Jerry L. Gray, *Educational Psychology* (Dubuque: William C. Brown, 1977), pp. 55–59; McDonald, "The Influence of Learning Theories," pp. 6–10.

7. Douglas J. Navarick, *Principles of Learning: From Laboratory to Field* (Reading, Mass.: Addison-Wesley Publishing Co., 1979), pp. 60–66; B. F. Skinner, "The Science of Learning and the Art of Teaching," *Harvard Educational Review* 25, no. 2 (1954): 86–97.

8. Hilgard, *Theories of Learning and Instruction*, Chapter 3, pp. 54–77 for a discussion of *Gestalt* theory; Kurt Lewin, *A Dynamic Theory of Personality* (New York: McGraw-Hill, 1935).

9. Jerome Bruner, *The Process of Education* (Cambridge: Harvard University Press, 1960); Mason, *Contemporary Educational Theories*, pp. 136–75.

10. Jean Piaget, *The Origins of Intelligence in Children* (New York: International Universities Press, 1952); Nathan Issacs, *A Brief Introduction To Piaget* (New York: Agathon Press, 1961).

11. Carl R. Rogers, *On Becoming a Person* (Boston: Houghton Mifflin Co., 1961), pp. 107–24; idem, *Freedom to Learn* (Columbus, Ohio: Charles E. Merrill Publishing Co., 1969).

12. Abraham H. Maslow, *Toward a Psychology of Being* (New York: D. Van Nostrand Co., 1962), p. 129; William Glasser, *Schools Without Failure* (New York: Harper and Row, 1969).

13. James Coleman et al., *Equal Educational Opportunity* (Washington, D.C.: U.S. Government Printing Office, 1966); Christopher Jencks, *Inequality: A Reassessment of the Effect of Family and Schooling in America* (New York: Basic Books, 1972).

14. Leonard S. Cahen and Nikola N. Filby, "The Class Size/Achievement Issue: New Evidence and a Research Plan," *Phi Delta Kappan* 60, no.7 (March 1979): 492–96, 538. See also Robert Ebel, ed., *Encyclopedia of Educational Research* (New York: MacMillan, 1969), pp. 141–45.

15. John C. Moracco, "The Relationship Between the Size of Elementary Schools and Pupils' Perception of Their Environment," *Education* 98, no. 4 (Summer 1978): 451–54.

16. Gene V. Glass and Mary Lee Smith, *Meta-Analysis of Research on the Relationship of Class Size and Achievement* (Boulder, Colo.: Laboratory of Educational Research, University of Colorado, September 1978); Martin N. Olson, "Ways to Achieve Quality in School Classrooms: Some Definite Answers," *Phi Delta Kappan* 53, no. 1 (September 1971): 63–65. The Educational Research Service (ERS), a nonprofit group serving mainly school administrators, disputes the Glass findings, and has issued an 80-page report entitled *Class Size Research: A Critique of Recent Meta-Analysis.* (See *Phi Delta Kappan* 62, no.1 (September 1980): 70, for more details.)

17. Catherine E. Loughlin, "Understanding the Learning Environment," *The Elementary School Journal* 78, no. 2 (November 1977): 124–31; Arthur Wise, *Rich Schools, Poor Schools* (Chicago: University of Chicago Press, 1968).

18. Robert Rosenthal and Lenore Jacobson, *Pygmalion in the Classroom* (New York: Holt, Rinehart and Winston, 1968); J. E. Brophy and T. L. Good, *Teacher-student Relationships: Causes and Consequences* (New York: Holt, Rinehart and Winston, 1974).

19. General references include: Charles Galloway, *Silent Language in the Classroom* (Bloomington, Ind.: Phi Delta Kappa, 1978); Dorothy Henning and Barbara Grant, *The Teacher Moves: An Analysis of Non-Verbal Activity* (New York: Teachers College Press, 1971); A.D. Edwards and V.J. Furlong, *The Language of Teaching: Meaning in Classroom Interaction* (Exeter, N.H.: Heinemann Educational Books Ltd., 1978).

20. G. Nuthall and I. Snook, "Contemporary Models

of Teaching," in Robert Travers, ed., *Second Handbook of Research on Teaching* (Chicago: Rand McNally and Co., 1973), pp. 46–76.

21. B. Rosenshine and Norma Furst, "Research on Teacher Performance Criteria," in B. O. Smith, ed., *Research in Teacher Education: A Symposium* (Englewood Cliffs, N.J.: Prentice-Hall, 1971), pp. 37–72; Michael J. Dunkin and Bruce J. Biddle, *The Study of Teaching* (New York: Holt, Rinehart and Winston, 1974). See also Neville Bennett, *Teaching Styles and Pupil Progress* (Cambridge: Harvard University Press, 1976), esp. pp. 11–36, "Does Teaching Style Make a Difference?"

22. E. Paul Torrance and R. E. Myers, *Creative Learning and Teaching* (New York: Dodd, Mead and Co., 1972); Jack Frymier, *Motivation and Learning in School* (Bloomington, Ind.: Phi Delta Kappa, 1974).

23. Daniel L. Duke, ed., *Classroom Management*, Seventy-eighth Yearbook, Part II, National Society for the Study of Education (Berkeley, Calif.: McCutchan, 1979); Robert G. Wegmann, "Classroom Discipline: An Exercise in Maintenance of Social Reality," *Sociology of Education* 49, no.1 (January 1976): 71–79. Some states or districts have policies limiting corporal punishment. See Chapter 13 and the discussion on student rights.

24. J. S. Kounin, *Discipline and Group Management in Classrooms* (New York: Holt, Rinehart and Winston, 1970).

25. United States Office of Education, *PREP Report No. 22* (Putting Research Into Educational Practice) (Washington, D.C.: U.S. Government Printing Office, December 1972), preface.

26. David C. Berliner, "Impediments to the Study of Teacher Effectiveness," *Journal of Teacher Education* 27, no. 1 (Spring 1976): 5–13.

27. Validity refers to whether the instrument measures what it purports to measure. Reliability refers to the degree to which the test can measure the same attitude or achievement level from one time to the next. Discrimination is defined as the ability of the test to distinguish between high and low performers on the instrument.

28. Hazel Davis, "Evolution of Current Practices in Evaluating Teacher Competencies," in Bruce J. Biddle and William J. Ellean, eds., *Contemporary Research on Teacher Effectiveness* (New York: Holt, Rinehart and Winston, 1964), pp 41–66.

29. Richard Shavelson and Nancy Atwood Russo, "Generalizability of Measures of Teacher Effectiveness," *Educational Research* 19, no. 3 (June 1977): 171–83; Pi Lambda Theta, *The Evaluation of Teaching* (Washington, D.C.: Pi Lambda Theta, 1967); Michael J. Dunkin and Bruce J. Biddle, *The Study of Teaching* (New York: Holt, Rinehart, and Winston, 1974).

30. Richard P. Manatt, Kenneth Palmer, and Everett Hildebaugh, "Teacher Performance Evaluation with Improved Rating Scales," *The Bulletin*, National Association of Secondary School Principals 60, no. 401 (September 1976): 21–24.

31. Donald M. Medley, "Indication and Measure of Teaching Effectiveness: A Review of the Research," (ERIC No. ED 988 844), 1971.

32. John McNeil and James Popham, "Assessment of Teacher Competencies," in Robert Travers, ed., *Second Handbook of Research on Teaching* (Chicago: Rand McNally, 1973), pp. 218–44.

33. Gerald Bryant and Frank Haack, "Appraisal: Peer-Centered and Administrator-Centered," *Educational Leadership* 34, no. 8 (May 1977): 608–12; F.L. Ulschak and R.G. Weiss, "Interpersonal Aspects of Evaluation," *Educational Technology* 16, no. 11 (November 1976): 18–25. As many sources point out, one major problem with using test scores for teacher evaluation is that teachers may "teach for the test." Rather than provide a broad range of educational experiences, the teachers are likely to focus on very specific, review-type activities.

34. Bruce W. Tuckman et al., "Teacher Behavior Is in the Eye of the Beholder: The Perceptions of Principals," (ERIC No. ED 137 928), April 1977.

35. Stuart Keeley and M. Neill Browne, "Improving Student Evaluation Forms: Related Need for Critical Thinking Emphasis and Trained Raters," *Peabody Journal of Education* 55, no. 4 (July 1978): 305–9; Norma Jo Campbell, "The Relationships between Students' and Teachers' Behaviors in the Junior High Classroom," *Journal of Instructional Psychology* 5, no. 1 (Winter 1978): 16–20.

36. Sandra Feldman, *Teacher Evaluation—A Teacher Unionist's View* (Princeton, N.J.: Educational Testing Service, 1972), introduction.

FOR FURTHER STUDY

Bigge, Morris L. *Learning Theories for Teachers*. 2nd ed. New York: Harper and Row, 1971.

Borich, Gary D. *The Appraisal of Teaching: Concepts and Process*. Reading, Mass.: Addison-Wesley, 1977.

Bugelski, B.R. *Some Practical Laws of Learning*. Bloomington, Ind.: Phi Delta Kappa Educational Foundation, 1977.

Gage, N.L. *The Scientific Basis of the Art of Teaching*. New York: Teachers College Press, 1978.

Chapter Six

Kash, Marilynn, and Borich, Gary D. *Teacher Behavior and Pupil Self-Concept.* Reading, Mass.; Addison-Wesley, 1978.

Kolesnik, Walter B. *Motivation: Understanding and Influencing Human Behavior.* Boston: Allyn and Bacon, 1978.

Lancaster, Otis E. *Effective Teaching and Learning.* New York: Gordon and Breach, 1974.

Morris, Joseph. *Psychology and Teaching: A Humanistic View.* New York: Random House, 1978.

Peterson, Penelope, and Walberg, Herbert J., eds. *Research on Teaching: Concepts, Findings, and Implications.* Berkeley, Calif.: McCutchan Publishing Co., 1979.

Rogers, Carl R., and Lyon, Harold C. *On Becoming a Teacher.* Columbus, Ohio: Charles E. Merrill Publishing Co., forthcoming.

7

Assessment of Learning

We do not say, "If you can't measure it, it doesn't exist." We do say, "If you can't define it clearly, you cannot teach it purposefully or measure it validly."

Robert Ebel

"Feedback" is a popular term in many fields today, among them computer technology, medicine, politics, and education. Individuals want to learn how their actions were perceived and whether the actions were effective. Chapter 6 noted teachers' concern about effective teaching and evaluation of their performance. This chapter focuses on the methods of assessment of student achievement.

For most students, the grading system is the assessment technique that comes to mind first. Possibly you have had some anxieties or difficulties with grading procedures, and you may be wondering already what improvements you might make if you should become a teacher. We discuss why the commonly used systems of grading emerged and mention some of the alternatives that are coming into practice.

Grades reflect tests, and the second section of the chapter discusses teacher-made tests and standardized tests, with more emphasis on the latter. Most college students took the Scholastic Aptitude Test (SAT) or the American Collegiate Test (ACT) for admissions. You also may have tried for a scholarship by taking a test such as the National Merit Examination. Earlier you took regularly scheduled IQ and achievement tests. After looking at the extent of such tests today, we discuss their value to individuals and society. Also, we investigate whether there is a cultural bias in standardized tests.

A growing phenomenon is the use of regional and national testing. The final portion of the chapter examines state efforts to institute minimum competency examinations and the National Assessment of Educational Progress project. Careful attention should be paid to the rationale and methodologies used in these approaches to the evaluation of learning.

Two educational issues permeate the chapter. First, you are asked to consider the difficulty of providing for students a fair evaluation that does not stifle their interest in learning. Second, you must weigh the costs and benefits of regional and national assessment efforts and ask yourself whether they are necessary and meaningful.

After you have read Chapter 7, you should be able to (1) identify at least five types of grading systems, (2) state three benefits and three limitations of teacher-made tests and standardized tests, and (3) describe how the National Assessment of Educational Progress conducts its research and list some of its major findings.

GRADING SYSTEMS

The A-to-F grading system, so familiar to Americans, is in many respects a novel approach to rating a student's performance. Historically, it is only one of many tried in this country, a system that has been widely used only since the 1880s. Comparatively few countries use the A-to-F method. Instead, students are marked on a 1-to-10 scale, ranked numerically in class, or periodically given national or system-wide examinations. Why has the United States adopted the A-to-F system, and what are some other grading systems that might be used?

Development of Grading in the United States

In the colonial period and early years of the new republic, there was little need for written evaluations of students. The small class size, the close proximity of teachers and students, and the fact that few students received extensive education, encouraged mostly oral reporting. For those few going to college, written examinations were used occasionally for the screening of applicants.

One of the earliest accounts of a report card is found in Horace Mann's *Common School Journal* in 1840, in which the writer of an article thought it would be appropriate to have parent responses to the teacher's account about the students' work. In time, schools began to issue "reward of merit" cards.

By the Civil War, the practice of using percentages was coming into favor. The scores on tests were averaged, and the percentages (with 100% as the perfect mark) were used to indicate student performance. Eventually, the percentages were accompanied by a letter grade or given in conjunction with a letter-grade scale: "A" having represented 95 to 100%, "B," 85 to 94%, and so on. By 1900 the practice of assigning letter grades was firmly established, and by 1940 four-fifths of the elementary schools in America had discontinued the use of percentages. During the 1930s a modification of the system was introduced. "S" for satisfactory and "U" for unsatisfactory performance were added to reports in some districts (usually for deportment categories), or substituted for the A-to-F system in other districts.[1]

Why this system and its modifications? In part, it was related to the mass-education movement and the increasing numbers of students compelled to go to school. A quantifiable score could alert parents to their offspring's efforts. As more students sought higher education, colleges became

Reward of Merit Cards. Then gold stars. What do we use today?

more selective in admitting applicants and increasingly used grades and transcripts. Businesses, too, wanted the schools to notify them of the performance levels of prospective employees. By the 1920s, teachers had come to the widespread belief that one of their functions was to be a "sorting agent," to separate the better academic students from the poorer ones.[2]

The development of the grading system and its increasing importance to outside agencies became a concern for some teachers and researchers. As early as 1912 studies were done on the validity of grades. Starch and Elliot, for example, sent duplicates of two English compositions to 200 high schools, asking that an English teacher at each school mark both papers. The scores of one paper ranged from 64 to 98 points, with the average 88.2, and the other paper was graded from 50 to 97 points, with an average score of 80.2. Starch and Elliot, concerned that critics would discount the findings by arguing that English was a subjective discipline, tested two geometry papers. The scores on these papers had an even greater range—from 28 points to

95 points. Some teachers deducted points for neatness, form, and spelling, as well as for incorrect answers.[3]

Current Methods for Grading and Evaluation

Although other studies also have challenged the validity of grading systems, they have expanded. In 1972 one survey concluded that 73% of schools sampled used letter grades in grades 4 to 6. There have been efforts to use other evaluation techniques, however, spurred by such factors as the free school movement and the student movement of the 1960s. Now, in general, the emphasis in grading has turned from the negative (what the students have failed to accomplish) to the positive (what they are doing). What follows is a brief account of the predominant systems of evaluation with descriptions of their advantages and disadvantages.[4]

1. *The A-to-F system.* This is by far the most common approach. There are a number of variations with honors (H) being added by some districts, or the "D" category being dropped by others. The advantages of this system are that it is widely known (understandable on transcripts), and it gives the student fairly precise information about how he or she compares with other students, especially when the + or − signs are used. The major disadvantages are that it doesn't inform the student about what knowledge or skills are mastered and that it encourages cheating.

2. *The pass-fail option.* Tried more at the collegiate level than in secondary schools, the pass-fail option was popular during the 1970s. One study found that this approach encouraged more creativity in students and was perceived as being more equitable than the A-to-F system. It is opposed increasingly because it doesn't discriminate sufficiently between levels of competence, and it is thought to tempt students to do minimal work.[5]

3. *Written evaluations.* The practice of writing comments about students has a long history and is still regarded highly by school administrators. During the 1970s there was a trend toward *not* converting the written evaluations into letter grades. In some schools, selected evaluations are included in the students' files and sent to college admissions offices and/or employers as the need arises. This system can provide more meaningful information to the student and parents about the quality of the pupil's work and social attitudes, and it does demand that teachers think about the individual students when they prepare their reports. Written evaluations, however, can be filled with broad generalities and, if done properly, require more of the teachers' time.

4. *Parent-teacher conferences.* This appears to be an increasingly popular method in elementary schools. Parents meet with the teacher several times throughout the school year to discuss their child's progress. In some districts teachers are required to write their evaluations and share them with the students before the parents have their conference. Usually, at conference time, parents are able to see samples of their child's work. This procedure is very time-consuming for the teacher and usually requires cutting some portion of the regular school schedule to arrange conferences. Further, in some circumstances the conferences become little more than informal chats between parents and teacher.

5. *Contracts.* With this approach the teacher outlines the type, quantity, and occasionally, quality of work expected, and sets the grade levels for such work. For example, a "C" might be based on attendance, one book report, and one theme. An "A" might require, in addition, an 8- to 10-page research paper. Presumably, contracts lower student anxiety since criteria are clearly spelled out. They encourage students to explore a variety of topics and use more methods of presentation, since the emphasis is on *what* the student produces rather than on the student's preselected responses. A drawback to this system can be the emphasis upon quantity, which promotes minimal effort. William Yarber concluded that the contract is neither superior to nor inferior to traditional grading.[6]

6. *Mastery or competency grading.* Similar to the contract approach, mastery evaluation begins with clear indicators to students of what is expected in a course. However, rather than stating the quantity of work required (number of reports or experiments), the emphasis is upon the skills to be mastered. For example, the teacher might specify a certain level of reading comprehension, the demonstration of successful operation of a shop tool, or the ability to swim a certain distance in a specified amount of time. Frequently, a checklist is used to mark the skills the students have gained. Some teachers choose to assign letter grades for various degrees of competence; others prefer to convert the performance of students into a simple pass or fail. Mastery grading's advantages are that it emphasizes successes rather than failures, it is objective, and it helps the teachers to think clearly through course objectives. Its disadvantages are that it can become far too specific about performance requirements, and it does not readily discriminate between levels of performance.

7. *Self-evaluation*. The students, on a systematic basis, individually write progress reports for their various subjects. This means that students must carefully consider what has been accomplished and what remains to be done. Usually students will be asked to compare their self-assessments with the teacher's evaluation. Still another option is to allow students to write open-ended answers to test questions and then to have time in class to defend their points of view. Such a system requires a great deal of time and, some might argue, would equate the students' "expertise" with that of the teacher.[7] Finally, self-evaluation is not necessarily the same as self-grading. A self-grading system implies just that—that the students give themselves grades, while self-evaluation means only that students submit reports on their work habits to the teacher as one element to be incorporated in the teacher's grade.

Of course, schools and teachers use combinations of these various grading approaches. Teachers may decide that specific units are better evaluated by one procedure than another. One interesting proposal is to grade the same course according to the goals of the individual students. If a student takes a course for general comprehension, he or she might be graded by objective examinations graded either S-U or P-F. A student needing the same course for vocational training might be evaluated by mastery tests. The student taking the course for personal growth (as an elective) could be graded by a written self-evaluation (if the student turns in a paper describing his or her feelings about the value of the course), or merely be given credit for attendance.[8]

The Issue of Marking

There is little disagreement among educators that most individuals want to receive some evaluation of the work they do in school. Mousley lists the kinds of questions parents ask (which may or may not be the ones their sons and daughters want to have answered, too): Where does my child stand in relation to national norms? Where does he or she stand in relation to his or her own ability? What required skills did my child master during the school year? What important concepts did my child acquire in this class? What skills and con-

Should students evaluate their own work?

Chapter Seven

cepts should I expect my child to develop next year? What kind of ongoing evaluation is being used that will clearly indicate the dynamics of my child's changes, mastery levels, and achievements? If the district's grading system answers these questions, Mousley argues that it is an effective system.

Goldstein and Tilker offer another set of questions that they believe, if answered in the affirmative, indicate an effective system of evaluation. Does the grading system provide the student with sufficient information about his or her performance? Does the system provide the motivation, inspiration, or incentive for the student to perform well? (Or does the system generate anxiety, tension, or undue pressure on the student?) Does it serve to encourage or foster creative, novel, or imaginative performance? Does the system encourage students to learn information to meet their needs and interests, or does it encourage memorization just to pass examinations? Is the system fair to all students? (Are some students graded more easily than they should be and others graded more harshly?)[9]

Those who defend the use of a grading or marking system might concede that any approach has some limitations, but they will argue that our mass educational system must employ some evaluation techniques. Why? First, marking gives students some sense of the quality of their performance. Second, marking systems help students decide which curriculum to follow by flagging the areas in which they will be strong and weak. Third, some students need motivation, even if it is negative. If presented properly, grades can be a positive inducement to learning. Fourth, grades aid society in predicting individual success in advanced schooling by helping colleges make decisions on admissions. Fifth, grades are a mechanism for insuring minimum competencies. Sixth, grades, especially the A-to-F approach, are relatively easy to understand by those outside as well as inside education.[10]

Those who oppose marking systems believe these arguments do not hold up.

By Clem Scalzitti in *Phi Delta Kappan*, February 1976, p. 412. Reprinted with artist's permission.

"Burke, about your grading stamps. . . ."

First, grades are imprecise, and what they typically measure is ability to recall information, not ability to reason. Second, grades encourage cheating and poor attitudes toward learning. Low grades deter students. Third, grades build extrinsic motivation rather than intrinsic motivation. They foster undue competition among students. More experiences in education should be based on cooperation rather than competition.

Fourth, school grades are not the best predictors of success on the job or in life generally. Fifth, some studies indicate that grades and transcripts are no longer critical to college admissions or employment. If other indices of performance are provided (written evaluations, scores on standardized tests, previous employer recommendations), grades lose their importance.[11]

ACTIVITY 7-1
Making the Grade

Since grading (marking) is one of the most frequent complaints by students about the educational system, you might find it valuable to explore some facet of the issue. Prepare a position paper for a class debate, in which you answer such questions as how the grading system should be structured and which grading alternatives are most satisfactory today.

You might begin by reading relevant chapters in books on teaching methods. The *Education Index* will contain articles referring to marking policies and practices. See also the Ebel and Karmel references in the "For Further Study" section at the end of this chapter.

FORMAL TESTING

As a student you have experienced many types of evaluation. Most were formal tests—written quizzes, essay exams, multiple-choice tests, personality inventories, rating scales, college entrance tests, and questionnaires on vocational preference. If you become a teacher, you will probably agonize over the tests you construct and wonder whether they are really valuable and valid; you'll probably also administer some of the standardized tests to your students.

After a brief review of rationale for tests and a look at general problems regarding teacher-constructed tests, this section will concentrate upon the controversies of standardized testing. In particular we shall look at the debate about the cultural bias of such tests, as well as the much-discussed decline in achievement levels.

Why Tests?

Tests in education should have as their general purpose the improvement of instruction. If, after all, we believe that education means changing students' lives through exposure to a variety of viewpoints and by increasing knowledge and improving problem-solving abilities, then we should be concerned about documenting changes. Specific tests, whether teacher-made or standardized, have been developed for a variety of immediate purposes. Some guide students in their choice of a curriculum or an occupation; others help select candidates for admission to college or special programs. In the classroom, there are tests to diagnose learning problems and thus place students in the most appropriate study groups. Certain instruments are designed to reveal students' attitudes and values. From the teacher's perspective, some tests are valuable in providing information about the progress of students toward course objectives. The results from such tests can be used to improve the instructional performance of the teacher or to modify and redesign the curriculum.

Since tests have many purposes, testers must be careful to select an instrument that accurately meets their needs. Teachers, administrators, and counselors must consider the types of tests available and the many techniques that might be employed. There are three types of tests. *Aptitude tests* are primarily designed to predict success in some future learning activity, while *achievement tests* measure the individual's present level of knowledge, skills, or performance. (Most teacher-made tests are a form of achievement test.) Tests that assess interest, personality, and attitude are sometimes called *inventories* because they gauge affective elements rather than factually right or wrong answers. Within each of these categories there are oral and written, essay and objective, mastery, survey and diagnostic, individual and group performance, verbal and nonverbal, speed and power tests. Testing methods include interviews, observations, use of anecdotal records, checklists, rating scales, and group-relationship surveys (sociometric procedures).[12]

After the type of test is tentatively chosen, the fundamental question is whether the test is valid. *Validity* refers to the extent the test measures what it purports to measure. How truthful or accurate is it? If it is supposed to determine whether students know how to treat a snakebite, but instead measures their ability to classify snakes, it is not a valid test. A second question is whether the test is reliable. *Reliability* means that the test is consistent. If a teacher gives the same test on Monday and Friday with similar results, or if different instructors independently test

the same students with an identical instrument and get similar results, the conclusion is that the test is reliable. Educators must also consider *usability*. Is it practical in terms of time needed for administering? Is it economically feasible? Can it be scored quickly?

Besides validity, reliability, and usability, test users must consider whether they want to use norm-referenced or criterion-referenced instruments. A *norm-referenced test* is an instrument whose interpretation is based on an external standard of performance. The norm may be the class (the average score of all students), by community or district (the average score of all fifth grades), by state, or by nation. A teacher reporting the results of a norm-referenced test to a parent might say, "Juan did better than 80% of the state's fifth graders on a test of addition of whole numbers." Often, norm-referenced tests cover cumulative and/or relational types of knowledge (e.g., how well students see the relationship of increasingly complex theories.) Their primary advantage is that they provide perspective on student performance on very specific *areas* of achievement. On the other hand, the *criterion-referenced test* is an instrument whose interpretation is based upon an internal level of performance, or degree to which a predetermined task is mastered. If it were a criterion-referenced test, the teacher might say to Juanita's parent, "She had 70% of the items correct on the test." The chief advantage of such tests is that they provide information on individual pupil achievement. Their main drawback is that the test items may not always be valid for the specific instructor or district goals.

Teacher-made Tests

Teachers who prepare their own tests face some of the issues discussed, particularly those of validity, reliability, and usability.

There are other questions that are unique to teacher-made tests. Our intent here is to probe the general problems teachers have when they design their own instruments. How to construct test questions is the domain of your methods courses. As the cartoon suggests, students realize that the quality of test items can vary markedly.

All future educators need to be concerned about testing. Lamentably, some prospective teachers from such areas as preschool education and the arts ignore this important topic because they make little use of essay and multiple-choice examinations. Regardless of your teaching field, you'll soon learn that parents expect some report on their child's progress. Students want to know, too, how they are doing. You will find it helpful to know a variety of evaluation techniques and their advantages and disadvantages. Structured interviews and systematic observations are just two types that are effective with younger children. A variety of mastery tests can be used with students in the performing arts.

Here is a partial listing of some of the questions teachers must resolve when they prepare their own tests:

1. What is the purpose of the test? Is it to determine how well the students have learned a unit of study? Is it primarily to rank the students in the class in a specific body of knowledge? Is it a diagnostic tool to determine individual students' strengths and weaknesses? Answers to these ques-

tions influence how many test items will be constructed, and what level of difficulty will be built into the choices.

2. To what extent are my tests compatible with those given by other instructors (in the same instructional area)? Would it be advisable to have periodic departmental exams?

3. Should students be asked to contribute test items? How beneficial is it to keep a file of test items? Should students be shown old exams?

4. When is it best to use an essay exam and when is it more appropriate to offer an objective examination? (Table 7–1 offers some general advice, while demonstrating the point that the teacher has numerous factors to weigh in designing a test.)[13]

Current Status of Standardized Tests

Almost every school district conducts some standardized testing each year. It is estimated that as many as 150 companies are now producing tests, including many subsidiaries of major publishing firms. In 1976 approximately 17 million students were tested, at a cost of $2 for each test.[14]

Testing would not have reached such proportions unless a number of educators and the public were convinced that it was worthwhile. One of the staunchest advocates of standardized testing is Robert Ebel, professor of educational psychology at Michigan State University and a past-

Chapter Seven

Table 7–1.

Summary of characteristics of essay and objective examinations

	Essay	Objective
Abilities Measured	Requires the student to express himself in his own words, using information from his own background and knowledge.	Requires the student to select correct answers from given options, or to supply an answer limited to one word or phrase.
	Can tap high levels of reasoning such as required in inference, organization of ideas, comparison and contrast.	Can *also* tap high levels of reasoning such as required in inference, organization of ideas, comparison and contrast.
	Does *not* measure purely factual information efficiently.	Measures knowledge of facts efficiently.
Scope	Covers only a limited field of knowledge in any one test. Essay questions take so long to answer that relatively few can be answered in a given period of time. Also, the student who is especially fluent can often avoid discussing points of which he is unsure.	Covers a broad field of knowledge in one test. Since objective questions may be answered quickly, one test may contain many questions. A broad coverage helps provide reliable measurement.
Incentive to Pupils	Encourages pupils to learn how to organize their own ideas and express them effectively.	Encourages pupils to build up a broad background of knowledge and abilities.
Ease of Preparation	Requires writing only a few questions for a test. Tasks must be clearly defined, general enough to offer some leeway, specific enough to set limits.	Requires writing many questions for a test. Wording must avoid ambiguities and "give-aways." Distractors should embody most likely misconceptions.
Scoring	Usually very time-consuming to score.	Can be scored quickly.
	Permits teachers to comment directly on the reasoning processes of individual pupils. However, an answer may be scored differently by different teachers or by the same teacher at different times.	Answer generally scored only right or wrong, but scoring is very accurate and consistent.

From *Making the Classroom Test: A Guide for Teachers.* (Princeton, N.J.: Educational Testing Service, 1959), p. 16. Copyright © 1959, 1961, 1973 by Educational Testing Service. All rights reserved. Reprinted by permission.

president of the American Educational Research Association. In a *Kappan* article in 1975, he debated a colleague at Michigan State about the merits of standardized testing and concluded the following:

1. Tests in education, to a reasonable extent, are valid and reliable. Too often it is the poor teachers who complain that the tests are invalid and unreliable.

2. The emphasis upon cognitive knowledge is acceptable and, indeed, desirable. Those who argue that standardized tests are too narrowly focused and who ask for additional testing in affective areas (emotions, attitudes, values) forget that the primary function of the public schools is to provide cognitive skills.

3. Norm-referenced tests, generally speaking, do not need to be replaced with criterion-referenced tests.

4. The idea that tests foster too much competition between students and give undue publicity to differences between groups is wrong.

5. There is not sufficient evidence to show that standardized tests are culturally biased.[15]

Others writing about standardized testing concur with Ebel that it is useful, and that the solution to problems with standardized tests is not to abandon them, but to improve them. Tests—any tests—are only one tool the schools use to evaluate student performance.[16]

Jonathan N. Goodrich has summarized seven general shortcomings of standardized tests: (1) they are culturally biased in favor of white, middle-class Americans; (2) knowledge is measured only on narrow topics; (3) they have little relationship to skills required in many business fields; (4) they don't measure intelligence; (5) they don't measure the student's ability to learn; (6) few assess oral and written communication skills, research capacity, motivation,

or leadership qualities; and (7) they promote the assumption that intelligence is inherited, not developed.[17]

Other critics feel that standardized tests, forced on the schools by state and federal education bureaucrats and testing companies, turn schools into "plodding, pedestrian, soul-destroying" places. Moreover, aptitude tests are woefully imprecise in predicting future performance levels. Tests stifle creativity and encourage too much competition. Furthermore, the critics say, history informs us that teachers will "teach to the test" if they believe that their promotions in any way depend upon student outcomes.[18]

As you can see, there is extensive debate about the use and value of standardized tests. Particular attention has been paid to the vast use of the Scholastic Aptitude Test (SAT). In June 1926, 8,040 candidates for college took the first SAT exam. In 1979, 1 million prospective college students completed the SAT. The increase is a reflection of higher enrollments, but also of greater use of such examinations. In January 1980, Ralph Nader's Learning Research Project Center released a critical analysis of the Educational Testing Service, the United States' largest producer of standardized tests such as the SAT, the Test of English as a Foreign Language (TOEFL), and many admissions tests for professional schools. The 554-page report charged that the tests were biased against minority-group and lower-income students and excluded disproportionate numbers of these students from higher education; that coaching could improve students' performance on the tests, giving an advantage to wealthier students who could hire tutors; that these tests were poor predictors of college performance; and that the tests discriminated against poor test-takers.[19]

Because standardized tests play a role in college and graduate school admissions, a number of consumer groups have fought to have "truth-in-testing" bills enacted in their states. Test companies say that to reveal the test questions and individual test results will place a heavy financial burden upon them (because of the expense of constructing new tests), and they have been restricting the number of times they will give the test in states that have passed such laws (New York is the first).

The controversies over truth-in-testing and colleges' use of standardized tests relate to two other issues. First, are IQ tests biased? Second, do standardized tests like the SAT prove that there is a decline in the academic ability of American students?

IQ Tests and Cultural Bias. As a teacher you may be asked by parents and members of the community how you feel about IQ tests. Probably that question will come after parents ask you what their child's IQ is. You should be prepared to cope with both questions.

First, there is consensus among educators about the purpose and limitations of intelligence tests. The basic function of IQ tests, historically as well as currently, has been to measure the student's ability to succeed in cognitive school assignments. According to most researchers, these tests do *not* measure innate abilities, nor can a single test indicate the overall intelligence of an individual. There are many kinds of intellectual activities—among them reasoning, verbal knowledge, spatial perceptions, number ability, memory, and creativity.[20]

This consensus was challenged in 1969 by Arthur Jensen, a professor of psychology at the University of California at Berkeley. He argued that the battery of intelligence tests then available provided a sufficient vehicle for measuring the general intelligence of individuals. Two of his most controversial findings were that heredity plays the dominant role in determining intelligence (environment is minor), and that

blacks are genetically inferior in intelligence to whites. Jensen discounted the arguments about the cultural bias of the tests. He argued that blacks consistently average 10 to 15 points below whites on IQ tests, a condition he attributed to genetic makeup.[21]

While his point of view was welcome ammunition to racists, most of the academic community immediately disputed Jensen's claims. Psychologists said Jensen misinterpreted data from Burt's studies of separated twins. Social scientists argued that the test instruments themselves were culturally biased, favoring white middle-class children. For example, consider these questions from intelligence tests: Why is it better to pay bills by check instead of cash? Who wrote *Romeo and Juliet*? What is the meaning of the word chattel? What is a cream pitcher? (This last item was to

The debate continues. . . . Are standardized tests biased? Is there a difference in intelligence among racial groups?

be identified by preschool children.) Jensen's opponents pointed to numerous IQ-test questions that favored children from white middle- and upper-middle-class homes.[22]

What is most upsetting to those who believe Jensen is wrong is that his interpretation encourages the misuse of intelligence tests. Based on test scores, some students are erroneously placed in classrooms with severely retarded children. Some school districts have organized classes by the scores on such tests. Certain studies show that teachers have more negative feelings about students with low IQs; poor self-fulfilling prophecies are bound to result, say the critics. Some courts have forced schools to discontinue the use of IQ tests. Some efforts have been made to design "culture-free tests," but that movement appears to be slowing in the belief that as long as the public schools reflect white middle-class culture, minority students and children from lower-class backgrounds will probably continue to score low on such tests.[23]

No doubt the issues of whether intelligence can be measured and whether intelligence tests are culturally biased cannot be answered completely. Continued research in these areas interests educators and the general public, especially as the schools grapple with such concerns as equal educational opportunity and individualized instruction. (See Chapters 15 and 13.)

ACTIVITY 7–2

How Intelligent Am I—About IQ Tests?

This discussion may have stimulated your interest to learn more about intelligence tests. Consult the sources cited in the Notes and in the "For Further Study" section at the end of the chapter.

For your own satisfaction, or for a class discussion, you may wish to write your responses to these questions: What is intelligence? Are you convinced that the IQ tests accurately measure what they purport to measure (i.e., academic aptitude)? If so, respond to the charge that IQ tests are culturally biased.

The Decline in Test Scores. At least for the immediate future, the nation's schools will have standardized tests, and members of the press, like parents, will want to know how students compare with each other. Headlines during the past few years have thundered a disconcerting message—test scores are declining.

The declining scores referred to, most of the time, are those obtained from the SAT and ACT. We first should clarify just what such tests measure. Both are designed to assess general educational development and the ability to do college-level work. The SAT, scored on a scale of 200 to 800 points, stresses verbal comprehension and mathematical problem-solving skills. The American College Testing program's instrument consists of four tests (English, mathematics, social studies, and natural sciences); a Student Profile Section; and an Interest Inventory. Scores range from 1 to 36, and 20 was the average score of college-bound first-semester high school seniors in 1975. The overall average score dropped to 18.6 by 1978 but the composite score climbed to 18.9 in 1980–81. Results in three of the four areas (English, mathematics, and social studies) declined during the period of 1975–80, but the natural sciences rose from 20.6 to 21.3. From 1963 to 1980, the average verbal SAT score plummeted 54 points (to 424), and math SAT scores dropped from 492 to 466.[24] Results on other tests have not always declined, but these two tests have gained the most publicity.

Why the decline? Reasons advanced have included more difficult test items, less incentive to work hard to get high scores, increase in television viewing time, decrease in stress on more rigorous college-preparatory courses such as physics, advanced math, and foreign languages, changes in family life, and "national turbulence." One of the most frequently mentioned explanations is the increase in the number of lower-ability students taking the exams. However, the Education Testing Service, which sponsors the SAT, has stated that the decline in scores affects the previously high-scoring groups as much as the lower-scoring groups.[25]

The decline in scores has not been universal. The National Association of Secondary School Principals sponsored a study of 34 high schools whose students have done exceedingly well on the SAT. The study concluded that the schools, which ranged in location from affluent neighborhoods to blue-collar communities, had resisted educational trends to loosen their rigorous academic programs. The 34 schools had emphasized writing, grammar, spelling, vocabulary, and literature. This study's conclusion has been challenged on grounds that the administrators' answers were subjective and that the number of tested students was small and unrepresentative.[26]

It is important to note again that the ACT and SAT tests are college predictor tests. The bulk of standardized tests are achievement tests in such areas as reading, writing, and mathematical skills. Some of these tests show that the test scores have not declined. For example, in addition to increases in the ACT natural science scores,

the Iowa Test of Basic Skills (early grades) and some of the NAEP (National Assessment of Educational Progress) tests, such as reading achievement, have shown gains.[27]

REGIONAL AND NATIONAL EVALUATION EFFORTS

As informative as SAT, ACT, and intelligence tests are, they do not describe clearly the changes in school performance of the nation's young people. Most of the tests discussed so far are aptitude rather than academic achievement tests. Moreover, the students who take ACT and SAT exams are not representative of the American pupil population. Even the widely used achievement tests (like the Iowa Test of Basic Skills) are more popular in some parts of the country than others, and they test very specific learning concepts. In short, most of these tests emphasize how a single student responds to many test items, and do not inform us of how groups of students react to typical school academic tasks.

This section highlights two efforts to increase both regional and national information on student performance, beginning with the National Assessment of Educational Progress, a project that attempts to develop a national profile of student achievement. The more recent movement, developed at the state level, is for minimum competency examinations.

National Assessment of Educational Progress

Planning for the NAEP began in 1964 by the Education Commission of the States (ECS). ECS at the time was composed of representatives of 47 states, and its members included governors, chief state school officers, legislators, and lay people. NAEP funding initially came from the Carnegie

Corporation of New York, the Ford Foundation, and the U.S. Office of Education. Major funding now is provided by the National Center for Education Statistics.[28]

Through annual achievement surveys, NAEP measures the educational attainments of four age groups: 9-year-olds, 13-year-olds, 17-year-olds, and young adults (ages 26 to 35). The assessments measure educational achievement in 10 learning areas, including 3 basic skill groups (reading, writing, and mathematics), 4 general subject-matter areas (social studies, citizenship, science, and career/occupational development), and 3 humanities and fine arts disciplines (literature, art, and music).

In preparing the tests, NAEP first asks groups of teachers, scholars, and concerned lay people to develop general and specific objectives for each of the 10 areas. There must be agreement that the objectives reflect acceptable teaching goals, that they are important for young persons to know in today's world, and that they are meaningful in the subject area. Then test items are constructed; some are quite unlike those on typical achievement tests. Students and the young adults may be required to view a motion picture segment, read a television guide, fill out a ballot, balance a checkbook, be interviewed, write an essay, use scientific apparatus, sing and play an instrument, or draw a picture. Test results are evaluated with the help of subject-matter experts like the National Council of Teachers of English. Each of the 10 areas is reassessed every 3 to 5 years.

When the National Assessment project was first proposed, some opposition was voiced by educators who thought that the tests might lead to district-by-district and building-by-building comparisons. Data and findings on individual students and districts are never published. Results are available for four geographic regions. Other variables in the published NAEP reports include level of parental education, race, sex, size and type of community.

What are the major findings of the assessments? Typically, high achievers live in the Northeast or Central regions, attend schools in the affluent suburbs, are the sons and daughters of parents who had considerable formal education, and are white. Low achievers very often live in the Southeast, attend inner-city or rural schools, have parents who had little formal education, and are members of minority groups. Students from high socioeconomic backgrounds do better in the 10 areas measured in the NAEP studies than students with low socioeconomic status—a confirmation of the Coleman Report (see Chapter 15).

What are some of the more specific findings? While it is true that the Southeast usually ranks lowest, it is normally no more than 5% below the national average. Generally, the inner-city students score lowest, and the rural youth perform below the national average in most areas. The affluent suburban students are consistently above the national average, especially in mathematics. The differences between young men and young women vary, with the women scoring higher in most learning areas. In science and mathematics, men score higher. Blacks, in recent years, have improved in reading comprehension.[29]

There are also important differences in schooling performances by the various age groups. Here is a partial summary of some of the students' abilities:

● Nine-year-olds are learning many things during their first few years of schooling such as the basic reading and writing skills. They can read simple stories and write letters to their friends, and they know a variety of subject-matter facts. Moreover, they are tolerant of other people's cultural differences and believe in an orderly society.

● Thirteen-year-olds can read, write, add,

7. A. Below are three ads from the Help Wanted section of a newspaper. Read all three ads and choose which job you would like best if you had to apply for one of them. Fill in the oval beside the ONE job you choose.

○ -Help Wanted- OFFICE HELPER: Experience in light typing and filing desirable but not necessary, must have 1 yr. high school math and be able to get along with people. $2.50/hr. to start. Start now. Good working conditions. Write to ACE Company, P.O. Box 100, Columbia, Texas 94082.

○ -Help Wanted- SALESPERSON: Some experience desirable but not necessary, must be willing to learn and be able to get along with people. $2.50/hr. to start. Job begins now. Write to ACE Shoestore, P.O. Box 100, Columbia, Texas 94082.

○ -Help Wanted- APPRENTICE MECHANIC: Some experience working on cars desirable but not necessary, must be willing to learn and be able to get along with people. $2.50/hr. to start. Job begins now. Write ACE Garage, P.O. Box 100, Columbia, Texas 94802.

B. On the next two pages, write a letter applying for the job that you choose. Write the letter as if you were actually trying to get the job. Use the name Dale Roberts.

Objectives:

VII. *Career and Occupational Skills*

E4. *Demonstrates ability to prepare a job application, letter or form.*

From Demo Booklet, Year 08, p. 30 (above); Demo Booklet, Year 09, p. 13 (right).

8.

Here are a tin can and a ball:

Here is how each looks from the side:

Draw how each looks when you are directly above them.

Objectives:

    C. Shape, Size and Position

      II D. Making geometric manipulations

          Spatial Visualizations

(Mathematics -- Ages 9, 13, 17)

subtract, divide and multiply when told to do so. However they do not, by themselves, use these skills in order to solve everyday problems. They have these skills and knowledges necessary to accomplish routine tasks at home and at school. They have developed some study skills and know a variety of useful facts, but the idea that they could use these skills and knowledges to make their daily lives more interesting and productive is not always obvious to them.

● Seventeen-year-olds have mastered the basic skills and know many specific facts in all school subjects, but have difficulty organizing and applying their skills and knowledges. They have some knowledge of the world of work, have thought about their futures, and know what attitudes and behaviors are expected of them in our society. They know a number of facts about our government and legal system, and know some specific scientific facts. They have difficulty reading long passages and have limited vocabularies when writing. They can read, write and compute in well-structured situations but they have difficulty applying their knowledge to new situations.[30]

What implications from the NAEP statistics are important to teachers? As indicated earlier, data reveal that family background is of prime significance. A major inference from the studies is that there are numerous variables associated with school performance, and it is simplistic (and perhaps dangerous) to attribute declining scores or improved performance to any one factor, such as a lack of discipline or a particular curriculum. Teachers and the schools do make a difference in pupil performance, as some of the data show. However, there is evidence also to suggest that students in many of the areas have not learned to apply school information to out-of-school situations. Finally, NAEP data show that concerted school efforts can change performance. In the Far West, for example, reading scores that had been on the de-

cline began to improve again. Evaluators believed a combination of changes in school programs and policies helped to reverse the trend.

Minimum Competency Examinations

The public and its lawmakers, although often unaware of the findings of the NAEP, sensed in the mid-1970s that not enough was demanded of students. With little support from educators, they enacted in more than 30 states a strategy—minimum competency tests—that they believed would both measure student abilities and boost student achievements.

Assuming that a high school diploma was little more than a certificate of attendance, the people who favored legislation for competency wanted tests prepared in such basic skills areas as reading, writing, and mathematics. In certain states, "survival or life skills" tests in swimming and consumer math were devised. Variations

GRIN AND BEAR IT   by Lichty & Wagner

"We've been instructed to give oral exams to all seniors who haven't yet learned to read and write "

Table 7–2.

State minimum competency testing standards, 1978

States Using Minimum Competency Testing	Government Level Setting Standards	Grade Levels Assessed	Expected* Uses of Standards		
			Grade Promotion	High School Graduation	Other
Alabama.......	State	9-12		X	
Arizona........	State and local	8, 12		X	X
California	State and local	4-6, 7-9, 10, 11		X	X
Colorado	Local	9-12			X
Connecticut....	State and local	3, 5, 7, 9			X
Delaware	State	11		X	
Florida	State and local	3, 5, 8, 11	X	X	X
Georgia	State	4, 8, 11			X
Idaho	State	9-12			X
Illinois	Local	Local option			X
Indiana........	Local	3, 6, 10			X
Kansas........	State	2, 4, 6, 8, 9, 11, 12			X
Kentucky	State	3, 5, 8, 11	X	X	X
Louisiana	State	4, 8, 11			X
Maine	State	11		X	
Maryland	State	3, 7, 9, 11	X	X	
Massachusetts .	Local	Local option			X
Michigan	State	4, 7, 10			X
Missouri	State	8			X
Nebraska......	Local	5-12			X
Nevada........	State	6, 9, 12		X	X
New Hampshire	State	4, 8, 12			X
New Jersey	State	3, 6, 9, 11			X
New Mexico....	State	Local option			X
New York	State	3, 6, 8, 9, 10, 11, 12		X	X
North Carolina..	State	1, 2, 3, 6, 9, 11		X	X
Oregon........	Local	Local option		X	
Oklahoma	Under study	3, 6, 9, 12			X
Rhode Island...	State	4, 8, 12			X
South Carolina .	State	1, 2, 3, 8, 11			X
Tennessee.....	State and local	4, 5, 6, 8, 11, 12		X	X
Utah	Local	Local option		X	
Vermont	State	1-12		X	
Virginia........	State and local	K-6, 9-12		X	X
Washington	Local	4, 8			X
Wyoming	Local	Local option		X	

*In most states, uses of standards will be phased in and are not yet in effect.

From Education Commission of the States, Department of Research and Information, *States Activity—Minimum Competency Testing*, January, 1979.

exist: some states test only in the 11th or 12th grades; other states test in the 3rd, 7th, or 9th grades. Realizing that the students who failed the exams would need remedial help before they could retake the tests, most states provided funds for districts to spend for such programs.

By 1980, 38 states had mandated minimum competency exams. (See Table 7–2.) Challenges to the movement arose, centering mainly on the validity of the tests being used.[31]

Florida was the first state to develop and administer statewide competency tests in communication skills and mathematics. The first time they were given in 1977, 8% of the students failed the communications segment and 36% failed the mathematics portion. Because black students had a high failure rate, the issue of cultural bias was raised and the National Association for the Advancement of Colored People (NAACP) initiated a lawsuit. In a U.S. District Court decision in 1978, Florida was prohibited from using a literacy test as a prerequisite to graduation from high school. However, the *Debra P.* v. *Turlington* ruling does not prohibit Florida from still using its minimum competency tests. After a year and one-half of remediation efforts, Florida education officials claimed that student performances improved dramatically. The failure rate decline to 3% in communications skills and 26% in mathematics.[32]

Those who are enthusiastic about minimum competencies believe that the examinations help students and teachers know what and how well work should be done. Parents and the public often feel they have more leverage over the schools (i.e., they can tell the schools what they want taught and how well they want it covered), and that tests with simple mathematics problems and reading comprehension selections should not be too difficult to create. Another dividend of this move-

ment, advocates hold, is that there can be earlier identification of student deficiencies.[33]

In opposition, "Reason and evidence don't justify the belief that minimum competency testing will help poor students to learn or poor teachers to teach."[34] Specifically, opponents ask the following questions:

1. Precisely what is to be tested? (Basic skills, life skills, or a combination? Depending on the answer, quite different tests have to be devised.)

2. Who sets the standards (i.e., cutoff points)? Also, what are the specific criteria for judging competency? Most educational researchers believe it is sounder to measure progress from one point to another rather than to declare minimums.

3. Are the costs of remediation affordable? In light of inflation and the costs of providing a basic education, is it feasible or even possible for local districts and states to spend millions of dollars annually for remediation programs?

4. What happens to local control? (Even states that allow or require local districts to set minimum standards find that state or national tests are being used with greater frequency, and that funding is coming from other-than-local sources. With that funding, it is argued, comes outside control.)

The fundamental issue, regardless of the future of minimum competency testing, is what are the best ways to ensure that students have successfully completed their course of study? Some people no longer feel confident that standardized test scores and accumulation of courses are adequate. Are mastery tests that much better?

ACTIVITY 7–3

Minimum Competency Today

Has minimum competency sufficient support to become rooted in the educational land-scape of America, or is it a passing fad? What are your feelings about such examinations? How would you feel as a teacher if you were in a district or state employing such a procedure?

Answer one or more of these questions in any form you choose (formal report, library research, interview with local or state educational official). You might begin the activity by exploring the current status of competency exams in your state and perhaps even obtaining a copy of an exam and testing your own competency.

SUMMARY

As a student, you probably had and have your share of unfair evaluations from instructors. As you consider teaching as a career, you must consider how you will assess student progress. Of course, you will not have sole responsibility for choosing a grading system, since the district and state may mandate some policies.

This chapter indicated that evaluation of pupil performance has a long history. There are many forms of evaluation—grades, standardized test, and minimum competency tests, to name a few. Further, efforts continue in educational research to determine how to improve student achievement. Underlying our discussion are such questions as whether all this assessment is necessary and whether it can be done fairly.

In the section on marking systems, it was noted that the predominant approach, the A-to-F scale, is a relative newcomer. Arguments in favor of and against this system and other grading procedures were cited. There is relatively little disagreement about the necessity for some sort of evaluation in the schools.

The use of standardized tests seems to be under more attack than are grading systems. The principal reasons appear to be that the tests may not measure what they purport to measure and that they may be culturally biased. Those who favor standardized tests acknowledge that they must be carefully interpreted, especially in such matters as assessing and predicting student performance.

Reflecting the public's dissatisfaction with testing procedures (from the teacher-made tests to the standardized tests), efforts have been made to better evaluate students on a systematic basis. The National Assessment of Educational Progress is one example. Evaluation items are based on generally agreed-upon classroom objectives in 10 learning areas. A second movement is the minimum competency testing that many states have adopted. Although popular because such tests give easily understandable results, the tests are being questioned by some who state that the emphasis is upon minimum performance and arbitrary decisions about passing scores and appropriate test items.

If anything is to be underscored in this chapter, and Part 2 as a whole, it is that teaching is a vocation that requires more preparation and dedication than is usually imagined. If you want to be an effective teacher, you must be concerned constantly about the best ways to assess student performance, just as you want to be fairly judged for your abilities.

Chapter Seven

NOTES

1. Wilson F. Wetzler, "Reporting Pupil Progress," *Grade Teacher* 77, no. 8 (April 1959): 14–16.

2. Howard Kirschenbaum, Rodney Napier, and Sidney B. Simon, *Wad-ja-get?* (New York: Hart Publishing Co., 1971), pp. 49–67.

3. Ibid., pp. 55–56.

4. Woodrow Mousley, "Report Cards Across the Nation," *Phi Delta Kappan* 53, no. 7 (March 1972): 36–37; Jessie Dubois, "Rise Up Red Pencil, Right On!" *Language Arts* 53, no. 6 (September 1976): 666–67; Kirschenbaum et al., pp. 292–307.

5. Philip T. Bain, "An Investigation of Some Assumptions and Characteristics of the Pass-Fail Grading System," *Journal of Educational Research* 67, no. 3 (November 1973): 134–36.

6. William L. Yarber, "Comparing Contract and Traditional Grading Techniques for Ninth Grade Students," *Education* 95, no. 4 (Summer 1975): 363–67.

7. Robert A. DiSibio, "A Different Approach to Grading," *Education* 92, no. 2 (November-December 1971): 34–35; James L. Leary, "Assessing Pupil Progress: New Methods are Emerging," *Educational Leadership* 32, no. 4 (January 1975): 250–52.

8. Norman M. Chansky, "Resolving the Grading Problem," *The Educational Forum* 37, no. 2 (January 1973): 189–94.

9. Mousley, "Report Cards," 36–37; Kenneth Goldstein and Harvey Tilker, "Attitudes Toward the A-B-C-D-F and Honors-Pass-Fail Grading Systems," *Journal of Educational Research* 65, no. 3 (November 1971): 99–100.

10. Duane M. Giannangelo, "Make Report Cards Meaningful," *The Educational Forum* 39, no. 4 (May 1975): 409–16.

11. Sidney Simon and Lois Hart, "Grades and Marks: Some Commonly Asked Questions," *Science Teacher* 40, no. 6 (September 1973): 46–48; Joseph C. Pentecoste, "From Competition to Cooperation: Toward a New Methodology in Education," *The Negro Educational Review* 26, no. 2 (April-July 1975): 110–15; Gehard Prause, *School Days of the Famous: Do School Achievements Foretell Success in Life?* (New York: Springer Publishing, 1978).

12. Norman E. Gronlund, *Measurement and Evaluation in Teaching* (New York: MacMillan, 1964), pp. 10–11, 18; William A. Mehrens and Irvin J. Lehmann, *Standardized Tests in Education* (New York: Holt, Rinehart, and Winston, 1973), p. 115.

13. John A. Jones, "How to Write Better Tests," *Instructor* 89, no. 3 (October 1979): 66–71; Edward Burns, *The Development, Use, and Abuse of Educational Tests* (Springfield, Ill.: Charles C Thomas, 1979).

14. Terry Herndon, "Standardized Tests: Are They Worth the Cost?" *Education Digest* 42, no. 1 (September 1976): 13–16; M.C. Kirkland, "The Effects of Tests on Students and Schools," *Review of Educational Research* 41, no. 4 (October 1971): 303–50.

15. Robert L. Ebel, "Educational Tests: Valid? Biased? Useful?" *Phi Delta Kappan* 57, no. 2 (October 1975): 83–88, 93.

16. John R. Kazalunas, "What's Right with Testing," *National Association of Secondary Principals Bulletin* 62, no. 420 (October 1978): 57–63; Parker Damon, "Questions You Should Ask About Your Testing Program," *The National Elementary Principal* 56, no. 1 (September/October 1976): 47–53.

17. Jonathan N. Goodrich, "American Standardized Tests: Pseudo Indicators of Ability?" *Educational Technology* 15, no. 12 (December 1975): 23–25; George F. Madaus et al., "The Sensitivity of Measures of School Effectiveness," *Harvard Educational Review* 49, no. 2 (May 1979): 207–30.

18. Arthur S. Laughland "Two Principals Look at Standardized Tests," *The National Elementary Principal* 54, no. 6 (July-August 1975): 88–90; Robert L. Green, "Tips on Educational Testing: What Teachers and Parents Should Know," *Phi Delta Kappan* 57, no. 2 (October 1975): 89–93.

19. Educational Testing Service, *The Story of the College Board Scholastic Aptitude Test*, a pamphlet of ETS, Princeton, N.J., published originally in 1961–62, and updated annually. Allan Nairn and Associates, *The Reign of ETS: The Corporation That Makes Up Minds* (Washington, D.C.: Learning Center, 1980). See also the ETS position papers, "An Overview: Test Use and Validity," and "Test Scores and Family Income: A Partial Response to the Nader/Nairn Report on ETS," in *Phi Delta Kappan* 61, no. 9 (May 1980): 649.

20. Benjamin Bloom, *Stability and Change in Human Characteristics* (New York: John Wiley, 1964); Richard R. Skemp, *Intelligence, Learning, and Action* (New York: John Wiley, 1979).

21. Arthur R. Jensen, "How Much Can We Boost IQ and Scholastic Achievement?" *Harvard Educational Review* 39, no. 1 (Winter 1969): 1–123; idem, *Bias in Mental Testing* (New York: Free Press, 1980).

22. Reactions to Jensen were printed in *Harvard Educational Review* 39, no. 2 (Spring 1969): 272–356.

23. N. J. Block and Gerald Dworkin, eds., *The IQ Controversy: Critical Readings* (New York: Pantheon, 1976); Jensen, *Bias in Mental Testing*.

24. *College Student Profiles* (Iowa City, Iowa: American College Testing Program, 1966–67), p. 23; *College Student Profiles* (Iowa City, Iowa: American *College Testing Program* 1978–79), p. 15; 1980–81 data from ACT obtained in a telephone interview, 10 October 1980; *The Chronicle of Higher Education* 21, no. 7 (6 October 1980): 4. For discussion of the validity of the SAT tests, see Rex Jackson, "The Scholastic Aptitude Test; A Response to Slack and Porter's 'Critical Appraisal,' " *Harvard Educational Review* 50, no. 3 (August 1980): 382–91; Warner V. Slack and Douglas Porter, "Training, Validity, and the Issue of Aptitude: A Reply to Jackson," *Harvard Educational Review* 50, no. 3 (August 1980): 392–401.

25. Robert L. Ebel, "Declining Scores: A Conservative Explanation," *Phi Delta Kappan* 58, no. 4 (De-

cember 1976): 306–10; Albert Shanker, "Test-score Declines: A Cause for Concern," *American Teacher* 60, no. 9 (May 1976): 6; Paul Copperman, "The Achievement Decline of the 1970s," *Phi Delta Kappan* 60, no. 10 (June 1979): 736–39.

26. John A. Black, "When Is a Study Not a Study? An Examination of *Guidelines for Improving SAT Scores*," *Phi Delta Kappan* 60, no. 7 (March 1979): 487–89.

27. R.B. Ingle, M.R. Carroll, and W.J. Gephart, eds., *Assessment of Student Competence* (Bloomington, Ind.: Phi Delta Kappan, 1979); Gordon Cawelti, "National Competency Testing: A Bogus Solution," *Phi Delta Kappan* 59, no. 9 (May 1978): 619; Leo A. Munday, "Changing Test Score: Basic Skills Development in 1977 Compared with 1970," *Phi Delta Kappan* 60, no. 9 (May 1979): 670–71.

28. We wish to thank J. Stanley Ahmann, former Director of NAEP, for his contributions of materials and information. In addition to his comments from interviews, we have used his articles such as J. Stanley Ahmann, "Differential Changes in Levels of Achievement for Students in Three Age Groups," *Educational Studies* 10, no. 1 (Spring 1979): 35–51, and materials from NAEP.

29. J. Stanley Ahmann, *How Much Are Our Young People Learning?: The Story of the National Assessment of Educational Progress* (Bloomington, Ind.: Phi Delta Kappa, 1976): 14–16. For more specific information on test results, see detailed reports published by NAEP. For a brief summary of NAEP studies, see *The Condition of Education* published annually by the National Center for Education Statistics.

30. Ahmann, "National Achievement Profiles in Ten Learning Areas," *Educational Studies* 9, no. 4 (Winter 1979): 362.

31. "The Minimum Competency Testing Movement," special issue, *Phi Delta Kappan* 59, no. 9 (May 1978): 585–625; *New York Times*, 13 March 1980.

32. Thomas H. Fisher, "Florida's Approach to Competency Testing," *Phi Delta Kappan* 59, no. 9 (May 1978): 599–602; Ralph D. Turlington, "Good News from Florida: Our Minimum Competency Program is Working," *Phi Delta Kappan* 60, no. 9 (May 1979): 649–51; "Florida Will Appeal Competency Test Delay," *Phi Delta Kappan* 61, no. 2 (October 1979): 143.

33. John Fremer, "In Response to Gene Glass," *Phi Delta Kappan* 59, no. 9 (May 1978): 605–06, 625; see also 609–13.

34. Arthur E. Wise, "Minimum Competency Testing: Another Case of Hyper-Rationalization," *Phi Delta Kappan* 59, no. 9 (May 1978): 598.

FOR FURTHER STUDY

Ebel, Robert L. *Practical Problems in Educational Measurement.* Lexington, Mass.: D.C. Heath and Co., 1980.

Eysenck, Jans J. *The IQ Argument: Race, Intelligence, and Education.* New York: Library Press, 1971.

Haney, Walt, and Madaus, George. "Making Sense of the Competency Testing Movement." *Harvard Educational Review* 48, no. 4 (November 1978): 462–84. (The article encompasses more topics than the title suggests and includes an excellent historical review of testing.)

Hoffman, Banesh. *The Tyranny of Testing.* New York: Crowell-Collier, 1962.

Ingram, F. Cregg. *Fundamentals of Educational Assessment.* New York: D. Van Nostrand, 1980.

Karmel, Louis J., and Karmel, Marylin O. *Measurement and Evaluation in the Schools.* New York: MacMillan Publishing Co., 1978.

National Assessment of Educational Progress, Education Commission of the States, 1860 Lincoln St., Suite 700. Denver, Colo. 80295.

Tarczan, Constance. *An Educator's Guide to Psychological Tests, Descriptions and Classroom Implications.* Springfield, Ill.: Charles C Thomas, 1972.

Testing, Teaching, and Learning: Report of a Conference on Research on Testing. Washington, D.C.; Government Printing Office, 1980.

Chapter Seven

Part 2
Self-Assessment

*Date*_____

1.0 Decision on Teaching as a Career

Since reading Part 2, my decision on becoming or not becoming a teacher has been—

( ) confirmed, because—
( ) somewhat modified, in that—
( ) drastically changed, because—
( ) made more difficult, because—

2.0 Philosophy of Education Statement

Since reading Part 2, my opening statement about education has been modified on the following points (write about only those that have changed; in this unit, 2.3, 2.4, and 2.5 are most likely):

2.1 goals of education

2.2 the curriculum

2.3 the role of the teacher

2.4 perceptions of learning

2.5 educational policies and procedures

3.0 The School as a Social Institution

3.1 Since reading Part 2, my understanding of the school has—

( ) not been altered. I still believe the school to be—
( ) become more appreciative. For example,—
( ) become more critical. I now feel—
( ) been expanded. I now realize why the school—

3.2 Regarding the social relationships in the school, I have changed my views on (write about only those that have altered, most likely 3.2.2 and 3.2.4 in this part):

3.2.1 student-student

3.2.2 teacher-students

3.2.3 teacher-teacher

3.2.4 teacher-administrator

3.2.5 administrator-school board

3.2.6 school-community

4.0 Information Gained

4.1 What specific information or concept(s) mentioned in Part 2 did you personally find most significant or interesting?

4.2 What information did you find of least interest?

5.0 Reflection on an Educational Issue (select only one)

5.1 (Chapter 4) Who should control teacher education?

5.2 (Chapter 4) Is there a teacher surplus?

5.3 (Chapter 5) What role should teachers have in determining their salaries, working conditions, and educational policy?

5.4 (Chapter 6) What criteria should be used in determining effective teaching performance?

5.5 (Chapter 7) Are national assessment evaluations (minimum competency examinations, NAEP, standardized tests) necessary and/or valuable?

Part 3

Teaching Today

To know your priorities and to have a thorough understanding of classroom responsibilities will enhance your chances of being a successful educator, as Parts 1 and 2 have implied. Effective teachers likewise should have a clear understanding of the school as a social institution.

You must go into teaching with your eyes wide open; know why schools do things the way they do, what the lines of authority are, and how they manage their finances. Moreover, you must understand the process by which the school changes its goals and what trends appear likely in curriculum. These matters may not seem relevant to you now. We believe, however, that learning the ways schools have developed and how they have chosen policies and curriculum may help you to avoid many frustrations later on. One of our saddest experiences as teacher educators is talking to promising young teachers who have decided to quit because they had not comprehended what the school system meant.

Part 3 provides an overview of the structure of schooling today or, in the vernacular, "the rules of the game."

AMERICA'S EDUCATIONAL HERITAGE

Chapter 8 is a historical introduction to the American educational system. It focuses on the formal school patterns, but also describes the informal ways that individuals and groups have been educated. A traditional chronological format is used, conveying the theme that the school system mirrors the predominant values and needs of the culture.

THE GOVERNANCE OF SCHOOLS

One of the favorite American myths is that there is local control of education. Chapter 9 explains the relationship between education and politics, which many assume are separate. Our schools, which are an agency of government, are influenced by decisions at the federal and state levels as well as at the local level. Local school boards, superintendents, and other administrators retain much of the control and responsibility for operating local schools. The final part of the chapter describes how nongovernmental groups have an impact on different aspects of the public school program.

THE EXTENT AND COST OF EDUCATION

You probably take for granted the size of the school system in this country; that is, you may assume that every industrialized nation is as committed to a universal system of schooling as the United States. Chapter 10 examines what America's commitment to mass education means in terms of citizen involvement and cost. Is it worth the expenditure? What about students who are dropping out? Are there ways to reduce the expenses of education without jeopardizing the quality of instruction?

EDUCATIONAL GOALS

At the heart of any educational system are instructional goals. In some communities they have been carefully developed and articulated over the years; in others, never publicly discussed but just as real. As the priorities of local districts and the nation change over the years, educational goals alter, too. Chapter 11 focuses on commonly held educational goals in American communities and how those goals are changed. The formal process for identifying goals and determining which ones will be implemented—*needs assessment*—is discussed in detail.

Related matters are treated. We examine what the public believes are the strengths and weaknesses of the schools. The closing section gives examples of other methods individuals and groups use to alter the school curriculum. Instruction in citizenship education, values education, teaching about religion, and the issue of censorship are mentioned.

THE SCHOOL CURRICULUM

Curriculum is affected by changes in the society and its educational goals. Chapter 12 examines the evolving curriculum in the nation's schools since colonial days and when various subjects began to be taught. The emphasis, however, is on recent trends and contemporary concerns, including curriculum reform projects, the preschool and middle-school movements, back to basics, career education, and multicultural and bilingual education. Selected methodologies and materials such as the use of textbooks, computers, and educational television are also considered. Some attention is given to an analysis of why certain curriculum innovations are successful while others, after briefly flourishing, fail to be widely implemented in schools.

8

America's
Educational Heritage

The common school is the greatest discovery ever made by man.

Horace Mann

American education . . . is, and was, universal, tax-supported, free, compulsory, bureaucratic, racist, and class-biased.

Michael Katz

The building depicted in Winslow Homer's *Snap the Whip* is a far cry from the carpeted, many-roomed school of today. "School Days, School Days," describing how the three R's (readin', ritin', and 'rith-metic) were "taught to the tune of a hickory stick," doesn't parallel the many-faceted curricula in modern schools.

But are the differences in schools really significant? Are the values that the schools transmit today distinct from those of the colonial period? Were the basics of the mid-nineteenth century fundamentally different from those of the mid-twentieth century? The essential question in the chapter is: Why do schools do what they do?

A simple question, but one that provokes interpretations.[1] Most historians of education, Ellwood P. Cubberley and R. Freeman Butts among them, envision the public school as a progressively better institution, training future citizens consistent with the aims of a democratic society. Their accounts of the schools are frequently

Chapter Eight

couched in the lexicon of battles—the fight for public tax support, or the triumph of higher teacher standards.

Other historians of education, including Lawrence Cremin and Henry Perkinson, have argued that schools change erratically, making a number of minor improvements and a few major improvements over the years. These historians see the school as a flawed institution in a generally positive light. According to these interpreters, schools do teach conformity to society's values, but they also liberate individuals.

Still other historians say that the changes schools have made are only cosmetic, similar to rearranging furniture in a house. Michael Katz and Joel Spring, among others, believe that the schools are controlled by business interests and favor white upper-class members. If anything, the schools are repressive, not progressive.

This chapter can be only a brief overview of our country's three and one-half centuries of schooling. Consider what changes education has made and is likely to make, its pressures and potentials. As you read the following, keep in mind how the historians (and the historical views they represent) might interpret the data. See the "For Further Study" section for additional historical references if you want to pursue any of the topics.

Considering the amount of material to be covered, it is best to use a straightforward chronological framework built around the theme that the school reflects society's dominant values. The nation, educationally as well as socially and morally, has faced value decisions in five major areas in its history: its religious foundation, its political creed, its relationship to technology, its global economic power, and its ecological standards. Following are the five eras discussed in this chapter.

● Colonial America: 1607–1776—The New Kingdom of God on Earth

● The Early Republic: 1777–1865—The Great Democratic Experiment

● New Frontiers: 1866–1918—The Expansion in Technology and Land

● Industrial America: 1919–1956—The Adjustment to a New World of Work

● America Today: 1957-present—The Exploration of Space and Environment

To facilitate the comparison of what took place during these periods, each will be studied by looking at—

● *the cultural climate.* What economic, social, intellectual, and political factors caused the schools to add or delete curriculum? What national goals and personal priorities seemed most evident?

● *other educational agencies.* What non-school organizations and institutions influenced the shape of education? What was the relationship of the school to the agencies? What were they doing or not doing that caused the school to take on some of the agencies' duties?

● *forms of schooling and building designs.* How did the school evolve? Why did certain types of schooling persist and others (like the academy) disappear? What clues about the needs and goals of local communities can we obtain from building designs?

● *curriculum and textbooks.* What was the basic curriculum in each period? What school books were the best-sellers? What court cases affected school curriculum?

● *students.* What type or types of persons were the schools likely to graduate? What knowledge, skills, and attitudes did society want graduates to have?

After you have read Chapter 8, you should be able to (1) summarize the cultural climate of each of five periods in American history and outline, with examples, how the climate influenced the forms of schooling, curriculum, and student populations within each period; and (2) identify a nonschool educational agency in each period.

COLONIAL AMERICA: 1607–1776

Cultural Climate: The New Kingdom of God on Earth

As the colonies were settled in the 1600s, their founders brought a variety of religious backgrounds, business interests, and literary traditions.[2] The invention of the printing press aided the spread of literary works such as the King James Bible and Shakespeare's plays. Worldwide travel and colonial exploration generated great interest in such subjects as astronomy and surveying.

The religious ferment that had driven the Puritans to America and the geography of the new land forced the settlers to reexamine their traditional ways of thinking and acting. The Protestant thrust of the seventeenth century, which often promoted established churches, was countered in the eighteenth century by the Enlightenment, which encouraged individuals to act as their consciences directed them.[3]

Where colonists settled colored their life-styles. Southerners developed patterns of education different from those in the close-knit communities of the middle colonies or New England villages. Somewhat later, the Spanish in the Southwest and Far West, steeped in Roman Catholicism and eager to convert the native American Indians, organized mission schools.[4]

During these traumatic years of settlement in a new land, the schools were not the dominant educational force. Individuals and groups tried to maintain the ways in which they had educated their young in the Old World. In most communities, schools were introduced when other forms of education collapsed or proved inadequate.

Other Educational Agencies

The prime educator was the family. Children learned to read within the household. There also, values and manners were transmitted, and vocational skills were learned. There is some debate among historians whether most colonial families were nuclear or extended; that is, whether the family typically included only the parents and their offspring, or encompassed grandparents, uncles, aunts and apprentices. Bernard Bailyn has argued that as the extended families became smaller, the task of educating children shifted from parents and grandparents to outsiders.[5]

In Europe the apprenticeship was used extensively by poor families who wanted greater educational opportunities for their children. Sometimes beginning when children were 7 or 8 years old, there were apprenticeships not only for skilled crafts, but in management of shops, farms, and for girls, households. The master would serve *in loco parentis* (in place of the parent) for his apprentices. Many colonies passed laws obligating masters to instruct their charges in basic reading and writing as well as vocational skills.

The educational influences of the home and the apprenticeship system were reinforced by the church. Especially in the New England colonies, Sunday services frequently lasted two or three hours. There were a host of special services and catechism instruction for the young during the week. Children and adults were expected to memorize the doctrines stated in the catechism.

In the South families were often isolated; thus, educational opportunities depended mostly on the choices made by each family unit. Most families taught their children at home. Many wealthy and upper-class families hired live-in tutors.

Besides basic academic skills, the landowners' children were expected to learn social graces from the tutors. A typical text of the time was *The Compleat Gentleman*, which instructed the future plantation masters in the proper ways to entertain guests and treat workers. Young men who wished higher education often went abroad.

Some families sent their children to schools sponsored by the Society for the Propagation of the Gospel in Foreign Parts (SPG), the missionary division of the Church of England. The SPG was committed to providing schools for Indians and blacks. The emerging pattern of slavery, however, along with laws prohibiting slaves from learning to read, slowed the efforts to have a literate black population.[6]

Forms of Schooling

In the middle colonies such as New Netherlands, the churches were more important than in the South. In the 1600s each religious denomination in the middle colonies supported schools for members of its faith, and instruction was often in Dutch or German (depending on the cultural group). Charity schools were sponsored by the Dutch Reformed Church for children whose parents could not afford private instruction.

In the 1700s schools began shifting to instruction in English. The growth of trade and the mercantile needs of the expanding colonies promoted the formation of private entrepreneurial schools, which taught more job-oriented subjects. By the mid-eighteenth century, private teachers and evening schools flourished in such cities as Philadelphia and New York, providing courses in accounting, navigation, French, and Spanish as well as the more traditional basic subjects.[7]

In New England people lived closer to each other than in the other colonies. Frequently they had been bound together in a covenant of faith, and new members could be admitted to the community only upon the vote of those already present. Many such towns had "dame schools" in which local housewives cared for neighborhood children in their homes, and taught them reading, writing, and numbers. For the girls, sewing was added. Most girls did not go beyond the dame school. Their samplers of letters and stitches, for practical purposes, symbolized graduation. Typical of the legislation regarding schools during this period was the "old Deluder

In the colonial world schools often resembled homes.

School House & Watch House 1648.

Satan" law passed by the Massachusetts Commonwealth in 1647. It required communities with 50 families to provide a schoolmaster who would teach children to read the Bible so they could avoid the clutches of the old Deluder Satan.

Reading and writing schools were available for boys in many communities. The schools were funded partly by public monies and partly by fees. The teachers in such schools frequently held other positions to supplement their salaries. Reading exercises were based on the *New England Primer*, catechisms, and the Bible. Arithmetic lessons were problems that students solved according to prescribed steps committed to memory.

In seventeenth-century America, a Latin school similar to the classical schools of Europe provided the equivalent of today's secondary instruction. The Latin grammar school was a college preparatory program for the future leaders of the colonies. Those who finished the grammar schools were expected to read and understand at sight Latin authors, speak Latin in prose and poetry, and conjugate Greek verbs. The grammar school modified its curriculum in the eighteenth century and became more like the private so-called English schools that taught sciences, mathematics and modern languages. The form of secondary schooling did not change much during this period. The school hours were long, sometimes from 7:00 until 11:00 A.M. and from 1:00 until 5:00 P.M. The education in these schools was often of an uneven quality. To improve their chances for college, some boys learned Latin from their ministers.

In 1749 Benjamin Franklin published an essay entitled *Proposals Relating to the Education of Youth in Pensilvania* [sic], which advocated a new type of school—an academy—that was to have a vocational focus and a more practical curriculum. The curriculum still included the classics, natural sciences, mathematics, and history. Franklin did not want Latin, but the trustees insisted on it. Although his idea that many classes were to be taught in English was implemented at first, in a few years the curriculum was offered in Latin.[8]

As towns and villages blossomed in the wilderness, schools were located in places other than homes, churches, or town meeting halls. Structures built specifically as schools usually looked like homes or churches complete with steeples and bells. The typical floor plan had a raised platform at one end of a rectangular room. On the platform was a lectern and desk and chair for the teacher. Facing the front of the room were benches. Such a design focused attention on the teacher and conveyed the idea that students were to accept the teacher as authority.[9]

Curriculum

Examining the textbooks of the period, especially the hornbook and the *New England Primer*, it is easy to see that religious concerns were central.[10] The Bible was used frequently to teach reading. Catechisms, too, were found in numerous colonial classrooms, as teachers were expected to inculcate students with moral

The text of the New England Primer had numerous biblical references.

B Heaven to find,
The Bible Mind.

C Chrift crucify'd
For finners dy'd.

D The Deluge drown'd
The Earth around.

E ELIJAH hid
By Ravens fed.

precepts and religious doctrines. The most common method of instruction was the lecture. To see that students had mastered their assignments, memorization drills and recitation periods were employed.

The colonists were concerned with other matters, too. Many wealthy and well-educated persons had libraries filled with books on science, navigation, architecture, and the arts. Newspapers and almanacs expanded to aid the settlers in determining which crops to plant and when to harvest.

Students

In this era America's settlers most frequently saw themselves as a religious colony, a replacement for the old Israel. The belief that America was the new Kingdom of God permeated the school curriculum and molded the future graduates to be saints, knowledgeable about the Scriptures and committed to serving God in all aspects of life.

This did not mean that all studies were religious. The new country needed well-trained diplomats, merchants, surveyors, and lawyers as well as ministers. The New World forced its citizens to expand the school curriculum to include new forms of mathematics and science, and new styles of literature. The graduate was to be a literate saint.

THE EARLY REPUBLIC: 1777–1865

Cultural Climate: The Great Democratic Experiment

The years from the War of Independence through the Civil War were truly revolutionary times. A new nation was born and political leaders referred to the country as "the great experiment." The Louisiana Purchase doubled the nation's size. Population expanded 10 times, from approximately 4 million to 40 million. People moved westward. Those who left the eastern cities and towns were replaced by immigrants who wanted to escape poverty in Europe. They provided the labor force in expanding factories. Inventions such as the cotton gin and the reaper changed farming practices and spurred greater production by the factories.

Urbanization and industrialization were accompanied, however, by social problems. Reformers called for the nation to correct the abuses of its experiments in technology. New institutions emerged—mental asylums, orphanages, prisons, and police departments. Writers and orators crusaded against the injustices of the economic systems, especially the "peculiar institution"—slavery.[11]

Other Educational Agencies

As families moved, it became increasingly difficult to rely upon relatives for emotional, educational, or financial support.[12] The opportunities in the West, symbolized by the California Gold Rush, jeopardized the apprenticeship system because individuals were often left on their own to learn trades and crafts. The professions such as law and medicine were still learned at the side of the practitioner.

The movement west and the new immigrant population forced religious groups to adopt new strategies in the education of the young. Major religious denominations joined efforts in 1824 to form the American Sunday School Union, which attempted to provide religious instruction across the country and especially on the frontier. Sunday schools were often stocked with libraries of suitable books to prevent the conquest of the new lands by "barbarians."[13] Denominations also competed with each other. Ministers were active in founding hundreds of academies and colleges of a religious character. However, many were short-lived because they could not maintain sufficiently high student enrollments.[14]

Individuals sometimes banded together, as had Benjamin Franklin and his Junto study group, to improve themselves. They often used newspapers or magazines brought to them by the expanding mail system and railroad lines. The lyceum movement, begun in the 1820s, was an attempt to implement the self-study concept for larger audiences. Josiah Holbrook and other organizers guaranteed a series of monthly speakers to communities; townspeople each would pay $1.00 for the entire series, which might include such renowned speakers as Ralph Waldo Emerson.[15]

The diverse forms of learning were examples of the democratic spirit permeating education. There were cooperative programs; there were competing forms of religious and secular education. But society's desire for education in a democracy brought the common school into prominence.

Forms of Schooling

In the early decades of the nineteenth century, the dominant sentiment was that parents who could afford it should pay for the education of their children. The town schools still existed in Massachusetts, while in other states charity schools served orphans and the children of the poor. The sparse population of· the fledgling nation, the difficulties of travel, the inability of state governments to exercise control, and the widespread belief that education was a private matter, resulted in a variety of formal schools.

The district school was the most common type. Townships were divided into districts and each district elected or selected a board to determine the curriculum, hire the teacher(s), and levy taxes to finance the school. The district school re-

placed the dame school and reading and writing schools.[16]

At the secondary level, academies gradually assumed the function of the Latin grammar schools and expanded along the lines Franklin had proposed earlier. Many of the early academies had both Latin or classical departments and English departments. The English department taught reading, writing, arithmetic and grammar. The Latin department was responsible for instruction in mathematics and classical languages. By the middle and certainly at the end of the period, however, girls were being admitted to Latin classes. The academies charged tuition and usually boarded students. They reflected a variety of interests in response to their clientele. Some stressed a collegiate preparatory curriculum; others catered to young women and were called female seminaries. Emma Willard, Catharine Beecher, and Mary Lyon founded such schools.[17] The curricula varied; some institutions served as finishing schools and others promoted a rigorous academic program. Many academies, including the United States Military Academy at West Point, provided practical vocational programs. Nevertheless, some parents desired a free secondary English education, and the first public high school opened in Boston in 1821.

In the early part of the nineteenth century, the Lancastrian or monitorial system of instruction was popular in some urban elementary and secondary schools. Joseph Lancaster of England believed that schools could be more efficient if they were run like factories. He designed a school so that one teacher could instruct several hundred students. The teacher lectured until the students filled both sides of their slate boards with notes. At the sound of a signal, usually a handclap, students moved to small groups where older students, called monitors, reviewed the notes on the slate boards and corrected errors. Sometimes the teacher taught the lesson

Chapter Eight

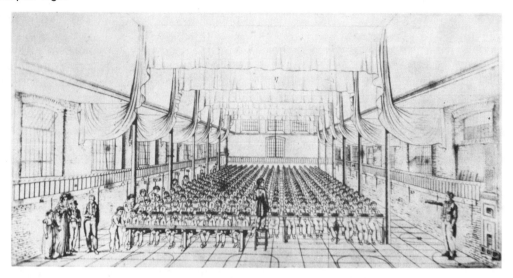

A Lancaster class in session. The instructor is on a plat-form, and the monitors are standing at the side of the room.

to monitors who then repeated it to their groups. The advantages appeared substantial—low cost, quality control (i.e., immediate correction of efforts), and a standard curriculum. This effort to cope with mass education of the poor had obvious limitations—a premium on rote memorization, lack of individual attention to students, and inordinate expectations of the young monitors.

During the 1830s and 1840s, the spirit of reform that swept the new nation captured the schools. Under the leadership of Horace Mann of Massachusetts and Henry Barnard of Connecticut, the public or "common" school emerged as the dominant educational institution. Mann, Barnard, and others hoped that the common school would bring together the daughters and sons of the rich and poor, the descendants of the original settlers and the offspring of the new immigrants, by providing high-quality free education in local schools financed by taxes from the whole community. Such schools were to be controlled by local boards elected from the community.[18]

Mann, who became Secretary of the Massachusetts Board of Education in 1837, attempted to convince his fellow citizens that state-supervised, but locally controlled, schools would diminish political and economic evils and help the nation to fulfill its mission to become the world's best example of democratic civilization. Mann's efforts, which included curriculum changes, teacher training proposals, and new designs for school buildings, were not universally applauded. He was accused of being antireligious and a captive of the social elite, and promoting a system that benefitted the wealthy and power interests of the day at the expense of the poor.[19]

Curriculum

Reformers advocating the common schools believed that the curriculum needed major revision. The push for distinctly American books had already begun in the 1700s, when most textbooks were published in England. One of the most popular texts of the period was Noah Webster's "blue-backed" speller, first published in 1783. Webster's goal was to build an American language by eliminating the various colonial dialects that reflected the "corrupt" European past.

Increasingly, books were using illustrations, and some, such as *Marmaduke Multiply's Merry Method of Making Minor Mathematicians*, tried humorous verse to teach multiplication tables. McGuffey's *Eclectic Readers* were introduced in the 1830s. These popular texts contained many moral stories and patriotic tales to heighten the feelings of American children that they were citizens of a chosen nation.

The country's need for surveyors, accountants, tradesmen, and managers led the schools to increase the number of subjects they offered. An 1827 Massachusetts law required that high schools offer United States history, bookkeeping, algebra, geometry, and surveying. Besides these basic courses, schools in towns having 4,000 or more residents were required to offer Greek, Latin, history, rhetoric, and logic.[20]

Students

Graduates of the schools in the early republic were expected to be loyal citizens and hard workers. Inculcating patriotism rather than religious doctrines was the primary goal of common schools. In secondary schools teachers began to emphasize oratorical skills so that the students could debate political philosophies. The college graduate was expected to help the great experiment in democracy at the local level as well as support it at the state and national levels.

The nation realized it could not grow by words alone. To compete with other countries the United States needed a strong economy. While the students were not yet instructed in trades and crafts directly (most instruction was still rote memorization), they were asked to develop skills that would benefit the nation.

ACTIVITY 8–1
The Nation's Textbooks

The textbooks of the nation's schools reflect the values of the society. Use your campus and community resources to find textbooks from various periods. Compare texts in your field and write your responses to the questions below.

Some of the famous American textbooks include the *New England Primer*, Webster's *Spelling Book*, McGuffey's *Eclectic Readers*, Muzzey's *American History*, and the Dick and Jane series of Scott, Foresman. Many of these books are now available in reprints.

• Do the authors have similar backgrounds (e.g., social class, occupation, and regional location)?
• What skills and basic knowledge are students expected to learn?
• How are native American Indians, blacks, women, and different religious and ethnic groups treated?
• What are the dominant values in these texts?

NEW FRONTIERS: 1866–1918

Cultural Climate: The Expansion in Technology and Land

Many social changes occurred in America from the end of the Civil War until the end of World War I. Probably the most obvious was the change in population. Between 1866 and 1918, America increased by 68 million persons. Immigration alone accounted for 2 million to 8 million people a decade. Many were from rural areas in southern and eastern Europe. The newcomers often could not speak English and were not familiar with a democratic government. Those factors, plus the Catholicism of many of them, caused the dominant Protestant culture to push for public schools to assimilate immigrant children. Urban education in particular was expanding, as Americans moved from farms and small towns to cities.[21] In short, America was like a gangling adolescent, growing everywhere at once—on the frontier, in the city, and, with the Spanish-American War and our involvement in World War I, on foreign soil.

Many new inventions and discoveries aided the technological expansion of the nation—the telegraph, typewriter, and electric light bulb, to name just a few. Giant corporations, new forms of trade such as the department store, and holding companies emerged. Ida Tarbell's *Standard Oil Company* and Upton Sinclair's *The Jungle* documented the excesses of two industries. The increasingly violent labor strikes were a reaction to the abusive expansion of capitalism.

The world of ideas was also in ferment. The scientific spirit of the age also included Darwin's concepts of evolution, which challenged the religious beliefs of many and resulted in a widespread adoption of a social philosophy of the "survival of the fittest."[22] The importance of the Bible as a guidebook for moral behavior was lessened for some by the work of scholars using scientific research. During these years the nation wrestled with the concept that women had a right to political and social equality, even as they were already increasingly employed in the work force.

Other Educational Agencies

A world with so many new frontiers in time and space placed great strains on fami-

lies and religious agencies. Increased educational and employment opportunities for women brought traditional family roles into question, as did the findings from such new disciplines as psychology.[23] Sunday schools continued to flourish, but the power of churches to dictate social policies, such as closing of businesses on Sunday, diminished.

In the cities, settlement houses such as Jane Addams's Hull House offered programs for immigrants. The Young Men's Christian Association (YMCA) was formed to provide wholesome experiences for males moving to the cities. The Chautauqua movement was the prime example of adult education with a religious basis. Founded as a training program for Sunday School teachers in 1874, it soon became a summer resort community in southeastern New York State with a platform open to the world's most famous speakers. The nation's first successful book club, the Chautauqua Literary and Scientific Circle, was formed there in 1878.

Reading clubs and libraries expanded throughout the country. Improvements in the printing presses brought new kinds of magazines and popular dime novels. Book publishers were able to offer the reading public fiction writers such as Mark Twain. The number of newspapers increased markedly. Special interest groups, such as labor unions, began to produce their own publications.

Forms of Schooling

While other agencies continued to educate Americans, formal schooling made dramatic gains in scope and importance, as reflected in enrollment, in the number of days students attended school, and in the amount of money society spent on pupils. To keep track of the nation's expanding educational system, Congress created a federal Department of Educa-

An early Chautauqua meeting where rural America received "culture under canvas."

tion in 1867.[24] Business giants such as George Peabody and John F. Slater established funds to improve educational opportunities in the devastated South. Others—including Johns Hopkins, John D. Rockefeller, Andrew Carnegie, and Leland Stanford, none of whom had gone beyond the eighth grade—provided money to start some of today's major universities and philanthropic foundations.

By the 1870s, public tax support for elementary education was widespread, but such was not the case for high schools. The high school curriculum stressed college preparatory subjects, and a number of citizens still expected parents to pay for their children's secondary education. High school was still considered a luxury by many families, and they did not want to finance it. (See Chapter 10 for a discussion of financing schools.) Eventually more people accepted the idea that secondary education was of general benefit to the community.

Such arguments for public education did not convince everyone. The academies, the mainstay of secondary education, remained popular. Until 1888, there were more students in academies than high schools. The variety among academies was immense—some offering little more than the basics, others specializing in a college preparatory program. A number were boarding schools, while a host of new schools in the East were day schools (see Chapter 15). As the nineteenth century closed, the high school became more and more of a competitor. Increasingly, the academy was identified as a rural institution while the high school was an urban phenomenon.[25]

The parochial school movement gained momentum during this period. Believing, with some justification, that they were being unfairly treated in public schools, Catholics began their own schools. The Third Plenary Council of Bishops, meeting in Baltimore in 1884, issued a statement urging

Chapter Eight

Catholics to send their children to parochial schools. Other religious groups, such as Lutherans and German evangelicals who wished to maintain their language, religion, and culture, also favored parochial schools.[26]

During this period new forms of schooling emerged at the preschool and elementary levels. In urban centers like St. Louis, kindergartens were established, in part because more mothers were working in factories. Some settlement houses started preschool programs. In 1892, John and Alice Dewey started a laboratory school in Chicago that stressed learning by doing.[27]

At the secondary level, manual trade schools, commercial high schools, and vocational schools began. The movement toward more manual skills, or industrial education, was prompted by the perception that Europeans were outdistancing American business.[28] The junior high school was begun in this period, although it was not widely adopted until the 1920s. There is some dispute over the reason for this new level of schooling. It may have been the creature of overcrowding. Some school officials, citing psychological and physiological evidence, argued that the differences between elementary and secondary students were too great to have them in close contact with each other.

The most impressive component in secondary education was the public high school. In 1875 there were fewer than 25,000 students in such schools; by 1900 there were 500,000 in 6,000 buildings. By 1920 there were over 2.2 million such students. The curriculum was broadened, although it remained more attuned to college preparation than vocational training.[29]

In the South, public schools, which had

Students receiving instruction in the use of the typewriter. Business interests brought other changes in the early 1900s.

Freedman's schools were begun in many Southern communities following the Civil War.

not been popular prior to the Civil War, were opened. There and in some border states, a dual system of public schools was instituted to ensure segregation of blacks and whites. In other parts of the country, separate schools were maintained for native American Indians and Chinese.

As enrollments grew, school buildings became larger. In the rural areas, of course, most schools were still one-room. In the cities, however, schools were often several stories high, made of brick, and some had decorative towers. Increasingly, the rooms became more specialized, with libraries, science laboratories, and shops.

Curriculum

The elementary textbooks of the period, most notably the McGuffey series of *Eclectic Readers*, often contained stories about hard work, respect, and punctuality, important virtues for an industrial society. Though the number and availability of textbooks steadily increased, some poor school districts used the Montgomery Ward's cat-

alog for reading instruction. At the secondary level, the watchword was still

Cartoon by Ford Button in *Phi Delta Kappan*, January 1975, p. 315. Reprinted with permission.

"Our architect has come up with an interesting concept in building design that might create an atmosphere in which students could achieve excellence."

Chapter Eight

"mental discipline" (see Chapter 6). Latin was overtaken by science, but even after 1900, four years of Latin grammar, prose, and poetry were the common core of many college preparatory programs. Algebra and geometry also were considered essential for mental discipline. English grammar was emphasized (sentence diagramming first was introduced in 1870), although literature entered the scene by the turn of the century.[30]

The sciences gradually became accepted in the curriculum. By 1900 physics and chemistry were established high school courses. Courses like zoology and botany were taught through the memorization of laws and theories.

Progressive schools at the elementary level were more inclined to use in-class experiments and out-of-class field trips to promote student curiosity in the sciences. At the Deweys' laboratory school, students constructed models of ancient boats, cooked favorite foods of other cultures, and dramatized events from ancient civilizations for their social studies classes.

Most schools were not prepared to build a curriculum as child-centered as the laboratory school's. Many schools affirmed the recommendations of the National Education Association's "Committee of Fifteen" Report in 1895, which specified that the five basic subjects should be grammar, literature, arithmetic, geography, and history. That committee agreed in principle with another that had earlier issued some recommendations for college preparatory work. The Committee on Secondary School Studies had proposed a partial elective system with four parallel courses of study—classical, Latin-scientific, modern language, and English—any one of which should qualify students for college.[31] While the committees felt certain subjects were important, they recognized that the curriculum should be broadened to allow for the various life goals of students.

The curriculum expanded in other ways. Calvin Woodward introduced manual training education in St. Louis in 1879. In response to the needs of the business community, school curriculum began to offer courses in typewriting, stenography, bookkeeping, commercial law, and business arithmetic. The Smith-Hughes Act of 1917 provided funds for agriculture, home economics, and vocational education in high schools. Art and music slowly gained acceptance in the curriculum, as did physical education and athletics.

By 1918, the nation had been through a traumatic war, had experienced another great influx of immigrants, and had witnessed mounting high school enrollments. It is not surprising, then, that another NEA national committee issued a call for a revision in the goals of American secondary education. The "seven cardinal principles," as they were commonly called, included worthy home membership, health, worthy use of leisure, command of fundamental processes, vocational training, citizenship, and ethical character. These aims reflected the broadened curriculum. Further, this Commission on the Reorganization of Secondary Education recommended comprehensive high schools rather than separate vocational schools.[32]

The scientific spirit so present in business permeated education in several critical areas. Standardized testing was initially developed to discriminate between those who would succeed and those who would fail in school. To make school programs more comparable, the "Carnegie unit" was adopted. A unit was given for a subject studied 45 minutes, 4 or 5 days a week for at least 35 weeks. The business world supported the development of the A-to-F grading system and the 100-point numerical scale because the companies felt this was a good way to have their future employees screened.[33]

Ironically, many people recall this era

Home economics, also known as domestic science in its formative years, was supposed to bring the latest technological advances to the home.

as one that featured one-room schoolhouses. Indeed, since there were still 200,000 one-teacher schools in 1916, there is some validity in that recollection. It is important to recall, however, that the expansion in territory and technology which marked the period also brought with it significant efforts to standardize the formal educational process. Local districts, states, teacher organizations, and businesses joined forces in efforts that would unify the curriculum and financing of schools.

Students

There were many frontiers between the years 1866 and 1918, resulting from urbanization and industrialization. The expansions, first westward and then abroad, demanded a new kind of graduate from the schools. America, increasingly urban and pluralistic, needed citizens who could fit easily into the corporate state as manual laborers, clerks, managers, or executives.

Was the graduate of this period significantly different from those of the two previous periods? Some revisionist historians (Greer, Spring, and Violas—see "For Further Study") argue that schooling during this time became decidedly dehumanized.

INDUSTRIAL AMERICA: 1919–1956

Cultural Climate: The Adjustment to a New World of Work

By the end of World War I, America had become a world military power. Aided by expanding economic markets in Europe and in the Pacific, the country's political influence soon spanned the globe. This influence was slowed by the debilitating depression in the 1930s, but revived after World War II. The Cold War that followed and the Korean conflict also hindered American corporations wanting to build international economic organizations.

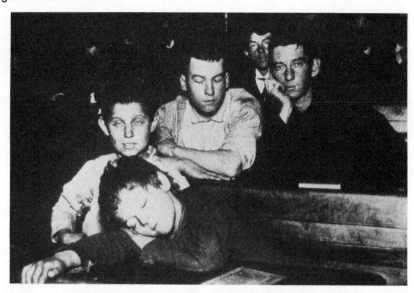

Immigrant children, after working all day at the factory, were forced to attend night schools in some cities.

The power and prestige of America abroad were tarnished at times during these years by the internal struggle for civil rights. Minority group members, subject to violence and harrassment or neglect, resorted increasingly to the courts to obtain their rights. Some gains were made, including the monumental 1954 decision against segregated schooling in *Brown* v. *Board of Education.*

The novelty of the radio wore off; increasingly, it came to be viewed as a vital communications system.

Technology provided new media to enhance communication throughout the period. Silent movies gave way to talkies, and radio became another form of popular mass entertainment. In 1922 an estimated 40 million Americans attended a movie each week. The coaxial telephone cable helped to shrink the world, so that events in Europe one day were reported as news in the United States the next. The expanding network of newspaper chains could relay stories about the work of Freudian psychologists and biblical scholars in Europe as well as political events.[34]

The depression and the automobile together moved more rural Americans to the urban centers of the country. By 1956 there were 55 million cars, compared with only 10 million in 1920. Lindbergh's 1927 flight foreshadowed commercial routes. The airplane, like the automobile, became a fact of daily life rather than a fad.

Other Educational Agencies

During the years from 1919 to 1956, America's population grew by almost 50% and the number of families increased accordingly. The birth rate rose dramatically following World War II. The needs of these families were many, and a host of private, civic, corporate and governmental agencies sought to help. Nothing better reflected the birth rate phenomenon than the era's best-selling book, Benjamin Spock's *Baby and Child Care*, first published in 1945.

Religious and civic institutions experienced membership gains that exceeded the population growth rate. By 1956, of 100 Americans, 60 claimed affiliation with a church or synagogue, and Sunday school enrollments topped 40 million. Programs offered by scout troops and other family service groups such as the YMCA and YWCA also expanded.[35]

During the 1920s two major book clubs were founded—the Book of the Month Club (1922) and the Literary Guild (1927). Symbolic of the growing interest in lifelong learning opportunities was the formation in 1925 of the American Association for Adult Education. By 1955 it was estimated that there were 50 million adult students in the country.[36]

The depression and World War II prompted new federal intervention in education and stimulated industry-related instructional programs, such as on-the-job training. Started in 1933, the Civil Works Administration built or improved 40,000 schools, employed teachers for urban adult-education classes, and hired artists and writers to demonstrate and teach their skills throughout the country. During the war the federal government sponsored day-care centers. Industries, besides offering job-related training, provided leisure-related courses for employees.[37]

Forms of Schooling

The most obvious change in public education during this and the earlier period was the gradual increase in students. (There was a decline during the late 1930s and early 1940s, but the baby boom in the late 1940s resulted in large enrollment increases in the 1950s.) By 1956, 99.3% of the 7- to 13-year-olds were in school. During the late 1940s, American schools reached the 50-50 point, with as many students graduating from high school as dropping out. By 1956, 88% of the 14- to 17-year-olds were in school.[38]

The elementary and secondary schools had some changes in format. As the nation became more urban and as transportation improved, the number of small rural schools declined. While there were approximately 196,000 one-room schools in 1918, concern about schools' cost-efficiency led to the consolidation of the number of districts to 55,000 by 1956. Meanwhile, the length of the school term increased. In 1870 the average number of days schools were in ses-

180

sion was 132; in 1920 it was 162, and by 1956 it was 178.[39]

The depression years were difficult for all schools, with teachers being reduced in salary or laid off, and schools closing for all or portions of the year. During the 1932–33 school year, for example, 81% of the children in white rural schools in Alabama did not attend regularly. Over a thousand schools with an enrollment of 170,000 were closed in Georgia. Dayton, Ohio schools were open only three days a week in early 1933. During the depression, the Civil Works Administration hired 50,000 teachers to keep rural schools open and used its funds to employ all the teachers who had been fired in cities like Boston.[40]

The depression was as hard on private and parochial schools as it was on public schools. Those that did not close often went to a reduced schedule. They hired more inexperienced teachers and got by with fewer textbooks and instructional aids. However, the nonpublic schools did not suffer a loss in their percentage of total school enrollments. For example, in 1919–20 nonpublic schools enrolled 8.5% of the students in grades 9 to 12. In 1955–56 their proportion had climbed to 11%. The baby boom also benefited the parochial schools. In 1919–20 Catholic schools enrolled 1.8 million elementary students and 130,000 secondary students. By 1955–56 the enrollment in Catholic schools had surpassed 4 million elementary students and 800,000 secondary students.[41]

American schools during this time were segregated in the North as well as in the South. Residential housing patterns and laws resisted desegregation. Over 60% of the black school children of the country were attending a school, in 1954, that was 90% to 100% minority population. In some cities, over 90% of the black students were in a school 90% to 100% black. (By 1976, 40% of the blacks were attending a school 90% to 100% minority.)[42]

The exterior designs of school buildings changed relatively little during this period. More were constructed of brick, had more windows, and were larger than earlier schools. Inside, new features included gymnasiums, kitchens, science laboratories, movable desks, and better lighting and ventilation systems. In the cities, schools resembled the headquarters of corporations. In smaller communities, they were more homelike in style. Some included fireplaces and had patios, gardens, and recreation rooms.

Curriculum

By the end of World War I, educators who favored the classics and a general education were on the defensive. Two groups presented alternative curriculum plans for the future. One group, sometimes called the business-efficiency or management advocates, wanted a more practical curriculum that would be vocationally centered. The second group, the child-centered progressives, also supported career-directed curriculum and scientific testing, but wanted more attention paid to the interests of students. Elements of both curriculum designs influenced textbooks and classroom practices during the next several decades.

Along with a change in school organization (from the 8–4 elementary-secondary model to the 6–3–3 model that featured junior high schools), the schools of the nation expanded their curricular and extracurricular offerings. Elementary schools still taught reading, writing, spelling, and arithmetic, but with less emphasis upon drill and memorization. Subjects such as drawing, painting, music and dance were used to enhance instruction, and audiovisual devices gradually were introduced. Probably the major change in curriculum was its reorganization, especially in elementary schools. Instead of being taught as separate disciplines, it was presented in terms of "areas of living," or "projects."

Schools operated under many restraints during World War II, including a lack of teachers. The baby boom following the war would bring other kinds of problems.

Examples of study units might be "How People Live and Work in Our Neighborhood" and "Heat," the latter covering such diverse points as building fires and understanding the principles of combustion.[43] Schools favored such terms as *language arts, social studies,* and *general sciences* to describe their integrated curriculum.

While the progressive education leaders probably influenced the elementary level more than the secondary level, here too were changes. The Progressive Education Association commissioned an eight-year study (1932–40) that compared the graduates of 30 innovative high schools with 30 more traditional high schools. The 30 experimental schools tended to allow students more elective courses, and tried a battery of projects (from a Denver class filming the making of bread to a New York class touring the Tennessee Valley Authority). The study concluded that the graduates of the experimental schools were as well-prepared, if not better prepared, for college-level work than the graduates of

the more prescriptive course of study.[44]

The business-efficiency group also had an impact on changing the curriculum, mainly at the senior high level. Its encouragement of practical, job-related skills coincided with increased federal support of vocational programs in schools. The nation's international economic interests supported increased use of standardized testing techniques. There was a decided emphasis upon societal goals rather than personal fulfillment.[45]

In summary, there were numerous curriculum changes during this period. Critics sometimes contend that the problems of education in this country relate to the "Dick and Jane" readers widely used in the 1940s and 1950s. Such readers reflected the dominant white middle-class values (a two-parent family, stereotyped sex roles of father as breadwinner and mother as homemaker, the advantages of a suburban life-style, and avoidance of controversy). Critics tend to forget that the curriculum was broader than Dick and Jane.

Chapter Eight

Students

During the years between World War I and the launching of Sputnik, America made a clear commitment to universal education. This resulted, first, in larger numbers of students. Second, those who came to school stayed longer. Third, the profile of students changed. No longer were schools filled only or primarily with the children of the wealthy or middle class. Increasingly, schools around the country were enrolling children from minority families and students with special needs.[46]

These students and such events as two world wars and a major depression brought changes in the perceptions of what the graduate ought to be. Vocational preparation became far more important and a general liberal arts background less important. To fill expanding world markets, the nation's industries needed more specialized workers. Yet the frantic pace of life also produced efforts to see that the students were better prepared to cope with problems at home and in society.

ACTIVITY 8–2
Profile of a Famous Educator

Throughout this chapter you have read about the ideas and accomplishments of some famous educators. Listed in this Activity are some of the individuals we have already discussed and others who have had an impact upon American education. Prepare an oral or written report on one of them. Use several sources to gain a detailed impression of the significance of the figure you select. Consider reading a biography or autobiography, a biographical reference work (such as the *Dictionary of American Biography*), a history of education textbook or monograph, or a recent journal article.

Consider what kind of education, including family training, this individual received. What events, cultural as well as personal, most influenced this person's educational outlook? What were his or her significant educational contributions?

Jane Addams	W. E. B. Du Bois	Caleb Mills
Henry Barnard	Benjamin Franklin	Col. Francis Parker
Catharine Beecher	Samuel G. Goodrich	Elizabeth Peabody
Mary M. Bethune	G. Stanley Hall	George Peabody
Andrew Carnegie	William T. Harris	Edward L. Thorndike
James G. Carter	Bishop John Ireland	Booker T. Washington
James Conant	Thomas Jefferson	Noah Webster
George Counts	William H. Kilpatrick	Emma Willard
Leonard Covello	Horace Mann	Ella Flagg Young
John Dewey	William H. McGuffey	

AMERICA TODAY: 1957–PRESENT

Cultural Climate: The Exploration of Space and Environment

When the Russians launched Sputnik in 1957, the world embarked upon a new era. The years since have been marked by a host of explorations in space, in medicine, and in personal freedoms. Not only have men walked on the moon, there have been heart transplants, test-tube babies, and experimentation with a variety of drugs.

Politically, the years since 1957 have been violent and unpredictable. The trauma of the Vietnam War, Watergate, the women's movement, student protests and draft-card burnings, the crises in the Middle East, and the assassinations of John Kennedy, Malcolm X, Robert Kennedy, and Martin Luther King have brought criticisms and doubts about the nation's policies.

Social and personal value systems are being reexamined. The civil rights movement has forced society to consider the relationships of our culturally different groups. Individuals are trying new religious styles—from born-again evangelism to eastern mysticism. A variety of therapy approaches are in evidence. Symptomatic of the search for new priorities are the shifts in popular music, from folk songs to Beatlemania, from rock to country and western, from disco to punk. The concern about environmental pollution and the use of energy are indications of our changing priorities.

Other Educational Agencies

Many claim that the family is losing its influence. They cite evidence about the divorce rate (one in three marriages end in divorce) and the increasing number of individuals living together (over one million in the mid-1970s) to suggest that the family is not the stable institution we have thought it to be. Others argue that the family has changed, but that it still has an immense impact on the total culture. Some commentators believe that the youth culture has not received enough investigation considering its influence.[47]

The media's influence is of increasing concern. Studies indicate that by the time children begin kindergarten, they already have watched 4,000 hours of television and are asking for things by brand names. By the time students graduate from high school, they will have spent more hours

watching television than in school. The research on television's impact on violent behavior continues. Some question the benefits of such educational programs as "Sesame Street." The impact of other media should not be ignored. For example, it is reported that the average American home has four radios, and that each family member listens to the radio 10 hours a week.[48]

A number of corporations have established educational programs. These vary from General Motors' formal schools of engineering to the leisure courses such companies as Texas Instruments or Johnson and Johnson provide for their workers (examples include fly casting or auto repair). Labor unions have extensive training programs for apprentices and members.

The military has a large educational enterprise. A study in the 1960s reported that there were more than 300,000 personnel taking courses at more than 300 military schools, a figure that only declined slightly in the 1970s. This figure did not include schools for military dependents. All these programs pale in comparison with adult and lifelong learning opportunities supported by libraries, school districts, and other educational agencies.[49]

Forms of Schooling

The mobile American society demands consistency in its institutions. Just as it wants each McDonald's or Holiday Inn coast to coast to offer the same food or facilities, so it expects its schools to have similar standards and programs.

Such a sentiment is obvious even at the preschool level. Working parents and educators, aware of the learning potential of young children, demand both academic preparation and training in social skills. In 1976–77 there were 18,307 day-care centers in the United States, with a total enrollment of 897,733. There has been an explosion of Operation Headstart programs, Montessori schools, nursery centers, and kindergartens.[50]

The middle school, begun in this period, is growing in popularity. Based on the belief that American children are maturing earlier, the middle school usually is organized for grades five or six through eight (ages 10 to 14). In 1971 there were an estimated 2,000 middle schools in the United States.[51]

At the secondary level other reforms have been introduced, principally the alternative or free school such as Summerhill (see Chapter 15). Open classes have been tried within the public school. Building designs have changed, too. The pod shape exterior became a popular design because it was less expensive than the rectangular building. The more frequent use of carpeting and brightly colored walls is meant to create an informal atmosphere. Another popular construction technique in the early 1970s was the open-space design that eliminated many interior walls. In theory,

students and teachers had more freedom to move around, flexibility in lesson presentations (large group or small group), and easier access to centrally located resource centers. Open-space schools appear to be declining, however, because of the noise level and visual distractions. Future school buildings probably will be constructed with even fewer windows, due to concern about increased costs of vandalism, energy, and maintenance.

Curriculum

America's problems since the late 1950s—the conflict with international communism, an unpopular war, a volatile economy, and a deteriorating environment—dictated in the late 1970s a renewed interest in a more structured curriculum. At the elementary level it was usually called a return to the basics; at the secondary level it was a movement toward disciplines (specific subjects). Society wanted highly trained specialists and technicians to solve these major problems. On the other hand, there was

Some schools today employ a variety of media, including closed-circuit television systems and elaborate projection techniques.

the realization that complex problems required interdisciplinary efforts. The discovery technique was advocated in science and social studies classes. Furthermore, there was an interest in humanizing classrooms, based on the realization that knowledge alone does not always produce the best answers.

Among the specific curriculum changes were major revisions in science and mathematics, spurred in no small measure by the space race. In 1958 Congress passed the National Defense Education Act that provided funds for laboratories, workshops for math and science teachers, and scholarships for guidance counselors (who were then to direct students into math and science careers). The so-called new math and new science curricula often bore the initials of committees that had produced them: BSCS (Biological Sciences Curriculum Study); PSSC (Physical Science Study Committee); and SMSG (School Mathematic Study Group).[52] Language laboratories and computer-assisted instruction were technological developments in this era. (See Chapter 12.)

Interest in solving the problems of spaceship Earth and the desire to humanize education promoted a number of curriculum revisions such as energy education and environmental studies. Greater emphasis was placed on career and family life education. A number of states, responding to discrimination against minorities, have mandated that public schools provide a multicultural, nonsexist curriculum. This is consistent with federal laws such as the Civil Rights Act of 1964 and Title IX of the Education Act of 1972, which bans sex discrimination. (See Chapters 12 and 13.)

A thrust of the curriculum in this period is toward individualized instruction (see Chapter 13). Flexible-modular scheduling was introduced to give students more time to investigate a variety of subjects. Recognizing the needs of special-education students as well as the talented and gifted, schools began to offer curriculum in self-paced programs.

Students

The student, like the teacher, is expected to be a flexible specialist. While students must master basic subject matter and possess certain academic skills, they also must have the ability to learn on their own. In some ways, it is a paradox; they are expected to be creative conservatives. They should be highly trained in order to find a specific job or to be admitted to the best colleges and universities, but unencumbered enough to make career changes easily.

SUMMARY

Our interpretation of the development of the American school is that the system has changed markedly over its three and one-half centuries because it reflects the nation's shifting priorities. The changes come slowly for the most part, because the school mirrors society's slow-changing values. Revisionist historians such as Michael Katz and Joel Spring would maintain that the changes are only superficial. Moreover, they claim changes made since the common school was introduced have not necessarily improved educational opportunity. More likely the changes have reinforced the power of those who control the school's goals—the white, upper-middle class.

This introduction to the American school system will help you weigh a number of important questions about education. Is the school given too much credit or blame, compared with other educational institutions, for the nation's well-being? Has it really changed since colonial days? Why do schools do what they do?

Chapter Eight

Notes

1. For an excellent review of the problems and issues facing historians of education, see Parts 1 and 2, Donald R. Warren, ed., *History, Education, and Public Policy* (Berkeley, Calif.: McCutchan Publishing Co., 1978), pp. 1–53.

2. Lawrence A. Cremin, *American Education: The Colonial Experience* (New York: Harper and Row, 1970), pp. 176, 231n, 533, 540–49.

3. Samuel E. Morison, *The Intellectual Life of Colonial New England* (Ithaca: Cornell University Press, 1960), pp. 4–26.

4. Daniel J. Boorstin, *The Americans: The Colonial Experience* (New York: Random House, 1958); Louis B. Wright, *Everyday Life in Colonial America* (New York: Capricorn Books, 1966).

5. Edmund S. Morgan, *The Puritan Family* (New York: Harper Torch Books, 1966); Bernard Bailyn, *Education in the Forming of American Society* (New York: Vintage Press, 1960), pp. 22–29; Cremin, *American Education*, pp. 113–37.

6. John Calam, *Parsons and Pedagogues: The S.P.G. Adventure in American Education* (New York: Columbia University Press, 1971). The education of blacks and native American Indians will be discussed in more depth in conjunction with the issue of equal educational opportunity (see Chapter 14).

7. Carl Bridenbaugh, *Cities in the Wilderness: The First Century of Urban Life in America, 1625–1742* (New York: Ronald Press, 1938); Carl F. Kaestle, *The Evolution of an Urban School System: New York City, 1750–1850* (Cambridge, Mass.: Harvard University Press, 1973).

8. John H. Best, ed., *Benjamin Franklin on Education* (New York: Teachers College Press, 1962), pp. 123–51.

9. Erwin V. Johanningmeier, *Americans and Their Schools* (Chicago: Rand McNally Publishing Co., 1980), pp. 51–56.

10. The hornbook was a paddle-shaped piece of wood the size of a hand which allowed printed pages to be placed under a thin, protective slice of animal horn. For pictures of hornbooks and other early texts, see Clifton Johnson, *Old-Time Schools and Schoolbooks* (New York: MacMillan, 1904). A reprint of Johnson's text is available in paperback (Dover, 1963).

11. Frederick M. Binder, *The Age of the Common School, 1830–1865* (New York: John Wiley, 1974).

12. Bernard Wishy, *The Child and the Republic: The Dawn of American Child Nurture* (Philadelphia: University of Pennsylvania Press, 1968).

13. Robert W. Lynn and Elliott Wright, *The Big Little School* (New York: Harper and Row, 1971).

14. Donald Tewksbury, *The Founding of American Colleges and Universities Before the Civil War* (New York: Teachers College, Columbia University, 1932).

15. C. Hartley Grattan, *American Ideas about Adult Education, 1710–1951* (New York: Teachers College, Columbia University, 1959), pp. 26–36.

16. Robert L. Church, *Education in the United States: An Interpretative History* (New York: Free Press, 1976), pp. 3–22.

17. Willystine Goodsell, *Pioneers of Women's Education in the United States* (1931; reprint ed., New York: AMS Press, 1970).

18. Jonathan Messerli, *Horace Mann: A Biography* (New York: Alfred A. Knopf, 1972); Vincent P. Lannie, ed., *Henry Barnard: American Educator* (New York: Teachers College Press, 1974).

19. Lawrence A. Cremin, ed., *The Republic and the School: Horace Mann on the Education of Free Men* (New York: Teachers College Press, 1957); Michael B. Katz, *Class, Bureaucracy, and Schools: The Illusion of Educational Change in America* (New York: Praeger, 1971), pp. 28–29, 94–95. Katz is typical of the revisionist or radical historian of education who sees Mann as an unwitting if not active participant in using the common school as a socialization tool of the dominant business interests of the day.

20. Ellwood P. Cubberley, *Public Education in the United States* (Boston: Houghton Mifflin, 1919), pp. 193–94.

21. David Tyack, *One Best System: A History of American Urban Education* (Cambridge, Mass.: Harvard University Press, 1974).

22. The widespread application of the theory of evolution to social problems is ably recounted in Richard Hofstadter, *Social Darwinism in American Thought* (Philadelphia: University of Pennsylvania Press, 1944).

23. Virginia Tufte and Barbara Myerhoff, eds., *Changing Images of the Family* (New York: Yale University Press, 1979); Sigmund Diamond, ed., *The Nation Transformed* (New York: George Braziller, 1963); Oscar Handlin, *The Uprooted* (Boston: Little, Brown and Co., 1951).

24. Donald Warren, *To Enforce Education: A History of the Founding of the United States Office of Education* (Detroit: Wayne State University Press, 1974).

25. Edward A. Krug, *The Shaping of the American High School, 1880–1920* (Madison: University of Wisconsin Press, 1969), pp. 3–5, citing data from the Commissioner of Education *Annual Reports*, notes that in 1884–85 there were probably more than 1,600 academies in the country. Johanningmeier, *Americans and Their Schools*, p. 247; James McLachlan, *American Boarding Schools: A Historical Study* (New York: Scribner's, 1970).

26. Glen Gabert, *In Hoc Signo: A Brief History of Catholic Parochial Education in America* (Port Washington, N.Y.: Kennikat Press, 1973); Neil G. McCluskey, *Catholic Education in America* (New York: Teachers College Press, 1964); Lloyd P. Gartner, *Jewish Education in the United States: A Documentary History* (New York: Teachers College Press, 1970).

27. Evelyn Weber, *The Kindergarten: Its Encounter with Educational Thought in America* (New York: Teachers College Press, 1969); Katherine Mayhew

and Anna C. Edwards, *The Dewey School: The Laboratory School of the University of Chicago 1896–1903* (New York: Atherton Press, 1966).

28. Marvin Lazerson and W. Norton Grubb, eds., *American Education and Vocationalism: A Documentary History* (New York: Teachers College Press, 1974).

29. U.S. Bureau of the Census, *Historical Statistics of the United States, Colonial Times to 1957* (Washington, D.C.: U.S. Government Printing Office, 1960), pp. 207–210, 214.

30. Robert S. Zais, *Curriculum: Principles and Foundations* (New York: Thomas Y. Crowell, 1976), pp. 50–51.

31. Krug, *American High School*, pp. 27–34.

32. Lawrence A. Cremin, *The Transformation of the School: Progressivism in American Education, 1876–1957* (New York: Vintage, 1961), pp. 93–94.

33. Clarence Karier et al., *Roots of Crisis: American Education in the Twentieth Century* (Chicago: Rand McNally, 1973), pp. 6–19.

34. John W. Dodds, *Life in Twentieth Century America* (New York: Capricorn Books, G.P. Putnam's Sons, 1973); U.S. Bureau of the Census, *Historical Statistics of the United States, Colonial Times to 1970*, (Washington, D.C.: U.S. Government Printing Office, 1975), Series H-873, p. 400.

35. Will Herberg, *Protestant-Catholic-Jew* (New York: Doubleday, 1956), pp. 47, 51; Edwin Nicholson, *Education and the Boy Scout Movement in America* (New York: Teachers College, 1941); C. Howard Hopkins, *History of the Y.M.C.A. in North America* (New York: Association Press, 1951).

36. Malcolm Knowles, "An Overview and History of the Field," *Adult Education* 7, no. 4 (Summer 1957): 219–30.

37. William E. Leuchtenburg, *Franklin D. Roosevelt and the New Deal* (New York: Harper and Row Torchbook edition, 1963), pp. 121–24. In 1945, 1.6 million children were enrolled in federally funded day-care centers. Harold F. Clark and Harold S. Sloan, *Classrooms in the Factories* (Rutherford, N.J.: Institute of Research, Fairleigh-Dickinson University, 1958).

38. National Center for Education Statistics, *Digest of Educational Statistics, 1977–78*, (Washington, D.C.: U.S. Government Printing Office, 1978) pp. 36, 371–72; U.S. Bureau of the Census, *Historical Statistics of the United States, Colonial Times to 1970*, pp. 371–72.

39. U.S. Bureau of the Census, *Historical Statistics, Colonial Times to 1957*, pp. 207–8.

40. Leuchtenburg, *Franklin D. Roosevelt*, pp. 121–23.

41. NCES, *Digest of Educational Statistics 1977–78*, pp. 44, 47.

42. U.S. Commission on Civil Rights, *Racial Isolation in the Public Schools* (Washington, D.C.: U.S. Government Printing Office, 1965), pp. 2–12; NCES, *The Condition of Education, 1979* (Washington, D.C.: U.S. Government Printing Office, 1979), p. 56.

43. Zais, *Curriculum*, p. 60; Cremin, *Transformation*, pp. 306ff.

44. Wilford M. Aikin, *The Story of the Eight-Year Study* (New York: McGraw-Hill, 1942).

45. Raymond Callahan, *Education and the Cult of Efficiency* (Chicago: University of Chicago Press, 1962).

46. NCES, *Digest of Educational Statistics 1977–78*, pp. 44, 60.

47. Kenneth Keniston, *All Our Children: The American Family Under Pressure* (New York: Harcourt Brace Jovanovich, 1977); Mary Jo Bane, *The Family Is Here to Stay* (Cambridge, Mass.: Harvard University Press, 1978).

48. George Comstock, *Television and Human Behavior* (New York: Columbia University Press, 1978); *Broadcasting* 96, no. 21 (21 May 1979): 86; *Broadcasting Yearbook, 1979* (Washington, D.C.: Broadcasting Publications, Inc., 1979), C-341 and C-344.

49. Harold F. Clark and Harold S. Sloan, *Classrooms in the Military: An Account of Education in the Armed Forces of the United States* (New York: Teachers College, 1964); Franklin D. Margiott, ed., *The Changing World of the American Military* (Boulder: Westview Press, 1978). Malcolm Knowles, *The Adult Education Movement in the United States* (New York: Krieger, 1976).

50. Sar A. Levitan and Karen C. Alderman, *Child Care and ABC's Too* (Baltimore: Johns Hopkins, 1976); Edward Ignas and Raymond J. Corsini, *Alternative Educational Systems* (Itasca, Ill.: Peacock, 1979); NCES, *The Condition of Education, 1980* (Washington, D.C.: U.S. Government Printing Office, 1980), p. 200.

51. Robert R. Leeper, ed., *Middle Schools in the Making* (Washington, D.C.: Association of Supervision and Curriculum Development, 1974), p. viii; Paul George, ed., *The Middle School: A Look Ahead* (Fairborn, Ohio: National Middle School Association, 1977).

52. J. D. Lockard, ed., *Seventh Report of the International Clearinghouse on Science and Mathematics Curricular Developments: 1970* (College Park, Md.: University of Maryland, 1970).

FOR FURTHER STUDY

Cohen, Sheldon S. *A History of Colonial Education, 1607–1776.* New York: John Wiley, 1974.

Dewey, John and Dewey, Evelyn. *Schools of Tomorrow.* 1915. Reprint. New York: E.P. Dutton, 1972.

Chapter Eight

Elson, Ruth. *Guardians of Tradition.* Lincoln, Neb.: University of Nebraska Press, 1964.

Graham, Patricia A. *Community and Class in American Education, 1865–1918.* New York: John Wiley, 1974.

Greer, Colin. *The Great School Legend: A Revisionist Interpretation of American Public Education.* New York: Basic Books, 1972.

Madsen, David L. *Early National Education, 1776–1830.* New York: John Wiley, 1974.

Nasaw, David. *Schooled to Order: A Social History of Public Schooling in the U.S.* New York: Oxford University Press, 1979.

Sizer, Theodore R. *The Age of the Academies.* New York: Bureau of Publications, Teachers College, Columbia University, 1964.

Spring, Joel H. *Education and the Rise of the Corporate State.* Boston: Beacon Press, 1972.

9

The Governance of Schools

Most people don't know who controls American education because little attention has been given the question by either educators or the public. Also because the question is not easily or neatly answered. . . . Yet the problem of how education is controlled is more important than most of the other educational problems that concern Americans.

James Koerner, 1968

Who controls American education? Who runs the schools? As we shall see, there are no simple answers to these questions. But it is important for teachers—and all citizens—to have an understanding of the control and organization, or governance, of American schools.

Education is a major governmental activity and accounts for a significant share of state and local taxes. Constitutional provisions, court decisions, laws, official rules and regulations, and school codes are the legal bases for our system of schooling. We must consider not only the formal, legal structure of education, but also the political realities at each level of government and within school systems. Interest groups, private corporations, and quasi-public organizations, as well as teachers, administrators, and other public employees all influence educational policy making. Thus, we will examine the governance and politics of public education at national, state, and local levels and the organizational or internal administrative structure of schooling. Brief attention will be given also to nonpublic schools.

Chapter Nine

The pervasive issue is the extent that citizens control their local public schools. As the federal government and states have increased their involvement, how much local control remains? What is the role of teachers and other professional educators in making school policy? What are the processes by which educational policy is determined? Before considering these questions, reflect briefly on the relationship between education and the political system.

Many people have felt that public education should not be involved in politics and· politics should be kept out of the schools. Others have argued that it is a myth to expect that they can be separated completely. To a considerable extent, however, schools have been shielded from partisan politics. Education has been traditionally unique in government. Most local school boards are fiscally independent with their own authority to levy taxes. Many school districts have boundaries that are not identical with other governmental units. School elections often are held separately from general elections, and candidates usually do not run with political endorsements by the Democratic or Republican parties. Such practices have enabled schools to maintain a degree of independence from partisan politics.

Yet as governmental agencies, public schools inevitably are involved in the political process. School districts are the most numerous type of governmental bodies in America, far surpassing the number of villages, towns, or cities. Literally thousands of elections are conducted every year for seats on school boards and for school budgets, tax levies, and bond issues. Education competes for the taxpayers' dollar in local communities and in state and federal legislatures. Moreover, in recent decades education has become increasingly politicized. Many of society's battles over desegregation and community control are fought in the schools. Blacks have demanded multiethnic readers and black history courses, while women's groups have attacked sexism in the curriculum. Teachers who have organized for collective bargaining and political activity have contributed also to politicizing education.[1] (See Chapter 5.)

Politics and education now are less often regarded as completely separate entities. Educators are more conscious of the politics of education, and political scientists are more interested in studying education. The political process is concerned with power, policy decisions, and the allocation of resources. Politics, to repeat an aphorism, essentially focuses on who gets what, when, and how. More specifically, as one analysis concluded, "At its heart, then, the phrase 'the politics of education' refers to the on-going struggle over who shall control the schools and to what ends."[2] These are basic questions for the educational system and our society.

After you have completed Chapter 9, you should be able to (1) explain the responsibilities and involvement of the local board of education and federal and state governmental agencies in public schooling, (2) describe the administrative structure within a local school district, and (3) list several organizations and interest groups and explain how each influences education.

FEDERAL ROLE

The United States Constitution does not mention schools or education. Under the 10th Amendment, therefore, education is reserved to the states or the people. American schools thus are primarily a state and local responsibility. For many years the federal government's role was very limited, but its involvement in education has increased substantially in recent decades.

From the beginning of our country, the national government set aside land to aid schools and education, and for over a century it has collected statistics and other information on education. You've already read in Chapter 8 about federal aid to vocational education, which began with the 1917 Smith-Hughes Act, and federal depression programs in the 1930s that benefited education. During World War II and continuing under various so-called impact laws, schools in communities near military bases or defense industries receive special federal assistance. The aid in lieu of taxes goes to schools enrolling children who live on federal property or whose parents are federal employees or work on federal contracts. The federal contribution to public elementary and secondary schooling was less than .5% of total revenues in the 1920s and less than 2% through the mid-1940s.[3]

Federal expenditures for schools considerably increased in the post-World War II years. One important impetus for broader federal involvement was the Soviet Sput-

nik. Many blamed our lag in space on America's educational system and its failure to train enough scientists and engineers. The National Defense Education Act in 1958 provided substantial funds to improve guidance services, science, math, and modern foreign-language instruction. College tuition-loan programs and summer institutes supported teacher education. Subsequent reenactments extended aid to English, social studies, and other subjects. With the Vocational Education Act of 1963, federal appropriations to the states for vocational and technical schools also increased.

A new and broader program of federal aid began in 1965 with the Elementary and Secondary Education Act (ESEA). Most of the funds were designated for special programs for the educationally disadvantaged in an effort to equalize educational opportunity. (See Chapter 14.) ESEA also provided money for textbooks, library resources, and instructional materials; guidance, remedial, enrichment, and health services; research and development; and

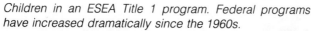

Children in an ESEA Title 1 program. Federal programs have increased dramatically since the 1960s.

state departments of education. Students attending nonpublic schools also received shared services and textbooks.

Traditionally, federal assistance usually has been for special purposes ("categorical aid") with money designated for specific programs. ESEA included such broad categories of assistance that it was virtually general aid and represented a major breakthrough for federal aid to schools. ESEA more than doubled the federal government's expenditures for elementary and secondary schools. Subsequent amendments and other education appropriations maintained the federal share of total school revenues at approximately 8% through the 1970s. In the District of Columbia and some states, including Alabama, Alaska, Mississippi, and New Mexico, the federal government provides more than 15% of education revenues. The proportion is less than 5% in some other states.[4]

Virtually all local school districts receive some federal funds that influence their programs. Through selective financing, the federal government encourages districts to provide programs such as vocational education and remedial services. Without such federal assistance, districts are less likely to offer them. Federal funds also may be used to shape educational policy. The 1964 Civil Rights Act prohibits discrimination on the basis of race, color, or national origin, while Title IX of the Education Amendments in 1972 prohibits sex discrimination. Since federal funds can be withheld from schools (and other institutions) violating these laws, most districts try to comply with federal nondiscrimination policies rather than lose federal aid.

President and Executive Branch

In education, as in other areas of national policy making, presidential leadership is important. Lyndon B. Johnson wanted to be known as the education president. His

commitment and political skills resulted in extensive education legislation during his administration. Presidential budget recommendations for education are important. Presidents may show leadership and exert influence by convening White House conferences on education, or naming presidential commissions to study specific issues and presidential task forces to make legislative recommendations.

Within the executive branch, the Secretary of Education and the Department of Education shape educational policy by drafting legislation, securing support from educational interest groups and Congress, setting guidelines and regulations, and implementing and administering programs. The U.S. Office of Education nearly tripled in size in the decade after Sputnik, reflecting the growth in the federal government's role in education.

The growing importance of education in the federal government was reflected in the creation of a Cabinet-level Department of Education in 1980. (The Office of Education, headed by a Commissioner of Education, had been in the Department of Health, Education, Welfare.) Shirley Hufstedler became the first Secretary of Education. The government consolidated many of its education programs in the new department. For example, Education took over responsibility from the Defense Department for operating one of the nation's largest school systems, which serves dependents of military personnel stationed abroad. Some educational programs, including Head Start, the National Science Foundation, and Indian schools, remain in other federal agencies.

Congress

Usually, education legislation in Congress is initially the responsibility of the House Committee on Education and Labor and the Senate Committee on Labor and Pub-

The Governance of Schools

Federal Courts

Decisions of the Supreme Court and federal judiciary system also affect schools throughout the country. To quote the Court:

> It is, of course, quite true that the responsibility for public education is primarily the concern of the states, but it is equally true that such responsibilities, like all other state activity, must be exercised consistently with federal constitutional requirements as they apply to state action.[6]

Some have called the Supreme Court the nation's unofficial school board because of its important role in setting educational policy. The single most important court decision for education was *Brown* v. *Board of Education* in 1954, which affected not merely segregated schools in the South, but ultimately all laws mandating racial segregation in our society. Other court decisions on civil rights and education have dealt with the desegregation of northern schools, busing for racial balance, and bilingual education. (See Chapter 14.)

A number of Supreme Court cases have involved religion and education, often centering on the meaning of the First Amendment provisions. In the *Vitale* and *Schempp* decisons in the early 1960s, the Supreme Court ruled that prayers and Bible-reading in public schools were religious exercises and violated the establishment clause.[7]

Numerous court decisions have involved relations between the government and religious schools, the most controversial concerning financial assistance. The Court has upheld providing textbooks, transportation, and various specific services to students attending nonpublic schools under the "child benefit" concept, but it has overturned state laws subsidizing salaries of teachers of secular subjects in religious schools on the grounds that such laws created an "excessive entanglement be-

Seal of the Department of Education

According to the Department of Education, the acorn symbolizes an individual's ability to learn, nurtured by the mound of earth representing education. The sun and sky are the learning atmosphere, while the mature oak tree symbolizes the results of these efforts.

lic Welfare. Many of the curriculum reform projects of the 1960s were federally financed. (See Chapter 12.) In the 1970s, Congress enacted (and the presidents approved) many education measures. Examples include laws relating to bilingual education, ethnic heritage studies, drug abuse education, and teacher education. As already mentioned, when the federal government wishes to stimulate specific types of programs or curricula, the availability of federal funds encourages districts to undertake them. The federal government does not always provide sufficient funds, however, to implement policies it mandates. The 1975 Education for All Handicapped Children Act (Public Law 94–142), for example, required most districts to provide increased services, including an individually prescribed program for each handicapped child, but did not cover the increased educational costs.[5]

tween government and religion."[8] (See Chapter 10.)

The Supreme Court ruled in a case involving Chinese-speaking children in San Francisco schools that when there are substantial numbers of non-English-speaking children, a district must provide special instruction or bilingual education.[9] Supreme Court decisions also have dealt with academic freedom, financing of education, and student rights. (For discussions of these issues, see Chapters 5, 10, and 13.)

The legal governance of education at the federal level is a combination of the three branches—the president and the Department of Education in the executive branch, Congress, and the Supreme Court and federal judiciary. Their roles are interwoven in our system. After Congress passes a law and the president signs it, the Department of Education draws up guidelines and regulations to implement the law. Guidelines specify the meaning of the legislation in greater detail. Court rulings provide further interpretations and determine whether the law and its guidelines are constitutional.

Although the federal government's share of education funding is still relatively small, it has been exerting increasing influence. Curriculum reform projects, the emphasis on the disadvantaged, and career education are among the specific programs the federal government has encouraged in recent years. Federal legislation, regulations, and court decisions have particularly benefited black and minority students, the handicapped, the non-English-speaking, and female students. Federal aid to education is now widely accepted. Although some people are critical of federal regulations and federal control, few oppose additional federal support for schools. Indeed, the NEA seeks to increase the federal share to one-third of total revenues. The growth of the federal government's role has affected both the state and local levels of school governance.

STATE RESPONSIBILITY

Education is primarily a state function and responsibility in America. Hence we have 50 different systems of public education and variations in the patterns of state organization and governance. Hawaii is unique in having only one school district. Other states delegate to local educational authorities the actual administration and operation of schools in conformity with state (and federal) laws and regulations.

The real beginnings of state supervision and systems of education accompanied the common school movement in the middle third of the nineteenth century. The states created state boards of education led by full-time executive secretaries. Under the pioneering leadership of Horace Mann, Henry Barnard, and other state commissioners of public instruction, genuine state systems of public schools were established. As state appropriations for schools increased, so did state supervision and regulation.[10]

The increased state involvement in education can be seen in the increasing proportion of state aid. In the 1920s, states contributed less than 17% of total revenues while local districts raised over 82% of the funds for schools. The state share increased to 30% by 1940, and by the 1950s to nearly 40%. The proportion from local revenues meanwhile declined. By 1980 the state share surpassed the amount raised locally.[11]

Yet there is considerable variation in the extent of state funding. Hawaii, which provides most of its schools' funds, has a highly centralized education system, which reflects its history of a centralized government. Localism has remained strong in certain New England states where local schools long antedated the state system. On the other hand, state systems in the South were established after the Civil War, with little prior tradition of local public schools. These historical patterns affect both the extent of state financing and relative state power over local school districts.

More than half of the states had established a state board of education by 1900, and today only Wisconsin does not have a state board. In two-thirds of the states, members of the state board are appointed by the governor. Most of the rest are elected by the people or, less frequently, the legislature. The size of the board ranges from 3 to 24 members. (Texas has the largest.) State boards typically have 7 to 9 members serving 4- to 6-year terms. Most boards meet quarterly, though some are in session more frequently. Members serve part time and are unpaid except for expenses. Many state board members previously have served on local boards of education or have had experience as professional educators. The overwhelming majority are white, male, college-educated professionals.[12]

State constitutions and statutes establish the legal authority of state boards to make policy and govern elementary, secondary, and, usually, vocational education. (Higher education is under a separate board in all but four states.) Specific duties, responsibilities, and practices vary. Most state boards rely on their chief state school officer and the state education department to execute policy.[13]

State boards of education have legal jurisdiction over schools and have considerable prestige, but they exert relatively limited political influence and power in most states. The legislature, rather than the board of education, is often the ultimate school board for the state, because the board is dependent on the legislature for money to implement its proposals and policies. State school boards in New York, Texas, and Minnesota have taken the lead in certain matters, but generally state boards play a minor role in making educational policy and serve primarily to legiti-

mate the proposals of the chief state school officer.[14]

State Superintendent and Education Department

All states have a chief state school officer. The title may be state superintendent of public instruction, state commissioner of education, or state superintendent of schools. The state superintendent is either appointed by the state board of education or the governor, or elected in a statewide election, which may be nonpartisan. (The trend in selection has been toward appointment.) The term of office ranges from 1 to 5 years (4 years is the most typical) or is indefinite, at the pleasure of the appointing authority.[15]

Most state superintendents have worked as local superintendents and have served in the state education department. The state superintendent heads the state education department.

The chief state school officer usually wields considerable power, and his or her leadership and influence is greatest with the state school board and state education department. Elected superintendents tend to have both more formal power and greater influence on legislation than the appointed superintendents. Most chief state school officers are more influential as leaders of the state education department than in successfully influencing educational policy in the state legislature.[16]

The education department implements and administers the state's responsibilities in education in accord with policies adopted by the state board of education, laws enacted by the legislature, court decisions, and federal laws and regulations. Under the direction of the chief state school officer, the department also adopts rules and regulations affecting schools.

State education departments differ in size and degree of importance. Until the late

Chapter Nine

1950s, most were relatively small and weak. All expanded with the influx of new federal appropriations. Most federal education programs have been channeled through the state education departments, and ESEA specifically included funds to strengthen the state education departments. They more than doubled in staff size in the late 1960s. By 1970, over 40% of the internal operating budgets for state education departments came from the federal government. In some individual states, the percentages were much higher. Size variations remain. In 1972, staff numbered fewer than 100 in nine states, for example, and more than 1,000 in three states.[17]

Specific duties of the education department vary among the states. Virtually all are involved to some degree in certifying teachers, accrediting schools, apportioning state and federal funds, disseminating information, supervising instruction, and generally maintaining education standards in accordance with state laws and regulations. Some operate special state schools for the blind and deaf, and a state library or museum.[18]

Laws and Regulations

The state legislature enacts education laws. A brief description of the process illustrates the involvement of many officials and groups in the process. Appropriations for education are usually a perennial concern in the capitol. The state board of education may make its recommendations, often with the assistance of the state superintendent and state education department. Education is a significant component in the governor's budget recommendations. Legislative committees will consider new education proposals and perhaps changes in the state aid formula or a reform of the system of financing education. Interest groups such as the state teachers' organization and school boards' association may testify at committee hearings and mobilize

members to write their representatives to support bills. Eventually a law is passed, signed by the governor, and the state education department then implements and administers it.

Financial support or state aid will affect the scope of education offered in local districts. For example, does the state provide funds for kindergartens? Are they full- or half-day? (Many states count kindergarten children as one-half of a student for state-aid purposes, assuming a half-day kindergarten session.) Does the state support other preschool programs? Postsecondary programs? Adult education? Transportation costs? Lacking financial incentives from the state, many local districts will not provide such education services even if there is permissive legislation.

State education codes, including state laws and education department regulations, cover a broad scope. The state sets local district boundaries and may require districts to merge or encourage consolidation by providing financial incentives. Regulation of curriculum may range from laws requiring study of state history and the observance of certain holidays, to issuing state curriculum guides and lists of state-approved textbooks. (See Chapter 12.) Academic standards may be enforced by minimum competency exams and other statewide achievement examinations, required subjects, and minimum graduation requirements. States mandate the years of compulsory attendance and may require that schools be in session a specific number of hours per day and days per year. Other laws may establish minimum salaries for teachers, a system of tenure, and rules for dismissal of teachers. Regulations may establish standards for school buildings, including the minimum amounts of land and space and the need for state approval of new building plans. State laws may regulate educational expenditures of local districts by specifying the maximum tax levy, procedures for budget approval, and limits on borrowing.

About half the states have an intermediate form of school administration between the state and local school district. Traditionally these involved a county superintendent of schools and school board. In recent years many have been abolished or consolidated to serve more than a single county. (In many states, especially in the South, the local school district *is* a county school district; these are not considered intermediate units.) Some of the intermediate units provide cooperative services for districts (e.g., Wisconsin's Educational Service Agencies or New York's Boards of Cooperative Educational Services, which operate regional vocational and other special schools).

By these various officials, boards, agencies, laws, regulations, and appropriations, states carry out their responsibility to create and support a system of public education. The states delegate to the local school district much of the responsibility for implementing the laws and administering education.

LOCAL SCHOOL DISTRICTS

Historically, our schools developed as local enterprises, and the tradition of local control is firmly embedded in our heritage and beliefs. In the colonial era, town officials or the local school committee hired teachers, levied taxes, and collected fees from parents of students for tuition or fuel costs. In the early years of the republic, only about half the states even mentioned education in their constitutions. As we have seen, the states began to increase their supervision (and financial support) in the nineteenth century, and significant federal involvement has come within the last few decades. This trend toward greater state

and federal financing and regulation has led some commentators to argue that local control of schools today is a myth. Local school districts are subject to the laws, regulations, and minimum standards established by the state and must conform to federal guidelines if they wish to qualify for federal funds. Within these constraints, what are the powers and prerogatives of local school districts? One of the first problems is the difficulty of generalizing, since districts vary greatly.

Local school districts vary in name, type, and scope. Town, city, and county districts have boundaries coterminous with political subdivisions, but most school districts are special independent subdivisions or communities. County districts are most common in the Southeast. Common school districts, which are generally in rural areas, provide elementary schooling (kindergarten or first grade through sixth or eighth). Some states and areas have separate elementary and high school districts, but the more common pattern is a unified K–12 system. A central school district generally represents a consolidation or merger of two or more districts. Nonoperating districts have school boards but no schools. If there are students in the district, the board contracts with a neighboring district for their education and pays tuition charges from its revenues.

School Board

The legal governing body for the local school district is the school board. The title may be board of education, school committee, school trustees, school inspectors, or school commissioners. Each state has laws governing school boards and sometimes within states there are differences depending on the type of district. There are many similarities in the operation of school boards as well, and generalizations are possible.

School boards are accountable to those who elected or appointed them.

Most school boards have five, seven, or nine members, though size ranges from one trustee to more than 20 members. The usual term of office is between 2 and 6 years. Overlapping terms provide a continuing board with some experienced members. In the absence of resignations, a complete turnover of board membership would require several years.

In the overwhelming majority of districts, voters elect members of the board in nonpartisan elections. Many are uncontested elections. Some school boards, especially in large cities and in some southern states, are appointed by the mayor, city council, county court, or other governmental body. The majority of board members are lay persons rather than professional educators. Many states prohibit teachers from serving on the school board in the district where they are employed because of conflict of interest. Board members must be residents of the district and generally must be qualified voters. Some states specify minimum education (e.g., literacy), and in a few states members must have children in school or own property.[19]

A national survey in 1979 indicated that board members were usually white (91%), male (72%), college graduates (72%), and over 40 years old (69%). Only 13% had annual incomes of less than $20,000, while 59% had incomes over $30,000. According to an earlier survey, two of every three board members were in professional or technical occupations, business managers, officials, or proprietors.[20]

Before their service on the school board, many members have been active in other community organizations, especially the Chamber of Commerce, a service club (e.g., Rotary, Kiwanis, Lions), the United Fund, a PTA, or a local citizens' advisory committee on education. Board members generally are not paid, but their expenses in board service usually are reimbursed. In a few large districts, members do receive several thousand dollars in salaries.

Most school boards meet regularly, at least once a month, usually in the evening. Additional special meetings often are required, especially when preparing the budget or dealing with a controversial issue. The meetings are open to the public, and so-called sunshine laws now usually restrict the closed executive sessions to discussion of specific sensitive issues such as a denial of tenure. All formal decisions must be made in open public meetings, and the official minutes are a matter of public record.

Local boards of education make policy and are legally responsible for the operation of schools consistent, of course, with state and federal requirements. They hire personnel, grant tenure, adopt the budget, authorize construction or renovation of schools, purchase textbooks and supplies, pay bills, approve the curriculum, set the school calendar, and generally oversee the management of the local schools. Most boards are fiscally independent in the sense that they have the power to levy taxes and issue bonds. Some districts are financially dependent on the city or other government for their local revenues.

A local board may decide to exceed the state minimum standards. For example, teachers must meet certain requirements to be certified by the state, but a local district may require teaching experience or a graduate degree besides certification. Whatever policy it adopts, the board generally delegates much of the responsibility for implementing it to the administrators. Thus, administrators recruit, interview, and select teachers who meet state and locally determined qualifications. An administrator's job offer is subject to approval by the board, which has the final authority to hire teachers and other personnel.

One of the most important decisions a school board makes is the selection of a superintendent of schools. It may seek assistance from consultants for initial screening of applicants, but the board members usually interview a number of candidates in person and select their own chief school officer.

Although the basic work of budget preparation usually is done by the administrators, the board generally makes major budget decisions. One of the board's most important tasks is to gain community support for the budget, since in many communities citizens vote on the budget or need to approve the tax levy. In fiscally dependent districts, the mayor and city council will become involved. They usually are interested, however, only in the bottom line—the total budget rather than specific components.

Sometimes board meetings seem very routine and votes are often unanimous. Some issues may be discussed, but consensus is the general pattern. However, should the board not adequately reflect the desires of the community, or should there be a shift in the population of the district and a resulting change in values and expectations toward education, there may be contested elections, eventually the defeat of incumbents, and often dismissal of the superintendent.[21]

Many boards in recent years have felt increasingly powerless. The growing role of state and federal government regulations, laws, and court decisions seem to restrict their decision making. While this is true to some extent, many important decisions still are made at the local level. One example is the selection of teachers and administrators. Moreover, as the closest and most responsive educational agency, it is the local school boards that become centers of controversy when demands are pressed by elections, local interest groups, or individual parents and citizens. With education becoming more politicized, some boards are dealing more directly with demands from teacher organizations, civil rights groups, student protesters, and citizen groups.

Relations between the school board and superintendent have been investigated in many communities. In practice, the lines

Chapter Nine

between the board's policy-making role and the superintendent's administrative role rarely can be drawn sharply. In small districts especially, members of the board may become intimately involved in the day-to-day operations of the schools. At the other extreme, the board may become a rubber stamp sanctioning the superintendent's recommendations. Since most board members have limited time to devote to their duties, they usually must rely a great deal on the superintendent and the administrative staff whom they have appointed. In virtually all districts, the professional educators supply information to the board and thereby influence policy.

Cartoon by Ford Button in *Phi Delta Kappan*, September 1974, p. 47. Reprinted with permission.

"As an administrative assistant, one of your jobs is to see that the school board doesn't come poking its nose in here."

ACTIVITY 9–1
Attend a School Board Meeting

Attend a meeting of a local school board. You may want to supplement your observations by visiting the district's administrative offices for background information. Speak with board members or other knowledgeable people attending the board meeting. If you wish to go into greater depth for the assignment, consult questions listed in Donald J. McCarty and Charles E. Ramsey, *The School Managers*, pp. 255–67.

Share and compare your findings and observations with students who have visited other boards, by reporting in class or in discussion groups.

Try to answer these questions: How many members are on the board? What is their term of office? How many years have members served? What are their occupations and backgrounds? How does the composition of the board compare with national norms?

How many people attended the meeting? (Try to find out whether this was average and when attendance is highest.) Do students, teachers, and other district employees have official representatives at the meeting? What are their roles? Can you estimate how many district employees attended? How many parents? Was an opportunity provided for comments from visitors? What were their concerns?

What were the major issues at the board meeting? Was there a formal agenda? How much discussion took place? What was the role of the superintendent and administrators? What were the voting patterns? (Is there generally unanimity or disagreement?) Which individual members seem to be most influential? What is the dominant education issue in the district? Before or after the meeting, you might ask board members, administrators, and teachers about their views and compare their responses.

What are your impressions about the amount of control the local school board actually has? How many of their decisions are rubber-stamping state and federal policy?

Option: If there has been a recent controversial issue, you might want to focus your attention on it, reading pertinent articles, editorials, and letters to the editor in back issues of the local newspapers. Talk with one or more board members, school administrators, and other interested parties. Learn not only their views on the issue, but their perceptions of the decision-making process and which individuals and groups were influential.

ADMINISTRATIVE STRUCTURE

As schools grew, some degree of administrative structure became necessary. When enrollments increased in the nineteenth century and the one-room school expanded to a graded school with several classrooms and a number of teachers, boards generally appointed a "principal teacher" who both taught and was in charge of the school. Eventually the position developed into a full-time administrator, the building principal. When city boards of education sought assistance in the administration of their school system in the mid-nineteenth century, they appointed superintendents whose responsibilities initially were basically clerical.

Superintendent

Over the years the superintendency has evolved to include the roles of educator, business manager, chief executive, and chief professional advisor to the board of education. The official title is usually superintendent of schools, though in some districts it may be "executive head" or "supervising principal."

Virtually all chief school administrators have teaching experience and most have administrative experience, usually as principals. Superintendents in larger districts generally have administrative experience as an assistant superintendent in the central office or superintendent in a smaller district. State certification requirements for administrators usually specify teaching experience and graduate study. An increasing proportion of superintendents in larger districts have a doctorate, usually in educational administration or business management.

Some small districts do not have a full-time superintendent, while large city districts may have scores of administrators and several layers of hierarchy in the central district office. In a typical district, a superintendent is assisted by a business manager, an assistant superintendent for instruction, and an administrative assistant, as well as secretarial and clerical employees in the central office. Specific titles and functions, as well as the number of administrators, vary depending on the size and organization of the district.

Regardless of the number of administrators, it is the superintendent as chief executive officer who provides leadership, makes recommendations to the board, carries out board policy, and administers the operation of the school district. The superintendent generally sets and controls the agenda for board meetings and initiates proposals and recommendations. On some issues, a superintendent may provide more than one alternative. Boards do not always accept a superintendent's suggestions, but they seldom initiate their own.[22]

Chapter Nine

Cartoon by Ford Button in *Phi Delta Kappan*, February 1974, p. 395. Reprinted with permission.

". . . and besides the faculty meeting, principal's meeting, six requests for educational conferences, the overview on buildings and grounds, here are 72 happy valentine cards from the afternoon kindergarten at Neil Armstrong School."

When superintendents find that many of their recommendations are rejected by their boards, they are likely either to look for another position or to change their ideas to conform to the board's. Superintendents are appointed by and responsible to the local board of education. They have contracts for 2, 3, or sometimes 5 years; superintendents do not have tenure. The turnover of superintendents is high, with the average length of service in a position only a few years. The number of involuntary resignations or dismissals is increasing. Boards certainly do exert power in their key decision to select and dismiss the chief school administrator.

The superintendent's role varies depending on the district, individual personality, and the type of board and community power structure. Superintendents gain influence through professional expertise, PTA support, contact with community leaders (perhaps by membership in the local Chamber of Commerce), and most important of all, by virtue of their full-time status and access to other administrators and information about the school district.[23]

Although they have legal authority over the schools, many boards concentrate on buildings and finances and leave the remainder of educational matters to the superintendent and educators. Many studies conclude that in most systems the professional educators hold most of the power and influence. The superintendent is usually identified as the most powerful individual within the system. Some studies of large city districts, however, conclude that it is the educational bureaucracy that really controls the system. Teacher organizations, as we have already seen in Chapter 5, are increasing their role in the governance of schools.[24]

Administrative Hierarchy

The principal is the administrator in charge of the individual school building. Some principals administer two schools, while others are teaching principals. Large elementary schools usually have one or more assistant principals and perhaps grade-level chairpersons or team leaders who have administrative responsibilities. Similarly, secondary schools may have assistant or vice principals, deans, and department chairpersons in the administrative hierarchy. Specific responsibilities of these building-level administrators vary greatly. One assistant principal may be in charge of discipline, while another's primary responsibility may be supervision of instruction and evaluation of teachers. Chairpersons often assign teachers, determining classes, periods, and duties for members of the department.

Thus, teachers may be responsible to a department or grade-level chairperson, the building principal (and assistant principals), perhaps a number of district-wide

A major responsibility of a principal is development of good staff morale.

administrators such as the assistant superintendent for instruction and assistant superintendent for personnel, the chief school administrator, and, ultimately, the local board of education. Teachers are near the bottom of the organizational hierarchy within a school district. They do have authority over their students and are responsible for teaching the curriculum. Sometimes they may have limited authority over paraprofessional aides, secretaries, and custodians. In most districts teachers do have considerable freedom in their teaching methods, approach to subject matter, and individual emphases.

Funky Winkerbean by Tom Batiuk © 1975 Field Enterprises, Inc. Courtesy of Field Newspaper Syndicate.

Chapter Nine

Figure 9–1 is an organization chart from a school district enrolling 5,000 students in four schools. The district conducts an extensive program of recreation and adult education and its expenditures per student are considerably above average. Some of the positions are part time, e.g., the treasurer, clerk, attorney, auditor, and doctors. The director of physical education and athletics, system-wide chairpersons, and department chairpersons also teach, although fewer classes than the full-time teachers. Building principals have authority over custodians, cafeteria staff, and secretaries in their schools. The purpose of this administrative hierarchy is to teach large numbers of students effectively.

In most schools and districts, as with most organizations, there is also an informal power structure. Certain individuals hold power and authority inherent in their positions, but others also may be influential though they do not have an official title. Areas of interest and influence vary. The football or basketball coach may be very influential because of an ability to mobilize parents in the booster club to support interscholastic sports. Teachers may have influence because their experience and expertise leads others to defer to their judgment. An individual teacher may have connections with the power elite in the community. A certain custodian may be more influential than the principal or head custodian in some areas. A superintendent or principal may regularly consult with certain staff persons for advice and not with others. Moreover, the teacher union may be very influential in a district. A teacher or administrator must understand the informal power structure to operate successfully within the system.

No one single power structure exists in local school districts. There are many different types and varieties. Furthermore, whether in relations between the board and administration or internal organization,

power will vary depending on the issue. On matters of curriculum, for example, professional educators generally make the decisions. State laws and regulations affect the curriculum, and publishers influence content and availability of textbooks. Occasionally there will be controversies, such as the use of certain books or a sex education program, and citizens may become involved.

Nonetheless, curriculum matters are generally internal issues decided within the educational system. Teachers usually participate in these decisions through their involvement on curriculum planning committees and textbook selection committees, as well as by implementing or teaching the curriculum in their classrooms. Administrators also may be involved, particularly an assistant superintendent for instruction, supervisors, and principals. Often, in a formal legal sense, the board approves the curriculum, but it generally defers to the expertise of educators, except for the episodic issues where particular books or programs become controversial.

Nonpublic Schools

Our focus has been on the administration of public schools. However, about 1 of every 10 students and over 250,000 teachers are in private or nonpublic schools.[25]

Many of the religiously affiliated schools are under the control of the local church or a diocesan board, but there is usually also a parish school board or advisory committee. In some denominations there also may be diocesan or district superintendents and school boards with varying powers and responsibilities. Most independent schools, as well as some of the religious schools, are governed by a self-perpetuating board of trustees. (The board itself selects new members to fill vacancies.) Many of the trustees are alumni or parents of students, and fund raising is

Figure 9–1.
School district organization chart

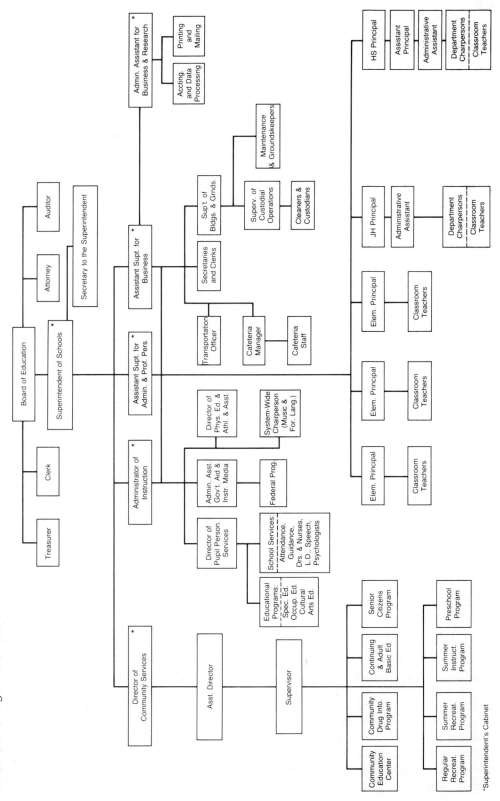

usually one of their primary responsibilities. Some schools are controlled by parents, while many private nursery schools are owned by individuals or business corporations.

Regardless of the type of control, a principal, headmaster, or headmistress is responsible for the day-to-day operation and administration of the school. Since the individual school is generally the basic unit rather than a system or number of schools, central office administrators are uncommon. Administrative structure tends to be less complex because of the relatively small size of most private schools. Many of the principals and other administrators also teach part time.

The National Catholic Education Association, National Association of Christian Schools, National Society for Hebrew Day Schools, and National Association of Independent Schools provide services to member schools, rather than act as governing or supervisory bodies. Although states do have regulations affecting private schools, they are generally less extensive than those governing public schools. Consequently, most principals and heads of private schools have more autonomy in their individual schools than do public school principals.[26]

EDUCATIONAL INTEREST GROUPS

Private and quasi-public organizations and special educational interest groups play important roles in shaping educational policy and decisions. Among the most important of these are teacher organizations whose role already has been examined in Chapter 5. The NEA and AFT are influential lobbying groups at the federal level. State teacher associations have been politically effective forces in state capitals for

many decades, while collective bargaining by local teacher unions has had a major impact in many districts in recent years.

Other groups also have had varying influence. Parents organizations, for example, have played an important role. The largest and best known is the National Congress of Parents and Teachers, better known as the PTA. As a result of the student movement in the late 1960s, PTAs have expanded to include high school students in Parent-Teacher-Student Associations. Mothers remain the backbone of the organization, however, and teacher involvement seems to have declined in recent years. Participation tends to be greater among parents of elementary school children.

One social scientist included the PTA among the 20 most influential organizations in the country, but most analysts do not feel it is so powerful, despite its large membership base. Its strength has been greatest in individual schools and local districts. The PTA has been a strong supporter of the schools and has lobbied at the state level for educational legislation. Principals and administrators often find the PTA among their staunchest allies in supporting school programs and budgets.[27]

There are professional organizations for virtually all levels and types of administrators. The Council of Chief State School Officers and the American Association of School Administrators (composed mainly of superintendents) are among the most prestigious and influential. Often there are state and county organizations as well as national groups for principals, supervisors, and other administrators.

Like the teachers, parents, and administrators, school boards have state and national associations that lobby for favorable legislation, hold annual conventions, and provide publications (e.g., *American School Board Journal*). The state associations tend to be more influential than their federation, the National School Board As-sociation, is nationally.[28]

The Education Commission of the States is a national educational interest group organized by the state governments. It has grown in importance since it began in the mid-1960s from a suggestion by James Conant in *Shaping Educational Policy*. States are represented by governors, legislators, educators, and lay persons. The commission administers the national assessment program and is concerned about educational issues and policies.

Professional accrediting associations are influential in American education. The standards of the National Council for the Accreditation of Teacher Education (NCATE) affect the preparation of teachers in many public and private institutions of higher education (see Chapter 4). Regional accrediting associations, such as the North Central Association of Colleges and Secondary Schools, accredit high schools and colleges on the basis of either written reports by the schools or periodic self-evaluation studies supplemented by a visit by a team of educators. Accreditation provides some measure of educational quality, and students from an unaccredited high school may have difficulty being admitted to college.[29]

College admission requirements affect the high school curriculum. (See Chapter 12.) The private Educational Testing Service administers the various College Board exams including the Scholastic Aptitude Test, Achievement Tests, and Advanced Placement Examinations. Because many colleges require students to take the SATs or American College Testing Program exams for admission, these exams affect the high school curriculum. For example, some schools gear content in regular courses to these exams or even offer an elective "Preparation for College Boards" course.[30]

Other tests also may have an impact.

Achievement tests may be used to determine a student's class placement or promotion. Results of these exams may be used to evaluate teachers and principals. Thus, these tests and the organizations that produce them influence school curriculum and practices.

Private philanthropic foundations have financed innovative programs and provided seed money for educational reforms. The Ford Foundation, which has been particularly active, invested $30 million in 25 projects in the 1960s to encourage team teaching, flexible scheduling, compensatory education, and other educational reforms. The Carnegie Foundation financed national assessment programs, and the Charles S. Mott Foundation supports community education programs.[31]

Civil rights groups have been active nationally in supporting litigation and legislation for desegregation. These groups also have pressured publishers to integrate their textbooks, produce multiethnic readers, and give adequate attention to black history. Similarly, many women's groups have sought to eliminate sexism in the curriculum.

Publishers influence school curriculum through the content of textbooks and other instructional materials. General Electric, IBM, Xerox, and other private corporations have entered the knowledge industry in recent years, and educational technology has expanded to include audiovisual materials and computer-assisted instruction. Publishers provide a proliferation of duplicating masters of prepared exercises for the elementary grades. (See also Chapter 12 on the role of publishers in curriculum.)

Interest groups have an important role in state educational politics. In some states, the state organizations of teachers, school boards, administrators, and PTAs join in a coalition to support increased state aid to education and other school legislation. Many of the education coalitions fragmented and became less effective in the 1970s as a result of labor-management splits and collective bargaining in most local districts. Nonetheless, the education lobby is among the most influential interest groups in state legislatures.

The most important education interest groups generally are the state organizations of teachers, school boards, and administrators. Among these, teacher organizations have the advantage in the number of members, financial resources, and size of professional staff. They generally are the most effective groups. The professional staff for each of the groups may include lobbyists and researchers, but the groups' most frequently used means of persuasion are contacts by local members with state legislators. Staff contacts and information are important sources of political strength for the education interest groups.[32]

At the local level there are literally thousands of ad hoc organizations and interest groups involved in local schools. Boards of education often create citizen advisory committees to encourage wider citizen participation and to gain support for the schools. The committees are sometimes focused on particular concerns such as a school building program or planning committee. Some boards created student advisory councils in response to the student movement in the late 1960s. Booster clubs in local districts support athletic teams by their attendance at games and by pressuring for adequate budgets for the sports activities. Local taxpayers' associations or budget committees often resist increases in school taxes or recommend more efficient operation of schools. Parents have organized boycotts and picketed the schools on some issues.

Other organizations are not focused on education, but they exert influence on a particular issue or in a specific community.

A local chapter of the American Association of University Women or the League of Women Voters may sponsor a nonpartisan caucus of representatives of community groups to select candidates for the board of education. Individual citizens, sparked perhaps by John Birch Society or Christian Crusade literature, may demand that certain books be removed from the schools. Thus, many different organizations and interest groups are concerned about education at different levels and with varying degrees of involvement and influence. Interest groups in our society are a means of broadening citizens' access to the political structure and making policy more responsive to demands.[33]

Citizens do turn out at school board meetings when an issue of deep concern arises.

ACTIVITY 9–2

In Whose Interest?

Select one of the organizations or interest groups mentioned in this section to investigate further. Locate recent articles about the organization, read some of its publications, and, if possible, interview a leader or member of the group. What are its views on education? What is the relationship of the organization to the formal legal structure of education? How does the group try to exert its influence? Can you determine how successful it is in achieving its goals? Do you feel its activities benefit education? Make an oral or written report of your findings.

Option: Contact your state legislators and ask them which groups and individuals (within and outside the legislature) are most influential in securing educational legislation. You may want to focus on the most recent state aid-to-education appropriations or other specific legislation. Or you may want to interview people such as a superintendent of schools, president of a local teacher organization, or other educational leaders about *their* perceptions of political influences in the state capital.

Ask about specific officials and organizations, including persons in official positions of authority and power. Compare your findings with other students from your state. Are certain individuals or groups on everyone's list? Are there consistent differences between the responses of legislators and those of educators? What tentative generalizations can you make concerning the politics of education at the state level and the influence of special interest groups?

SUMMARY

The governance of American schools is undergoing change. The politics of education deals with the control of the schools. The federal government's role in education has been expanding in recent decades through Supreme Court decisions and increased federal aid to education. The federal involvement will continue to expand in the 1980s with the Department of Education. However, federal support will probably fall far short of the NEA's goal of one-third of total public school revenue.

The states, too, have increased their responsibilities in public schooling. Various pressures probably will lead to more funding from the states and a further decline in the proportion of school revenues raised locally. More state aid may mean increased state control. Nonetheless, responsibility for the operation of schools will remain at the local level. Despite those who assert

that local control is a myth, there remains an important role for the local board of education in the governance of public schools. Indeed, as education becomes the focal point of political controversies, boards find themselves more involved in educational policy making than ever before.

Administrators, particularly the superintendent of schools and principals, provide leadership for local districts and schools. The administrative hierarchy may be a complex bureaucracy in a large city district or a single administrator in a small rural district. Nonpublic schools have varying patterns of governance.

Local patterns of influence are changing in the relations between school boards, superintendents, and the public, but it is difficult to generalize about trends. As teacher organizations become more powerful, they press for a greater role in educational decision making (see Chapter 5).

Many private or quasi-public interest groups seek to influence and affect schools and educational policy at the national, state, and local levels.

Professional educators likely will remain influential in the control of American schools. The balance of power may shift, however, and controversies can be expected among professional educators at different levels—in the federal and state education departments, in state and local superintendencies, and in the classroom. Educational politics and governance will continue to reflect kaleidoscopic patterns of shared federal, state, and local responsibilities, lay and professional participation, and influence by school boards, superintendents, educators, citizens, education organizations, and interest groups.

NOTES

1. Thomas H. Eliot, "Toward an Understanding of Public School Politics," *American Political Science Review* 52, no. 4 (December 1959): 1032–51; and Laurence Iannaccone and Frank W. Lutz, *Politics, Power, and Policy: The Governing of Local School Districts* (Columbus, Ohio: Charles E. Merrill, 1970), pp. 1–28.

2. Frederick M. Wirt and Michael W. Kirst, *Political and Social Foundations of Education* (Berkeley, Calif.: McCutchan, 1975), p. 253. (The earlier version of this book was entitled *The Political Web of American Schools* and was published by Little Brown in 1972.)

3. Sidney W. Tiedt, *The Role of the Federal Government in Education* (New York: Oxford University Press, 1966), pp. 14–27; and U.S. Bureau of the Census, *Historical Statistics of the United States, Colonial Times to 1970, Bicentennial Edition, Part 2* (Washington, D.C.: U.S. Government Printing Office, 1975), p. 373.

4. National Center for Education Statistics, *The Condition of Education 1979* (Washington, D.C.: U.S. Government Printing Office, 1979), p. 146; and *Financial Status of the Public Schools, 1979*, NEA Research Memo (Washington, D.C.: NEA, 1979), p. 18.

5. *New York Times*, 29 July 1979, p. 19.

6. Quoted in David Fellman, ed., *The Supreme Court and Education*, 3rd ed. (New York: Teachers College Press, 1976), p. vii.

7. *Engel* v. *Vitale*, 370 U.S. 421 (1962) and *Abington School District* v. *Schempp*, 374 U.S. 203 (1963).

8. *Lemon* v. *Kurtzman, Earley, V. Dicenso*, 403 U.S. 602 (1971).

9. *Lau* v. *Nichols*, 414 U.S. 563 (1974).

10. Roald F. Campbell et al, *The Organization and Control of American Schools*, 4th ed. (Columbus, Ohio: Charles E. Merrill, 1980), pp. 63–66.

11. U.S. Bureau of the Census, *Historical Statistics*, p. 373; and NCES, *The Condition of Education, 1979*, p. 146.

12. Roald F. Campbell and Tim L. Mazzoni, Jr., *State Policy Making for the Public Schools* (Berkeley, Calif.: McCutchan, 1976), pp. 29–33; and Ralph B. Kimbrough and Michael Y. Nunnery, *Educational Administration* (New York: Macmillan, 1976), pp. 234–38.

13. Campbell and Mazzoni, *State Policy Making*, pp. 50–51.

14. Ibid., pp. 28–80, 257.

15. Kimbrough and Nunnery, *Educational Administration*, p. 238; and Campbell and Mazzoni, *State Policy Making*, p. 82.

16. Campbell and Mazzoni, *State Policy Making*, pp. 81–133.

17. Wirt and Kirst, *Political and Social Foundations of Education*, p. 120; and Mike H. Milstein, *Impact and Response: Federal Aid and State Education Agencies* (New York: Teachers College Press, 1976), pp. 13–15.

18. Kimbrough and Nunnery, *Educational Administration*, p. 243.

19. Ibid., pp. 258–59.

20. Kenneth E. Underwood et al, "Portrait of the American School Board Member," *American School Board Journal* 167, no. 1 (January 1980): 24; and L. Harmon Zeigler, M. Kent Jennings, and G. Wayne Peak, *Governing American Schools: Political Interaction in Local School Districts* (North Scituate, Mass.: Duxbury Press, 1974), p. 28. The general pattern, although not the same percentages, has been true historically. See, for example, a summary of earlier studies on social status of board members in Keith Goldhammer, *The School Board* (New York: Center for Applied Research in Education, 1964), pp. 89–94. The proportion of women board members has increased in recent years.

21. Laurence Iannaccone, *Politics in Education* (New York: Center for Applied Research in Education, 1967), pp. 84–92.

22. Donald J. McCarty and Charles E. Ramsey, *The School Managers: Power and Conflict in American Public Education* (Westport, Conn.: Greenwood, 1971), pp. 163, 177; and Zeigler, Jennings, and Peak, *Governing American Schools*, p. 154.

23. Zeigler, Jennings, and Peak, *Governing American Schools*, p. 150.

24. See, e.g., Marilyn Gittell, *Participants and Participation: A Study of School Policy in New York City* (New York: Praeger, 1967); and David Rogers, *110 Livingston Street: Politics and Bureaucracy in the New York City School System* (New York: Random House, 1968).

25. NCES, *The Condition of Education, 1979*, p. 80; see Chapter 10 on enrollments.

26. Otto F. Kraushaar, *American Nonpublic Schools: Patterns of Diversity* (Baltimore: The Johns Hopkins University Press, 1972); and Campbell et al, *The Organization and Control of American Schools*, pp. 425–35.

27. James D. Koerner, *Who Controls American Education?* (Boston: Beacon Press, 1968), pp. 147–50; Campbell et al, *Organization and Control of American Schools*, pp. 325–29; and Kimbrough and Nunnery, *Educational Administration*, pp. 386–87.

28. Kimbrough and Nunnery, *Educational Administration*, pp. 388, 391; Campbell et al, *Organization and Control of American Schools*, pp. 329–32.

29. Joel Spring, *American Education: An Introduction to Social and Political Aspects* (New York: Longman, 1978), pp. 198–201; Koerner, *Who Controls American Education?*, pp. 51–59; and Campbell et al, *Organization and Control of American Schools*, pp. 415–17.

30. Roald F. Campbell and Robert A. Bunnell, eds., *Nationalizing Influences on Secondary Education* (Chicago: University of Chicago, Midwest Administration Center, 1963), pp. 18–19, 57–72; and Campbell et al, *Organization and Control of American Schools*, pp. 409–14.

31. Kimbrough and Nunnery, *Educational Administration*, p. 390; and *A Foundation Goes to School: The Ford Foundation Comprehensive School Improvement Program, 1960–1970* (New York: Ford Foundation, 1972), a very candid assessment of the success of Ford's grants.

32. Iannaccone, *Politics in Education*, p. 48; and Jane Aufderheide, "Educational Interest Groups and the State Legislatures," in Campbell and Mazzoni, *State Policy Making*, pp. 177–215.

33. Michael O. Boss et al, "Professionalism, Community Structure, and Decision-making: School Superintendents and Interest Groups," *Political Science and School Politics*, ed. Samuel K. Gove and Frederick M. Wirt (Lexington, Mass.: Lexington Books, D.C. Heath, 1976), pp. 39–60.

FOR FURTHER STUDY

Bailey, Stephen K. *Education Interest Groups in the Nation's Capital.* Washington, D.C.: American Council on Education, 1975.

Brodinsky, Ben. *How a School Board Operates.* Bloomington, Ind.: Phi Delta Kappa Educational Foundation, 1977.

Heald, James E., and Moore, Samuel A., II. *The Teacher and Administrative Relationships in School Systems.* New York: Macmillan, 1968.

Mosher, Edith K., and Wagoner, Jennings L., Jr., eds. *The Changing Politics of Education.* Bloomington, Ind.: McCutchan-Phi Delta Kappa, 1978.

Nunnery, Michael Y., and Kimbrough, Ralph B. *Politics, Power, Polls, and School Elections.* Berkeley, Calif.: McCutchan, 1971.

Scribner, Jay D., ed. *The Politics of Education.* 76th Yearbook of the National Society for the Study of Education, Part II. Chicago: University of Chicago Press, 1977.

Strahan, Richard Dobbs, *The Courts and the Schools.* Lincoln, Neb.: Professional Educators Publications, 1973.

Thomas, Norman C., *Education in National Politics.* New York: David McKay, 1975.

Zeigler, Harmon, and Johnson, Karl. *The Politics of Education in the States.* Indianapolis: Bobbs-Merrill, 1972.

10

The Extent and Cost
of Education

Children are not the private property of parents, but the wealth of the state.

Chinese proverb

Our schools are, in a sense, factories in which the raw materials [children] are to be shaped and fashioned into products to meet the various demands of life. The specifications for manufacturing come from the demands of the twentieth-century civilization, and it is the business of the school to build its pupils according to the specifications laid down. This demands good tools, specialized machinery, continuous measurement of production to see if it is according to specifications, the elimination of waste in manufacture, and a large variety in output.

Ellwood P. Cubberley

These two quotations focus our attention on the role of the school as an agent of society. Schools offer not merely personal benefits, but are organized and managed to provide certain economic returns and social dividends for the nation.

Even among the technologically advanced countries, few have rivaled the extensive commitment of the United States to formal education. America leads the world in total numbers of students, the percentage of youth in school, the money spent per learner, and the facilities and resources provided for higher education. Other nations, past and present, have offered elementary schooling to all and secondary and higher educational opportunities to an elite, but it is rare to find countries that offer education on the scale that the United States does.

Chapter Ten

This chapter's purpose is not to give mere patriotic accolades, but to describe and analyze the extent of education America offers its citizens. More specifically, this section discusses the implications of the trends in the reduction of school districts, declining student populations and faculties, and the dropout problem.

The second segment of the chapter details the amounts of money provided for schools, stressing the actual cost of various educational components (such as buildings, instructional salaries, and classroom materials). Part of this segment raises questions about the ways in which individuals and groups determine whether the school is worthy of the investment.

The final part of the chapter discusses what is a major problem at all levels of education—how to raise more money for schools. It explains the current emphasis upon the property tax, which most states use to raise revenue for their schools, and why the courts have objected to this system. Alternative methods for supporting schools are discussed briefly.

Even if you are concerned about the cost of education, economic data and statistics on education don't seem very exciting. We do believe that this information is crucial, however, if you are to comprehend the issues facing teachers tomorrow; thus, we shall emphasize the implications of the data in each section. Are we doing enough to reduce the number of dropouts? Is the way we pay for schooling fair? Is universal education worth our investment?

After you have read Chapter 10, you should be able to (1) state the enrollment trends in American schools, (2) provide a general description of how much American public schools cost, and (3) describe the process by which Americans pay for their public schools.

THE EXTENT OF EDUCATION

Unlike most industrial countries which have

Miss Peach by Mell Lazarus. © 1972 Field Enterprises, Inc. Courtesy of Mell Lazarus and Field Newspaper Syndicate.

national systems of education, the United States has 50 independent state systems and a vast number of nonpublic schools. Keeping tabs on the size and scope of these units has always been a vexing problem; indeed, it was one of the reasons the United States Department of Education was founded. Today, the National Center for

Education Statistics gathers much of the data about schools.

School Districts

The data that follows should convince you that it is hard to speak of or plan for (if that were legally possible on a national scale) the American school system. Districts vary greatly in size as well as financial resources; hence, it is difficult to prescribe common remedies for similar educational problems.

Considering the phenomenal increase in student enrollments in the twentieth century, it is surprising to learn that the number of districts in the nation actually has been declining. In 1933 there were 125,000 districts. In 1977 there were only 16,112.[1] The decline reflects the trend toward centralization in metropolitan areas and consolidation in rural parts of the country.

Looking at size alone, the diversity among districts is mind-boggling. In 1980 the largest district was New York City, with 963,000 students. Enrollment in the fifth largest district, Dade County (Miami), Florida, was over 200,000, while the 50th largest district, Austin, Texas, was 58,000. Most districts have relatively small enrollments. For example, Nebraska has the nation's largest number of districts at 1,204, but a total student population of only 312,000. Twenty-five percent of the nation's districts have 300 or fewer students. The reduction in the number of districts has increased the average district size. In 1945–46 the average number of students per district was 230, but 2,700 in 1976.[2]

Similarly, the number of students in buildings has increased while the total number of school buildings has declined. In 1930 there were 275,000 schools, of which approximately 150,000 were one-teacher units. In 1976 the total number of buildings was 106,000, with fewer than 1,200 one-teacher buildings (Nebraska had 477 of them in 1978).[3]

This overview of the system does not reveal the condition and value of the school facilities. A report on schools in 15 large cities of the country in 1967 disclosed that 36% were built prior to 1920 and 12% before 1900.[4] Many old schools were built of brick and had high-quality woodwork inside. While that may seem commendable, it also means that it is difficult to modernize buildings for energy conservation or for educational innovations such as renovation of libraries into instructional resource centers. Suburban communities will not have the same maintenance problems as urban ones, although they now may be faced with having too many facilities.

School buildings reveal that education is a large enterprise in this country. For example, in 1975–76, public school districts invested $6 billion on construction of new buildings and nearly $7 billion for plant operation and maintenance. It was estimated in 1979 that the capital outlay for public K-12 schools was $10.5 billion.[5]

Student Enrollments

Just as a business carefully counts its customers from year to year, so the school partially judges its health in terms of enrollment. For years, rising student enrollments meant that a school's main worry was how to take care of its growth. Now the problem facing many districts is what to do with their excess facilities. Since most students are in the public schools, we shall examine that data first; but because a large number of students in America attend nonpublic schools (and you may teach someday in such a school), we shall include separate figures for them. Finally, we shall examine some enrollment figures from other countries.

Public School Enrollments. The period from 1870 to 1970 showed a steady increase in the total number of elementary and secondary students enrolled in the country's schools. In 1870 there were 6.9 million public school students, representing 58% of the 5-to-17 age group. Elementary and secondary enrollment peaked in 1970, when 51.3 million students, approximately 92% of the 5- to 17-year-olds, attended kindergarten through 12th grade.[6]

Another perspective on the extent of schooling is the percentage of the 17-year-old population graduating from the nation's high schools. In 1869–70, 16,000 students, only 2% of the country's 17-year-olds, completed their studies. The proportion of 17-year-olds graduating from high school peaked in the late 1960s at approximately 75%. Increasingly, students who are having difficulty with a regular high school curriculum are taking examinations such as the Graduate Equivalency Diploma (G.E.D.) to get credit for their high school work. Seven percent of all high school completions come from such examinations. In some states, G.E.D. certificates constitute over 15% of all high school completions.[7]

Enrollment predictions for the 1980s can be based on recent births. Elementary school enrollments are more predictable than secondary enrollments because factors such as dropouts will affect the latter.

The U.S. Bureau of the Census projects that for the nation as a whole the number of children ages 5 to 17 will decrease until 1984. Beginning in 1985 the number of children and youth ages 5 to 17 will increase every year until the year 2000. This would result in an increase in elementary enrollments in the mid-1980s and the secondary schools in the 1990s.[8]

Nonpublic Enrollments. Of the total elementary and secondary students enrolled in 1889, the first year such statistics were gathered, 9.3% were in the nonpublic schools. The highest percentage was in 1964–65, when 13.9% of the nation's pupils attended nonpublic schools. Since then the percentage has declined. In fall 1978, 11% of those enrolled in elementary schools were in nonpublic schools, and 8% of the students at the secondary level were in nonpublic schools.[9]

Most of these schools have some religious affiliation. Approximately 90% of the nonpublic students are in Roman Catholic schools. Other denominations supporting schools include the Missouri Synod Lutheran, Seventh Day Adventist, Christian Reformed, and Amish (see Chapter 15 for a more extensive description of nonpublic schools). From 1965 to 1976, the Catholic elementary schools decreased by 2 million students. However, during the same period, enrollments in other nonpublic schools, including the Christian day schools, increased, but not enough to offset the large decreases in the Catholic schools. The net result is a decrease of 1.3 million students in all nonpublic elementary schools since 1965.[10]

Two important political implications are linked to nonpublic school enrollments. First, the 5 million nonpublic school students are not evenly distributed throughout the country. In certain northeastern cities, for example, they may represent as many as 40% of all K-12 students. In other portions of the nation, the nonpublic student population ranges from 10% to 30%. Envision the effect on public schools should nonpublic schools in some cities close. Second, the concentration of these students in the cities does not go unnoticed by political officials. Since 1968 Republican and Democratic presidential candidates have favored some form of public tax aid to nonpublic schools. In some districts, members of the public school board enroll their own children in parochial schools, and seek to ensure that the local district provides ESEA services and busing to nonpublic school children.

Figure 10–1.
Kindergarten to 12th grade enrollment

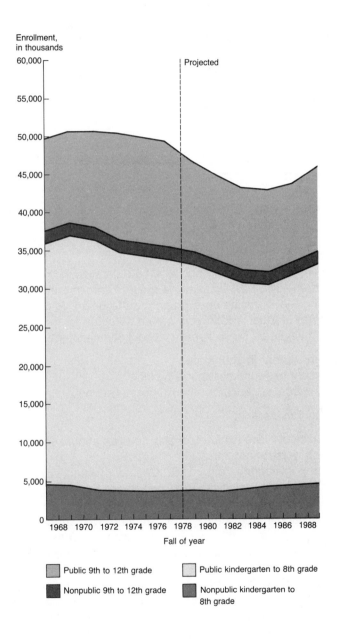

Enrollment,
in thousands

Public 9th to 12th grade

Public kindergarten to 8th grade

Nonpublic 9th to 12th grade

Nonpublic kindergarten to
8th grade

From National Center for Education Statistics, *The Condition of Education, 1980* (Washington, D.C.: U.S. Government Printing Office, 1980), p. 57.

Enrollments in Other Countries. Although many other industrialized countries offer universal elementary schooling, few have attempted to provide secondary education on the same scale as the United States. The tradition in most European countries and in many other parts of the world is to end students' formal schooling at age 13 or 14 and to have them enter the work force. Some students may begin a vocational training program. The percentage of students attending college is much higher in the United States than in any other country.

Statistics indicate that other industrialized countries are following America's model by providing more education for precollege youth. Only Japan has a higher proportion of its 15- to 19-year-olds in school than does the United States.[11]

ACTIVITY 10–1
Survey School Enrollment Trends

Although there will be a national decline in the number of school-age children, such a generalization does not allow for regional, state, or local trends in public school enrollments. Nor does it allow for consideration of the enrollment profile in your area for special types of schools, such as the Christian day school.

Make an enrollment projection of a specific school population. You should provide data from at least four dates—two past figures, the present enrollment, and at least one figure for the future. Putting the statistics on a graph may facilitate your projection. Be sure to indicate your source(s) of data. Add to your data a rationale for the projections you make.

You may wish to investigate these specific school populations:

- the total school enrollment in your state;
- the school enrollment in your local school district;
- the enrollment in a local Catholic or other nonpublic school.

Some sources you can consult:

- your local school district office (which probably does an annual school enrollment study);
- the state education department office;
- U.S. government publications, e.g., U.S. Census Bureau, *Statistical Abstract* and National Center for Education Statistics, *The Condition of Education*, each issued annually.

Attendance Patterns and Dropout Rates

Americans can be justly proud of the extensive educational enterprise they have erected, but a discussion of the system would not be complete without acknowledgement of two related problems—truancy and early school leaving, i.e., dropping out. Society's belief that education is so important it must be compulsory forces educators to wrestle with the question of what to do with and for those students who do not want to be in school and who are potential dropouts.

Truancy in the United States is much more extensive than you may realize; an estimated 2.5 million students miss school each day. Of course, reasons for the absences range from the understandable and legally excusable (illness, doctor's appointment, family emergency) to the inappropriate (going shopping, getting a haircut, or playing hookey). On an average school day, approximately 89% of the students are in school; but in some districts, such as large city systems, average daily attendance may be only 75% of those enrolled.[12]

Historically, attendance has improved over the years. In 1869–70, when few states had compulsory attendance laws and enforcement was lax, average daily attendance was only 58% of those enrolled. Prior to 1900 it never exceeded 70%; by 1959 and continuing through the seventies, the average daily attendance was about 90%.[13]

School officials, like parents, are concerned about the educational opportunities students lose when they miss school. Districts have developed various techniques to lower tardiness and absenteeism. Moreover, school officials are concerned about absenteeism because it also affects financing. Typically, local districts receive state funds based on their average daily attendance. The lower the average atten-

dance rate, the less money the district receives.

Compulsory Attendance Laws. In the mid-1970s a number of educators became quite concerned about the need for states to continue to require attendance in schools.[14] Some authors suggested that such laws were necessary when the country was primarily agrarian and farm families needed coercion to send their children to schools. Likewise, immigrants needed persuasion to keep their children out of the factories. Haven't we learned, these writers ask, that more and better learning occurs in a noncoercive environment? Doesn't the violence in the schools (Chapter 3) give us proof that some students do not want or need 10 to 12 years of schooling?

What are the attendance requirements today? While some variations exist, most states require that a person remain in school until age 16. Many states have spe-

Truancy has been a long-time problem for schools.

222

cial provisions for youth who have completed a certain level of education, usually the eighth grade or higher, and who are employed. As long as our society uses the schools to certify, in a sense, what types of employment our graduates fit best, it is unlikely that we shall totally eliminate compulsory attendance, as some of the critics urge.

Dropout Rates. Approximately one of four 17-year-olds in America does not graduate from high school. Is that figure high or low? Is it good or bad? Compared with other countries, it is very low. But if you assume that a high school education is the minimum needed to survive in our technological society, then you will be unhappy with such a high dropout rate.

As mentioned earlier, the dropout rate in America has declined sharply since the 1880s; however, it was not until 1940 that more students graduated (50.8%) than dropped out. Now approximately 78% graduate annually. Considering the 100 years from 1880 to 1980, you may feel that the reduction in dropouts has been substantial. On the other hand, if you think like Ralph Nader for a moment, can you accept that one in four students fails to graduate?

Before considering the characteristics of dropouts, note that the dropout rate var-

ies widely from state to state. It varies within states as well. Table 10–1 reveals that certain regional patterns exist: the far western and midwestern states have low dropout rates, while most southern states have high dropout rates.

Generally speaking, researchers find that social class distinctions are more significant than racial or ethnic factors in predicting who will drop out.[15] The overwhelming percentage of dropouts occur in the blue-collar, or lower class, although there is some evidence that class lines are blurring. Whites, compared with blacks and persons of Spanish origin, have higher school-completion percentages. Such statistics can be misleading; although the dropout rate among blacks is twice that among whites, four of five dropouts are white.

Are there certain in-school behaviors that potential dropouts are likely to display? Yes, say researchers. By the seventh grade they are two years behind their classmates in reading and mathematics; their grades are below average; they are likely to have failed one or more school years; they are irregular in attendance and frequently tardy; their performance is consistently below potential; they participate less in extracurricular activities; they change schools frequently; and their problems are more often disciplinary than academic.[16]

Table 10–1.

America's dropout rates 1976–77

States	Enrollment in 9th grade (Fall 1973)	Graduates 1977	Number and percentage of dropouts	
Alabama	67,660	46,763	20,897	31%
Alaska	6,483	4,526	1,957	30%
Arizona	42,552	27,223	15,329	36%
Arkansas	38,485	27,628	10,857	28%
California	357,817	266,143	91,674	26%
Colorado	47,035	36,647	10,388	22%
Connecticut	53,994	39,485	14,509	27%
Delaware	11,052	8,164	2,888	26%
District of Columbia	8,908	5,335	3,573	40%
Florida	132,056	88,137	43,919	33%
Georgia	93,216	62,234	30,982	33%
Hawaii	14,023	11,637	2,386	17%
Idaho	16,622	13,029	3,593	22%
Illinois	194,837	142,040	52,797	27%
Indiana	101,122	76,406	24,716	24%
Iowa	52,307	43,720	8,587	16%
Kansas	41,258	33,216	8,042	19%
Kentucky	62,479	41,755	20,724	33%
Louisiana	71,459	48,219	23,240	32%
Maine	19,664	15,205	4,459	23%
Maryland	72,350	55,503	16,847	23%
Massachusetts	98,815	75,386	23,429	24%
Michigan	176,341	135,162	41,179	23%
Minnesota	77,448	68,166	9,282	12%
Mississippi	45,108	27,639	17,469	39%
Missouri	87,019	64,471	22,548	26%
Montana	15,588	12,328	3,260	21%
Nebraska	27,339	23,067	4,272	16%
Nevada	10,989	7,992	2,997	27%
New Hampshire	14,503	11,477	3,026	21%
New Jersey	120,550	97,494	23,056	19%
New Mexico	24,406	17,988	6,418	26%
New York	295,601	215,100	80,501	27%
North Carolina	103,451	71,146	32,305	31%
North Dakota	12,764	10,839	1,925	15%
Ohio	199,688	156,220	43,468	22%
Oklahoma	50,680	38,577	12,103	24%
Oregon	41,028	30,258	10,770	26%
Pennsylvania	195,507	160,600	34,907	18%
Rhode Island	14,992	10,796	4,196	28%
South Carolina	53,382	37,780	15,602	29%
South Dakota	13,313	11,293	2,020	15%
Tennessee	71,910	49,290	22,620	31%
Texas	230,270	163,574	66,696	29%
Utah	24,188	19,801	4,387	18%
Vermont	8,138	6,699	1,439	18%
Virginia	90,256	66,738	23,518	26%
Washington	65,757	50,876	14,881	23%
West Virginia	34,122	24,719	9,943	29%
Wisconsin	86,198	72,367	13,831	16%
Wyoming	7,219	5,861	1,358	19%
Nationally	3,801,949	2,836,719	965,230	25%

Source: Data supplied to authors by staff of National Center for Education Statistics, 1980.

It is tempting for educators to look at these factors and others (such as family background or personality) and blame the victim for his or her problems with school. To what extent can or should the school and individual teachers be held accountable for failing or, as some charge, "pushing out" the student with problems? After all, the characteristics of dropouts are readily discernible by the time they are in the upper elementary grades (basic reading deficiencies, attendance patterns). Why aren't we more successful in providing remedial programs?[17] To what extent can we argue that certain individuals are just not school material?

ACTIVITY 10–2
Interview a High School Dropout

Most college students have been generally successful in school and were not high school dropouts. Interview someone who experienced difficulties in school to the point that he or she decided to drop out.

Following are examples of the kinds of questions you might ask.

1. What factor(s) caused you to leave school?
2. Was your dropping out your own decision? Did you feel that you were, in any way, pushed out? How did your family, friends, and teachers feel about it? Did your dropping out really surprise anyone?
3. How do you feel about dropping out now? Do you regard it as the best decision you could have made under the circumstances? Have you made any effort to return to school? Have you attempted to get an alternative diploma?
4. What is your opinion of school now?

Then ask yourself:

1. In what ways do you agree and disagree with the person you interviewed? Is the person a typical dropout who fits the characteristics described earlier?
2. Have you considered dropping out of college? What specific factors would convince you that you should drop out or that you should stay?
3. What should be done to help potential dropouts? (If you know a school district that has a program for dropouts, visit it; if not, consult the *Education Index* or some of the sources cited in this chapter for details of a program.)

Educational Professionals and School Staff

The numbers of teachers and other personnel employed to staff the nation's school programs confirm that education is a major societal enterprise. Public schools in 1976 employed 2,440,000 teachers, 168,000 administrators, 59,000 other professional staff, and 1,316,000 nonprofessional staff (custodians, secretaries, bus drivers, etc.). Another 247,000 teachers worked in nonpublic schools for a total of more than 4 million school personnel.[18]

Not included in these figures are those who serve as school board members or as volunteers with various school projects. A conservative estimate of school board members would be 100,000. When students, faculty, staff, and nonprofessional staff are added together, roughly 63 million Americans, one of every four persons, have a substantial involvement in education.

While it may appear logical to assume that as pupil enrollments drop, the size of the educational staff also will decline, that may not happen. The total number of teachers (K-12) has been steadily increasing. (See Figure 10–2.) This discrepancy is due to the decline in pupil-teacher ratios. (See Figure 10–3.) Average class size may be smaller, but more specialized staff are being employed to meet the needs of students (for example, in remedial reading and learning disabilities). Also influential are the teacher organizations that resist attempts to reduce the instructional staff.

At levels other than the local school districts, staff numbers have been increasing also. For instance, although the number of local school board members is declining (from approximately 150,000 in 1962 to 105,000 in 1974), the number of staff in state education departments more than doubled during the period (from nearly 11,000 to 23,000). The federal agencies likewise have expanded their staffs. Perhaps the major reason for the expansion of staffs is the increase of federal dollars for education, which requires more personnel to administer the programs.[19]

EDUCATIONAL EXPENDITURES

The following discussion has at least three lessons for you as a prospective teacher. By examining the country's expenditures on schooling, you may gain further insight into education's *real* importance. (In today's vernacular, you will see the "bottom line.") Second, the data on the realignment of support of education—the shift from local

Figure 10–2.
Classroom teachers in elementary/secondary schools

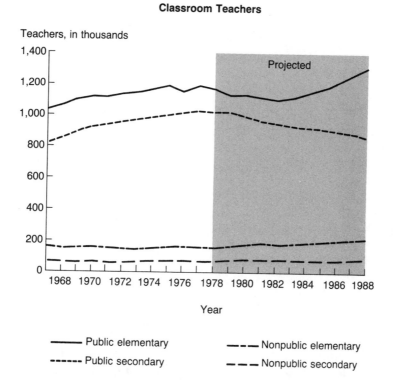

Classroom Teachers

From the National Center for Education Statistics, *The Condition of Education, 1980* (Washington, D.C.: U.S. Government Printing Office, 1980), p. 71.

Chapter Ten

Figure 10–3.
Pupil-teacher ratios for elementary and secondary schools

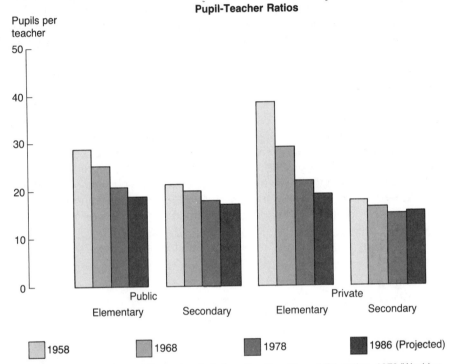

Pupil-Teacher Ratios

Pupils per
teacher

☐ 1958   ☐ 1968   ■ 1978   ■ 1986 (Projected)

From the National Center for Education Statistics, *The Condition of Education, 1979* (Washington, D.C.: U.S. Government Printing Office, 1979), p. 81.

revenue to state and federal funds—raises the question of who actually controls the schools. One wit has said it demonstrates the Golden Rule—he who has the gold makes the rule. The analysis of local school budget components makes clear still another point—that the largest portion of a school budget is for salaries, which has serious implications when a budget must be reduced. The concluding portion of this segment of the chapter discusses how individuals and society can weigh intelligently whether the immense expenditures America makes for education are worth the cost.

Funding for Education

It is estimated that $89.4 billion was spent in 1977–78 on public and nonpublic K-12

programs in America.[20] What does such a figure mean when it is compared with other personal and societal expenditures? How does that stand in relation to the educational expenditures in other countries?

We may begin by looking at schooling costs as a percentage of the country's gross national product (GNP), the total dollar amount of goods and services produced per year. In 1978 education accounted for just over 7% of the GNP, up considerably from its 3% level at the end of World War II. Compared with two other major governmental expenditures, education expenses are slightly below health costs, which are almost 9% of GNP, but more than defense spending, which is approximately 5% of GNP. In a comparative study done in the mid-1970s, only Canada and the Netherlands devoted a higher percentage of GNP to education than the United States. Other countries in that study were France, West Germany, Japan, Norway, Sweden, and the United Kingdom.[21]

Another way to analyze the economic impact of American educational costs is to compare how much state and local governments spend on education with what they spend on highways and social services. During the last quarter of a century, elementary and secondary education has commanded the largest single share of these state and local expenditures. In the late 1970s, 38 cents of every state dollar was earmarked for education. In many local districts, 50 cents or more from each tax dollar is spent on education.[22]

As mentioned in Chapter 9, the proportions of federal, state, and local monies for education have been undergoing a major realignment since World War II. As Table 10–2 shows, the state portion has been increasing to the point where it is nearly identical to the local share. The federal slice of the pie was about 8% in the 1970s.

The figures in Table 10–2 represent the national average every four years. The ranges between states are immense. For example, the state of Hawaii has *no* local funding, while in New Hampshire, local districts contribute 85% of school revenues. Massachusetts has the lowest percentage of federal funds (4.2) while New Mexico has the highest (23.0). A matter of deep concern for those committed to equal educational opportunity is, besides the range between states, the disparity between districts in the same state. Although the national average expenditure in 1977 was $1,278 per pupil, Tennessee spent $766 per pupil while Alaska spent $3,049 per student annually. Within states, some districts may spend twice or three times as much as other districts. For example, in Massachusetts, which averaged $1,560 per

Table 10–2.

Revenue sources for public elementary and secondary schools, 1942–78

| | Percentage distribution | | |
	Federal	State	Local
1942	1.4	31.5	67.1
1946	1.4	34.7	63.8
1950	2.9	39.8	57.3
1954	4.5	37.4	58.1
1958	4.0	39.4	56.6
1962	4.3	38.7	56.9
1966	7.9	39.1	53.0
1970	8.0	39.9	52.1
1974	8.5	41.7	49.8
1978	8.1	44.1	47.8

From the National Center for Education Statistics, *The Condition of Education, 1979.* (Washington, D.C.: U.S. Government Printing Office, 1979)

student per year, over 5% of the districts spent less than $1,200, while about the same precentage spent more than $2,600 per student.[23]

Perhaps these broad figures are bewildering to you. The data on school expenditures may be more meaningful when it is given in terms of how much money is spent per pupil. As Figure 10–4 indicates, the amount of money spent per student has increased significantly since 1930.

Another way to gain perspective on educational expenditures is to examine a local budget. The two studies in Table 10–3 show the variations that can exist. Also, there is a range between districts. For example, most districts may spend approximately 65% to 70% on salaries; others, as much as 80%. The relatively low percentage spent on instructional materials often surprises prospective teachers.[24]

In light of declining enrollments and inflation, it is important to consider the implications of these local budget figures. In a few states, residents vote on the local budget each year. If you had to make cuts in a budget (assuming you had a typical budget), where do you think cuts should

Figure 10–4.
Per-pupil expenditures of public school systems

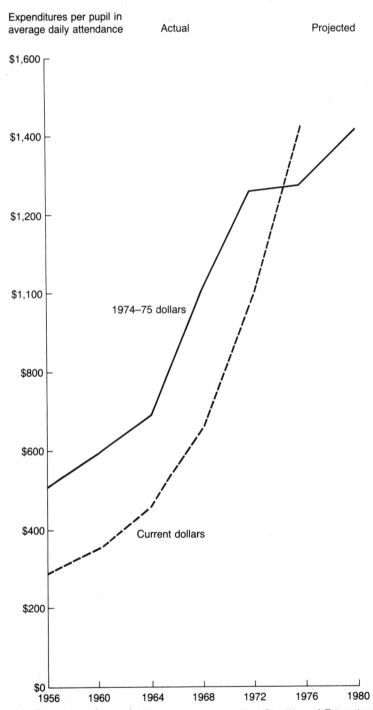

Current Expenditures of Public School Systems

Expenditures per pupil in
average daily attendance   Actual   Projected

From the National Center for Education Statistics, *The Condition of Education, 1976* (Washington, D.C.: U.S. Government Printing Office, 1976), p. 153.

be made? Where would you make the cuts? You would find, first of all, that much in a local budget is mandated and cannot be changed easily. For example, some states require that a percentage of the local budget be set aside for building repairs, future construction, and loan repayments. There are master contracts with teachers and other school employees that may cover several years. A major innovation requiring significant expenditures for new curriculum supplies may be cut or crippled when a district must reduce its budget. Finally, you will note that the largest portion of the budget is for teachers' salaries. When a school system must make extensive cuts, teachers will be directly affected.

The Benefits of Education

Are these costs of education worth it? All of us evaluate our educational experiences and decide whether we received any benefits from a particular course, a certain school, or a given extracurricular activity. Our judgments are essentially informal.

There are two formal methods, however, for determining the benefits of education to individuals and society.

The cost-benefit approach and the cost-effectiveness analysis share the premise that there are enough quantifiable elements in "human capital" so that one can reasonably estimate the return on individual and societal investments in schooling.[25] The cost-benefit approach is the more general, and it tends to use a relatively simple formula. For example, to determine whether your high school or college education has been worth it, add your costs and subtract the total from your gains, such as a higher salary. School districts thus may calculate whether an experimental program in remedial reading or dropout prevention is working. Besides computing the actual costs of the program, researchers may use interviews and observations to detect changes in student attitudes and performance on tests.

The cost-effectiveness method is much more specific and tends to use very spe-

When bond issues are proposed, public hearings are held.

Table 10–3.
Average local budget expenditures (as shown in two surveys)

National Center for Education Statistics		U.S. Statistical Abstract	
Item	Percentage of the local budget	Item	Percentage of the local budget
Instructional Costs*	66.5	Instructional Services*	73.0
Plant Operation and Maintenance	11.6	Plant Operation and Maintenance	8.9
Fixed Charges	12.9	Fixed Charges	8.0
Transportation	3.9	General Control (Superintendent's salary, legal expenses)	.2
Administration	4.1		
Attendance and Health	.9	Auxilary (library, health, transportation)	1.7
	100.0**	Debt Service	8.0
		Capital Outlay	.08
			100.0**

*Instructional costs include salaries of teachers (65% to 70%), and curriculum, which may be 1% to 3%.

**Due to rounding, totals will not equal 100%.

Note: Salaries other than teachers' are located in several categories. Salaries may reach 80% in some local budgets.

From NCES, *The Condition of Education, 1979* (Washington, D.C.: U.S. Government Printing Office, 1979), p. 156; U.S. Bureau of the Census, *Statistical Abstract of the United States*, 1979 (Washington, D.C.: U.S. Government Printing Office, 1979), p. 158 ff.

cific instruments to measure the degree of payoff. For example, a cost-effectiveness study of a dropout prevention program may analyze whether it is more beneficial to hire a teacher with an additional year of experience or one with higher verbal skills. Another cost-effectiveness tool is the case study, in which the contrasting administrative styles of two neighboring school districts are examined to see whether one is more efficient than the other. Media specialists may use cost-effectiveness techniques to determine whether a particular medium (e.g., film) is more effective than another format (slides or audiotape).[26]

Individual Benefits. Most persons regard increased earnings as the most tangible benefit of advanced schooling. According to studies done in the 1950s and 1960s, those who completed high school had lifetime earnings approximately 40% higher than those who had not gone beyond the eighth grade. College graduates had lifetime earnings roughly 60% above the earnings of high school graduates. Studies done in the 1970s show that the differences have become less pronounced, although average income differentials between high school and college graduates range from 33% to 52%. There are six times more college graduates than non–college graduates who hold jobs paying $25,000 or more. Moreover, higher paying jobs typically offer other economic advantages such as more generous sick leave, health insurance, longer vacations, and better retirement benefits.[27]

Other research suggests that college graduates derive additional noneconomic benefits from their advanced education. They include more contentment with life in general, a greater number of friends and acquaintances, and more skills in relating to others. Some evidence suggests that persons with more education have higher job satisfaction.[28]

Social Benefits. An individual can calculate, formally and informally, what benefits he or she has gained from education. It is harder to determine the benefits society or the public gains from education. Even so, there are some measures that can be applied, beginning with the financial benefits. Often in smaller communities, the school district is the largest employer. The rising investments in education already noted can positively influence the economy of many communities.

Another perspective on the social benefits of education is to consider what would happen if society did not have schools. Would the crime rate be higher? Would more people be on welfare? Would the standard of living be reduced? Many supporters of American schooling assume that there would be an increase in societal problems if educational programs were not provided.

These social benefits can be measured by several methods. One is to rely upon the testimony of graduates. Another is to use surveys to determine how, in fact, persons with different levels of schooling act differently. Table 10–4 suggests that participation in community activities is positively related to educational attainment. If data were available for adults who had not completed high school, their participation would be even lower.

Table 10–4.
Political and social participation of young adult high school graduates, by level of education: 1976

Activity	No college	Some college, no degree	Bachelor's degree or higher
	Percent		
Registered to vote	59.5	76.7	87.4
Voted in government election	54.4	74.2	82.2
Participated in or belonged to:			
Political club or organization	5.1	9.9	16.0
Youth organization	6.1	10.9	13.6
Work-related organization or student government association	17.7	23.8	42.4
Church or church-related activity (excluding worship services)	30.6	33.1	38.4
Community, service, or organized volunteer work	16.3	25.9	39.6
Social, athletic, arts, or discussion group	38.8	51.2	60.0

From the National Center for Education Statistics, *The Condition of Education, 1979* (Washington, D.C.: U.S. Government Printing Office, 1979), p. 36.

Chapter Ten

ACTIVITY 10–3

Is Your Schooling Worth It?

Attempt to figure the costs and benefits of your last year of high school and/or a year in college. Consult some of the economics books mentioned in the "For Further Study" section for more details on how to figure the costs of education.

Most economists would include tuition and fees, special clothes (uniforms, for example), books and supplies, and personal expenses related to schooling (travel). Be careful if computing room and board charges to include only the difference between those costs and the expense if you were living at home. Include opportunity costs or foregone earnings. These imputed costs are the amount of money you could have earned if you were working rather than attending school. (Be sure to deduct from your opportunity costs any part-time earnings during the school year and vacations.)

Then calculate what you might earn for the four years after your anticipated college graduation date. (This will require you to project *both* what you would have made if you had not gone to school as well as what you anticipate your salary will be when you graduate.) Reach a final figure of what college will have cost you and what financial benefits you will have gained by then. Is it worth the cost? What noneconomic benefits will you receive?

FINANCING SCHOOLS

The financial problems of schools may not be an immediately relevant issue for you, but as soon as you become a teacher they will be. You may have heard about some of the financial crises facing the schools and wondered why someone hasn't done something sooner to rectify education's monetary problems. This portion of the chapter emphasizes the ways schools are financed. What is underscored is that a variety of methods have been tried over the years, each one having its drawbacks as well as advantages. After focusing on the current methods to raise funds for schools, the section closes with consideration of some of the financial issues facing tomorrow's schools.

From the beginning, schooling in America has been paid for in many ways. New England settlers were accustomed to a variety of traditions—rents from land, subsidies from the Church of England and the Crown, local taxes, and tuition fees paid by parents and guardians. Parents or guardians usually paid in cash, but they sometimes provided goods or services (a cord of wood or boarding the teacher). The colonists even tried lotteries to finance schools. As the education system became more formal and extensive in the 1800s, communities increasingly turned to property taxes. The high court in Michigan ruled in 1874 that the general welfare of the state justified asking the *entire* population to support the high school, which some school patrons in Kalamazoo had thought should be supported only by those who had children in school.

Not only were local communities using the property tax more frequently in the nineteenth century, but the states were increasing their support of local schools. Even before Horace Mann had persuaded the legislature in Massachusetts to increase state support in the 1840s, Connecticut had sold her Western Reserve lands and put the receipts in a permanent school fund. States used a variety of techniques for raising school monies—the sale of public lands, property taxes, income taxes, and sales taxes.

KALAMAZOO HIGH SCHOOL

States continue to modify the ways school funds are raised. In recent years some have raised funds from lottery revenues or horse race receipts. States not only provide monies for schools, but they have the power to limit school budgets as well. For example, some states have placed a ceiling on the percentage that a local school district might increase its budget from one year to the next. If states do have tax limits, they may permit local communities to pass referenda to exceed the state-imposed ceiling.

Methods of Paying for Schooling

The various laws of the 50 states and the diverse financial situations of 16,000 school districts encourage a variety of methods of paying for schooling. Although states and districts seem ever-changing in their approaches to financing schools, there are many similarities. The constant interest in school finance is in part due to pressures from individual taxpayers and special interest groups claiming inequities in the system, and in part due to two perennial problems.

The first problem concerns the type of tax that is most commonly used to pay school costs—the property tax. At the local district level, an average of 90% of school funds raised locally come from property taxes. At the state level, about half of the funds returned to local districts are raised through property taxes. Most tax experts consider the property tax a regressive tax, i.e., it is increasingly *less* burdensome on the wealthy. Some feel that greater use should be made of income taxes or sales taxes.[29] Another aspect of the property tax is that it is based on the assessed value of property, which is a subjective determination. Property owners generally tend to feel that they are overtaxed and others are undertaxed.

The second major problem with financing schools is equalization. As previously discussed, there are widespread differences among local districts in the ability to raise funds. Such factors as the general economy, the geographical and economic givens of a region, and population shifts complicate the tax base of a district. In addition, some districts are willing to tax themselves at a higher rate than their neighbors.[30] What is a state to do with the great disparity among districts within its borders? Historically, states have tried to equalize educational funding rather than ignore the vast differences.

Major Funding Plans. Aware of these problems, states generally have used two methods to compensate for the differences in local school district expenditures. In 1977–78 about 60% of the states used a *foundation* plan. This guarantees a minimum annual amount to each district for each enrolled student (based on average daily attendance), regardless of the amount of tax money raised locally. The foundation plan does not include consideration of local district tax efforts. The rationale behind the foundation plan is that it is to the state's benefit to see that a minimal education is received by all children, and that the state can most easily do this by distributing funds to each district. While the states employing the foundation plan recognize the chief criticism that it exacerbates the differences between districts ("the rich get richer"), these states believe that there are too many complications if they begin to evaluate local district policies and tax procedures.

In practice the foundation plan is administered more firmly in some states than others. In 1977 the states that strictly followed the foundation plan included Arizona, Florida, Indiana, Iowa, Minnesota, New Mexico, North Dakota, South Carolina, Tennessee, Utah, and Washington. Some states, including California, Maine, Missouri, Montana, South Dakota, and Texas have so-called modified-foundation plans; the al-

lotment to the local district depends upon its tax base and to what extent the district exceeds what the state determines is the minimal education level.[31]

The second major funding program that states use is called *district power equalizing* (DPE). Colorado, Connecticut, Illinois, Kansas, Michigan, New Jersey, Ohio, and Wisconsin are among the states using this approach.[32] The heart of DPE is that local district differences, including local tax efforts, are taken into account by the state. The wealth of the district is noted, and richer districts will not be provided the same amount of money as the poorer districts.

The states not mentioned here have either variations of these approaches or some other form of funding. Hawaii is an exception, since it is a state system with just one district. Your instructor can provide information and details about school finance in your state.

Reforming School Finance Plans. In the 1970s at least half the states attempted reform of their plans for funding schools. The *Serrano* case in California (1971) was one of the earliest manifestations of concern in the courts about the inequity of the property tax for funding purposes. The State Supreme Court in California did not abolish the property tax, as some have thought, but mandated that the state legislature reconsider its application. Civil rights leaders hoped that the U.S. Supreme Court, in the 1973 *Rodriguez* case, would declare the property tax method unconstitutional because it discriminated against the poor. However, the high court held that education was not a fundamental right under the Constitution and that each state was responsible for determining its method of financing schools. With that verdict, reformers shifted their attention to the state courts and continued their efforts to change state laws. New Jersey courts ruled in the

Robinson case in 1973 that the system of financing education in that state violated the state constitution.[33]

The major reform to date has been the revision of the state aid formulas. A second reform in the 1970s was the increased recognition in financial aid programs of the students who require special education, compensatory education, or bilingual-bicultural education services. Florida, Indiana, New Mexico, and South Carolina have passed bills that add special funds for local districts having children with special needs. Illinois and Minnesota, to aid compensatory education programs, allocate greater dollar amounts per pupil as the number of poverty students increases in local districts.[34] (This is also the principle used in many of the federal ESEA programs.)

Due to inflation in the 1970s, some states have added features to their plans to keep educational revenue in line with rapidly changing local economies. Michigan, for example, provides additional state aid to school districts where tax rates for non-education items exceed the statewide school tax rate by more than 25%. Missouri has amended its formula for low-income districts to give them more of a tax break than the high-income districts. Florida has instituted a cost-of-living index in computing its tax rates.

One other attempt to reform the basic school-financing plans should be mentioned. It is based on the issue of alignment of government support for schools. Some advocates of reform argue that our system is archaic and grossly inefficient. They propose that the states take over the funding of schools, much as Hawaii has already done. This model is called the Full State Assumption plan. Others argue for a different form of realignment. The National Education Association, for one, believes that educational needs of the country would be served best if local, state, and federal revenues were equal (33% each). Critics

of these plans are concerned about the likely concomitant increase in state and federal control and the loss of local decision making.[35]

School Finance Problems: Today and Tomorrow

Inflation. Reductions in state aid. Collective bargaining. Declining enrollments. What school district today has not encountered at least one of these problems? This brief section examines some of the remedies that different types of districts are applying today to their particular financial problems, and closes with a financial issue likely to affect all parts of the nation—financial aid to nonpublic schools.

Urban Schools. Seven of 10 students in the country attend schools in what the census defines as an urban area. For practical purposes this includes both city and suburban areas. Metropolitan school districts have been severely crippled in recent years because of the cities' financial crises. New York City's near bankruptcy resulted in layoffs of teachers. Chicago's schools were closed by strikes when teachers missed several paychecks after that

Cartoon by Randy Glasbergen in *Phi Delta Kappan*, November 1977, p. 170. Reprinted with permission.

"That school budget deficit must be more serious than we thought. They just installed coin-operated teaching machines!"

city's schools could not get revenue bonds. Cleveland and St. Louis also experienced long strikes precipitated by urban economic issues. In both Ohio and Oregon, major city school systems decided to close school after Thanksgiving when they ran out of funds. (Bond issues repeatedly failed at the polls.) These schools were reopened in January after state funds were received.[36]

In these districts and in suburban districts experiencing declining enrollments, what other remedies have been tried? Anticipating that their enrollments will not rise for the foreseeable future, some districts attempted to solve their problems by reducing their teaching staffs, i.e., RIF—reduction in force. Others closed schools. Still others tried to keep schools open by consolidating old programs or adding new courses to allow for special interests. For example, special education classes for the talented and gifted are located in one building while previously offered science special interest classes are moved to a central location.[37]

Rural Schools. In the rural districts of the nation (over 40% of the districts have fewer than 600 students), declines in enrollment usually have resulted in teacher reductions. Some small districts try to remain independent as long as possible. State regulations usually specify a minimal curriculum, and to maintain that, as enrollments drop, the cost per student escalates. At some point, the economic disadvantages outweigh the advantages—such as personal attention to the individual students. Then consolidation, or school reorganization, is considered, although it is not a popular remedy.

The issue of the relationship between size of a district and a good curriculum is interesting since it often relates to educational costs. Some educational experts, like James Conant, have argued that a quality comprehensive high school requires a graduating class of at least 100 students. Those who favor consolidation believe that it provides more curricular opportunities at a reduced cost. A major study has found, however, that small districts can be as efficient and no more expensive to operate than the consolidated districts. At least one organization has been formed—PURE (Persons United for Rural Education)—to work with state legislatures and the federal government to maintain small districts.[38]

Aid to Nonpublic Schools. Our attention thus far has been focused on the financing of public schools. Considering the extent of nonpublic education, some mention should be made of the issue of public aid to nonpublic schools. You may have heard of "separation of church and state" and assumed that the matter of public funds going to nonpublic schools had been settled by the writers of the Constitution.

Not so. Nonpublic schools, primarily at the local level, have received public tax monies since the colonial era. State funds have gone to such schools for a variety of purposes since the mid-1800s. In *Cochran* v. *Louisiana State Board of Education* (1930), the U.S. Supreme Court ruled that textbooks could be provided to students in parochial schools because it would benefit the child rather than the school. This "child benefit" theory was extended in 1947 in the case of *Everson* v. *Board of Education*, when it was held that certain transportation costs for nonpublic students paid for by a public school district were legal.

To relieve the financial plight of nonpublic schools in their states, the Rhode Island and Pennsylvania legislatures attempted to bypass the restrictions of the First Amendment by purchasing secular services from private and parochial schools. Their plan was to reimburse the nonpublic schools for the teaching costs associated with secular subjects. In 1971, in *Lemon* v. *Kurtzman*, the U.S. Supreme Court declared such efforts illegal.

Where do things stand today? Many private schools receive federal funds, including monies for school lunch programs. Through the Elementary and Secondary Education Act of 1965, nonpublic schools have also received library books and the services of remedial specialists. Many state governments provide textbooks, and others cover transportation costs. Studies of support of parochial schools in 1968 and 1972 found that 14% of their revenues were from state funds.[39] More recently, the U.S. Supreme Court struck down a New Jersey law that had given taxpayers a tax deduction up to $1,000 for each child's tuition in a nonpublic elementary or secondary school. The U.S. Congress has debated a bill that would allow parents to receive a tax credit for their expenses in sending their children to nonpublic elementary and secondary schools. These cases and examples suggest that the matter of nonpublic aid from public tax sources will be more intensely debated. Some predict that if widespread funding of nonpublic education is permitted, public education, as we know it today, will collapse (see Chapter 15).

SUMMARY

America's school system is a massive enterprise, involving one of four persons in a direct way. The historic growth of the system is impressive by virtually any measure. Its size and scope, however, may be its major problem. Can a quality education be given to 50 million students in 16,000 school systems?

In examining enrollment figures, we learned that the percentage of the age group attending school is very high—much higher than a century ago. Yet it is disturbing to realize that about 25% of students do not finish secondary school. There are numerous reasons why students leave school, not all of which can be explained as the fault of the dropout. The question remains: Can or should society do more to prevent dropouts?

Education is a major investment in the United States. Educational expenditures constitute 7% to 8% of the GNP. The United States is among the leaders in terms of per pupil expenditures.

The proportions of federal, state, and local support for schools have been changing, with the state and federal levels increasing in recent years. The financial disparities among states and among districts have brought reform efforts in the funding of school programs. Over half the states have changed their systems in efforts to make them more equitable.

The complex matter of financing public schools and America's treatment of nonpublic schools are continual problems for our society as we try to balance educational costs against educational benefits.

NOTES

1. National Center for Education Statistics [hereafter cited as NCES], *The Condition of Education, 1979* (Washington, D.C.: U.S. Government Printing Office, 1979), p. 78. Some officials maintain that 10,000 school districts could efficiently manage the nation's schools.

2. Educational Research Service, *Bulletin*, April 1980, p. 4; NCES, *Digest of Education Statistics 1977–78* (Washington, D.C.: U.S. Government Printing Office, 1978), pp. 12, 34.

3. NCES, *The Condition of Education, 1978* (Washington, D.C.: U.S. Government Printing Office, 1978), pp. 82, 83. The Nebraska data is from a Nebraska State Department of Education Report, reported in the *Des Moines Register*, 17 July 1978.

4. Ben E. Graves, "The Decaying Schoolhouse," in *The Schoolhouse in the City*, ed. Alvin Toffler (New York: Praeger, 1968), pp. 61, 62.

5. NCES, *Digest*, p. 69; U.S. Bureau of the Census, *United States Statistical Abstract, 1979* (Washington, D.C.: U.S. Government Printing Office, 1979), p. 136.

6. Bureau of the Census, *Historical Statistics of the United States, Colonial Times to 1970* (Washington, D.C.: U.S. Government Printing Office, 1975), pp. 369, 379; NCES, *The Condition of Education, 1979*, p. 52.

Chapter Ten

7. NCES, *Condition of Education, 1978*, pp. 50, 92; NCES, *Digest*, p. 44.

8. Susan Abramowitz, *Declining Enrollment: The Challenge of the Coming Decade* (Washington, D.C.: National Institute of Education, 1978), pp. 47–61; National Education Association, *Research Memo: Population Trends and Their Implications for Association Planning, 1980* (Washington, D.C.: National Education Association, 1980), p. 4.

9. Census, *Historical Statistics*, pp. 368–69; NEA *Population Trends, 1980*, p. 7; NCES, *The Condition of Education, 1980*, p. 56.

10. NCES, *Projections of Education Statistics to 1986–87*, (Washington, D.C.: U.S. Government Printing Office, 1978) p. 9.

11. NCES, *The Condition of Education, 1978*, p. 260. For information on education in other countries, see Edmund King, *Other Schools and Ours*, 4th ed. (New York: Holt, Rinehart and Winston, 1974).

12. National PTA, "Where Have All the Students Gone?" a pamphlet issued by the National Office of the PTA, no date, c. 1976.

13. Michael S. Katz, *A History of Compulsory Education Laws* (Bloomington, Ind.: Phi Delta Kappa, 1976), pp. 17–18.

14. D. J. Chase, "Compulsory Attendance: Sense or Nonsense," *Nation's Schools* 93, no. 4 (Spring 1974): 41–43; Robert Everhart, "Compulsory Education, Not Compulsory Attendance," *National Association of Secondary School Principals Bulletin* 60, no. 396 (January 1976): 71–75.

15. NCES, *Condition of Education, 1978*, p. 22.

16. Lucius F. Cervantes, *The Dropout* (Ann Arbor: University of Michigan Press, 1965); Solomon Lichter et al., *The Drop-outs* (New York: Free Press, 1962); Daniel Schreiber, *The School Dropout* (Washington, D.C.: National Education Association, 1964). Delbert S. Elliott and Harwin L. Voss, *Delinquency and Dropout* (Lexington, Mass.: Lexington Books, 1974).

17. Examples of some successful remedial programs include: "70001: Caring for Dropouts," *School and Community* 64, no. 7 (March 1978): 12, 13, a program providing students with part-time jobs; "Program Lifeline of the Real World," *American Education* 14, no. 1 (January/February 1978): 35ff, a program for young Spanish women.

18. NCES, *Condition of Education, 1978*, p. 166.

19. Ibid., p. 85.

20. NCES, *The Condition of Education, 1980* (Washington, D.C.: U.S. Government Printing Office, 1980), pp. 36, 38.

21. NCES, *Condition of Education, 1978*, p. 41; NCES, *The Condition of Education, 1976* (Washington, D.C.: U.S. Government Printing Office, 1976), p. 173.

22. NCES, *Condition of Education, 1979*, pp. 146, 147.

23. NCES, *Condition of Education, 1979*, p. 164.

24. For an overview of budget breakdowns, see Charles S. Benson, *The Economics of Public Education* (Boston: Houghton Mifflin, 1961), pp. 475–502.

25. Charles S. Benson, *The Economics of Public Education*, 3rd ed. (Boston: Houghton Mifflin, 1978), pp. 203–17.

26. Ibid., pp. 212–15.

27. Aaron Alexander, "Why Go to College," a pamphlet published by the New York State United Teachers/American Federation of Teachers, 1979, pp. 10, 11; Joe L. Johns and Edgar L. Morphet, *The Economics and Financing of Education*, 3rd ed. (Englewood Cliffs, N.J.: Prentice-Hall, 1975), pp. 95–96; Howard R. Bowen, *Investment in Learning: The Individual and Social Value of American Higher Education* (San Francisco: Jossey-Bass Publishers, 1977).

28. Herbert H. Hyman et al., *The Enduring Effects of Education* (Chicago: University of Chicago Press, 1975), compares the attitudes and behaviors of various students in terms of knowledge of public affairs, television viewing habits, interest in politics, etc., as indices of the values of education; see also NCES, *Condition of Education, 1979*, p. 32.

29. Charles Benson and Thomas A. Shannon, *Schools Without Property Taxes: Hope or Illusion?* (Bloomington, Ind.: Phi Delta Kappa, 1972).

30. Tax effort is essentially the degree of commitment that a local district is willing to make to finance its governmental programs. Contrary to popular belief, poor districts (i.e., those with lower tax bases) often make a greater tax effort than rich districts. That is, the assessed value of property in poorer districts is less, but even though they may tax themselves at higher rates than wealthier districts (i.e., make a greater tax effort), their total revenues will be lower.

31. Educational Finance Center, Education Commission of the States, *School Finance Reform in the States: 1978* (Boulder, Colo.: Education Commission of the States, June 1978), p. vii.

32. James Guthrie, *Equality in School Financing: District Power Equalizing* (Bloomington, Ind.: Phi Delta Kappa, 1975).

33. David C. Long, "Litigation Concerning Educational Finance," *The Courts and Education*, ed. Clifford P. Hooker, 77th Yearbook of the National Society for the Study of Education, Part I (Chicago: National Society for the Study of Education, 1978), pp. 217–47.

34. Education Commission, *School Finance Reform*, pp. vii-x.

35. Charles Benson, *Equity in School Financing: Full State Funding* (Bloomington, Ind.: Phi Delta Kappa, 1975); Phi Delta Kappa, *Financing The Public Schools: A Search for Equality* (Bloomington, Ind.: Phi Delta Kappa, 1973), pp. 42–44.

36. Casey Banas, "The Chicago School Finance Catastrophe," *Phi Delta Kappan* 61, no. 8 (April 1980): 519–22.

37. David L. Martin, "RIF: Out of a Job, Out of Teaching," *Learning* 5, no. 8 (April 1977): 22–28; William F. Keough, *Declining Enrollments: A New Dilemma for*

Educators (Bloomington, Ind.: Phi Delta Kappa, 1978).
38. James B. Conant, *The American High School Today* (New York: McGraw-Hill, 1959), pp. 37–38, 77–85; Jonathan P. Sher, *Education in Rural America* (Boulder, Colo.: Westview Press, 1977).

39. George A. Kelly, *Government Aid to Nonpublic Schools: Yes or No?* (New York: St. John's University Press, 1972), p. 8; Daniel J. Sullivan, *Public Aid to Nonpublic Schools* (Toronto: Lexington Books, 1974), pp. 22–24.

FOR FURTHER STUDY

Adibe, Nasrine, and Stone, Frank A. eds. *Expanding Dimensions of World Education.* Storrs, Conn.: World Education Project, 1976.

Burrup, Percy E. *Financing Education in a Climate of Change*, 2nd ed. Boston: Allyn and Bacon, 1977.

Cohn, Elchanan. *The Economics of Education.* Cambridge, Mass.: Ballinger Publishing Co., 1979.

Dersh, Rhoda E. *The School Budget: It's Your Money; It's Your Business.* Columbus, Md.: National Committee for Citizens in Education, 1979.

Garms, Walter. *School Finance: The Economics and Politics of Public Education.* Englewood Cliffs, N.J.: Prentice-Hall, 1978.

Squires, Gregory D. *Education and Jobs: The Imbalancing of the Social Machinery.* New Brunswick, N.J.: Transaction Books, 1979.

Willett, Edward J., et al. *Modernizing the Little Red Schoolhouse: The Economics of Improved Education.* Englewood Cliffs, N.J.: Educational Technology Publications, 1979.

Woodring, Paul. *A Fourth of a Nation.* New York: McGraw-Hill, 1957.

11

Educational Goals

The schools of America are the temples of a living democracy.

Angelo Patri

The correct concern for a school is not education or preparation for later life, but the present lives of children.

George Dennison

The chapters you have read in Part 3 have emphasized how the educational system has evolved, how it is controlled, and how it is financed. The remaining two chapters shift gears in that they stress how American schools change—how they set their goals and modify their curriculum.

As a veteran of schooling and a teacher education candidate, you probably have given some thought to how you would like to improve the system if and when you have the chance. Think of your future role in terms of a movie producer making a sequel to *The Graduate*, in which Dustin Hoffman played a person who had accumulated course credits and a degree, but who had no purpose in life. If you become a teacher, you will have the chance to produce many "graduates." You will not be doing it alone; indeed, there will be many others influencing how the graduates come out. Like the movie producer, you will be hearing about what the public wants; others will advise you on keeping costs at a minimum; still others will be telling you to do your job in different ways. It is imperative that you do gain a clear perspective on *what* you think the graduates of tomorrow should be like—what knowledge they should have, what attitudes and values they should hold, what skills they should gain.

Chapter Eleven

The information in Chapter 11 will guide you toward reaching some of your conclusions about the goals of education. Specifically, it will ask you: In what ways is the public contented with what schools are doing? In what ways is it not pleased? What are the goals that the public and professional educators have set? How are these goals translated into classroom objectives? How are conflicting goals resolved?

As you consider these questions, you will be formulating your answer to the issue that permeates the chapter: What are schools for? For some, the answer is summed up in the word socialization. For others, education means growth and personal fulfillment of individuals. Still others believe schools should not be concerned about social adjustment, but only provide academic skills for students. Can it be only one of these goals? To what extent can the school provide both a broad-based education and vocational training?

After you have read Chapter 11, you should be able to (1) formulate five goals you hold for American education; (2) describe the needs assessment process; and (3) explain the terms *accountability* and *cognitive*, *affective*, and *psychomotor objectives*.

THE PUBLIC'S ATTITUDES TOWARD SCHOOLING

You may have the impression that there is widespread dissatisfaction with schools. But is that an accurate perception? In the past decade, for example, can we say that there was more criticism than praise of schooling policies and practices? It is difficult to determine.

What is easier to state is that throughout history, there have been critics of the school, although few of them have made systematic evaluations of the schools be-

fore launching their attacks. One who did was a New York pediatrician, Joseph M. Rice, who wrote one of the first extensive evaluations of American schools. His articles appeared in *Forum* magazine in 1892–93. After examining 36 city systems and 1,200 teachers, Rice reported that schools offered poor instruction and were controlled too often by political leaders.[1]

Interviewing the public about their attitudes toward the public school is a more recent phenomenon. Since 1969 the Gallup poll has conducted an annual survey of the public's attitudes toward the public schools.[2] This section relies mainly upon the evidence gathered from the Gallup polls.

The Schools Compared to Other Institutions

Before seeing how the public views various aspects of schooling, we should consider how people rate the school in comparison with other social service agencies. As Figure 11–1 reveals, the public believes that schools are providing more adequate services than they are receiving from public transportation, hospitals and health clinics, and fire and police protection. Moreover, Figure 11–1 indicates the importance of schools. If schools were inadequate, a higher percentage of people would move as a result than if other community services were poor quality.

When asked if they would pay higher taxes to improve services from various institutions, one-third of all Americans said they would be willing to pay *more* taxes for improved services from schools, more than for any other agency mentioned. In 1980, the public's confidence in the school ranked second only to the church (and ahead of the courts, local, state, and national governments, labor unions and business). Another indicator of the respect for schools is the amount of confidence the public has in educators. Leaders in edu-

Figure 11–1.
The schools compared to other institutions

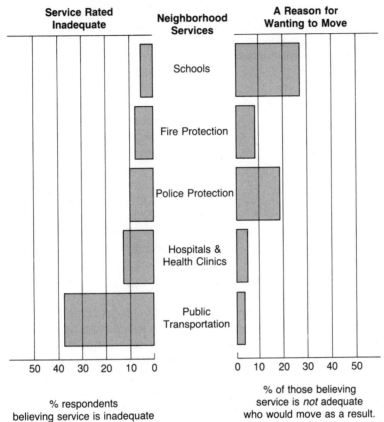

% respondents
believing service is inadequate

% of those believing
service is *not* adequate
who would move as a result.

From the National Center for Education Statistics, *The Condition of Education,*
1978 (Washington, D.C.: U.S. Government Printing Office, 1978), pp. 10–11.

cation, when compared with a group of professionals and service occupation personnel in a 1977 poll, ranked second only to medical professionals.[3]

How School Policies and Practices Rate

The public is generally positive about what schools do, and the public indicates that it would be willing to help the local schools. Ninety percent of the respondents indicate they would be willing to work on citizen advisory groups for the schools. With some exceptions, to be discussed later, the public believes the school is offering an adequate curriculum. It is interesting to note that respondents who have the most contact with schools—parents of public school students—have the most confidence in the schools. According to researcher Ned Hubbell, the lack of confidence among those who have little contact with schools is due to an "information gap." They do not know how schools are financed, and they may not even know the names of school administrators, much less understand how school policies are set and implemented. Citing the projection that by 1990 one of every five Americans will be 55 or older, Hubbell implies that there is likely to be less support for school programs in the future, because more individuals will be less familiar with their day-to-day activities.[4]

The public's confidence in schooling has been dropping in the past few years, but is still strong, according to the Gallup polls. Since 1974, respondents have been asked this question: "If the public schools were graded for quality of their work, just as students are, what grade would you give them—A, B, C, D, or Fail?" Following are the national averages:

	1974	1976	1978	1980
		(percentages)		
A rating	18	13	9	10
B rating	30	29	27	25
C rating	21	28	30	29
D rating	6	10	11	12
Fail	5	6	8	6
Don't know	20	14	15	18

An analysis of the responses indicates that the lowest ratings of public schools come from parents who send their children to private or parochial schools. Northern blacks give schools the worst ratings of all: 33% believe public schools deserve D's or F's.[5]

One of the most publicized findings of the annual Gallup poll is the ranking of problems facing the public schools. In all but one year, lack of discipline has been mentioned as the chief problem. Other major difficulties have included integration, finances, drugs, and getting good teach-

ers. Apparent concern over declining test scores and the interest in back-to-basics resulted in poor curriculum reaching third place in the list of problems in the 1980 survey.[6]

There are inherent problems in analysis of the data. First, what do the terms mean? Can we be sure that those interviewed have a common understanding of "lack of discipline" or "poor curriculum"? The answer is no, because the interviewers do not explain the terms. Another caveat is the overemphasis upon the negative findings. For example, in no year have more than 30% of the respondents stated that discipline is a problem. Does that mean that 70% or more feel that discipline is adequate in their schools?

Are the innovative efforts of the public school generally supported by its patrons? The Gallup polls suggest that the public wants the schools to change their curricula from time to time. A majority of respondents encourage career education, moral education, and programs to help parents understand what their children are experiencing in schools. Another poll indicates that resistance to desegregated education is lessening in the North as well as in the South. Two innovations not supported by the public in the 1970s were child-care centers held on school premises and early leaving plans whereby students could

From *Newsday*, 7 February 1980. ©1980, Archie Comic Publications, Inc. Reprinted with permission.

ARCHIE

graduate early if all requirements were met.[7]

Parents and citizens are very concerned about declining standardized test scores. Most people are not convinced by explanations that point to different types of tests or the different composition of student bodies today from those of 20 years ago. The public, by a 2-to-1 margin, believes that standardized tests are correctly measuring a decline in the quality of education—a point of view not shared by many educators. Interestingly, 58% of elementary students and 45% of secondary students do not think their homework is hard enough. The decline in performance, according to the public, is not so much the fault of the school as lack of parental concern and "too much television."[8]

On balance, the public seems satisfied with what the school as an institution is doing, although there are some disquieting signs that it is growing less content. Obviously, individual communities may have greater or lesser confidence in their public schools.

GOALS FOR SCHOOLS

Polls of attitudes toward education usually focus on public reactions to what *is* being done by the schools. As we have just noted, the public generally approves what the schools are doing. But *what* does the public want the schools to do? The 1979 Gallup poll included a section on the ideal school, which revealed the following requirements: state board examinations for new teachers; periodic reexaminations for all teachers; strict discipline; curriculum emphasizing the basics; more homework as well as more in-school assignments; better school-home-community interaction; more career guidance; and more meetings to inform the public of school programs. It is interesting to compare these sentiments

with the findings of sociologist Wilbur Brookover in 1955. It was his opinion that Americans had developed seven expectations, or functions, of schools. The public school is to provide vocational training, instruct students in the basic skills, transmit accepted cultural values, train socially adjusted persons, demonstrate methods for social mobility, cure social problems, and be a source of entertainment.[9]

Brookover did not say that the schools would achieve all of these goals; in fact, he intimated that these were the ideals, and that in various periods in American life, the American public would rank these functions differently. Some of his seven functions need further explanation. To train socially adjusted persons is another way of saying the schools are expected to socialize individuals. Critics like Jerry Farber and Jonathan Kozol argue that socialization is a polite word for indoctrination. (See Chapter 15.) That the nation uses the schools to try to cure social ills was demonstrated in Chapter 8; when we have a problem—whether it's a sexual revolution, drug abuse, large numbers of highway fatalities, or a war—we are likely to turn to the schools to prepare citizens to cope with the problem. Brookover's final point requires only a brief comment. The local school, especially in small towns and rural districts, is often the cultural center of the area, the place where community identity is preserved through athletic teams, plays, and special events.

Few would dispute that the schools in America are expected to meet these seven functions today. Which ones are met and in what priority, reflect the public's philosophies of education.

Philosophies of Education

Developing a philosophy of education is valuable because it can have a great impact upon schooling practices. Your philosophy as a teacher, coupled with that of the school district, will influence what goals are set for pupils, what subjects are emphasized, what methods of instruction are used, and what types of evaluation are employed. For some individuals, philosophy has little value because it raises more questions than it answers. At its best, philosophical inquiry helps discern truth from falsehood, and meritorious views from the frivolous. Philosophy can serve as a road map of the best routes to take on intellectual journeys and social missions.

We urge you now to continue to develop your philosophy of education. A good way to begin is to look briefly at four popular philosophies of education. This introduction to the four diverse ways of looking at schools is not intended to be more than a cursory treatment of these philosophies. Note that there are some similarities between the philosophies and the learning theories discussed in Chapter 6, where the emphasis was upon *how*, not *what*, students learn. Finally, there is an additional link between what you will read here and what will be covered in Chapter 15, where we discuss some of the ideas of critics of education.

It makes the most sense to treat these philosophies in chronological sequence. That way you will understand what one generation of educators was trying to reform. Each description opens with general educational beliefs that arise from the philosophy, then treats some of the ideas of proponents of that philosophy, provides some specific examples of classroom practices consistent with the philosophy, and closes with comments showing how it compares and contrasts with the other points of view.

From "Children," a Pictorial Archive from 19th Century Sources. Dover Publications, Inc., New York.

What subjects, if any, should all students be required to take?

Perennialism. The roots of perennialism go back to ancient Greece and the ideas of Plato and Socrates. They averred that:

- Truth remains the same (i.e., perennial or everlasting). Reality is universal; it is everywhere and at the same moment the same.

- Life is purposive. There is meaning to life. Each person, like an acorn growing into an oak, has a destiny, and it is the responsibility of the teacher to help the individual find his or her purpose in life.

- Teaching students to recognize the truth can best be done through disciplined study. To discover the meaning of life and what purposes their lives have, students must study the great books of the past to see how others have attempted to solve the mystery of life.

- Basic curriculum will include the study of and practice in making ethical decisions.

- The goal of education is the development of rational powers.

- An educational program as just described is not meant for everyone. Its academic demands may result in society's producing an intellectual elite.

A favorite technique of Socrates and Plato was to ask their students question after question, constantly forcing them to justify their beliefs and actions. Thomas Aquinas, a medieval Catholic priest trying to prove the existence of God, developed a metaphysical justification for the church. His system of reasoning encouraged an educational system that relied heavily upon logical analysis. In the twentieth century, Robert M. Hutchins, who was president of the University of Chicago, advocated a classical curriculum that would be considered perennialist. All of these philosophers would argue that if truth is eternal, then the task for human beings is to develop reasoning skills to understand the truth. Learners must attempt to solve such problems as the nature of being and causality. To engage in this search for meaning, students must learn how to examine syllogisms (through deduction) and postulate theories (through induction).

For the perennialists, the primary purpose of schools should be the building of skills in mental discipline. Logical analysis and abstract thinking are prized. Memorization and drill are good instructional techniques. In elementary schools, perennialists would ask that grammar, logic, and rhetoric—what we would call communication skills today—be emphasized. At the secondary level, the sciences, history, geography, and foreign languages would be stressed. Literature would be taught through use of classics. Since not all students are interested in or have the capability for the necessary degree of intellectual study, schools should provide two types of curriculum—general education and vocational. The goal of education, the perennialists would conclude, is preparation for life, and the function of the school is to provide students with the tools so that they can make personal decisions about vocations and participation in society.[10]

Perennialism today is attacked on two grounds. It is considered outdated; that is, few believe that the world is ordered in the same way that the medieval scholars saw it. In the minds of many, technology has brought a new world that does not have the same values as the world of the past. The second argument is that perennialism is elitist, in that it implies that there is a higher form of knowledge available to the chosen few, which results in most students taking a more practically based (vocational) curriculum that is inferior. This attitude, it is argued, runs counter to the democratic principle of equality of opportunity for all.

Essentialism. In the Middle Ages, opposition to the perennialist point of view began to develop. In part it stemmed from an attempt to free philosophical inquiry from presuming a divine origin to life. A growing number of philosophers could not accept the concept that truth could not be modified. Gradually a new philosophic outlook arose on these presuppositions:

- We should learn from the past, and it is therefore important to transmit the ideas of culture to the new generation.

- There are basic subjects to be taught, but this core curriculum may vary from one generation to another.

- It is better to have a curriculum that is organized by disciplines than issues or students' interests.

- Individuals and societies have an obligation to search for truths that are the foundations of life. These truths may be natural or divine.

- The chief goal of education should be mastery of basic academic knowledge and rational skills so that students can become contributing members of society.

- Students should also have vocational guidance.

Essentialism developed two branches—idealism and realism. Idealism underscores the importance of being: How do we know what really *is*? Idealists conclude that only what the self discovers to be real is true. The realists argue that there are truths that some individuals will not correctly perceive. The goal of knowledge is to learn what are the accurate concepts of life and what are the precise relationships between facts.[11]

In the 1930s, essentialists were active in the country, in part due to their reaction to the growing popularity of progressivism. Essentialists believed there were absolutes to be promoted, and they wanted more attention paid to cognitive learning processes and mastery of certain subject matters. Leaders such as William Bagley

and Harry Broudy pressed for a sequential, systematic curriculum that would promote a democratic way of life. Unlike the perennialists, they believed that the curriculum of past generations could be changed. However, it was necessary for society to agree on what was essential for the present day. Critics of essentialism pointed out that the essentialists tended to bequeath an irrelevant culture based on questionable natural and divine laws.

Today the Council for Basic Education is the leading group espousing this philosophy. Its literature reveals a concern about both the lack of formal training in basic communication skills (much as the perennialists would be upset) and excessive attention to personal adjustment (building a good self-concept and happy peer relationships). Although the council does not like to be labeled as a prime example of a back-to-basics proponent, its members would agree with some of the criticisms by such advocates. For example, they favor more rigorous spelling and reading programs. Also, they favor a broad-based education, but not the heavy use of behavioral objectives and competency programs some schools use today. They believe these are too mechanistic.[12]

Progressivism. In the seventeenth and eighteenth centuries an increasing number of philosophers challenged one of the key tenets of perennialism and essentialism—that education begins with subject matter. Writers such as Jean Jacques Rosseau were convinced that the person was the starting point of learning. Those who became known as progressives believed that:

- The curriculum should be built upon students' interests rather than the traditional disciplines.

- The major goal of education is to teach rational problem-solving skills to pupils to enable them to become contributing citizens.

- Schools must teach social values as well as individual values.

- The future will be better than the past.

- People can learn from mistakes, and societies can be improved. (Life is not merely cyclical.)

- Learning must take into account the whole child, i.e., his or her needs as well as his or her interests.

- Learning by doing, i.e., experiential activities, is the most effective method of instruction.

According to this philosophy, change is inevitable and therefore it is incumbent upon individuals to open themselves constantly to self-analysis and their societies to continual reflection of shifting values and priorities. Absolutes and, to a large extent, authorities, are rejected. Progressivism is closely aligned with two other philosophical positions, pragmatism and experimentalism, which hold that ideas are meaningless unless they make a difference in individual and group experience. In other words, knowledge is not possible apart from consequences.

Progressivism is often misunderstood when it is applied to education. Critics have accused progressivism, and its foremost advocate, John Dewey, of promoting a child-centered curriculum that ignored the findings of the past. Dewey did not reject the study of history, geography, and the sciences. He argued that the teacher must be flexible enough to take into account where the students were, in terms of knowledge and interests, as they structured the learning experience.

One of the best illustrations of Dewey's point of view was the work of a teacher in a New York school in the 1930s. Learning that her students had spent much time with boats in the summer, the teacher planned a curriculum that touched on the

design of boats, cargos that ships carried, what propelled boats, and the uses of boats. As the students engaged in projects from building model boats to presenting plays about famous voyages, they obviously were exposed to numerous traditional disciplines.[13]

Progressives believe that education is life. Said another way, what happens in the classroom should be as similar to everyday life as possible. To teach mathematics, for example, some progressive schools built model grocery stores. The students would buy canned goods, learning numbers through the counting of the change they received from the store clerks.

The excesses of some progressive educators brought discredit to the term *progressive* by the 1950s; it was associated with being too *permissive*. Many instructional practices that progressives devised, however, are still used by teachers. Interest corners and display areas that students construct, field trips and discussion groups are just a few. An emphasis upon arts and crafts, the performing arts, and such new subjects as sex education are also linked to progressive education.

Reconstructionism. Some philosophers acknowledge the effort of the progressives to make the educational process more active, but they believe that the fatal flaw in all three philosophies is that their purpose is to help students adjust to the world *as it is*. The reconstructionists hold that:

- It is better to be future oriented than past oriented.

- A world culture is more important than nationalism (especially in this nuclear age).

- People must be ready to transform society thoroughly (including engaging in revolution if need be).

- The goal of education should be a new social order founded on democratic principles.

Chapter Eleven

In the twentieth century American experience, reconstructionism is an extension of progressivism. Like progressivism, it believes in the importance of experience. A number of its leaders, such as Theodore Brameld and George Counts, find much of value in the Judeo-Christian tradition.[14] Because of their belief in the need to reform society, however, there is much emphasis upon the social sciences in the curriculum. In schools where a reconstructionist philosophy has been adopted, efforts are made to have a student population reflecting cultures from around the world. Many of the classroom implications of reconstructionism are similar to progressivism. There is much classroom interaction between teacher and students, and students with each other. As much as possible, the community is used for field trips, speakers, and resource help. The emphasis of the curriculum is upon action.

This discussion is meant to raise questions about the structure of education, or what should be taught. Our key assumption is that what you believe about human nature (Is it essentially good or bad?), reality (Are there absolutes?), ends (What gives meaning to life?), and what should be taught, can and will make an impact on your classroom. Quite understandably, you may feel that you have much to learn about one or more of these philosophies. If so, Activity 11–1 will help clarify some of your questions as you formulate your personal philosophy of education. Even if you do not do the activity, you should test yourself now. Can you formulate five goals you think are important to have in education? Can you justify their inclusion over other goals?

ACTIVITY 11–1
Education for ?

Using the sources below, or the references cited in the "Notes" and the "For Further Study" sections, explore either a philosophy of education or the position of one philosopher.

Write a short statement summarizing the major points of the philosophy. Be sure to include several illustrations of its educational implications.

Green, Thomas. *Work, Leisure, and the American Schools.* New York: Random House, 1968.
Monson, Charles H., Jr., ed. *Education for What?* Boston: Houghton Mifflin, 1970.
Park, Joe, ed. *Selected Readings in the Philosophy of Education*, 4th ed. New York: Macmillan Publishing Co., 1974.
Phenix, Philip, ed. *Philosophies of Education.* New York: John Wiley and Sons, 1961.
Phenix, Philip. *Realms of Meaning.* New York: McGraw-Hill, 1964.
Schroder, Harold M.; Karlins, Marvin; and Phares, Jacqueline O. *Education for Freedom.* New York: John Wiley, 1973.
Ulich, Robert, ed. *Three Thousand Years of Educational Wisdom.* Cambridge, Mass.: Harvard University Press, 1963.

Goals and Objectives Statements

Eventually a general philosophy of education must be reduced to specific tasks for instructional purposes. While some educators use the terms *goals* and *objectives* interchangeably, more commonly *goals* refers to long-range outcomes that a school system or a national organization (such as the PTA or NEA) might expect students to achieve. *Objectives* are usually the short-range, very specific changes teachers expect students to make. A school district, for example, may set as a goal, "Students will learn how to communicate effectively." An objective of a senior high English class in that district may be, "Students will be able to write a letter applying for a job."

Those who want individual districts, states, and national groups to set goals and teachers to plan objectives believe this is valuable for many reasons. The goal-setting process requires input from many individuals, which helps clarify the purposes of the school for its patrons. Research studies indicate that students appreciate teachers who provide clear objectives, and that teachers are more comfortable when they know what the district expects them to accomplish in the classroom.[15]

There are critics of these efforts, especially of the attempts to formulate long-range goals. The critics argue that such statements are often vague, although positive. Who, for example, is opposed to schools promoting "good health," or building "student self-concepts," or encouraging "a democratic way of life"? Such statements are frequently found in national pronouncements and individual school district literature, but they are rarely spelled out. Another problem with goal setting is that, in the short-range teacher objectives, too much stress is placed on measurable results. In turn, questions can be raised about whether the specific objectives are related to the goals statements. What often results is a disproportionate number of objectives on minor academic skills and very few related to attitudinal outcomes such as "appreciates literature" or "has an interest in science." Another criticism is that goal statements usually are so general that they are irrelevant to local situations.[16]

Students, as well as their parents, like to know what is expected in the classroom. That can be one reason why some educators advise teachers to share objectives with learners.

Historical Goals Statements. Probably the most famous statement of educational goals developed in this century was "the seven cardinal principles" of a National Education Association committee in 1918.[17] The seven goals included good health, command of fundamental process (what we would call the basics), worthy home membership, vocational direction, citizenship, worthy use of leisure, and ethical character.

In 1938, the Educational Policies Commission of the National Education Association released another statement of goals, *The Purposes of Education in American Democracy*.[18] The writers of the report tried to be specific, to the point of illustrating what was intended by each of four major goals. The goals, with two illustrations each, were—

- *Self-realization.* The educated person

has an appetite for learning, i.e., an inquiring mind. The educated person appreciates beauty, i.e., displays aesthetic interest.

- *Good human relationships.* The educated person enjoys a rich, sincere, and varied social life (friendships). The educated person observes the amenities of social behavior (courtesy).

- *Economic efficiency.* The educated producer knows the satisfaction of good workmanship (work). The educated consumer is an informed and skillful buyer (efficiency in buying).

- *Civic responsibility.* The educated citizen is sensitive to the disparities of human circumstance (social justice). The educated citizen has defenses against propaganda (critical judgment).

In the wake of World War II, there were more statements on educational goals. Some educators promoted what came to be called the *life adjustment* movement. They were concerned that young men and women needed strong academic programs, but they believed that more emphasis should be placed upon relating the curriculum to everyday life. Their publications called for greater attention to career preparation and more aid to students in preparing to be heads of families. One widely circulated report in the 1950s urged the schools to give more attention to moral and spiritual values.[19]

The historical statements of this century focus on preserving a democratic way of life, adjusting to the world of work, improving the family, and gaining basic academic skills. In short, there is a remarkable consistency in the statements—a consistency that seems repeated in recent statements. As the critics note, however, such statements are vague, and we may wonder how helpful they are.

Current Goals Statements. Various state departments of education, colleges and universities, local districts, and national organizations develop goals statements for their constituents in the belief that such efforts will improve instruction. For example, in 1976 Pennsylvania issued a statement on 10 goals of quality education. The University of California at Los Angeles, through its Center for the Study of Evaluation, has prepared an instrument that helps local units determine their educational priorities. A fraternity for educational professionals, Phi Delta Kappa, has prepared a list of 18 goals, which numerous districts have used to assess their future plans.[20]

The NEA formed a new committee in 1976 to reexamine its 1918 list of seven cardinal principles and to ask what changes might make the statement relevant today. The committee concluded that safety and ecology should be stressed as functions of good health; that command of fundamental processes should be expanded to include skills in humanistic interactions, skills in using computers, and an understanding of political power; that worthy home membership should include awareness of new roles for women and an expanded definition—worthy *family* membership; and that citizenship should include an appreciation of world cultures.[21]

Types of Objectives. As stated earlier, short-range goals are often called objectives. For many educators, objectives refer to observable behaviors of students in the classroom or school setting. Beginning in the 1950s, Benjamin Bloom and others developed taxonomies of cognitive, affective, and psychomotor objectives.[22] (A taxonomy is a system of classification, from the simplest to the most complex.) Bloom acknowledged that separating cognitive processes from the affective realm, or the psychomotor from the affective, did not imply that the three domains are entirely separate. They do overlap. Bloom and his associates argued that in education, especially in the cognitive domain, different intellectual tasks or levels of knowledge could be identified. Recalling an historical date is not as difficult as being able to apply a theory to new data. Similarly, formulating a hypothesis from what appears to be unrelated data is more complex than restating a concept in one's own words.

Just as in the cognitive domain, so in the affective domain of feelings, emotions, attitudes, and values, there is a similar ladder of difficulty. It is easy to be willing to listen to a new form of music; it is more difficult to spend one's money to buy records or tapes. A student may learn to appreciate a poet's style, but it is a greater challenge to write verse that imitates the master. One level in the affective domain (valuing) implies that a student may join a group (possibly an interest club in the school) that offers some of the things that the student likes. When the student becomes a leader in the club, sharing the group's philosophy with others, he or she has moved to the next highest level (organization).

Psychomotor skills involve some physical dexterity. For example, the home economics student must know how to blend ingredients properly or roll a pie crust. The swimmer or golfer must put together a series of movements to achieve greater speed and/or power. The industrial arts student must master certain competencies to operate a drill press or lathe properly. Teachers in this area will usually tie their objectives to a level of competence (degree of accuracy or speed).

While there is much acceptance of classroom teachers' planning ahead, even to the point of using objectives, there is still debate over *behavioral* objectives. Writing objectives may help teachers organize their material better, and it may help students understand what is expected in their courses, but are all worthwhile outcomes of education observable? Can teachers tell when

a student appreciates the scientific method or establishes better peer relationships? Far too often, the critics contend, the use of objectives is too time-consuming, far too specific about minor points, and artificial (separating the cognitive, affective, and psychomotor areas).

MEETING AND CHANGING GOALS

However worthy and well-stated educational goals are, they will need revision from time to time. Teachers will want to modify their objectives periodically. But what about the public? What if the community believes that the school's program needs revitalization? What is the process to change the goals to produce a better educational program? Such questions are discussed below through the consideration of the accountability movement, the introduction of needs assessment in the schools, and a brief look at how other methods are used to change the system.

Accountability

In the late 1960s, due in part to the increasing costs of education and in part to a negative response to student protests, more and more citizens asked what the schools were accomplishing. Parents and taxpayers wanted to hold school systems accountable. They expected schools to teach the types of courses and values mentioned in the previous section, and they asked for more instruction in the basics (see Chapter 12). They were upset with declining standardized test scores, and they increasingly criticized teachers. There are two sides to the coin of accountability: one dimension is *what* curriculum the community wants; the other is *how well* teachers and administrators are transmitting the curriculum to the students.

Almost every state now has a law that, in theory, ensures accountability to the pa-

Chapter Eleven

trons of a district. The states vary, as usual, in the way accountability is obtained, but these are the essential steps: the public tells school officials what types of knowledge, skills, and attitudes it wishes the district to teach students; the district sets the goals and resulting objectives; and an evaluation measures how effectively the goals were achieved. This approach to implementing new goals in the schools seems quite reasonable. Accountability, however, has promoted two phenomena: malpractice suits against teachers, and censorship cases. Teacher organizations and professional educators respond to the matter of accountability with the reaction that their academic freedom is often infringed upon, that the public does not realize how complex education is, and that success depends upon many variables.

Before examining in detail the malpractice and censorship issues, we should consider some of the arguments, pro and con, regarding accountability. Proponents argue that it reinstates the proper relationship between the home and the school, i.e., teachers and administrators will become more responsive to the needs of the community. It promotes better instruction since teachers will prepare lessons more carefully to meet the desired goals and objectives at the appropriate age and ability levels. Moreover, there will be improved communication between teachers in the same system, as they promote students from grade to grade. Duplications of materials and concepts will be reduced. Finally, accountability counters the excuse used by some teachers and administrators that the home, and not the school, has more responsibility for what children learn. Teachers must be willing to earn their pay and not blame their failures on the home.[23]

Accountability is another simple answer to a complex problem, critics respond. Learning is a continuous process, and it

Cartoon by Randy Glasbergen in *Phi Delta Kappan*, March 1979, p. 526. Reprinted with permission.

"He fell in the hall. I kissed his boo-boo. That didn't make it feel any better. Now he wants to sue me for malpractice."

is extremely difficult to isolate and measure the effectiveness of specific units of instruction. Team teaching, or the fact that a secondary level teacher has a student for only one period a day, compounds the problems. Several arguments relate to academic freedom. Consider that teachers are unlike professionals such as doctors and lawyers, who have clear control over what they prescribe for their patients or advise their clients. Frequently, teachers must follow state-mandated curriculum guides or use a textbook adopted by their school systems. Attempts to identify what teachers have accomplished have resulted in greater use of standardized tests, a questionable pedagogical practice. If teachers perceive that they are evaluated on the basis of their students' reaching specific objectives, they are likely to concentrate on minimal objectives that are the most easily measured (simple recall items or easy psychomotor skills). Moreover, such tests do not measure affective objectives. Finally, educators insist that it is unfair to hold them accountable for all or most school failures. It is virtually impossible to force people to learn.[24]

Some parents, feeling that their children have not had a proper education, have filed lawsuits. The most notable case involved Peter Doe (pseudonym), a student in San Francisco. He had been granted a high school diploma, but his parents discovered that their son did not have sufficient writing skills to fill out a job application, nor sufficient reading skills to comprehend the simplest questions on job questionnaires. The parents filed suit against the superintendent of schools of San Francisco and the school board members (not Doe's individual teachers). In this and a number of similar cases, the courts have rejected such challenges, usually on the grounds that it is too difficult to assess blame on specific educators. Nonetheless, educators feel that malpractice suits are likely to increase.[25]

It is unlikely that the accountability movement will go away. The growing use of the courts to correct alleged wrongdoings will probably mean that more schools and teachers can expect to face malpractice suits. Increasingly, teachers must be able to defend their objectives and demonstrate that they have made reasonable efforts to help every student reach them.

Needs Assessment

Needs assessment is a procedure or process to gain the maximum input from school patrons, staff, and students regarding the school system's goals and objectives. Phrased differently, it is the measure to assess the accountability that the communities want.

Most state laws mandate that needs assessment begin with an information-gathering procedure. Some districts may use public meetings; others may resort to a mailed questionnaire. One procedure is to select a random sample of the public, in addition to a cross-section of teachers and students, and have them attend a special meeting. Under any of the formats, sug-

gestions for district goals are solicited from the participants. Some districts, however, choose to be guided in their deliberations by previously prepared goals statements. The UCLA program, mentioned earlier, has a different goal printed on each of 114 cards; participants place the cards in priority piles. Phi Delta Kappa has a list of educational goals that are ranked at the meetings.

A second procedure is often employed after the ranking of goals. Participants judge how well their district is meeting the goals. For example, the community members may indicate that their highest priority is reading comprehension, consumer math skills second, and learning a foreign language third. The participants then may determine that their first goal is being met adequately, that the second is not being achieved at all, and that the third priority is available only on an elective basis. The discrepancies between the perceived needs of the district and their current implementation should determine the district's curriculum priorities in the next few years.

Studies indicate that in this phase of needs assessments, most respondents—parents, faculty, staff, or students—rank the basic skills as the highest goal. Moreover, many district assessments reveal that participants believe that their systems are doing an adequate job of instruction in the three Rs. Interesting, two or three of the top five goals are generally in the affective domain, and it is these affective goals that school patrons believe most need immediate attention.[26]

The second phase in a needs assessment program typically is curriculum revision. Districts often involve teachers, organizing them into horizontal committees (teachers from the same level or grade) or vertical committees (representatives in the same subject areas from kindergarten to 12th grade. The committees write new performance objectives, modify the sequence of the curriculum, focus on critical skills, and contruct a curriculum that is flexible enough to allow for individual student needs.

Some districts utilize a third phase in the needs assessment process—essentially, evaluation. They may begin by studying whether the district is fully using all its resources—human, financial, and material. A variety of assessment instruments, from achievement test scores to self-reports by the students, may be used to see whether the districts have met their goals. Most state laws on needs assessment require some type of report to the state department of education. Occasionally, states will aid the local districts by preparing standardized report forms and evaluation instruments. Working with Phi Delta Kappa, the New Jersey Department of Education developed a series of standardized tests that parallel the 18 goals on the Phi Delta Kappan form.[27]

ACTIVITY 11–2
School Needs

Now that you have learned about needs assessment and seen some statements on possible goals and objectives, consider developing some of your own. First write a description of a school situation—your home district or the type of school in which you would like to teach. Is the district rural, urban, or suburban? Is it under public or private control? How many of its students are college-bound?

What do you believe should be five goals of the educational system you describe? If you borrow from any of the statements in the text, rewrite them in your own words.

Other Ways to Change Goals and Objectives

The needs assessment process for changing school goals is rather formal and quite systematized. You should not have the impression that this process is the only or major way school curriculum changes occur. The classroom teacher has many opportunities to restructure the curriculum. We can recall a former student who was so successful in her home economics teaching that her students opened a restaurant (on the school grounds, serving the public during the lunch hour Monday to Friday) to try the new recipes learned in class.

Some school districts, anticipating special demands, have standing committees ready to respond to requests to add or delete curriculum. Many public and nonpublic school systems have a curriculum committee that reviews new instructional materials and makes recommendations for new policies. To deal with an individual or a group wanting some curriculum eliminated (censorship), many districts have a clearly stated and widely circulated procedure as part of school board policy. Typically, the procedure's first step is the completion of a form to specify the reason or reasons for requesting a change in curriculum. If the local administrator cannot resolve the difference, a committee of teachers and, perhaps, citizens consider the request. If the protesting group or individual is not satisfied with the committee's decision, an appeal to the school board is made and a public hearing is held.[28]

As Chapter 12 reveals, it is more likely that schools will be asked to add rather than delete curriculum. The broad area of values best illustrates the many ways individuals and groups pressure schools to modify course offerings on citizenship training, moral decision-making skills, and religion. As you will see, those who want to add something to the curriculum usually try such strategies as financially supporting pilot projects, seeking federal funds or state grants, sponsoring contests for students, and bringing law suits when all else fails. Those who wish the schools to delete some curriculum resort to letter-writing campaigns (from the local to the national level), demonstrating at school board meetings, supporting political candidates who will adopt their plank, seeking legislation, and again, resorting to legal action.

A constant theme in American education since the formation of the common school has been that citizenship training is needed. Historically, interest in specific citizenship training programs has been greatest in wartime and periods of high immigration. Yet leaders of the country are rarely contented with the results of the programs, and so call for additional efforts. For example, in 1977, B. Frank Brown, editing the report of the National Task Force on Citizenship Education funded by the Danforth and Kettering foundations, wrote: "An abundance of research data indicates that the nation's young people have scant knowledge about the responsibilities of citizenship or how to become involved in government. Data also reveal an increasing disrespect among the youth for the most important institutions of society."[29]

The country has witnessed a number of pilot projects and curriculum efforts to foster greater patriotism as well as knowledge about the political process. Introduced in the 1930s, political socialization programs explain to students the functions and roles of governmental representatives, from congressmen to police officers. Foundations have supported projects such as "Law in a Free Society" to instill appreciation of

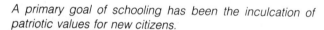
A primary goal of schooling has been the inculcation of patriotic values for new citizens.

the democratic system. Professional educational organizations, such as the Association for Supervision and Curriculum Development (ASCD), have guidelines for teachers and districts to use in building citizenship competencies. A relatively new group, the Center for Citizenship Education in Washington, D.C., seeks both federal and state legislation to require more citizenship training in the nation's schools. Research for Better Schools, Incorporated, a Philadelphia-based organization that has received both federal and private foundation grants, has sponsored national conferences of leading educators in this area, and has published monographs reporting on the effectiveness of moral, ethical and citizen education programs. The American Legion has sponsored Boys State and Girls State programs, and the Daughters of the American Revolution has sponsored essay and oratorical contests on the values of the American way of life.[30]

Efforts to have the schools help students improve their skills in moral decision making are, like citizenship training programs, likely to peak in periods following wars, when there is a general societal concern that the values of the nation may have declined. No doubt Watergate, as well as Vietnam, sparked a renewed interest in values education in the 1960s and 1970s. Advocates of values education and moral development programs, which incidentally have included large numbers of teachers and counselors as well as parents, claim that such programs result in improved self-concepts for students, better school morale, more respect for authority figures, as well as reduced incidents of vandalism, violence, and drug usage.

A conservative estimate is that at least 10,000 teachers have attended a one-day workshop on topics such as values clarification, character education, or moral development. While some schools have introduced elective courses in these areas,

the current trend is to integrate the discussion of moral issues into regular subject matter courses. English, history, and government classes have been the most common courses for such discussions. School counselors have also used certain values education programs (curriculum kits) with students having problems adjusting to school. Critics of moral decision-making programs, such as that developed by Lawrence Kohlberg of Harvard, contend either that the school has more important things to do (i.e., academic preparation of students) or that such programs become far too personal.[31]

The opposition to moral education programs is minor compared to the heated debates regarding the appropriateness of religion in public schools. Not infrequently, those who favor religious practices in public schools, as well as those opposed to such practices, turn to the courts. Legal solutions are sought because the First Amendment specifies that there shall be "no law respecting an establishment of religion, or prohibiting the free exercise thereof." There are many dimensions of the church-state issue, but those that relate most directly to school curriculum revolve around prayers in schools and Bible reading.

In 1962 the U.S. Supreme Court ruled in *Engel* v. *Vitale* that a prayer prescribed for use in New York public schools was illegal on the grounds that the power of government was being used to force a devotional practice upon students (i.e., it was establishing a religion.) The decision did not declare that spontaneous prayers offered by students were illegal.[32] Nevertheless, the verdict of the court shocked many Americans who assumed that the public schools had a silent partnership with the mainline denominations of the country to support religious practices. Extensive letter-writing campaigns were begun to persuade Congress to alter the First Amendment to allow prayers in public schools. Efforts continue to circumvent the so-called Regents prayer case decision. Several state legislatures (notably Massachusetts and Florida) have modified their constitutions to permit moments of private meditation as well as prayers. Such practices are being challenged in the courts. The issue of praying in schools is strident enough that some political candidates have made it a plank in their platforms.

In the *Schempp* case in 1963, the U.S. Supreme Court decided that a practice of the Abington School District in Pennsylvania—reading 10 verses of the Bible to open the school day—was illegal because that practice, too, was establishing a religion. In reaching their verdict, the justices had developed a question that is now taken as the standard for judging what religious studies are acceptable in public schools. What is the purpose and primary effect of

Grin and Bear It by Lichty & Wagner, © 1980 Field Enterprises, Inc. Courtesy of Field Newspaper Syndicate.

"I would have made better on my report card if I'd been allowed to pray during the exams."

the practice? If the intent of the activity is devotional, it is illegal; if it is informational, it is legal. If the primary purpose of singing religious hymns, for example, is to celebrate the birth of Jesus Christ, it would be illegal in a public school. If, on the other hand, the intent of listening to various religious hymns or viewing religious paintings is to increase knowledge and understanding of the role of religion in western culture, it would be legal. Justice Clark, writing the majority opinion, listed the types of instruction about religion that would be legal in a public school: comparative religion, the Bible as literature, and the history of religion. The one reservation of the Court was that any teaching about religion had to be objective.[33]

These court decisions have brought some changes in public school curriculum. One study indicates that since 1963 more than 1,000 high schools have added courses and/or units on such topics as The Bible as Literature, World Religions, and Religion in American History. A number of states, including Pennsylvania, have mandated some form of instruction about religion in social studies units. Groups of educators in Wisconsin, Michigan, Ohio, and Iowa, have formed organizations which promote the academic study of religion. Eight states have some form of certification (usually a minor) for those who wish to teach about religion.[34]

Despite the Court's ruling in the *Schempp* case, and the curricular efforts just cited, there is still the widespread conviction that religious topics cannot be discussed in public schools. Members of conservative religious groups have organized campaigns in a number of states, including California, Tennessee, Indiana, Minnesota, and Iowa, to institute state laws that would require that "scientific creationism" (essentially the accounts of creation mentioned in Genesis, chapters 1 and 2) be discussed whenever the origin of the world or the origin of humankind is mentioned in a science classroom.

Lack of religious values or violation of Judeo-Christian religious principles has been cited often as a reason for opposing specific curriculum in public schools. Some groups have demonstrated at local school board meetings against the MACOS social studies curriculum (Man: A Course of Study) because they were offended by the lifestyles depicted in the curriculum. Sex education courses have been attacked by such groups as POSSE (Parents Opposed to Sex and Sensitivity Education) and the John Birch Society because the programs allegedly promoted anti-Christian behavior. In West Virginia in the mid-1970s, a particularly violent confrontation over the goals of a district occurred because parents perceived certain textbooks as antireligious.[35]

For the teacher, it is important to remember that opposition to anything controversial that you propose to do in the classroom will come most likely from the local community. It is more likely to be a parents' group rather than some representative from a national organization that will oppose what you are doing. That says something about maintaining lines of communication with your students and their parents about your goals. It also says that you should alert your administration to any unusual procedure or curriculum that you plan to use.

SUMMARY

What are schools for? What should they do? Those two questions have been raised throughout the chapter. An indirect point of the chapter is that it is difficult to reach consensus among the American public on what should be taught in the schools. A second point was that changes can occur, and many states now have provided a mechanism (needs assessment) whereby

members of the public can alert schools to changes they wish.

The first section of the chapter discussed what the public thinks about the public schools. The popular impression is that the public is generally unhappy with the schools. Quite the contrary. While the public is concerned about the lack of discipline, financial problems and drug use in schools, it generally endorses its schools and school practices. Further, those who are in closest contact with the schools are most supportive of its efforts.

Philosophies of education developed over the centuries as men and women sharpened their ideas about schooling. In this country, four general philosophical approaches have been used in American education—perennialism, essentialism, progressivism, and reconstructionism. Teachers of tomorrow should begin to frame their outlooks of *what* should be studied, just, as we discussed earlier, they should begin to formulate their points of view about *how* people learn.

Various instruments have been developed to determine educational priorities. Schools are using both formal and informal ways of assessing their goals. Teachers need not fear trying approaches to learning and subject matter that they believe are important. They must be prepared, however, to defend what they do, since the public has increasingly voiced its opinions about what is and is not proper instruction.

NOTES

1. Joseph Mayer Rice, *The Public-School System of the United States* (New York: Century Co., 1893).

2. *Phi Delta Kappan* publishes the results of the latest Gallup poll on education every September or October.

3. Harold Hodgkinson, "What's Right with Education," *Phi Delta Kappan* 61, no. 3 (November 1979): 159; National Center for Education Statistics, *The Condition of Education, 1978* (Washington, D.C.: U.S. Gov-

ernment Printing Office, 1978), p. 9; George H. Gallup, "The 12th Annual Gallup Poll of the Public's Attitudes Toward the Public Schools," *Phi Delta Kappan* 62, no. 1 (September 1980): 35.

4. *Education U.S.A.*, 28 May 1979, p. 1.

5. George H. Gallup, "12th Annual Poll" *Phi Delta Kappan* 62, no. 1: 35.

6. Ibid., p. 34.

7. Vernon Smith and George H. Gallup, *What the People Think About Their Schools: Gallup's Findings* (Bloomington, Ind.: Phi Delta Kappa, 1977), pp. 11, 12, 30–33, 49, 53.

8. Ibid., pp. 27–28; National Center for Education Statistics, *The Condition of Education, 1979* (Washington, D.C.: U.S. Government Printing Office, 1979), p. 72.

9. Wilbur Brookover, *A Sociology of Education* (New York: American Book Co., 1955), pp. 53–63; George H. Gallup, "The Eleventh Annual Gallup Poll of the Public's Attitudes Toward the Public Schools," *Phi Delta Kappan*, 61, no. 1 (September 1979): 44, for description of the "ideal school."

10. Theodore Brameld, *Patterns of Educational Philosophy* (New York: Holt, Rinehart and Winston, 1971), pp. 263–341.

11. Harry Broudy, *Building a Philosophy of Education* (New York: Prentice Hall, 1954), p. 353, also Chapter 3; Brameld, *Patterns,* pp. 181–260.

12. Located in Washington, D.C., the Council for Basic Education publishes *Basic Education* 10 times a year, plus occasional papers and monographs.

13. John Dewey, *The Child and the Curriculum* (Chicago: University of Chicago Press, 1902); Brameld, *Patterns,* pp. 91–178; Lawrence A. Cremin, *The Transformation of the School* (New York: Alfred A. Knopf, 1961), p. 283.

14. Brameld, *Patterns,* pp. 346–511.

15. Robert Zais, *Curriculum: Principles and Foundations* (New York: Thomas Y. Crowell, 1976).

16. Maurice P. Hunt, *Foundations of Education: Social and Cultural Perspectives* (New York: Holt, Rinehart and Winston, 1979), pp. 456–59.

17. National Education Association, *Cardinal Principles of Secondary Education: A Report of the Commission on the Reorganization of Secondary Education,* Bulletin 1918, no. 35 (Washington, D.C.: U.S. Bureau of Education, 1918).

18. Educational Policies Commission, National Education Association, *The Purposes of Education in American Democracy* (Washington, D.C.: National Education Association, 1938).

19. U.S. Office of Education, *Life Adjustment Education for Every Youth* (Washington, D.C.: U.S. Government Printing Office, 1945); Educational Policies Commission, National Education Association, *Moral and Spiritual Values in the Public Schools* (Washington, D.C.: U.S. Government Printing Office, 1951).

20. Carl A. Guerriero, "Assessing Attitudes and Values in Pennsylvania Schools," *Educational Leadership* 34, no. 4 (January 1977), pp. 268–71. For information about the Phi Delta Kappa model, write to PDK, The Center for the Dissemination of Innovative Programs, 8th and Union, Box 789, Bloomington, Ind., 47401. For the UCLA model, write the Center for the Study of Evaluation, Director of Public Information, Graduate School of Education, UCLA, Los Angeles, Calif., 90024.

21. Harold Shane, "The Seven Cardinal Principles Revisited," *Today's Education* 65, no. 3 (September-October 1976): 57–72.

22. Benjamin Bloom, ed., *Taxonomy of Educational Objectives: The Classification of Education Goals, Handbook I: Cognitive Domain* (New York: David McKay Co., 1956), pp. 1–8; David R. Krathwohl, Benjamin S. Bloom, and Bertram B. Masia, *Taxonomy of Educational Objectives, Handbook II: Affective Domain* (New York: David McKay Co., 1956); Anita J. Harrow, *A Taxonomy of the Psychomotor Domain: A Guide for Developing Behavioral Objectives* (New York: David McKay Co., 1972).

23. See a symposium on accountability in *Phi Delta Kappan* 52, no. 4 (December 1970): 193–239.

24. Dave Darland, "Some Complexities of Accountability," *Today's Education* 64, no. 1 (January-February 1975): 21ff; Gerald J. Pine, "Teacher Accountability: Myth and Realities," *Educational Forum* 40, no. 10 (November 1976): 49–60.

25. Nat Hentoff, "Who's to Blame? The Politics of Educational Malpractice," *Learning* 6, no. 2 (October 1977): 40–9.

26. For studies about the PDK model, see note 20.

27. Test booklets are available from Phi Delta Kappa. These are in English and Spanish in arts and leisure, careers, civics, English language, general knowledge, human relations, life skills, reasoning, self-concept, and Latin American culture.

28. Such groups as the National Council of Teachers of English and the Intellectual Freedom Committee of the American Library Association provide guidelines for public agencies who must deal with censorship problems.

29. B. Frank Brown, *Education for Responsible Citizenship* (New York: McGraw-Hill, 1977), pp. 1–3. Some of the data Brown refers to was collected by the National Assessment of Educational Progress and published in 1975 and 1976. For an historical overview, see R. Freeman Butts, "What Should We Learn from the History of Citizenship Education in the United States?" *History of Citizenship Education,* Colloquium Papers (Philadelphia: Research for Better Schools, Inc., 1978), pp. 48, 49.

30. Charles E. Merriam, *The Making of Citizens* (Chicago: University of Chicago Press, 1931); Robert D. Hess and Judith V. Torney, *The Development of Political Attitudes in Children* (New York: Anchor Books, 1968), pp. 242–51; Richard C. Remy, *Handbook of Basic Citizenship Competencies* (Alexandria, Va.: Association for Supervision and Curriculum Development, 1980).

Chapter Eleven

31. Douglas Superka, *Values Education Sourcebook* (Boulder, Colo.: Social Science Education Consortium, 1976); Charles R. Kniker, *You and Values Education* (Columbus, Ohio: Charles E. Merrill, 1977); Edward B. Fiske, "Values Taught More Widely," *New York Times*, 4 March 1980, pp. C1, C4.

32. *Engel* v. *Vitale*, 370 U.S. 421 (1962).

33. *Abington* v. *Schempp*, 374 U.S. 203 (1963). In 1980, in *Florey* v. *Sioux Falls School District 49–5*, the 8th Circuit Court ruled by a 2–1 majority that it was permissible to sing traditional Christmas music in schools. The U.S. Supreme Court has since affirmed the lower court's decision.

34. Nicholas Piediscalzi and William Collie, *Teaching about Religion in Public Schools* (Niles, Ill.: Argus Communications, 1977): Paul Will, ed., *Religion Studies in Public Education Programs: A National Overview* (Missoula, Mont.: Scholars Press, 1980).

35. Franklin Parker, *The Battle of the Books: Kanawka County* (Bloomington, Ind.: Phi Delta Kappa, 1975); Catholic Bishops of Pennsylvania, *Public Education and Student Conscience: A Dilemma for Concerned Citizens* (Harrisburg, Pa.: Pennsylvania Catholic Conference, 1976), pp. 13–20.

FOR FURTHER STUDY

Association for Supervision and Curriculum Development. *The School's Role as Moral Authority.* Washington, D.C.: Association for Supervision and Curriculum Development, 1977.

Bailey, Stephen. *The Purposes of Education.* Bloomington, Ind.: Phi Delta Kappa, 1976.

Bernier, Normand R. *Beyond Beliefs: Ideological Foundations of American Education.* Englewood Cliffs, N.J.: Prentice-Hall, 1973.

Brown, L. M., ed. *Aims of Education.* New York: Teachers College Press, 1970.

Derr, Richard L. *A Taxonomy of Social Purposes of Public Schools: A Handbook.* New York: David McKay Co., 1970.

Jenkinson, Edward B. *Censors in the Classroom: The Mind Benders.* Carbondale, Ill.: Southern Illinois University Press, 1979.

Morris, Van Cleve. *Philosophy and the American School.* 2nd ed. Boston: Houghton Mifflin, 1976.

Phi Delta Kappa. *A Decade of Gallup Polls of Attitudes Toward Education: 1969–78.* Bloomington, Ind.: Phi Delta Kappa, 1978.

Sciara, Frank, and Jantz, Richard. *Accountability in American Education.* Boston: Allyn and Bacon, 1972.

12

The School Curriculum

The question of the course of study . . . is the most important question which the educator has before him.

William T. Harris, 1880

Learning in school differs from learning in life in that it is formally organized. It is the special function of the school to so arrange the experiences of children and youth that desirable learning takes place. If the curriculum is to be a plan for learning, its content and learning experiences need to be organized so that they serve the educational objectives.

Hilda Taba, 1962

What is the curriculum? Although popularly regarded as specific subjects or courses in the school program, curriculum in its broadest sense includes *all* educational experiences. Thus, sports and club programs often are viewed as cocurricular rather than extracurricular activities.

Authorities disagree on the precise definition of curriculum. Many would limit it to the *planned* learning experiences offered by the schools. Some feel this is too narrow because it excludes the unintended aspects of the "hidden curriculum." They would include the "totality of students' experiences in school." Others, who stress the distinction between curriculum and instruction, would narrow the definition of curriculum to "a structured series of intended learning outcomes." Still others define curriculum as a written "plan for action which guides instruction." All agree that curriculum is broader, however, than specific lesson plans.[1]

John Goodlad and his associates distinguish the abstract "ideal curriculum"; the "formal curriculum" of what should be done in the school; the "instructional curriculum" of teachers; the "operational curriculum" of what actually occurs in classrooms; and the "experiential curriculum"—student perceptions and outcomes.[2] Which of these definitions is the best depends on the particular situation or purpose.

You read in Chapter 8 about past curriculum changes in response to the changing needs of society. In this chapter we will look briefly at the development of curriculum, focusing on the twentieth century and emphasizing the curriculum reform projects and developments in the 1970s. A number of contemporary curriculum concerns then will be examined.

The central issue throughout the chapter is, What should be the school curriculum? What knowledge is most valuable? What should be taught? What are the basic or essential subjects everyone should know? Can the curriculum continue to expand? Has the curriculum responded adequately to the changing needs of society?

After you have completed this chapter, you should be able to (1) state three generalizations about how curriculum has changed in American schools, (2) give reasons for inclusion in the curriculum of three recent innovations, and (3) explain why some curriculum innovations succeeded and others failed to be fully implemented.

THE EVOLVING CURRICULUM

In the colonial era, education focused primarily on reading and religion. Most boys and many girls also learned penmanship or writing and some arithmetic. Boys preparing for college concentrated on Latin classics (in literature and history) and Greek. By the middle of the 1700s, arithmetic and the perfection of English language skills received some attention. Some boys studied mathematics, including algebra, trigonometry, and geometry, and perhaps navigation, surveying, bookkeeping, geography, astronomy, and modern languages. Girls learned sewing, cooking, and other housewifely skills at home. Young daughters of the well-to-do studied music and dancing, painting and French, as well as embroidery and other ornamental needlework.

The school curriculum expanded greatly over the years. Spelling, grammar, geography, and American history became standard in elementary schools even in the early years of national independence. All schools stressed moral education and development of character. Although most common schools in the nineteenth century had prayers and Bible readings, sectarian religious instruction became the responsibility of Sunday schools and churches.

In the academies and high schools, the number of subjects substantially increased. In New York State in 1850, for example, the subjects most frequently offered in the academies were Latin, physical sciences, algebra, plane geometry, chemistry, astronomy, French, composition, elocution, surveying, physiology, history, and philosophy. Other new school subjects included botany, English literature, debating, and rhetoric. The admission requirements of most colleges during the nineteenth century, however, focused on a narrower range of subjects. The usual college preparatory course included Latin, Greek, mathematics, English, history, some science, and, by the 1870s, perhaps a modern foreign language in place of Greek.

The standard process of curriculum design in the nineteenth century was accretion—adding new subjects. This expansion continued in the late nineteenth and early twentieth century. Music, drawing, physiology, nature study, and physical exercise became common in elementary schools. Secondary schools offered more sciences, modern languages, home economics, physical education, manual arts, commercial and vocational subjects, as well as music and art.

Relatively few subjects were dropped, but not all received equal amounts of time. According to an 1890 survey of elementary education in 83 large cities (where the curriculum was likely to be more standardized), reading and arithmetic received more time than other subjects in the eight grades. Geography and spelling received less than half as much time, with grammar, natural science, history, physiology, manners and morals, and singing receiving considerably less attention. Recess received the most time of all![3]

Some subjects have changed their names. Natural philosophy, for example, was the predecessor of physics, and zoology and botany replaced natural history in high schools. The content and emphasis in virtually all subjects have changed considerably. In the nineteenth century especially, textbooks provide the best indication of curriculum content. Many early geometry textbooks included trigonometry, although this virtually disappeared by the 1880s. Treatment of conic sections did not appear in geometry books until after 1837, and modern geometry not until after 1864. War was the most popular subject in most nineteenth century American history textbooks for elementary schools, and it received much more space than other topics until it was surpassed by government and politics in the early twentieth century. In English, grammar, composition, and literature have received varying degrees of attention at different grade levels and different periods of time.[4]

Another trend has been to shift subjects to earlier grades—from the colleges to the secondary schools or from secondary to elementary schools. The Committee of Ten, for example, recommended in 1893 that most high school subjects should be in-troduced in grades 7 and 8 of elementary school.

The literature about curriculum increased in the 1890s and expressed the concern of the progressive educators whose influence helped transform American schools in the first half of the twentieth century. The progressives deplored the drill, memorization, and rote recitation of abstract subjects in traditional education. They also sought to serve the growing number and diversity of secondary students by changing the narrowly academic curriculum.

The general thrust of progressive education was toward "expansion, election, activity, and utility in the curriculum." Elementary schools became more child-centered as the interests and needs of students became the bases for organizing the curriculum. Projects and the activity method became popular, while "learning by doing" and "creative self-expression" became popular slogans. Innovations and reforms of progressive education included a problem-centered core curriculum; correlation of work in different courses; fusion of subjects; integrated studies; broad fields rather than separate disciplines (e.g., social studies rather than history, geography, and civics; and English or language arts instead of grammar, spelling, and literature); individualized instruction; and teacher involvement in curriculum revision. The curriculum expanded to include new subjects appealing to many interests and a wide range of cocurricular activities—sports, music groups, and clubs.[5]

Progressive education reached the peak of its influence in the 1920s and 1930s and had its greatest impact on elementary schools. Not all the reforms were equally successful. Many schools adopted the slogans and terminology of the new approaches, but not the real substance. Even John Dewey decried the distortions and misinterpretations of progressive education in the 1930s. "Life adjustment" education

Chapter Twelve

emerged after World War II, focusing attention on the majority of students who were not in vocational or college preparatory programs. This emphasis in particular and progressive education in general came under severe attack in the 1950s, in books such as *The Diminishing Mind, Quackery in the Public Schools*, and *Educational Wastelands*. As a result of such criticisms and demands for higher standards and a return to fundamentals, the progressive education movement collapsed in the 1950s.[6]

Curriculum Reform Projects

The federal government, through its National Science Foundation, began to fund curriculum projects in the mid-1950s to develop new courses and materials for high school science and mathematics. The Soviet Sputnik increased public awareness and resulted in the National Defense Education Act (1958), which substantially increased federal aid to education. NDEA focused initially on science, math, foreign languages, and guidance. The goal was academic excellence, and emphasis shifted back to the disciplines.

The central thrust of most curriculum reform projects of the 1950s and 1960s is described in Jerome Bruner's *The Process of Education*. This report of a 1959 conference of representatives of many projects has been called a "curriculum manifesto." The emphasis was on understanding the *structure* of the disciplines—basic organizing concepts and their relations to each other. An inquiry approach, discovery method, and inductive teaching were advocated. Bruner maintained that "any subject can be taught effectively in some intellectually honest form to any child at any stage of development." The conference urged teaching basic ideas and themes earlier in a "spiral curriculum" that would be redeveloped in later grades. The goal was to have students experience the process of doing science or mathematics,

rather than merely memorize facts about the subject.[7]

The curriculum reform projects were led by university science and mathematics professors who were joined by scholars in psychology. Later, social scientists and English professors became involved in federally funded projects in their own disciplines. The Physical Science Study Committee under Jerrold Zacharias of the Massachusetts Institute of Technology developed a new physics course for high school students. The Biological Sciences Curriculum Study developed three different biology courses using cellular, molecular, and ecological approaches. The science projects had the greatest impact on high school curriculum. The new math was probably the most widely publicized

Two students use the inquiry method in a science course.

of the curriculum reform projects and had influence on elementary as well as secondary schools. Modern mathematics presented a new approach, new terminology, and a new content—set theory, congruences, matrices, and bases of number systems. Most of the curriculum reform projects produced textbooks and supplementary materials. Commercial publishers also incorporated some of the new approaches and updated the content of their regular textbooks.

The federal government financed many summer in-service institutes to familiarize science and math teachers with the new curricula. But many teachers were confronted with new curricula and texts without in-service preparation. Often they did not fully understand the principles involved. Parents also were not prepared. Some schools offered them new math courses so they could help their children with homework or at least understand what they were doing.

By the 1970s the new curriculum reform movement had peaked and disenchantment had set in. Enrollments in high school science classes were down both in numbers and in the percentage of students enrolled. Teachers and students at all levels had difficulty with the courses, believing that most of them were geared to above-average students. Math scores on college boards and standardized achievement tests declined, and complaints were widespread that students could not do computations. Although many schools returned to more traditional approaches, some elements of the reform projects were retained and the curriculum was updated.

Recent Trends

Other factors also contributed to the decline of interest in the discipline-centered reform projects. Attention had begun to shift by the mid-1960s from the academically talented to disadvantaged students

Cartoon by Ford Button in *Phi Delta Kappan*, October 1974. Reprinted with permission.

"Just when we knock the new math into their heads, along comes the metric system."

in response, in part, to the civil rights movement. The federally financed Project Head Start and Title I of the Elementary and Secondary Education Act of 1965 were among the most extensive compensatory education efforts. (See also Chapter 14.)

Furthermore, in response to criticisms (see Chapter 15), interest turned to a more functional curriculum geared to the problems and needs of the day. Relevance and a more humanistic education were the new watchwords. Open education, the free-school movement, alternative education, and interest in the affective aspects of education began to flourish in the early 1970s. Elective and mini courses proliferated in the high schools on every conceivable topic from filmmaking to witchcraft. The pendulum swings rapidly, however, and by the end of the 1970s, the cry was "back to basics," with behavioral objectives, minimum competency exams, and career education receiving attention.

Beginning in the 1960s, a growing number of districts replaced their junior high schools with a middle or intermediate school. The most common organizational pattern in American schools has been a 6–3–3 system—kindergarten or first grade through sixth grade in an elementary school, grades 7 to 9 in a junior high school, and grades 10 to 12 in a senior high school. (Some districts utilize the more traditional

8–4 arrangement of kindergarten or first grade through eighth in an elementary school, and a four-year high school of grades 9 through 12.) The middle school usually includes grades 5 or 6 through 8, resulting in a 4–4–4 or, more often, a 5–3–4 pattern.

The basic reason for creating middle schools was usually to end overcrowding in existing schools. Some large cities turned to middle schools to aid racial desegregation. A rationale soon developed for the middle school to distinguish it from the junior high school as a school serving the special needs of the 10- to 14-year-old age-group of younger adolescents. In many respects, however, curriculum in most middle schools is very similar to that in junior high schools. The most common innovations associated with middle schools are team teaching, provisions for independent study, and block-of-time scheduling or two or more classes.[8]

In some middle and junior high schools, but more often in senior high schools, modular scheduling has replaced the 40- to 45-minute five-day-a-week traditional pattern for more flexible programming. Although many classes may be scheduled for two 20-minute modules daily, others may span three or four modules, but meet fewer days a week. Some schools also are on six-day cycles or have rotating schedules that provide additional flexibility.

Traditionally, most American secondary schools have been comprehensive high schools, offering academic, commercial, and vocational programs within the same building. Some cities have had separate vocational schools and specialized academic schools. In the 1970s more districts began to provide specialized vocational schools, sometimes under regional cooperative agencies.[9]

As part of the broader effort to equalize educational opportunity, more attention has been directed to the special needs and education of handicapped and gifted and talented students. Most physical education, industrial arts, and home economics classes have become coeducational as a result of Title IX, which prohibits sex-segregated classes. (See Chapter 13.)

The curriculum continues to expand.

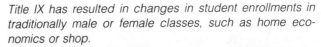

Title IX has resulted in changes in student enrollments in traditionally male or female classes, such as home economics or shop.

Many high schools have become virtual curriculum cafeterias offering a smorgasbord of courses, especially in English, science, and the social studies. Often these reflect contemporary social concerns such as ecology, energy education, environmental or ocean studies, consumer education, the holocaust, black history, ethnic studies, women's studies, and drug education. Among other new courses or topics are anthropology, psychology, law, futuristics, metrics, community-based learning, preparation for college entrance (SAT) exams, family-life or parenting education, and death and dying. Humanities courses, integrating literature and the arts, have become more popular in some high schools, and there has been more interest in the arts at all levels of education. Advanced-placement courses in high school enable seniors to receive college credit. Some elementary schools are teaching philosophy, and the values-clarification movement has influenced curriculum in both elementary and secondary schools (see Chapter 11). Other subjects receive new emphases. Physical education, for example, has put more stress on lifelong sports. Gymnastics has gained popularity as a result of television coverage of the Olympics. Movement education, which focuses on self-awareness and body control, has become popular in some schools.

Curriculum in high school has been influenced by college admission requirements. When colleges began to drop Greek and Latin as admission requirements in the late nineteenth century, many students opted for modern foreign languages. Greek and Latin enrollments declined. Many high schools no longer offer Latin and only rarely is Greek available. After many colleges dropped foreign language requirements for admission and graduation in the late 1960s, enrollments soon dropped in high school foreign language classes. Many districts also eliminated from their elementary schools the foreign language instruction that had been instituted in the post-Sputnik decade.

ACTIVITY 12–1
Analyze Curriculum

Explore in greater depth changes in your favorite subject in the school curriculum. (This may be one of the subjects you plan to teach. You may focus on the elementary or secondary level, depending on your own interests.)

Among the questions you might consider: When did the subject first begin to be taught in American schools? What changes have occurred? How has content changed? What seem to be the most recent trends?

You may want to speak with teachers who have been teaching in the area for more than ten years and ask them about changes they have observed. You should do some library research, also. Methods books often have a chapter on the historical background of the subject or you can read a chapter or two in a historical survey of the subject field you select. For current trends, read the appropriate chapter in a recent curriculum text or locate recent articles using the *Education Index* or by reading a professional journal in the field (e.g., *Social Education* for social studies, *Teacher* for the elementary curriculum).

The federal government has had a major impact on curriculum in recent decades. Federal funds have encouraged vocational education, compensatory education programs, the curriculum reform projects, career education, and many other programs. (See also Chapter 9.)

Since education is primarily a state responsibility, it is hardly surprising that virtually all states have laws and regulations affecting the curriculum. Some subjects are required by state law. More than half the states, for example, require U.S. history, state history, physical education, English, health education, the federal constitution, and instruction about alcohol and narcotics. A few states have laws that mandate Bible study, metrics, flag education, Bird Day, thrift, and traffic safety. Iowa, with 43 subjects required by law, has the greatest number of any state, while Montana laws do not prescribe any subjects.[10]

The states specify requirements for high school graduation. Many state education departments issue curriculum guides. Some states approve lists of textbooks that may be used. New York has statewide Regents exams in many high school subjects, directly influencing what is taught in these courses. State minimum competency test laws are a recent development (see Chapter 7) that affect the curriculum.

A study of educational changes in the twentieth century included 21 in curriculum, 15 of which originated in the first half of the century. The degree of successful implementation varied. One-third were classified as having permeated the system: driver education; the elective system; cocurricular activities; physical education; safety education; special education; and vocational and technical education. Another third of the changes had some, but not full, implementation: the British Infant School (open education); compensatory education; conservation education; environmental education; home economics; international education; and updating curriculum content. At the other end of the scale, three were judged to have made no permanent impact: the core curriculum; creative edu-

cation; and the Progressive Education Association's Eight Year Study experiment with 30 progressive high schools in the 1930s. Four left only a residue—the activity (or experience) curriculum, community school, sex education, and the unit method.

Although this study is not definitive, some of its findings are suggestive.

1. Many of the curriculum changes originated outside the educational system.

2. Some of the most successful had support from legislation or organized interest groups.

3. The addition of new subjects seemed to be more successful than changes in the basic organization of curriculum.

4. If a change involves a great deal of additional time and work for teachers, it is more likely to be resisted and not successful.

5. Change is more likely to be successful if it has support from all involved and encounters little opposition.

6. More of the changes in administration and organization were successful than in curriculum, but changes in instruction were more difficult to implement fully.[11]

What can we learn from this study and our overview of the evolving curriculum? Obviously, the curriculum has changed over the years, yet many of the recent curriculum reforms have had only limited success. How many did you experience in your own schooling? As we turn to examine contemporary curriculum concerns, keep in mind these findings to help assess the prospects for success of innovations.

CONTEMPORARY CONCERNS

The curriculum can be described as a plan by which a school seeks to achieve its goals. The basic concerns in curriculum are what should be taught and why. The politics of curriculum making and its influential participants were covered in Chapter 9. Curriculum design and textbooks are perennial concerns. Fads are prevalent in American education, and it has been estimated that the average life of an educational reform is about three years. We will examine selected aspects of some recent curricular innovations that seem likely to last: educational technology, early childhood education, the back-to-basics movement, career education, and bilingual and multicultural education.

Curriculum Design

Curriculum specialists usually develop curriculum. Committees of teachers within a district or school also may be involved in revising curriculum. The so-called Tyler rationale has been for many years the most widely accepted approach to curriculum development. Ralph Tyler set four questions to be considered:

1. What educational purposes should the school seek to attain?

2. What educational experiences can be provided that are likely to attain these purposes?

3. How can these educational experiences be effectively organized?

4. How can we determine whether these purposes are being attained?

The first step is to state objectives. These are derived from studies of learners, contemporary life, and the subject matter content—screened or filtered through one's philosophy of education. The next steps are to select learning experiences, then to organize them, and finally to evaluate whether the objectives have been realized.[12] Teachers should remember this logical approach to curriculum design as

they make their own unit and lesson plans to implement curriculum.

Textbooks

Despite the proliferation in recent years of audiovisual aids—filmstrips, records, cassettes, films, and sets of multimedia packaged materials—textbooks still reign supreme in most classrooms. Indeed, John Goodlad and other observers conclude that textbooks are still the primary determinants of the curriculum. Students spend more time with textbooks than any other learning aid.[13]

Textbooks, like the schools, reflect society as they help mold the knowledge, skills, and attitudes of the upcoming generation. Textbooks by nature tend to be conservative. Indeed, one study of nineteenth century schoolbooks is entitled *Guardians of Tradition.*[14]

Textbooks are produced by commercial publishers, who understandably are primarily interested in books that will have wide acceptance and hence large sales. A considerable number of states, particularly in the South and Southwest, have state adoption committees that approve lists of textbooks for the public schools. If Texas or California does not approve a particular text, that can represent loss of a significant part of the market. Most textbooks, therefore, tend to be bland, seeking to avoid controversy or antagonizing any interest group.

Nonetheless, sometimes textbooks become subjects of public debate when they conflict with particular beliefs and values. Sex education and evolution are classic examples. One of the new social studies programs for elementary students, "Man: A Course of Study" (MACOS) was attacked in Arizona and ultimately on the floor of Congress for the "alleged propagation of 'cultural relativism' and 'immoral behavior.'" Sales dropped precipitously.[15]

Chapter Twelve

The staple of most classrooms is still the text-book. Teachers today often provide more than one text for their classes.

Textbooks change; contents are updated and interpretations may be revised. Frances Fitzgerald's critical analysis of American history textbooks used in secondary schools traced changes in interpretation and approach. Books published in the 1960s and 1970s, she found, gave more attention to blacks, women, and ethnics in response to pressures from these groups and the broader changes in society that these reflect. Fitzgerald concluded, however, that the new social studies has had only a limited impact on history; some social science concepts are now in the narrative texts, and the newer inquiry texts reach about 15% of the market.[16]

Educational Technology

In the 1960s, television, teaching machines, computers, and other technological innovations seemed to be on the verge of transforming American education. Many districts, aided by federal and foundation funds, invested in tape recorders, overhead projectors, closed-circuit television, language laboratories, and media resource centers. By the 1970s, however, as a Ford Foundation report observed, the use of

Funky Winkerbean by Tom Batiuk © 1978 Field Enterprises, Inc. Courtesy of Field Newspaper Syndicate.

educational technology had declined and much of the equipment was "gathering dust." The quality of the software, or teaching materials for the machines, was a major problem. Moreover, the high purchase, maintenance, and utilization expenses for the new equipment lowered its cost-effectiveness for instruction. Students' exposure to media in their classrooms was much more likely to be the traditional films, filmstrips, and slides, rather than television, teaching machines, or learning kits.[17] The 1980s may be the decade when educational technology comes into its own.

Television. As one observer has concluded, "The educational potential of the electronic blackboard remains largely unfulfilled." Although there are several hundred public television stations that broadcast programs for schools, in fact their support and utilization by schools has declined.[18] Cable television is used effectively in some districts. Videotapes may prove more successful for schools than closed-circuit television systems were in the 1960s. Videotapes, like films, are apt to be more uniform in quality and can be utilized at the optimum time in the curriculum.

Probably the most successful of educational television's ventures has been "Sesame Street." Yet even this program has not reached all children, and most of the viewers are middle-class suburban children rather than the inner-city disadvantaged for whom it was designed.

Many have blamed television for the decline in reading scores. Children today spend more time watching television than they do in school. As educator Lawrence Cremin has observed:

> Radio and television stations have curricula—and by these curricula I refer not only to programs labeled educational but also to news broadcasts and documentaries (which presumably inform), to commercials (which teach people to want),

and to soap operas (which reinforce common myths and values).[19]

Obviously, television has a major impact on the lives and education of all of us.

Computers. The much-heralded teaching machines using the psychological principles of B.F. Skinner encountered many difficulties in the 1960s. By the 1970s the main survivors were a few self-paced, programmed learning texts. Computers are likely to have a greater impact on education.

Some high schools offer computer courses as part of the math curriculum. School districts use computers for administrative and managerial functions such as scheduling students and courses, and keeping attendance and grade records. But computer-assisted instruction (CAI) may have a.more permanent effect on curriculum. The computer can individualize instruction for drill and practice, tutorial instruction, and problem solving in many fields. Yet according to an NEA survey, fewer than 12% of secondary schools and only 4% of elementary schools were utilizing the computer for instruction in 1974.

Reasons for the lag in implementing CAI are related to high costs, the quality of the instructional programs (the software), teacher resistance, and technical problems. Several different CAI formats and programs are now available, including the Stanford Project, Interactive Training Systems (ITS), Programmed Logic for Automatic Teaching Organization (PLATO), and Time Shared Interactive Computer Controlled Information Television (TICCIT).

Computer costs are expected to decline in the 1980s, and as software improves, computers may be more widely used. Many effective CAI programs already have been developed in different subjects at all levels of education. Although it was estimated that more than half the students in high

Increasingly, students are being exposed to computers. How familiar are you with CAI?

schools in 1979 had access to a computer, many fewer actually used the computer for instruction. Whether computer-assisted instruction will revolutionize education remains to be seen.[20]

Simulation Games. Simulations or education games emerged in the 1970s as a promising method of classroom instruction. Students learn through their involvement and role playing the simulation of real-life situations. Motivation is usually high for this experiential learning. Some simulations use computers, but many rely on printed materials. (Noncomputer simulations or games are not considered new educational technology, but instructional innovations.) Games may take one or several class sessions or extend over several weeks.

The principles of an educational game may be clarified by describing one. WEB is designed for college students in an education course studying the organization of an educational bureaucracy. Participants are assigned various roles (school board members, citizens, superintendent, principal, and teachers). They are asked to deal with a number of crisis situations at a school board meeting (e.g., merit rating, denial of tenure, and sex education). "Teachers" must apply and be interviewed for a position by the "administrators" and decide whether to join the NEA or AFT. Background materials are provided on the community, situations, and procedures. In the process of playing the game, participants not only increase their knowledge about the organization and operation of school districts, but also have an opportunity to make decisions and act on their beliefs.[21]

Of simulations used in classrooms, probably the most popular are in the social studies. A recent survey of social studies teachers in Ohio indicated 58% were using simulations and many had developed their own. The 5% who had discontinued using simulations and the 37% of teachers who had never used them had doubts about the educational benefits and were concerned about the costs and time involved.[22]

Individualized Instruction. Many methods have been developed to individualize instruction, a goal that has again become popular in recent years. Independent study and contract plans may be used. Individualized Prescribed Instruction (IPI), Individually Guided Education (IGE), Individualized Mathematics System (IMS), and the Learning Activity Package (LAP) are different types of individualized, self-paced instruction. Typically, students take a placement test and then work at their own pace on the various learning materials, which may include cassettes, filmstrips, and games as well as more traditional printed and teacher-made materials. The computer, besides providing instruction, often is utilized for diagnostic purposes and to keep track of student progress. To enhance continuous progress under individualized learning, a nongraded organization of classes may be used.[23] (See also Chapter 13.)

ACTIVITY 12–2
Using Educational Technology

If your college has a media or curriculum resource center with simulation games or CAI programs, and if computer terminals are available, arrange with others to play a simulation game or to spend at least an hour doing CAI lessons in different fields.

Option: Watch several different programs on a public television station, preferably those designed for school instruction.

After you have finished, summarize and analyze your reactions. Was your interest sustained? What did you learn? How effective was the game, computer, or television as a learning device? Do you see any drawbacks or limitations to this method?

Early Childhood Education

Psychologists have emphasized the importance of the first four or five years of life to a child's cognitive development. These are crucial years because the development of intelligence is affected by early experiences. Head Start, the federally financed program of early intervention to aid disadvantaged children, provided an important impetus to early childhood education. Moreover, as the percentage of employed mothers with preschool children has increased, there has been greater demand for preschool programs and child-care facilities. Kindergartens and nursery schools have become more widespread.

More states now provide state aid for kindergarten in public schools, and enrollments have increased to more than three-fourths of the age group. The overwhelming majority are in public schools, with half-day sessions most common. The Educational Policies Commission of the National Education Association has urged that public schools extend their programs to 4-year-olds. The American Federation of Teachers has advocated putting day-care as well as early childhood services in the public schools.

Nursery schools traditionally have served middle-class children and have been play-oriented. The Montessori approach of a carefully planned environment is popular in many nursery schools. (See Chapter 15.) The participation in prekindergarten programs by 3- and 4-year-olds nearly doubled in the decade following the first Head Start programs. By the late 1970s, over 25% of 3-year-olds and 43% of 4-year-olds were attending preschool programs.[24]

About a third of these children attend publicly financed preschool programs that have focused on the disadvantaged. Head

Educational opportunities are expanding at both ends—preschool programs and programs in lifelong learning.

Start has been one of the most popular programs in early childhood education. It began as a summer program for 5-year-olds in 1965, but soon expanded to emphasize year-round programs serving mainly 3- and 4-year olds. Although a compensatory program designed to give children from disadvantaged backgrounds a "head start" in school, it also has provided important medical, nutritional, and social services, parent participation, and jobs for paraprofessionals from the community.

Some of the early evaluation studies of Head Start raised questions about the long-term effect on intellectual growth. After a few years of school, the initial gains seemed to dissipate. Project Follow Through began as a compensatory education program for elementary children who had been in Head Start programs. By 1980, however, longitudinal studies of Head Start children concluded that the programs have had "significant long-term effects on school performance." Compared with control groups, fewer Head Start children had been retained in grades or placed in special education classes, while more were in college or had acquired skilled jobs.[25]

Early childhood education includes the primary grades as well as the preprimary programs that are mentioned here. Concern has extended also to infants and parent education programs to improve child-rearing skills. Most of these programs work closely with mothers in their own homes. Television in homes has an important impact on young children. Studies of "Sesame Street" and "The Electric Company" have shown their effectiveness in teaching cognitive skills.

Child- and day-care centers also expanded in the 1970s in response to needs of working mothers. While custodial care may be the primary focus, many also encompass broader educational concerns for child development. Relatively few companies provide child-care centers for their employees, who then must arrange for their children's care by informal baby-sitting in private homes. Day-care became a national political issue in the 1970s. The federal government now allows tax credits for child-care expenses and has allocated some funds for day-care centers for low-income families, but the broader Comprehensive Child Development Acts in the 1970s were vetoed by Presidents Nixon and Ford.

Experts disagree on the most appropriate approach for early childhood education, particularly for children five years old and younger. Some emphasize socialization, enrichment, play, self-expression, and creativity, whereas others stress preparation and readiness for school in more structured programs. These differences obviously affect the curriculum for young children in kindergartens, nursery schools, and other child development centers.[26]

Back to Basics

One of the most popular slogans in American education in recent years has been "back to basics." The basics, however, have been interpreted in many ways. (Some of the differences should be obvious after reading the discussion in Chapter 11 on goals for schools and the various philosophies of education.) For many, the basics mean concentrating on reading, writing, and arithmetic skills in elementary schools, and English, mathematics, history, and science at the secondary level. Some also advocate stricter discipline, more drill and homework, minimum competency standards, and an end to social promo-

Cartoon by Ford Button in *Phi Delta Kappan*, November 1979, p. 207. Reprinted with permission.

"Did you ever have days when you'd just as soon go back to 'reading 'n writing 'n 'rithmetic, taught to the tune of a hickory stick'?"

tion. Others urge eliminating electives and so-called frills such as art, music, psychology, social issues, driver education, and guidance.[27]

What some call a frill, however, others feel is a basic and essential part of the curriculum. The Council for Basic Education (organized some two decades before the contemporary back-to-basics movement and in reaction to progressive education) supports a serious intellectual education and solid curriculum for all students. It includes geography, foreign languages, and the arts, as well as English, history, mathematics, and science among its basics. When the Gallup Poll asked the public what high school subjects were essential for all students, 97% said mathematics; 94%, English grammar and composition; 88%, civics and government; 86%, U.S. history; 83%, science; 81%, geography; 76%, physical education; and 60%, the interdependence of nations and foreign relations. A majority of those surveyed regarded music, foreign language, and art as "not too essential" for all students.[28] In fact, geography is taught infrequently in secondary schools, and art, music, and foreign languages are usually electives in high schools.

Not only is there disagreement over what are the basics, but even the most basic of the basics—the three Rs—are subject to varying emphases. Should writing, for example, stress spelling and grammar? Is penmanship important? Should typing be required? What about oral communication skills?

The back-to-basics movement began in the 1970s in part as a reaction to open education, the new math, and other curriculum reforms. Declining test scores (see Chapter 7), interest in accountability, and concern about the increasing costs of education also contributed to the popularity of the movement. The feelings of many back-to-basics advocates are reflected in the title of Paul Copperman's popular 1978 book, *The Literacy Hoax: The Decline of Reading, Writing, and Learning in the Public Schools.*[29]

Although educators would deny that they have ever neglected the three Rs and the basics, one of the most popular alternatives in public school districts is the fundamental or traditional school, which espouses aspects of the back-to-basics idea.

Another response to the back-to-basics movement is the minimum competency examinations that you read about in Chapter 7. These exams usually focus on reading, writing, and arithmetic skills, but may include other life-survival skills. The exams may be required for promotion at certain grade levels or for high school graduation.

Both back-to-basics and minimum competency exams have implications for the curriculum. Remedial work, proficiency tests, and performance-based curriculum are becoming more widespread. Schools are emphasizing reading, writing, and arithmetic and providing remedial work in these subjects for those who do not meet performance standards. The underlying assumption is that basic skills will improve. Critics fear that the results will be disappointing—teaching for the test, "minimal mediocrity," and dehumanizing education. Advocates hope that standards and achievement levels will rise as a result of the back-to-basics movement.

Career Education

Career education is a relatively new area that has been receiving widespread support. Career education received "overwhelming approval" from the public as early as the 1973 Gallup Poll on education. Ninety percent felt public schools should "give more emphasis to a study of trades, professions, and business to help students decide on their careers." Career education is broader than traditional vocational education. It includes all students and ideally begins in kindergarten or first grade. Its goal is to make education more relevant to careers and to have students think more realistically about the world of work. Students learn about career opportunities and sharpen career decision-making and development skills.[30]

Federal officials, particularly Sidney Marland, the U.S. Commissioner of Education in the early 1970s, have promoted career education to prepare students for the real world. Marland was primarily concerned about the large number of high school students who were prepared neither for college nor in vocational courses for jobs, but who had received only a general education. Marland was reluctant to define career education, preferring to describe its objectives, allow debate, and let various programs emerge.[31]

The belief has developed that all students should be taught skills that they can use to evaluate both work-related tasks and all daily decisions. It is recognized that students ask fundamentally different questions about life at different age levels (see the discussion of Piaget's findings in Chapter 6). Career education curriculum typically recognizes three phases in students' lives.

The first phase is *career awareness*. In the early elementary grades, children are exposed to problem-solving techniques and decision-making skills. They are asked to think about themselves, what they value, their priorities, and why they enjoy doing some things rather than others. Gradually, the curriculum may be supplemented with instructional materials that provide information about specific careers. School districts may utilize books, films, or television programs to depict a variety of careers. Parents and others may be invited to class to discuss their careers. Teachers and school librarians may design bulletin boards or construct career displays that are changed periodically. The main purpose of career awareness is to alert students to the immense variety of occupations in the world.[32]

As students move to the higher grades, teachers may introduce *career discovery* experiences. Guidance counselors often assist teachers with techniques to show students specific career possibilities. Students may be given information about careers, take vocational inventories, and use a computer match to relate their interests to various occupations. Some junior high schools have organized so-called shadow days when students visit a job site and follow a person through his or her routine.

The third stage, *career emphasis*, stresses the future applicability of particular skills. It hopes to arose students' curiosity about the competencies needed in various jobs. Curriculum in other courses may be refocused on careers. Mathematics books attuned to career education may use illustrations from baking and banking, while social studies texts may ask students to look at family and societal work patterns of various cultures. A career-oriented English text may include practice exercises for writing business letters, or show how a newspaper reporter constructs a story, or illustrate how advertising executives develop a commercial. Teachers also supplement their regular curriculum with career education materials that they have developed.

The emphasis in career education is more to help students weigh career possibilities than to prepare for an occupation. When careers are discussed directly, job *clusters* are often mentioned. Clusters include occupations in business and offices, marketing and distribution, communications and media, or manufacturing and service. For example, consider the family of occupations (or cluster) related to construction. Students may come to realize that they are interested in construction,

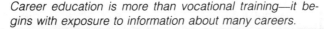

Career education is more than vocational training—it begins with exposure to information about many careers.

Chapter Twelve

but also that they do not want to make a premature choice to be a carpenter, mason, painter, plumber, or air conditioning specialist.

The U.S. Office of Education and state departments of education funded demonstration projects and model career-education programs. By the late 1970s, it was estimated that one or two of every four school districts had implemented some form of career education. Many districts incorporated only some aspects. Approximately half the states had allocated some funds for career-education programs. About half of the districts surveyed had indicated they had offered in-service workshops for their teachers on career education. Yet those programs have not always been effective, and they may be misunderstood by some of the public. In another Gallup poll, only 20% of high school students, according to their parents, received any career guidance from their school.[33]

Some educators have been critical of career education. They do not agree with its advocates who claim that it improves the students' self-concept, increases motivation, and improves work habits. Some point out the "historic continuities" and similarities of career education to traditional vocational education and its predecessor, manual training. Manual training in the 1880s also promised broad benefits, including more interest in school, retention of students, a better choice of occupations, material success, the end of labor problems, and improved status of occupations.[34]

Other educators are concerned, moreover, that career education may be a new means of tracking students, especially minority students, into manual trades and lower-status positions rather than college preparatory courses in high schools. Others question refocusing the entire curriculum around the concept of career: Is the relevance of schooling limited to work? And

the perennial question: Is job training (or in this case, career education) best learned in school or on the job?[35]

Bilingual and Multicultural Education

Significant numbers of students in our schools are from non-English-speaking backgrounds. Chicanos, American Indians, migrants from Puerto Rico, and immigrants from Latin America, Asia, southern Europe, and other areas often have difficulties when classroom instruction is in English. An English as a Second Language (ESL) approach provides special instruction in English language skills. Students receive additional work in written and spoken English and are instructed in English in the regular subject areas. A major limitation of the ESL approach is that many students nonetheless fall behind in science, social studies, and other subjects because of their deficiencies in English.

Bilingual education is instruction in two languages. Not only are English and the native language taught, but other subjects such as math and science may be offered in the native language until English skills are developed. Students may be in English-language classes in subjects which rely less upon language, such as music, art, and physical education.

The federal government promoted these programs in the Bilingual Education Act of 1968 (Title VII of ESEA), and some states, including Massachusetts, Illinois, Texas, and California, have mandated bilingual education. Moreover, in the 1974 *Lau* case involving Chinese-speaking students in San Francisco, the United States Supreme Court ruled that under the Civil Rights Act, districts must rectify those English-language deficiencies that exclude students from effective participation in education programs.[36] Later that same year, Congress revised and extended bilingual education to encompass bicultural education, and it increased appropriations. The Bilingual Education Act of 1974 officially defined a bi-lingual education program as:

> a program of instruction, designed for children of limited English-speaking ability in elementary or secondary schools in which ... there is instruction given in, and study of English and, to the extent necessary to allow a child to progress effectively through the educational system, the native-language of the children of limited English-speaking ability, and such instruction is given with appreciation for the cultural heritage of such children, and, with respect to elementary school instruction, such instruction shall, to the extent necessary, be in all courses or subjects of study which will allow a child to progress effectively through the educational system.[37]

History, literature, and other aspects of the students' cultural traditions are included to strengthen their self-concept and promote cultural pluralism in our multicultural society. Some criticize bilingual education as a crutch. Many bilingual programs are two- or three-year transitional programs and often fall short of providing a genuine bilingual, bicultural experience. Districts with few non-English-speaking children may provide remedial instruction or an ESL program to try to ensure access to the school curriculum. Whichever approach is followed, the ultimate goal, of course, is to equalize educational opportunity for students from non-English-speaking back-grounds. Many children, however, still do not attain adequate skills in English to realize their potential and to succeed in American society.

Besides implementing bilingual education programs, many districts have incorporated ethnic studies in their curriculum to provide a multicultural education for all students. Many elementary reading series are now integrated and better reflect our multicultural society. The social studies curriculum now gives more attention to America's diverse racial and ethnic groups than it did as recently as the 1960s. American Indians, blacks, and other minorities are more visible in American history textbooks, and world history has expanded beyond Europe. Elective courses on black history and Third World studies are available in some high schools.[38] These texts and courses tend to be most popular in schools enrolling students of different racial and ethnic backgrounds. They are equally important, however, to broaden awareness for those in more homogeneous districts.

These various changes reflect in part the civil rights movement and the rise of ethnicity in our society. Federal and state legislation supporting ethnic heritage studies have further promoted these curricular changes. NCATE, the teacher education accrediting association, has mandated multicultural education in progams preparing teachers for the schools.

ACTIVITY 12–3

Status of Curricular Innovations

Select one of the important contemporary curricular concerns (e.g., an aspect of educational technology, early childhood education, back to basics, career education, bilingual and multicultural education, or a more recent innovation) and determine its current status. You should read recent articles on the topic (locate through the *Education Index*). You may also want to focus on one particular school or district and talk with teachers or review changes in textbooks. What tentative conclusions can you make about the impact and implementation of curriculum change?

Chapter Twelve

SUMMARY

Changes in the school curriculum often are responses to changes in the society. Many schools abandoned teaching German during World War I and added courses in communism during the Cold War era of the 1950s. During the post-Sputnik education decade, myriad innovations and changes occurred. Many of the curriculum reforms were oversold and in practice fell far short of being the panacea promised. Head Start, for example, did not eliminate poverty nor equalize educational achievement for disadvantaged children. Disillusionment quickly followed.

Often the name, sometimes the form, but frequently not the substance of curriculum reforms have been adopted by schools. The latest change—new math, open education, back to basics, or career education—was quickly espoused, but often with relatively little significant change from previous practice.

Sometimes schools seemed to endorse change for the sake of change or for good public relations. Are innovations necessarily improvements? Schools invested in technological hardware because federal and foundation funds were available and having such equipment demonstrated that they were up-to-date. Did the technology improve learning? Was it worth the expense? Did students learn more effectively, for example, in language laboratories? Once the novelty of technological gadgets wore off or the machines broke down, they often went unused or were not repaired.

Many of the so-called new ideas and reforms in curriculum have their roots in earlier practices. The curriculum legacy of the progressive education movement is substantial and still influential in American education. The progressives, for example, were very concerned about individual differences, individualizing instruction, interdisciplinary approaches, problem solving,

motivation of students, and the involvement of teachers in curriculum development. These remain fundamental issues in the 1980s. Due to many changes in schools and society, today's answers will not be the same as yesterday's, but an historical perspective can be enlightening and useful.

The curriculum can be affected by laws or court decisions mandating policy (e.g., minimum competency tests, education of the handicapped, and the *Lau* decision). The availability of new funds targeted for special programs can further promote change. The federal government has encouraged many changes by financing the programs through various types of grants. However, it is probably easier to add new courses or emphases (e.g., career education, bilingual education) than to change the content or approach in existing courses (as the efforts of the curriculum reform projects demonstrate). Many of the programs fell far short of achieving their goals when implemented in various school districts.

Courses that have support, consensus, and endorsement within the educational community and among the public are more likely to be implemented successfully than when there is conflict and opposition. Driver education is very popular (and encouraged by more favorable rates from insurance companies), whereas sex education is a volatile issue in many communities.

Over a decade ago, John Goodlad, on the basis of observations in more than 150 classrooms, concluded that "many of the changes we have believed to be taking place in schooling [in the education decade] have not been getting into classrooms."[39] That statement probably still is true today, despite a great deal of attention in education literature to the change process. Leadership is a critical factor at all levels. Within a school, the principal is a key person, but teachers are in a strategic position to pocket-veto changes that they do not endorse. Changes may be more successful if teachers are involved in their development or at least in the decision to adopt. In-service training of teachers is crucial in implementing curriculum change, but it has often been slighted or ignored.

Finally, it is probably premature to expect recent changes to have fully permeated the schools and too soon to make final judgments on their success. Change takes time. The governance and organization of American schools make full implementation of reforms difficult. Nonetheless, the curriculum has changed and in the years ahead will continue to be shaped by the new needs of society.

NOTES

1. Robert S. Zais, *Curriculum: Principles and Foundations* (New York: Thomas Y. Crowell, 1976), pp. 6–14.

2. Frances Klein, Kenneth A. Tye, and Joyce E. Wright, "A Study of Schooling: Curriculum," *Phi Delta Kappan* 61, no. 4 (December 1979): 244–45.

3. David B. Tyack, *The One Best System: A History of American Urban Education* (Cambridge, Mass.: Harvard University Press, 1974), pp. 46–47.

4. John A. Nietz, *The Evolution of American Secondary School Textbooks* (Rutland, Vt.: Charles E. Tuttle, 1965), p. 74; John A. Nietz, *Old Textbooks* (Pittsburgh: University of Pittsburgh, 1961), p. 242.

5. Lawrence A. Cremin, "Curriculum Making in the United States," *Teachers College Record* 73, no. 2 (December 1971): 207–20; Lawrence A. Cremin, *The Transformation of the School: Progressivism in American Education, 1876–1957* (New York: Knopf, 1961); and James R. Squire, ed., *A New Look at Progressive Education* (Washington, D.C.: Association for Supervision and Curriculum Development, 1972). The best descriptions of showcase progressive schools are in John Dewey and Evelyn Dewey, *Schools of To-Morrow*, 1915 (New York: Dutton, 1962).

6. John Dewey, *Experience and Education* (New York: Macmillan, 1938); and Cremin, *Transformation of the Schools*, pp. 332–38.

7. Jerome S. Bruner, *The Process of Education* (New York: Vintage Books, 1960).

8. William E. Klingele, *Teaching in Middle Schools* (Boston: Allyn and Bacon, 1979), pp. 1–16; and Leslie W. Kindred et al., *The Middle School Curriculum* (Boston: Allyn and Bacon, 1976), pp. 70–81.

9. Daniel Tanner, "Splitting Up the School System: Are Comprehensive High Schools Doomed?" *Phi Delta Kappan* 61, no. 2 (October 1979): 92–97.

10. Montana repealed its curriculum laws in 1975 and gave the state education department responsibility. Earl J. Ogletree, "The Status of State-Legislated Curricula in the U.S.," *Phi Delta Kappan* 61, no. 2 (October 1979): 133–35.

11. Donald E. Orlosky and B. Othanel Smith, "Educational Change: Its Origins and Characteristics," *Phi Delta Kappan* 53, no. 7 (March 1972): 412–14.

12. John D. McNeil, *Curriculum: A Comprehensive Introduction* (Boston: Little, Brown, 1977), pp. 295–97. See also Hilda Taba, *Curriculum Development: Theory and Practice* (New York: Harcourt Brace & World, 1962).

13. John I. Goodlad, M. Frances Klein, and Associates, *Behind the Classroom Door* (Worthington, Ohio: Charles A. Jones, 1970), pp. 62–64, 81.

14. Ruth Miller Elson, *Guardians of Tradition* (Lincoln, Neb.: University of Nebraska Press, 1964).

15. Hillel Black, *The American Schoolbook* (New York: William Morrow, 1967); and William Lowe Boyd, "The Changing Politics of Curriculum Policy-Making for American Schools," *Review of Educational Research* 48, no. 4 (Fall 1978): 577–608.

16. Frances Fitzgerald, *America Revised: History Schoolbooks in the Twentieth Century* (Boston: Atlantic-Little, Brown, 1979).

17. Ford Foundation, *A Foundation Goes to School* (New York: Ford Foundation, 1972), p. 22; Fred M. Hechinger, "Where Have All the Innovations Gone?" *Today's Education* 65 (September/October 1976): 80–83; Barbara J. Benham, Phil Giesen, and Jeannie Oakes, "A Study of Schooling: Students' Experiences in Schools," *Phi Delta Kappan* 61, no. 5 (January 1980): 339.

18. Stuart A. Shorenstein, "Pulling the Plug on Instructional TV," *Change* 10, no. 10 (November 1978): 36–39; and Richard W. Smith, "Educational Television Is Not Educating," *Change* 10, no. 11 (December/January 1978/79): 62–63.

19. Lawrence A. Cremin, *Public Education* (New York: Basic Books, 1976), p. 22. Neil Postman develops the idea of a television curriculum in *Teaching as a Conserving Activity* (New York: Delacorte Press, 1979). See also Robert M. Liebert, John M. Neale, and Emile S. Davidson, *The Early Window: Effects of Television on Children and Youth* (New York: Pergamon Press, 1973); and Robert J. Blakely, *To Serve the Public Interest: Educational Broadcasting in the United States* (Syracuse, N.Y.: Syracuse University Press, 1979).

20. Fred L. Splittgerber, "Computer-Based Instruction: A Revolution in the Making?" *Educational Technology* 19, no. 1 (January 1979): 20–25; and Robert J. Seidel, "It's 1980: Do You Know Where Your Computer Is?" *Phi Delta Kappan* 61, no. 7 (March 1980): 481–85.

21. *WEB: A Simulation of Working in an Educational Bureaucracy* (Lakeside, Calif.: Interact Company, 1973); Robert E. Horn and Anne Cleaves, eds., *The Guide to Simulations/Games for Education and Training*, 4th ed. (Beverly Hills, Calif.: Sage Publications, 1980).

22. Jeffrey J. Blaga, "Simulation in the Teaching of Social Studies: A Dying Strategy?" *Phi Delta Kappan* 61, no. 1 (September 1979): 70.

23. McNeil, *Curriculum*, p. 36.

24. National Center for Education Statistics, *The Condition of Education, 1980* (Washington, D.C.: Government Printing Office, 1980), p. 206.

25. Nancy Rubin, "Head Start Efforts Prove Their Value," *New York Times*, 6 January 1980, Sec. 13, p. 13. See also Edward Zigler and Jeanette Valentine, eds., *Project Head Start: A Legacy of the War on Poverty* (New York: The Free Press, 1980).

26. Herbert Zimiles, "Early Childhood Education: A Selective Overview of Current Issues and Trends," *Harvard Educational Review* 79, no. 3 (February 1978): 509–27.

27. Ben Brodinsky, "Back to the Basics: The Movement and Its Meaning," *Phi Delta Kappan* 58, no. 7 (March 1977): 522–27.

28. James D. Koerner, ed., *The Case for Basic Education* (Boston: Little, Brown, 1959); and George H. Gallup, "The Eleventh Annual Gallup Poll of the Public's Attitudes Toward the Public Schools," *Phi Delta Kappan* 61, no. 1 (September 1979): 40–41.

29. See also Morris Klein, *Why Johnny Can't Add: The Failure of the New Math* (New York: St. Martin's Press, 1973); Frank E. Armbruster, *Our Children's Crippled Future: How American Education Has Failed* (New York: Quadrangle, 1977); and Council for Basic Education, *Empty Pages: A Search for Writing Competence in School and Society* (Washington, D.C.: Council for Basic Education, 1979).

30. Stanley Elam, ed., *The Gallup Polls of Attitudes Toward Education, 1969–1973* (Bloomington, Ind.: Phi Delta Kappa, 1973), pp. 163, 175.

31. Sidney P. Marland, *Career Education: A Proposal for Reform* (New York: McGraw-Hill, 1974).

32. Jeanne Wilson and Patricia Rutan, *Career Education: An Open Door Policy* (Bloomington, Ind.: Phi Delta Kappa, 1977), pp. 7–9.

33. Gallup, "The Eleventh Annual Gallup Poll," p. 42.

34. W. Norton Grubb and Marvin Lazerson, "Rally 'Round the Workplace: Continuities and Fallacies in Career Education," *Harvard Educational Review* 45, no. 4 (November 1975): 451–74; and Calvin M. Woodward, "The Fruits of Manual Training," (1883), reprinted in Marvin Lazerson and W. Norton Grubb, eds., *American Education and Vocationalism: A Documentary History, 1870–1970*), (New York: Teachers College Press, 1974), pp. 61–65.

35. Stephen P. Heyneman, "The Career Education Debate: Where the Differences Lie," *Teachers College Record* 80, no. 4 (May 1979): 659–88.

36. *Lau v. Nichols*, 414 U.S. 563 (1974).

37. Public Law 93-380, quoted in United States Commission on Civil Rights, *A Better Chance to Learn: Bilingual-Bicultural Education*. Clearinghouse Publication No. 51 (May 1975), pp. 186–87.

38. See, e.g., James A. Banks, ed., *Teaching Ethnic Studies: Concepts and Strategies*, Forty-third Yearbook of the National Council for the Social Studies (Washington, D.C.: National Council for the Social Studies, 1973); Nicholas Colangelo et al., eds, *Multicultural Nonsexist Education* (Dubuque, Iowa: Kendall/Hunt, 1979); and special issue of the *Journal of Negro Education* 48, no. 3 (Summer 1979), on multicultural education.

39. Goodlad et al., *Behind the Classroom Door*, p. 97.

FOR FURTHER STUDY

Davis, O. L., Jr., ed. *Perspectives on Curriculum Development, 1776–1976*. Washington, D.C.: Association for Supervision and Curriculum Development, 1976.

Lesser, Gerald. *Children and Television: Lessons from Sesame Street*. New York: Random House, 1974.

Ragan, William B., and Shepherd, Gene D. *Elementary Curriculum*. 5th ed. New York: Holt, Rinehart and Winston, 1977.

Roberts, Arthur D. *Educational Innovations: Alternatives in Curriculum and Instruction*. Boston: Allyn and Bacon, 1975.

Spodek, Bernard, and Walberg, Herbert J., eds. *Early Childhood Education: Perspectives and Issues*. Berkeley, Calif.: McCutchan, 1977.

Tanner, Daniel, and Tanner, Laurel, *Curriculum Development: Theory Into Practice*. 2nd ed. New York: Macmillan, 1980.

Trump, J. Lloyd, and Miller, Delmas F. *Secondary School Curriculum Improvement*. 3rd ed. Boston: Allyn and Bacon, 1979.

Part 3
Self-Assessment

Date _____

1.0 Decision on Teaching as a Career

Since reading Part 3, my decision on becoming or not becoming a teacher has been—
( ) confirmed, because_____.
( ) somewhat modified, in that_____.
( ) drastically changed, because_____.
( ) made more difficult, because_____.

2.0 Philosophy of Education Statement

Since reading Part 3, my opening statement about education has been *modified* on the following points (write about only those in which there are changes; in this unit, 2.1, 2.2, and 2.5 are most likely):

2.1 goals of education.

2.2 the curriculum.

2.3 the role of the teacher.

2.4 perceptions of learning.

2.5 educational policies and procedures.

3.0 The School as a Social Institution

3.1 Since reading Part 3, my understanding of the role of the school has—
( ) not been altered. I still believe the school to be_____.
( ) become more appreciative. For example, _____.
( ) become more critical. I now feel_____.
( ) been expanded. I now realize why the school_____.

3.2 Regarding the social relationships in the school, I have changed my views on (write about only those that have been altered, most likely 3.2.3, 3.2.4, 3.2.5, and 3.2.6 in this part):

3.2.1 student-student.
3.2.2 teacher-students.
3.2.3 teacher-teacher.
3.2.4 teacher-administrator.
3.2.5 administrator-school board.
3.2.6 school-community.

Chapter Twelve

4.0 Information Gained

4.1 What specific information or concept(s) mentioned in Part 3 did you find most significant or interesting?

4.2 What information did you find least interesting?

5.0 Reflection on an Education Issue (Select only one; be specific, including points made in class, or evidence cited in the book).

5.1 (Chapter 8) Has the American public school system changed substantially in the past 100 years?

5.2 (Chapter 9) To what extent do citizens control their local public schools?

5.3 (Chapter 10) Is the way we pay for public schools fair?

5.4 (Chapter 11) What are schools for?

5.5 (Chapter 12) What should be the school curriculum?

Part 4
Teaching Tomorrow

Now that you have learned about teachers' personal attributes, their classroom responsibilities, and the rationale behind the school's functions, you may wonder what will be the dominant concerns of American education in the future. The answer to that question will largely determine what you teach and how you organize instruction.

Before discussing what is in the chapters of Part 4, we should mention that it has one unique feature. In the introductions to Chapters 13, 14, and 15, you will find a list of competencies that are proposed for tomorrow's teachers. The schools of the future will require teachers who have special knowledge, skills, and dispositions. As you explore the issues of individualization, equality of educational opportunity, and freedom of choice regarding schools, consider carefully what these issues will mean to you and those who will be instructing tomorrow's citizens.

The common thread found in all the chapters of Part 4 is that teachers in coming years will be faced with a challenging dichotomy: they must maximize individual liberties yet fulfill societal needs. The opening chapter sets the stage by discussing how society perceives individuals today and how it expects the schools to treat individuals. Chapters 14 and 15 reveal divergent solutions to the problem of responding to differences in students' needs. Chapter 14 focuses on the remedies to the historic discrimination against minority students. Chapter 15 discusses proposals to provide more meaningful options in education, both public and nonpublic, to allow students choices more appropriate for their abilities and interests. An epilogue challenges you to formulate your answers to the two questions that opened the book: Is teaching for you? and What are schools for?

RECOGNIZING INDIVIDUAL NEEDS

A variety of phenomena have forced America to reexamine its traditional emphasis upon socialization in schools. Today's society is more concerned that individuals be free to explore their personal dreams, although it fears that this may deteriorate into narcissism. Within the schools there is much interest in humanizing education, individualizing instruction, and building positive student self-concepts. Teachers and administrators are aware of the educational and legal need for recognizing student differences. Student civil rights and sex discrimination have become important issues to parents and special interest groups.

Perhaps nothing today receives more attention than the education of special students. As a result of a 1975 federal law, handicapped students must be provided a public education in "the least restrictive environment." One consequence is the retraining of teachers to cope with new types of students "mainstreamed," as it is called, into the classroom. Furthermore, such legislation indirectly acknowledges that teachers must pay more attention to talented and gifted students as well. Can teachers and the schools realistically cope with the needs of each student?

IMPLEMENTING EQUAL EDUCATIONAL OPPORTUNITY

Not only must the schools take account of the special needs of handicapped students, the courts have stated that schools must provide equal educational opportunity for all students, regardless of their racial or ethnic background. Chapter 14 begins with an examination of racial isolation in the United States and explores the arguments surrounding school desegregation. Major court decisions and remedies for improving equal educational opportunities are discussed. Numerous researchers believe that, as pervasive and destructive as racial discrimination is in the schools, social class bias provides even more denial of equal educational opportunity. Important questions are raised for those who believe that teachers have a responsibility to promote equal educational opportunity.

OFFERING EDUCATIONAL CHOICES

Throughout history, schools have been the frequent object of protest and controversy. Socrates had to drink the cup of hemlock; students at early Italian universities threw spoiled fruit and vegetables at unpopular professors; truant officers in the nineteenth century locked up delinquent pupils; parents in the twentieth century have risked jail sentences as they opted for instruction of their children at home rather than in schools.

The first major section of Chapter 15 looks in depth at the arguments of school critics that emerged during the 1960s and 1970s. The charges against the schools remain virtually the same today. The remainder of the chapter will look at the alternatives that have been tried recently, such as open education and the school-within-a-school concept. Nonpublic options—private schools, parochial schools, and free schools—constitute the closing segment of the chapter.

13

Recognizing Individual Needs

We are guilty of many errors and many faults, but our worst crime is abandoning the children, neglecting the fountain of life. Many of the things we need can wait. The child cannot. Right now is the time his bones are being formed, his blood is being made, and his senses are being developed. To him we cannot answer "Tomorrow." His name is "Today."

Gabriela Mistral

Every person born into this world represents something new, something that never existed before, something original and unique. . . . Every person's foremost task is the actualization of his or her unique, unprecedented and never recurring potentialities, and not the repetition of something *that another, and be it even the greatest, has already achieved.*

Martin Buber

Part 3 detailed America's commitment to universal education. Some would say that the price of providing basic skills to millions of students has been the loss of creativity and individuality. The schools usually cater to the average and typical, and ignore or minimize treatment of students who have special needs or talents.

The central issue here is whether the public school system can have two major goals—the socialization of students and the encouragement of their individuality—at the same time. Can the interests of the public be compatible with the desires of individuals? Can the nation bear the burden of the costs and can teachers find the time to be truly responsive to the needs of all students? The American public seems to tell teachers that it wants the needs of individual students met first.

Chapter 13 opens with a brief overview of past efforts to recognize individual differences. That segment is followed by a description of the legal dimensions of individuality. Special attention is given to student civil rights and Title IX, the legislation designed to counteract sexual discrimination in the schools.

Shifting to classroom practices, the remaining portions of the chapter examine what is likely to happen when teachers individualize. Most attention is given to the ramifications of Public Law 94-142, the Education of the Handicapped law. Mainstreaming—of students with disabilities as well as the talented and gifted—is discussed in some detail.

After you have read Chapter 13, you should be able to (1) offer a plausible explanation of America's periodic efforts to humanize education, (2) briefly state the legal rights of students, (3) identify four areas in schooling where sexism exists, and (4) describe the classroom implications of Public Law 94–142.

One more thing. As you read Chapter 13, think about the type of person who will be needed in the classrooms of the future. Would you agree with the following list of competencies? Can you add anything to this list? (Answer the second question after you have read the chapter.)

Tomorrow's teachers should have *knowledge* of:

- the principles of humanistic education;
- a variety of teaching methods appropriate for individualized classrooms;
- students' legal rights;
- regulations pertaining to mainstreaming and sexism in schools;

- the physical, psychological, and academic needs of special education students;
- various professionals and agencies to whom students could be referred.

Tomorrow's teachers should have *skills* in:

- evaluating students' needs;
- identifying physical, mental, and social disorders;
- preparing and implementing individual education plans (IEPs);
- disciplining with persuasion rather than physical force.

Tomorrow's teachers should be *disposed* toward:

- creativity and inventiveness, considering the diverse interests of students;
- flexibility;
- cooperation and team teaching (for the many group projects);
- equal treatment of male and female students.

HUMANIZING EDUCATION

The effort to give greater personal attention to students may seem a mere reflection of today's so-called me generation and our alleged culture of narcissism. This is not a new phenomenon, however. Writers in the late 1800s frequently urged teachers to be concerned about each pupil's interests, feelings, and personal goals (see Chapters 8 and 12). An extensive statement about the dignity and worth of individuals as the fundamental value of this nation was made in the *Moral and Spiritual Values in Public Schools* pronouncement of the National Education Association in 1951.[1]

Today the term *humanistic education* is often used to convey these sentiments.

One source describes it this way: "In a humanistic atmosphere, both the teacher and the student cooperatively and reflectively identify the students' educational needs. In the process, the teacher involves the student in learning through choosing, investigating, discovering, creating, generalizing, evaluating, applying, and performing. This teaching-learning process also requires extensive sharing between teacher and student and student and student."[2] As this definition makes clear, when most educators today talk about humanizing instruction, they are talking about a process of interaction that seeks more shared responsibility (between teacher and student) for learning. The term should *not* be equated with humanism, a philosophy that espouses the perfectibility of human beings and denial of a divine power who is supreme.

You will recall from Part 3, however, that humanistic education has not always been one of the country's major educational goals. What conditions promote interest in a curriculum that is more keenly sensitive to the diverse personalities of students rather than a curriculum that can be taught to all? Kniker's research concluded that America wants affective educational programs most especially in periods following wars.[3] Evidently, the trauma of battle and the exposure to alternative value systems causes the nation to reexamine its traditions and priorities. The nation's economic status is likely to emphasize or deemphasize humanistic goals of the schools. Periods when the economy is expanding, or when the nation experiences a crisis (such as a war), may bring a concerted effort to have schools stress the basics. Yet another factor that may provide impetus for humanistic education is the changing populations of the schools. As different immigrant groups come into the country, or educators identify students with specific learning problems, school officials often ask that such pupils receive special instruction.

As you would suspect, humanistic education is defined and implemented differently in various schools, but three components seem common to most programs. Educators assume that there are significantly different styles of learning; that constant diagnosis and prescription of instructional materials must occur; and that students learn best through demonstration of what they have learned. Some humanistic educators believe that the third component should be the extensive use of students as teachers of other students.[4]

The beginning point is the assumption that students learn by quite different methods. Some begin with abstractions; others prefer to look at details and draw deductions. Some work best alone; others in groups. Some move at a rapid pace, others proceed cautiously and meticulously. Reissman found that many inner-city students, for example, have strongly developed nonaural senses (visual, tactile, and kinesthetic). They gesture actively and are very expressive in unstructured, spontaneous situations. They like to learn in active situations, such as work-study programs and field-based learning. Rather than a discussion or lecture on discipline, justice, and government, Reissman found that inner-city children enjoyed game-playing that, in this case, included a mock court.[5]

To meet the variety of learning styles, teachers in humanistic programs must spend much time in preparing materials and in diagnosing and prescribing assignments for students. A major problem is the huge amount of time needed by individual teachers and teaching teams for such tasks as orienting students to independent study opportunities; listening to student reports; observing pupils; and consulting with specialists in the district who are working with children with special needs. If teachers believe that individuals learn differently, then they must engage in these activities to monitor student progress.

Many of the programs in humanizing education encourage students to work together on specific lessons as well as extended research projects. There are benefits from such interaction. Students gain confidence as they are able to talk with their peers and are asked to share what they know. When older students are asked to help younger students, their preparation becomes a reinforcer of concepts they had been exposed to earlier. Programs that do not have the student-as-teacher concept usually provide students with training on how to evaluate their own work.

Some programs emphasize team teaching while others make extensive use of specialists. The assumption is that just as students are different, so are teachers different. A blend of teacher personalities will better meet the diverse needs of the students. The focus in programs can differ. For example, a math teacher who wishes to humanize his classroom may have all the students working with the same text, doing the same problems at different speeds. A history teacher may have her students involved with a choice of activities about ancient Rome (e.g., a drama about daily life in the city, or a report about military battles, or a discussion of the lives of the Caesars). In the same school a third teacher, who also wishes to humanize the classroom, may provide the greatest amount of choice by limiting the students only to projects that come under the heading of energy conservation.[6]

Are humanistic classrooms as practical at the secondary level as at the elementary level? You may think that it is more natural for this movement to work with younger children since their curriculum is not as structured as the high school curriculum. Numerous articles and books suggest it can work at both levels, with the

following results: vandalism declines, student academic performance increases, and the teacher dropout rate decreases.[7]

As you will note in Chapter 15, some critics are convinced that the schools are far too permissive and intellectually weak already. They would join those philosophers mentioned in Chapter 11 who are convinced that the goals of the schools should be strictly academic. They would add that in an educational enterprise the size of the United States, the public is only fooling itself if it believes that individual needs in the affective area can be met in conjunction with cognitive tasks that society expects to be accomplished.

PROTECTING STUDENT RIGHTS

To speak of humanizing the schools without mentioning the status of legal rights of youth would be a critical omission. Until recently, students had little legal standing and protection. In the eighteenth century, children were considered to be possessions—chattels of the family and wards of the state. Legally they were nonpersons bound by the decisions of their families. When others, such as schools, had responsibility for children and youth (even college students), they were considered to be *in loco parentis*, i.e., "in place of the parents."

The twentieth century has produced ever-increasing knowledge about the needs of children as the result of psychologists' research. Social services agencies documented abuses by parents. The student protest movement of the late 1960s and early 1970s resulted in court decisions securing the rights of demonstrators. Concern about the collapse of the family in the 1970s, the women's movement, and child abuse brought more legislation for the rights of children and youth. Many states now require medical personnel, social service workers, and educators who learn of child abuse to report it to police authorities.[8]

The U.S. Supreme Court decision that is the landmark case in juvenile rights is the *In re Gault* verdict in 1967, involving a 15-year-old boy who had made obscene phone calls. The finding of the court was that children are persons entitled to constitutional rights, including due process. Teachers must be concerned about the legal protections accorded to all citizens.

Court Cases on Student Rights

Two years after the *Gault* decision, the *Tinker* case from Des Moines, Iowa, ruled that "neither the 14th Amendment nor the Bill of Rights is for adults alone." Two Tinker children, together with several other students, had been suspended when they attended school wearing black armbands as a protest against the Vietnam War. The Supreme Court ruled this symbolic expression of free speech was protected by the 1st and 14th amendments since it did not disrupt school activities or invade the rights of others.[9]

More recent decisions have clarified students' rights in matters of personal and general conduct. Students can picket outside schools in an orderly fashion. School newspaper staffs, or individuals producing student underground papers distributed in schools, generally have been accorded the same freedom of the press as the media have. Regulating the length of boys' hair and establishing dress codes were major issues in many schools in the late 1960s and early 1970s. The courts were divided on these issues of personal appearance and student freedom. Generally speaking, the schools had to show that hair codes had some rationale and were applied fairly to all. Typically, hair codes and dress codes introduced by coaches have been upheld because participation in extracurricular activities has been regarded as an optional school program.[10]

Cartoon by A. L. Kaufman, Master's Agency.

"Now, Mr. Filbrick—just what's wrong with the way my daughter dresses for school?"

Chapter Thirteen

The matter of privacy in school has grown in importance as a legal issue. Congress passed the Family Educational Rights and Privacy Act (often called the Buckley Amendment) in 1974. It guarantees privacy of student records and grants parents the right to inspect all pupil records maintained by the school. The law restricts school personnel from releasing information about students to third parties without obtaining parental permission. There is some question whether teachers must allow parents to see records that they have maintained *just for themselves*. The privacy of student records does not extend to the matter of lockers. Administrative searches of student lockers have been upheld.[11]

Most teachers and administrators are concerned about classroom and school-related incidents that might involve them legally. A major court case concerns students' suspension. Another concerns school policy regarding corporal punishment. The *Goss* v. *Lopez* case, decided in 1975, has far-reaching implications for teachers and administrators because it concerns procedural due process that students must be granted. The decision by the justices was that students must have oral or written notice of the charges against them and some form of hearing. Students are entitled to confront the witnesses against them, have an impartial hearing, receive a full list of allegations, speak at the hearing, and, in the case of a suspension, have legal counsel present.[12]

The decision in *Ingraham* v. *Wright* (1977) concerned the right of a Florida school to spank its students. One student argued that his spanking was administered arbitrarily and was unduly harsh. The Supreme Court ruled that the school had the right to use corporal punishment, but that such punishment was not to be administered capriciously. The regulations regarding spanking were to be made known to the students and to their parents. In effect, the court said that corporal punishment can be legally administered even if a child's parents are opposed to it.[13]

You may think that it is increasingly difficult, if not impossible, for schools to discipline students. There are two reasons why that is not true. First, many parents and students do not know the due process regulations. Even when they know about due process, they often avoid it. The parents may fear that their sons and daughters will be harrassed by teachers or other students if they press legal charges.

The second reason, and perhaps the more important, is that the schools have legal responsibility for education. The courts have consistently upheld the schools' obligation for the safety and welfare of the students and staff. For example, there is little question that schools can set rules and regulations regarding health and safety (for example, equipment and clothing to be worn in shop and gymnasium, policies against fighting, conduct at school functions). Similarly, schools have been upheld in their authority to set policies regarding disruptions of the educational process. Students wearing provocative clothes to schools could be dismissed. In the *Tinker* case, however, the court held that the school cannot use the argument of potential disruption to curtail freedom of speech.

For the classroom teacher, it would appear that the courts have said that it is very important to be sensitive to students' rights. Even the teacher's recognized responsibility for managing a class does not give the teacher a license to mistreat students or deny them rights of citizenship. In the words of one writer, the Supreme Court "has carefully tried to carve out an area between parental dominion and state prerogatives, where certain adult rights can be extended to children under specific circumstances."[14]

Cartoon by Mike Elam in *Phi Delta Kappan*, April 1973, p. 543. Reprinted with permission of Phi Delta Kappa, Bloomington, Ind.

"It's only fair to warn you, Mr. Flint—everything you say is being recorded for my ACLU lawyer."

Sexism in Education and Title IX

Just as there has been much concern during the past two decades about children's rights, so there has been a cultural reconsideration of the role and status of women. The women's movement has led educators to examine sexism in schooling. Title IX of the Education Amendments of 1972 (which is related to the earlier Civil Rights Act of 1964) specifically barred discrimination on the basis of sex.

Prior to the passage of Title IX, there was growing concern about sexism in schools. Extensive documentation was gathered on the sex bias in school textbooks. Pioneering studies such as *Dick and Jane as Victims* analyzed the pictorial and textual content of children's readers. In its

1972 edition, *Dick and Jane as Victims* noted that 84% of the books pictured women in homemaking roles while only 16% showed women in professional roles. Typically, readers show boys doing vigorous activities, being in leadership positions, and pursuing more exciting careers. Girls are depicted as more likely to be spectators, engaged often in reading and daydreaming. Although some progress has been made, most texts still give greater prominence to males.[15]

In classroom interactions, teachers have tended to accept cultural stereotypes. Assuming that girls are more interested in academics, teachers asked them more questions. Teachers allow boys more leeway in not conforming to school disciplinary practices. Among the traditional sex-role stereotypes are that activity and aggression are characteristics more likely of boys than girls; that girls are better at reading and boys better at mathematics; and that girls are more emotional than boys. Are such tendencies, if they are accurate, biological or cultural? While research on the brain suggests that the sexes may have differences in the way they process information, are such differences so significant that they, and not the cultural stereotypes, determine student behaviors?[16]

How boys and girls are treated in the classroom, what courses they are advised to take, and what careers are suggested to them by their teachers and counselors, are factors that reinforce sex-role stereotypes. There is evidence to suggest that schools are gradually breaking down such stereotypes. In metropolitan centers, former vocational high schools for boys are admitting girls. In junior high schools, as a result of Title IX, home economics classes and shop courses previously segregated by sex have been integrated. Coeducational physical education courses likewise are being offered. Counselors are far less likely today to advise boys to become doctors and lawyers ｜but｜ girls to become nurses or teachers.[17]

Earlier (in Chapter 3) we looked at the numbers of teachers who are men and women. A preponderance of elementary teachers are women, while men are in the majority at the secondary level. What does not escape those concerned about discrimination is that only 18% of the school administrators in a 40-state survey were women. Further analyzed, the data show that women usually hold middle-management (from principals to assistant superintendents) positions rather than chief administrator jobs.[18]

School boards have been under pressure to reexamine policies that are sexist. Do their master contracts have provisions that discriminate against women (the medical clauses for pregnancy, for example)? Do job descriptions, together with tradition, favor men for certain positions (such as coaches)? Schools often have been willing to advertise scholarships that would be available to their students. Some scholarships have been designated for boys or girls. A number of districts have decided to forego advertising such scholarships and granting such awards.

The most controversial aspect of Title IX has been its application to athletics. The visibility of interscholastic athletics, the amounts of money spent on it, and the obvious sexism have made the problem a well-publicized one.[19] Title IX only stated that there should be no discrimination on the basis of sex. The Department of Health, Education, and Welfare issued guidelines defining discriminatory practices. Initially released in the mid-1970s and periodically revised, these guidelines have not been welcomed by male sports fans and some school athletic directors.

The earliest guidelines called for schools to provide equal opportunities for males and females. This was widely interpreted as a rule of balance. If 10 sports were provided for boys, 10 were to be available for girls. The guidelines further noted that if a school

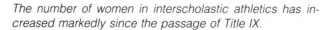

The number of women in interscholastic athletics has increased markedly since the passage of Title IX.

offered only one varsity team in a sport, it was to be open to both sexes, except for contact sports. (The football and wrestling teams, for example, could exclude girls.)

Has such legislation had an impact upon sports participation? Definitely. In 1977 the National Federation of State High School Associations reported that the number of girls taking part in high school sports had increased 459% since the 1970–71 school year, the year prior to the passage of Title IX.[20] Not only varsity interscholastic programs are affected, however. As mentioned earlier, physical education programs have been combined in most schools. Another effect of the law has been the membership stipulations of many extracurricular clubs in schools. Singing groups have been reorganized, and cheer squads now have male as well as female leaders.

Because Title IX applied to all educational institutions, and because most of the organized opposition to it came from the collegiate level, it is important that we consider at least two other dimensions. The National Collegiate Athletic Association (NCAA) lobbied extensively against the Department of Health, Education, and Welfare's efforts to require schools to spend equal amounts of money on men's and women's teams. Such actions, the NCAA argued, would ruin college and university programs. In 1979, HEW Department Secretary Patricia Harris announced new guidelines for Title IX. A proportionate amount of money was to be spent on the women in athletic programs. Thus, if 40% of a school's athletes were women, then 40% of the college's athletic budget should be spent on their programs. There is a real question whether this ruling will be applied at both the K-12 and collegiate levels.

How will the increase of women's athletics at the collegiate level affect high school sports? The lure of athletic scholarships has already prompted some parents to file lawsuits against one state (Tennessee) that maintains six-player girls' basketball. The parents of the high school players claim that this version of the game, which has three offensive and three defensive players, diminishes the chances that their daughters will be considered all-round players that the colleges want. There is considerable pressure in Iowa, another six-player state, to change the rules to make it a five-player game, despite the contention that more participate in six-player games.[21]

Sexism in education and Title IX symbolize another aspect of a significant educational problem that we have treated in this chapter—that students' individual needs must be recognized. These needs are not met when sexual stereotypes are widely accepted.

Cartoon by Ford Button, *Phi Delta Kappan*, September 1974, p. 47. Reprinted with permission.

"If you're serious about this women's lib bit, I might be able to get you a basketball scholarship."

Chapter Thirteen

ACTIVITY 13–1

Sexism in Education

How sensitive are schools today to the issue of sexism? You may wish to visit a school or the central administrative office of a school district to learn how the district is attempting to eliminate sexual discrimination. Before you make the visit, you should develop a list of questions to ask about various areas of concern, such as textbook materials, athletic policies, and faculty hiring. Consult the sources in the "For Further Study" section and below for possible questions.

Here are some possible questions for the evaluation of textbooks:

1. Do females appear as frequently as males?
2. Are females portrayed in a limited stereotyped manner?
3. Is the reader given the impression that interesting, acceptable, or achievement-oriented females are the exception?
4. Are people shown solely in traditional roles and life-styles? Are all adults married? Are any single-parent families shown?
5. (for social studies texts) Are the comments about women's contributions integrated throughout the text? Is history written solely in terms of wars rather than other areas where women have made contributions?

These questions have been adapted from Marjorie Stern, ed., *Changing Sexist Practices in the Classroom: Women in Education* (Washington, D.C.: American Federation of Teachers, 1971–72). Also, see *Cracking the Glass Slipper: PEER's Guide to Ending Sex Bias in Your Schools* (Washington, D.C.: NOW Legal Defense and Education Fund, 1978 – PEER is the Project on Equal Educational Rights of the National Organization of Women); Mary Berry, *Taking Sexism out of Education* (Washington, D.C.: U.S. Government Printing Office, 1978); Franklin and Betty June Parker, *Women's Education—A World View* (Westport, Conn.: Greenwood Press, 1979); Janice Pottker, ed., *Sex Bias in the Schools* (Rutherford, N.J.: Fairleigh Dickinson University Press, 1977).

PROVIDING FOR THE INDIVIDUAL NEEDS OF STUDENTS

Consistent with the feeling that education should be humanized and students given more rights is the effort to individualize the curriculum. Educational journals in the 1970s had many articles by teachers on how they individualized their classes.[22] More and more in the late 1970s, however, articles appeared about the education of exceptional children. (*Exceptional children* is a term referring to all special education students, including the talented and gifted, learning disabled, emotionally disturbed, mentally retarded, and physically handicapped youngsters.) The increase in attention to the needs of the exceptional children reflected the impact of the Education of the Handicapped law in 1975. This federal law already has had and will continue to have an immense effect on many classrooms.

Individualizing Instruction

There are numerous parallels between the basic format of a humanized classroom and an individualized classroom. Both acknowledge the importance of the individual student and wish to take that into account. Both give the individual student alternative ways to respond to general instructional objectives. The major difference, if one can call it that, is that the humanized classroom will allow the student a greater voice in determining the instruction objectives. Activities in an individualized classroom are very much structured by the teacher.

Helen D. Dell has identified five components that distinguish an individualized classroom from a group-centered classroom. Three of the components deal with curriculum materials and two with classroom involvement:

Curriculum.
1. a unit for achievement with specific objectives;

2. learning activities in a prewritten learning guide;

3. evaluation of student achievement;

Classroom.
4. teacher involvement;

5. student responsibilities.[23]

The heart of individualized instruction is the opportunity for the student to work at his or her own pace.

Dell explains each as follows: A unit for achievement should be brief enough so that the students can see their progress. A unit of achievement, therefore, might be a one-day or even a one-hour lesson built around a single instructional objective. This objective would state what the student would be expected to know or do. The objective might be broad enough to tell the student what sequence of steps he or she must master to gain the objective. The objective suggests the means by which both the student and the teacher will be able to measure the student's mastery of it. Instructional objectives are short-range goals that are part of the larger picture of the student's education. Students must be alerted to the terminal objectives, which may take from six months to several years to achieve. (Following are examples of terminal objectives: "Given a community issue, present a solution and the evidence that supports your solution;" or, "Use the elements of sentence structure when writing sentences.")

It is crucial that teachers develop a number of learning activities for their students. Not every student needs the same types of activities or the same number. At this point the teacher may find that there are commercially prepared curriculum sets that can be used besides activities that are developed by the teacher. The teacher may decide to assign a student a number of activities (a sequence), selected ones, or allow the student to choose one or two to gain an instructional objective. In many respects, this variety of activities is the heart of individualization.

Obviously, individualized instruction requires constant evaluation of the student's performance regarding the objectives. That does not mean necessarily that the teacher or teacher aide in the room checks each assignment. Self-check lists may be developed. The usual range of assessment techniques (see Chapter 7) can be employed—paper and pencil tests, achievement tests, development of reports to the class, and essays.

The points above stress teacher preparation. Such teacher preparation is essential to avoid chaos in the classroom. An individualized classroom, to the observer, may appear chaotic due to the variety of materials available, the movement of students throughout the room as they check on reference sources and confer with the teacher and their peers, and the higher level of noise. But such appearances mask, in an effectively prepared environment, the purposeful way students are working.

The teacher in the classroom will want to maximize his or her involvement with the individual learners. Dell suggests that various room arrangements facilitate better use of time and reduce the number of wasted trips by students. Likewise, the teacher in the classroom works toward establishing a record-keeping system that reduces needless trips by students to check on their progress. Unlike the group-centered classroom teacher who is lecturing much of the time, the teacher in an individualized classroom functions in three special areas in his or her interactions with students. The teacher counsels students about curriculum that will aid their course work. Since not all students have the same objectives, the teacher tutors individual students. Finally, teachers monitor and modify behavior. Recognizing that individuals work at different paces, the teacher must develop techniques that reward those students who achieve their instructional objectives, motivate those who lose interest, and rechannel the efforts of those who create disciplinary problems that interfere with other students.

Unlike the traditional classroom that puts little responsibility on the student, the individualized classroom encourages the student to be an independent learner. Students are therefore expected to manage

their own time, form constructive working relationships with other students, and on occasion, serve as tutors to other students.

This description is a general picture of what individualized classrooms will require of teachers and students. Specific programs may add other dimensions to individualized instruction. Some will use the school district's computer services to test students' comprehension in various subjects. Teachers may use the services of the system's or regional education agency's professional consultants to determine whether their students have learning or emotional disabilities. Some instructors in individualized classrooms make extensive use of mastery tests, diagnostic instruments, and attitudinal scales to discover the learning styles most appropriate for each student. Certain districts committed to individualized instruction use commercially designed computer programs, such as Westinghouse Corporation's PLAN, which provides prescriptive suggestions based on frequently given diagnostic tests. In systems without funds for such programs, some teachers design individual contract forms that students fill out, indicating what objectives they will accomplish by a certain date.

No doubt you have wondered what problems there might be with this approach to learning. As you can imagine, a major drawback is the time needed by teachers to prepare the individual materials. It is difficult, too, for many teachers to do the record-keeping and evaluation required without the aid of a paraprofessional. Individualized instruction, or what passes for individualized instruction, can be challenged because it does not truly provide *different* objectives for individual learners. If all materials are the same, but the students read them at different speeds, can that truly be called individualized instruction? The final criticism that can be leveled against individualized instruction is that it minimizes, to a dangerous level, the concept that there is a body of knowledge and a number of group experiences that all students should have. By dividing education into so many compartments and segregating individuals by ability levels and interests, that valuable part of schooling is curtailed.

Working with Talented and Gifted Students

Approximately 3% of the K-12 school population in the nation is talented and gifted (TAG), although typically only half that number are identified and given any special help in the classroom. Talented and gifted children have been defined as those "capable of high performance including those with demonstrated achievement and/or potential ability in any one of the following areas, singly or in combination: general intellectual ability, specific academic aptitude, creative and productive thinking, leadership, ability, skill in visual and performing arts, and psychomotor ability."[24]

Talented and gifted students may have some of the following attributes: a large vocabulary, ability to read before entering school with comprehension of what is read, ability to see several ways to handle a situation, enjoyment of the companionship of adults as much as peers, constant experimentation and extensive interests, a good memory, and good intuition. Contrary to the common assumption that these students find school work easy, a number of them are likely to experience difficulty. It may be due to boredom, but more likely they experience problems because of their different rate of physical, emotional, and mental development. It is erroneous to assume that these students, so capable in some areas, will be equally adept in all phases of school life.[25]

Just as students with other special needs are being recognized, so more educational leaders and legislators are coming to be-

lieve that the talented and gifted need special attention. (If a distinction is to be made between talented and gifted, it is that talented refers to one area, whereas gifted covers many areas.) Yet funding for TAG programs appears to be sporadic. While some legislators endorse funding plans, others oppose the grants because they feel such programs are a form of elitism. They also argue that our limited educational funds should be given to those more in need of special help.[26]

Those states and local districts that have instituted programs for the talented and gifted usually have tried one of four methods: acceleration, special grouping, enrichment, and individualized learning. Skipping grades, providing early entrance to school, and taking two years at one time are three types of acceleration. While this approach allows for rapid progression and may reduce boredom, its disadvantages are that students may experience gaps in their learning, and they may have problems developing friends in school.

Special groups have been used in this country for a variety of educational purposes, and special grouping would appear to offer numerous benefits to TAG students. Their peers would challenge them, and they would likely have a teacher with special training to provide appropriate curriculum for the interests. The drawbacks are that it promotes the charge of elitism, and it reduces the chances for the TAG students to interact with other students. As noted earlier, just because such students have academic skills does not mean they are adept in social relationships, which could be alleviated through contact with the rest of the population.

Enrichment programs essentially offer the same curricula used with other students, but the content is taken beyond what occurs in the traditional classroom. The student receives special work, and may have time apart from the regular class to work on individual projects. The greatest drawbacks are that the student is known as a "different" pupil, which may bring resentment, and that it involves additional work for the teacher.

The school district committed to a program of individualized instruction treats every student as a person with special needs and interests. To provide for those who are talented and gifted, the teacher may use some of the activities that allow the student to do extensive reading or work as a tutor with other students. Some school districts, finding that their faculty may not have the specialized expertise to work with TAG students, have arranged for additional tutors from the community.

Working with Handicapped Students

Who are the handicapped? The commonly accepted definition includes those who are mentally retarded, hearing-impaired, deaf, speech-impaired, visually handicapped (both the partially sighted and the blind), seriously emotionally disturbed, orthopedically impaired, and those who have limited strength, vitality or alertness due to chronic or acute health problems.[27] About 8% of all school-age children, or almost 4 million persons, are classified as handicapped. Figure 13–1 indicates the number by type of disability.

Many societies, including our own, have often denied full membership to those individuals who are handicapped. When families could not care for them or pay for private institutional care, the handicapped were relegated to special schools, state mental hospitals, and even prisons. When communities recognized a moral obligation to provide some education for those who were handicapped, they set aside within the public schools special units devoted solely to such students. The first self-contained classroom in the public schools

was in Cleveland, Ohio, in 1875. By 1890 such classrooms were located in many major cities.[28]

By the late 1960s researchers recognized that there were far more people with handicaps than were generally assumed; moreover, there were indications that educating handicapped persons in isolated centers was not preparing these individuals for the fullest participation possible. These findings do not mean that all handicapped children should be mainstreamed in regular classrooms. It is still recognized that some handicapped students will never be able to function adequately in a regular classrooms. Programs such as the Special Olympics, begun in 1968, are valuable in providing a setting for handicapped youngsters to succeed in that select competition.

The concern for the rights and needs of handicapped students in the 1970s was reflected in court decisions and federal legislation. Federal district court decisions in 1972 ruled that "all school-age children, regardless of the severity of their handicap, were entitled to a free public education." Prior to this time, some states had laws requiring education of all eligible handicapped, but others left it to local districts whether they would provide services to handicapped, or pay tuition of the students to private agencies.[29]

It was not until Congress acted in the mid-1970s that all children were entitled to a "free appropriate public education." Thus, even when a child is too severely handicapped to be placed in a public school and must be placed in a residential program, it will be at public expense for room and board as well as education. One federal law is often referred to simply as "Section 504." It is a provision of P.L. 93-112, the Vocational Rehabilitation Act Amendments of 1973. The law was designed to protect the civil rights of handi-

Figure 13–1.
School-age handicapped receiving special education

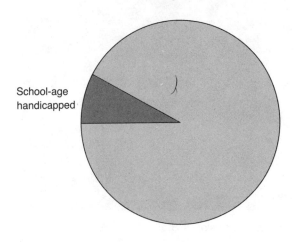

**Proportion of the Handicapped
in School-age Population**

School-age
handicapped

Number of Handicapped by Condition

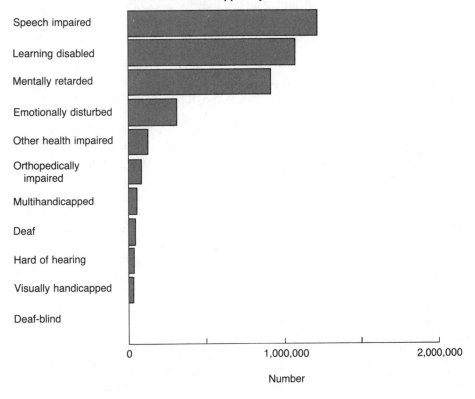

Speech impaired

Learning disabled

Mentally retarded

Emotionally disturbed

Other health impaired

Orthopedically
  impaired

Multihandicapped

Deaf

Hard of hearing

Visually handicapped

Deaf-blind

0   1,000,000   2,000,000

Number

From the National Center for Education Statistics, *The Condition of Education, 1980* (Washington, D.C.: U.S. Government Printing Office, 1980) p. 69.

Chapter Thirteen

A blind student using a Braille textbook.

capped Americans *of all ages*. The statute reads: "No otherwise qualified handicapped individual in the United States shall, solely by reason of his handicap, be excluded from the participation in, be denied the benefits of, or be subjected to discrimination under any program or activity receiving federal assistance." Two years later, a more specific bill applying to handicapped students under age 21 was passed. The Education for All Handicapped Children Act of 1975 (Public Law 94-142), establishes a set of minimum standards that must be followed by states and local educational agencies in the instruction of handicapped students.[30]

Three features of P.L. 94-142 should be emphasized. The first is that the law calls for the education of the handicapped with nonhandicapped children to the "maximum extent appropriate." This is often known as "the least restrictive environment" provision; that is, whenever possible the students should be mainstreamed in regular classrooms. The law does not automatically call for mainstreaming of all children, nor insist that all handicapped children be educated in the regular classroom.

A second provision of the law insists that local educational agencies (or whatever agency is responsible for the education of the handicapped) must develop "an individual education plan" (IEP) for each student. The IEP should clearly note the unique needs of each child and indicate the type of environment best suited for that student. If and when a student is moved from one environment to another that is more restrictive, the IEP document must show why such a move is required.

Further, special education committees of parents must be established on the local level. Such committees have become important to educators in advising them of parental concerns, and they are vital in building support for and understanding about the education of the handicapped.

As a potential teacher who will have handicapped children to instruct, you probably wonder what gains and problems have emerged since the passage of these laws. Much progress has been made, even with the severely handicapped. For example, great advances have been made in teaching daily living skills and personal care skills to the trainable and profoundly retarded. Autistic children have been brought into regular classrooms and, through their interactions with other students, gained many social skills. Technological breakthroughs have aided the education of the blind and deaf. For example, the Kurzweil Reading Machine for the blind is an electronic computer that scans and recognizes printed letters and then reads them aloud. What these techniques and devices point to, in the opinion of those who are advocates of mainstreaming, is that we have too often underestimated what will be accomplished.[31]

While there are few who oppose education of the handicapped, some raise questions of a so-called practical nature. They are concerned that harried teachers who can barely cope with a regular classroom will have to spend an inordinate amount of time with the handicapped students assigned to them. Moreover, they believe that requiring teachers to have a minimum number of hours in special education courses, as some states including Maryland, California, and Kansas now mandate, will not sufficiently prepare them. A few see a problem of more federal control of the schools. In summary, they ask, can the public schools take on this immense, albeit important, task without sacrificing the quality of education of regular students?

ACTIVITY 13–2
Special People

To increase your awareness of the wide range of students with special needs and potentials, consider doing one of the following:

Option A: Visit a school or institution having handicapped students or mainstreamed classes. In your report (written or oral), note what you observed. Be sure to include anything unexpected.

Option B: Contact a local, state, or national educational agency to find out what it is doing regarding special education. One national organization would be the Council for Exceptional Children.

Option C: If you cannot arrange for either of the other options, do a report on a famous person who had a handicap. Learn what problems the person had in school because of his or her handicap, and how they were overcome. Any of the following would be a good subject:

Alexander Graham Bell	Nelson Rockefeller
Isadora Duncan	Eleanor Roosevelt
Thomas Edison	Wilma Rudolph
Albert Einstein	Woodrow Wilson
Helen Keller	Stevie Wonder
George Patton	

SUMMARY

One of the clichés prominent in school literature during the 1970s was, "There is nothing more unequal than the equal treatment of unequals." It was good rhetoric, but did schools then and are schools today really providing individualized instruction for the nation's students?

America's long-term commitment to education has recognized that students' personal needs and interests should be taken into account. However, through most of our history, the schools have emphasized turning out good American citizens. Personal feelings and goals of students were of secondary importance.

For a variety of reasons, the schools in the twentieth century gradually became aware of the variety of needs and interests of their students. The thrust of humanistic education is that the student should be an active participant in determining the curriculum. The recognition of student rights is a parallel development. The most dramatic changes, from a legal point of view, occurred in the late 1960s and early 1970s. Children became officially recognized as persons with constitutional rights. During this period congressional action attempted to redress discrimination against women in education.

For years, students with special needs, ranging from the talented and gifted to those with physical and emotional handicaps, were slighted or isolated. There have been increased efforts to provide an appropriate education and to individualize instruction for those students. Education has been viewed as a vehicle that will increase opportunities for those who are handicapped, much as it was viewed as a means to improve the plight of the immigrants.

Chapter 13 shows that as much as society may favor recognizing and protecting individual needs, it also has some reservations. For example, it still wants students who are responsive to the authority of school administration. This dilemma between individual needs and societal needs may be dramatized by the apocryphal account of two parents who filed a lawsuit against a school district for discriminating against their children because they were normal—everyone else was receiving special programming. In other words, there is real concern that if the handicapped receive IEPs, shouldn't *all* students? Who knows, it may be that some features pioneered for the handicapped may extend eventually to all students. Already, normal children are receiving one benefit from mainstreaming; they are broadening their contacts with individuals who heretofore have been considered different.

NOTES

1. Christopher Lasch, *The Culture of Narcissism: American Life in An Age of Diminishing Expectations* (New York: W.W. Norton, 1979); Educational Policies Commission, National Education Association, *Moral and Spiritual Values in the Public Schools* (Washington, D.C.: National Education Association, 1951).

2. Weems A. Saucier et al., *Toward Humanistic Teaching in High School* (Lexington, Mass.: D.C. Heath and Co., 1975), preface.

3. Charles R. Kniker, *You and Values Education* (Columbus, Ohio: Charles E. Merrill, 1977), especially Chapter 1; Gerald Weinstein and Mario Fantini, eds., *Toward Humanistic Education: A Curriculum of Affect* (New York: Praeger, 1970).

4. Alan Gartner and Frank Riessman, *How to Individualize Learning* (Bloomington, Ind.: Phi Delta Kappa, 1977), p. 7.

5. Ibid., p. 11. For other descriptions of classroom practices, see A. L. Butler, "Humanistic Early Childhood Education: A Challenge Now and in the Future," *Viewpoints in Teaching and Learning* 55, no. 3 (Summer 1979): 83–90; Billy L. Abel, "Humanizing Secondary Schools: Words or Action?" *National Association of Secondary School Principals Bulletin* 60, no. 402 (October 1976): 63–68.

6. James L. Neujahr, *The Individualized Instruction Game* (New York: Teachers College Press, 1976), p. 2; Robert W. Wirtz, "Developing and Selecting Content Material," *Thrust for Education Leadership* 5, no. 3 (January 1976): 19–23.

7. See note 5; also, Carolyn Reece, "Meeting New Challenges—Making New Friends," *Children Today* 7, no. 4 (July-August 1978): 16–21; Bruce A. Middlebrooks, "A Principal Humanizes His School," *Peabody Journal of Education* 53, no. 1 (October 1975): 24–26; George W. Neill, "The Reform of Intermediate and Secondary Education in California," *Phi Delta Kappan* 57, no. 6 (February 1976): 391–94.

8. Hillary Rodham, "Children Under the Law," *Harvard Educational Review* 43, no. 4 (November 1973): 487–514.

9. *Tinker* v. *Des Moines Independent School District*, 393 U.S. 503 (1969); Paul E. Herbold, "Freedom of Expression, the Schools and the Burger Court," *Peabody Journal of Education* 51, no. 2 (January 1974): 124–31.

10. Bertram Bandman, "Some Legal, Moral, and Intellectual Rights of Children," *Educational Theory*

27, no. 3 (Summer 1977): 169–78; R.D. Mawdsley, "Constitutional Rights of Students," in C.P. Hooker, ed., *The Courts and Education*, 77th Yearbook, National Society for the Study of Education (Chicago: University of Chicago Press, 1978), p. 175.

11. John Walden, "Student Privacy: What Are Your Responsibilities?" *Instructor* 86, no. 1 (August/September 1976): 86–87.

12. David Schimmel and Louis Fischer, *The Civil Rights of Students* (New York: Harper and Row, 1975), pp. 228–63, for a general discussion; *Goss v. Lopez*, 419 U.S. 565 (1975).

13. *Ingraham* v. *Wright* 97. S. Ct. 1401 (1977); Thomas J. Flygare, "Corporal Punishment Is Not Yet Dead as a Constitutional Issue," *Phi Delta Kappan* 62, no. 1 (September 1980): 53, 54.

14. Rodham, "Children Under the Law," p. 497.

15. *Dick and Jane as Victims* (Women and Words and Images: P.O. Box 2163, Princeton, N.J.: 1972 and 1975, revised); John Warren Stewig and Mary Lynn Kniptel, "Sexism in Picture Books: What Progress," *Elementary School Journal* 76, no. 3 (December 1975): 151–65; Phyllis Arlow and Merle Froschl, "Women in the High School Curriculum: A Review of U.S. History and English Literature Texts," in *High School Feminist Studies*, ed. and comp. Carol Ahlum and Jacqueline Fralley, an introduction by Florence Howe, (Old Westbury, N.Y.: The Feminist Press, 1976), pp. xi–xxviii.

16. Eleanor Maccoby and Carol Jacklin, *The Psychology of Sex Differences* (Palo Alto, Calif.: Stanford University Press, 1974); Marcia Guttentag and Helen Bray, *Undoing Sex Stereotypes: Research and Resources for Educators* (New York: McGraw-Hill, 1976); Pauline B. Gouch, "Forty-one Ways to Teach About Sex Role Stereotyping," *Learning* 5, no. 5 (January 1977): 72–74, 77, 80.

17. Patricia Sexton, *Women in Education* (Bloomington, Ind.: Phi Delta Kappa, 1976), pp. 55–60.

18. Joseph M. Cronin and Sally B. Pancrazio, "Women as Education Leaders," *Phi Delta Kappan* 60, no. 8 (April 1979): 583–86.

19. Robert Cole, "Title IX: A Long Dazed Journey into Rights," *Phi Delta Kappan* 57, no. 9 (May 1976): 575–77, 586.

20. *Des Moines Register*, 2 January 1977.

21. "Text of Majority Opinion on Anti-Sex Bias Lawsuits," *Chronicle of Higher Education*, 21 May 1979, and "Sex, Sports, and Discrimination," *Chronicle of Higher Education*, 18 June 1979.

22. T.C. Roth, "Expanding the Concept of Individualized Education," *Educational Forum* 36, no. 1 (November 1971): 61–66; Michael Fedo, "For the Record: Individualized Learning," *American Education* 11, no. 5 (June 1975): 12–15; Donald W. Meintz, "The Task System in an Individualized Reading Class," *Journal of Reading* 20, no. 4 (January 1977): 301–4.

23. Helen D. Dell, *Individualized Instruction* (Chicago: Science Research Associates, 1972), pp. 5–17.

24. Edward L. Meyen, *Exceptional Children and Youth* (Denver, Colo.: Love Publishing Co., 1978), pp. 471–72. See Marsha M. Corell, *Teaching the Gifted and Talented* (Bloomington, Ind.: Phi Delta Kappa, 1978), p. 10, and Barbara Clark, *Growing Up Gifted* (Columbus, Ohio: Charles E. Merrill, 1979), pp. 136–38. The Office of Gifted and Talented (OGT) was established in the U.S. Office of Education and in 1974 the Education Amendments Section 404 Public Law 93-380 (part of the Special Projects Act) was passed.

25. Dorothy A. Sisk, "What If Your Child is Gifted?" *American Education* 13, no. 8 (October 1977): 23–26; C. June Maker, *Providing Programs for the Gifted Handicapped* (Reston, Va.: The Council for Exceptional Children, 1977), p. 95. It is estimated that as many as one of five gifted children could be classified as having educational problems, ranging from underachieving in particular subjects to experiencing alienation to the point that they choose to drop out of school.

26. Deborah Olstad, "The Pursuit of Excellence is not Elitism," *Phi Delta Kappan* 60, no. 3 (November 1978): 187–89, 229.

27. Joseph Ballard, "Public Law 94-142 and Section 504—Understanding What They Are and Are Not," a pamphlet from the Council for Exceptional Children, Reston, Va., 1978, p. 2.

28. Ted L. Miller and Harvey N. Switzky, "PL 94-142 and the Least Restrictive Alternative: An Interim Progress Report for Educators," *Journal of Education* 161, no. 3 (Summer 1979): 60–80; Jeffrey J. Zettel and Joseph Ballard, "The Education for All Handicapped Children Act of 1975 PL 94-142: Its History, Origins, and Concepts," *Journal of Education* 161, no. 3 (Summer 1979): 5–22.

29. Jeffrey J. Zettel and Alan Abeson, "The Right to a Free Appropriate Public Education," in *The Courts and Education*, ed. C.P. Hooker, p. 198.

30. William S. Kendell, "Public Law 94-142: Implications for the Classroom Teacher," *Peabody Journal of Education* 55, no. 3 (April 1978): 226–30.

31. "Mainstreaming Mary Ann," *American Education* 14, no. 9 (November 1978): 13–17; Henrietta Welden, "New Technology for the Handicapped," *American Education* 14, no. 9 (November 1978): 45–46; Barry Thomas, "Environmental Education for the Blind," *Instructor* 86, no. 9 (May 1977): 106–7.

FOR FURTHER STUDY

Balzer, Fred J., et al. *Human Relations Development: A Manual for Educators*, 2nd ed. Boston: Allyn and Bacon, 1977.

Brewer, Garry D., and Kakalik, James S. *Handicapped Children: Strategies for Improving Services.* New York: McGraw-Hill, 1979.

Dell, Helen D. *Students' Rights and Responsibilities.* Morristown, N.J.: General Learning Press, 1978.

Fishel, Andrew, and Pottker, Janice. *National Politics and Sex Discrimination in Education.* Toronto: Lexington Books, 1977.

Lamb, G., and Tiedt, S. W. *Humanizing Education.* Morristown, N.J.: General Learning Press, 1978.

Passow, A. Harry, ed. *The Gifted and the Talented: Their Education and Development*, 78th Yearbook of the National Society for the Study of Education. Chicago: National Society for the Study of Education, University of Chicago Press, 1979.

Reynolds, Maynard C., and Birch, Jack W. *Teaching Exceptional Children in All America's Schools.* Reston, Va.: The Council for Exceptional Children, 1977.

Stacey, Judith; Bereaud, Susan; and Daniels, Joan, eds. *And Jill Came Tumbling After: Sexism in American Education.* New York: Dell, 1974.

Talmadge, Harriet, ed. *Systems of Individualized Instruction.* Berkeley: McCutchan, 1975.

Vardin, Patricia, and Brody, Ilene, eds. *Children's Rights: Contemporary Perspectives.* New York: Teachers College Press, 1980.

14

Implementing Equal
Educational Opportunity

In these days it is doubtful that any child may reasonably be expected to succeed in life if he is denied the opportunity of an education. Such an opportunity . . . is a right which must be available to all on equal terms.

U.S. Supreme Court, Brown *v.* Board of Education, *1954*

In principle it is easy to agree that the individual needs of students should be recognized. In practice it is difficult to implement. Similarly, America can admit its discrimination and call, as Chief Justice Warren did, for equal educational opportunity for all students. It is quite another matter to achieve that ideal. The perceived lack of equal educational opportunity is a major issue facing the nation today. How well our society reaches that goal will just as surely affect you whether you are a citizen of suburbia, a business person in a small town, or a teacher in a desegregated school in a metropolitan area.

It has been said that the only social service America guarantees to all its citizens is education. The issue in Chapter 14 is whether the schools do provide an *equal* educational opportunity to all students. Other questions we can ask are whether schools can be used to rectify social discrimination and economic disparities between individuals, and whether the remedies introduced to overcome inequities are succeeding or failing. Also, what criteria should be used to determine the success or failure of the remedies?

Chapter Fourteen

The first section of the chapter, "Racism and the Schools," documents the isolation of America's minorities and cites some of the major studies on discrimination and the schools. When the schools perpetuated rather than corrected the injustices of society, the courts intervened. This segment describes the major court decisions and outlines the resulting remedies for desegregating the schools. The effects of busing and racial balance plans will be scrutinized. The section closes with a description of the methods to use in successfully desegregating a school system.

While the media have emphasized the problems of racial isolation and discrimination, most scholars believe that social class bias and equal educational opportunity are problems just as critical. Are we more of a classbound system than we might suspect? Are the poor being deprived of a fair chance for education? After examining studies on the relationship of family socioeconomic status and education, this segment of Chapter 14 explores those court cases and school programs that have attempted to alleviate social class bias.

The strategies highlighted include the compensatory programs of Title I of the Elementary and Secondary Education Act of 1965 and teacher training programs for the inner city.

After you have completed Chapter 14, you should be able to (1) state in your own words the rationale for desegregation remedies and (2) give three illustrations of the impact of social class upon school performance.

Racism and social class bias are two facts of American life, and so it is a safe prediction that if you become a teacher, you will encounter one or both of them—regardless of the type of system in which you are employed. Because schools are becoming more sensitive to these problems, future teachers will be expected to deal with them. As you read the chapter, think of the competencies you would want to have to cope with the situations described. Can you add anything to this list?[1]

Tomorrow's teachers should have a *knowledge* of:

● the ways social class is determined in the United States;

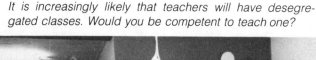

It is increasingly likely that teachers will have desegregated classes. Would you be competent to teach one?

- the contributions and concerns of various ethnic groups in America;

- the variety of desegregation remedies and resultant concerns (student assignments, assessment techniques, special curriculum);

- persons from various cultural backgrounds.

Tomorrow's teachers should have *skills* in:

- human relations, especially in knowing how to use a variety of group structures in classroom interactions;

- evaluating curriculum materials for race and sex bias;

- using a variety of instructional materials and approaches;

- working with parents of different racial, ethnic, and socioeconomic backgrounds.

Tomorrow's teachers should be *disposed* toward:

- avoiding stereotypes;

- justice for all students;

- using a multicultural perspective.

RACISM AND THE SCHOOLS

Racism exists in America. According to Robert Terry, racism occurs when any one color group, intentionally or unintentionally, "inequitably distributes resources; refuses to share power; maintains unresponsive and inflexible institution policies, procedures, and practices; and imposes an ethnocentric culture on any other color group for its 'supposed' benefit, and justifies its actions by punishing, blaming, ignoring, and/or helping the other color group."[2] If you accept that definition, it is hard to avoid labeling yourself a racist, because who among us has not at one time or another linked himself or herself

with "one color group" and intentionally or unintentionally engaged in a behavior that denied another color group something it was entitled to.

While racism is a fact, the term *race* is an abstraction. In other words, it is difficult, if not impossible, to find any individual who is a pure representative of a race. (Race usually refers to biological characteristics that include skin color, eye color, head shape, nose shape, hair color and texture, the presence or absence of body hair, and stature. Because there are so many variations within racial groups and because individuals are likely to have characteristics that can be associated with other races, anthropologists say that persons are *more or less* negroid, mongoloid, or caucasoid. Thus, race is a statistical and abstract concept rather than biological and genetic.[3]

While race is still recognized in U.S. Census data, it appears that there is increasing recognition that it is not the most useful categorization to use. It appears that there is more recognition of ethnicity, which refers to the shared experiences that a group of people have had. Because of the way data has been gathered and used in government documents pertaining to the census and affirmative action, the discussion in this section centers on four groups—black, Hispanic, Native American Indian, and Asian-American.

Racial Isolation

Approximately 25% of the nation's population belongs to the four groups:[4]

- 25,112,000—Black

- 18,300,000—Hispanic

- 1,387,000—Asian-American

- 793,000—American Indian

The racial groups are concentrated in certain areas of the country, and it is important to understand why they are clustered in such patterns. Blacks are located in the South or in metropolitan areas (where many moved after the Civil War to gain better employment opportunities). Cities such as Detroit, Philadelphia, and Chicago have large black populations. Four of five persons of Spanish origin live in metropolitan areas. However, they are concentrated in certain states—Arizona, California, Colorado, New Mexico, and Texas; almost 2 million more live in Florida and in the Northeast. Two-thirds of the American Indian population live on reservations; the remainder are about equally divided between rural and metropolitan areas. Asian-Americans tend to live in large cities on the East and West Coasts. This pattern of clustering is explained by racism. These groups were forced to live in ghettos when they came to the cities looking for work. Some who wanted to return home found that they were trapped economically and had to remain in the cities. (Who wants to hire a farm worker in Chicago?)[5]

The major educational implication of these demographic patterns is school segregation. Over 80% of the students in public schools in Atlanta, Newark, San Antonio, and Washington, D.C. are nonwhite. In fact, in the 26 largest cities of the United States, almost three of every four black young people are assigned to an intensely segregated school. In school districts of over 100,000 students, three of every five black students will attend a school that has over 90% black enrollment.[6]

Assuming district lines are not crossed, it becomes impossible to speak of any meaningful desegregation in such systems. Nationwide, there is some desegregation, although segregation of blacks is increasing. (*Desegregation* refers to the court-ordered efforts to bring together in the same school or social setting blacks and whites. This may or may not result in *integration*, which connotes a change in attitude so that individuals want to work together.)

Figure 14–1 shows the percentage distribution of black public school students, by region between 1970 and 1976. In the Northeast racial isolation increased, while other regions of the country (border states and D.C., Midwest, and West) showed a decrease. Figure 14–2 illustrates the percentage distribution of Hispanic public school students.

Historically, racist attitudes caused the development of segregated schooling. In colonial America there were numerous examples, in the South as well as the North, of black and white children attending the same schools and churches. But over the years, segregationist policies grew. In the South, specific laws prohibited education of blacks. After the Civil War, other laws established separate schools for blacks (de jure segregation). In the North, de facto segregation resulted from residential patterns. While modest efforts were made after World War II in the South to equalize the white and black schools, the courts

LUTHER

Figure 14–1.
Distribution of black students in public elementary and secondary schools

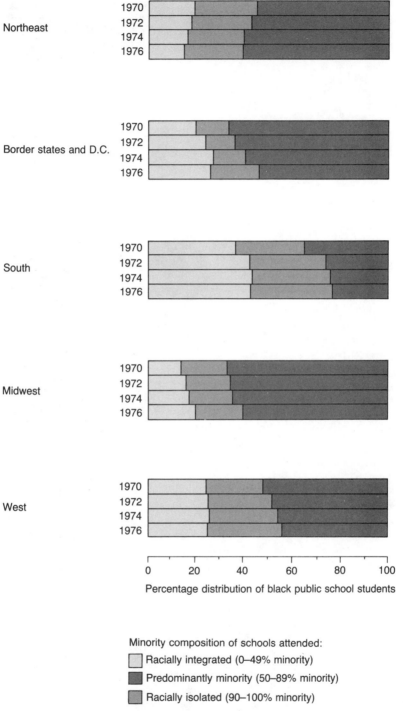

Percentage distribution of black public school students

Minority composition of schools attended:

☐ Racially integrated (0–49% minority)

■ Predominantly minority (50–89% minority)

▨ Racially isolated (90–100% minority)

From the National Center for Education Statistics, *The Condition of Education, 1979* (Washington, D.C.: U.S. Government Printing Office, 1979), p. 57.

Figure 14–2.

Distribution of Hispanic students in public elementary and secondary schools

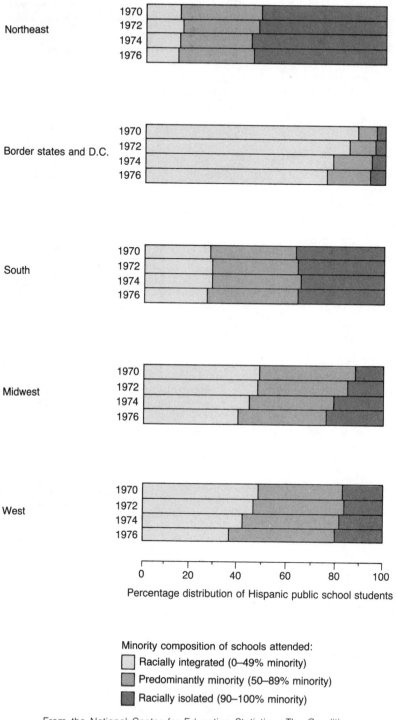

Percentage distribution of Hispanic public school students

Minority composition of schools attended:

☐ Racially integrated (0–49% minority)

▨ Predominantly minority (50–89% minority)

■ Racially isolated (90–100% minority)

From the National Center for Education Statistics, *The Condition of Education, 1979* (Washington, D.C.: U.S. Government Printing Office, 1979) p. 59.

increasingly recognized that segregation was not providing an equal educational opportunity for minority children. Study after study confirmed that white schools (or in the North, predominantly white schools) spent more money per pupil than black schools, and had better facilities, more instructional supplies, and teachers with more education. The minority schools had higher dropout rates, more suspensions, and fewer students attending college.[7]

These findings are ignored or minimized by racists, who argue that the poor performance of some minority students is their own fault. Some argue that blacks cannot

learn as well as whites (see Chapter 7). Others believe that the family or neighborhood environment is the chief cause of poor student behavior (in that no one in the family promotes education, for example). There are those who argue that desegregation is an admission that blacks cannot learn unless they attend schools with whites. The courts, citing research studies, disagree and are convinced that racial practices brought about unequal educational opportunity. Desegregating schools, they assert, would be the best insurance that *all* students would have at least an equal opportunity.[8]

ACTIVITY 14–1
Racist Practices

Can you identify examples of racist practices regarding schools today? Begin by rereading Robert Terry's definition of racism that opened this section. Terry emphasizes that typical responses of the majority, when "racial problems" emerge, are either to "blame the victim" and deny that there are problems, or to avoid the problem by pretending it doesn't exist. Here are some samples of denial and avoidance practices. Using media reports as well as your own experience, describe three current racist responses to educational issues.

(Denial: rejects the existence of a problem.)

1. "Our people have always been content. It was the outside agitators who got them to complain about school conditions."
2. "Minorities just want everything handed to them. They're too lazy to work for it."
3. "People get what they deserve. If we fixed the schools up, they would be vandalized tomorrow. They've brought it on themselves."
4. "We don't have any racial problems in our town."

(Avoidance: accepts the existence of a problem, but attempts to avoid it.)

1. "Sure, there is prejudice, and there has been some injustice. But it happened to my ancestors, too. It'll work out in time."
2. "Haven't they gone too far? After all, change has to occur gradually."
3. "I'm only one person. What can I do that makes a difference?"
4. "What we have here is a failure to communicate. Let's set up a committee."

Source: Robert Terry, Human Relations Consultant, Ypsilanti, Mich.

Court Decisions on School Desegregation

This brief review of judicial decisions about education and segregation of schools should be helpful to you in understanding the current efforts to provide equal educational opportunities. The courts are in a sense the nation's moral barometer, measuring our idealism as well as our racism. The decisions have called the country to live up to the Constitution, while others have mirrored the nation's fear of integration.

More than 100 years ago a northern state, Massachusetts, was the site of the nation's first segregated schooling case. The Roberts asked the Boston School Committee to allow their daughter to attend a nearby white school rather than the designated black school. In 1849 the state supreme court upheld the decision of the School Committee, which had denied the Roberts' request. The rationale of the committee and the court was that as long as "equal, but separate" facilities were provided, no injustice could be claimed.

That rationale was adopted by the U. S. Supreme Court in 1896 in *Plessy* v. *Ferguson*. In 1890 the state of Louisiana had passed a law that required that railroad cars provide separate accommodations for the white and colored races. Homer Plessy, who was seven-eighths white and one-eighth "African blood," protested that under the 14th Amendment, his equal rights had been violated. The majority opinion upheld the statute on the grounds that it was equally discriminatory for the whites as well as the blacks! As long as separate but equal transportation was provided, the Supreme Court concluded, the social conventions of the state could be upheld.

Thus the "separate-but-equal" doctrine was firmly entrenched in the American judicial system. It was the primary defense used by school districts that were challenged during the next 50 years for not providing equal educational opportunities. During this time the National Association for the Advancement of Colored People (NAACP) became the leader in using the legal system to address the evils of racism. In its earliest years, its founders, including W. E. B. DuBois, had attempted to

arouse the nation to correct racial injustices by publishing accounts of lynchings and discrimination in their journal, *The Crisis*. Increasingly, they found that change was more likely when it was mandated by the courts. Victories were slow in coming, but some progress was made.

The case that signaled the beginning of the end of the separate-but-equal doctrine was *Sweatt* v. *Painter* (1950).[9] A veteran of World War II, Herman Sweatt, wanted to become a lawyer in his native Texas. He was denied admission to the University of Texas law school because of his race and was referred to a newly created black law school, which was separate, but certainly not equal. The faculty did not have the reputation of the institution at Austin, the experience of the administration was less, the library holdings fewer, and the black school did not have the tradition or prestige of its "equal," according to the NAACP lawyers. In its verdict, the U. S. Supreme Court accepted the point that there were "certain intangibles in education" that had to be weighed as part of the equality of educational opportunity that was to be provided. The Court ordered the University of Texas to admit Sweatt.

The landmark case in desegregation occurred four years later in *Brown* v. *Board of Education of Topeka, Kansas*.[10] Linda Brown's parents were convinced by the time she was in fourth grade that the education she was receiving in the segregated schools in that city was decidedly inferior. They asked that she be transferred to a white school, a request that was denied. On behalf of the family the NAACP brought suit. In 1954 the U. S. Supreme Court ruled that racially separate educational facilities are "inherently unequal" and violate the equal protection clause of the 14th Amendment. The justices indicated, further, that in a technological society like the United States, education is a virtual right. Those

Numerous studies confirmed the fact that minority students received separate and unequal opportunities prior to 1954.

students who do not receive an equal opportunity for education are being discriminated against for life.

The implementation decision the following year (often called Brown II) mandated the federal courts to direct and oversee the transition to a "racially nondiscriminatory" or unitary system of public schools. The Court realized that its 1954 decision would bring a momentous societal change that would be difficult to achieve, and invited interested parties to submit suggestions on how to execute the 1954 verdict. The justices urged that desegregation proceed "with all deliberate speed."[11] This expression quickly became a legal loophole that reluctant districts used to delay desegregation. How does one define *deliberate* and/or *speed* legally?

Despite the publicized delay tactics of some southern systems, schools in the South were gradually desegregated. Ironically, northern school districts were becoming more segregated as whites moved

to the suburbs (de facto segregation). In 1969 in *Alexander* v. *Holmes County Board of Education*, the U.S. Supreme Court declared that the time for all deliberate speed was over and ordered an end to dual school systems.[12]

In the decisions prior to the mid-1960s busing was not addressed. The Civil Rights Act of 1964 increased the use of busing as one of the acceptable strategies to implement desegregation. In 1971 the Supreme Court held in *Swann* v. *Charlotte-Mechlenburg School District* that busing could be used to achieve desegregation. A 1974 decision involving Detroit, however, ruled that a city district could not force suburban districts to help it desegregate through a busing plan, in the absence of proof that the 53 suburban districts had deliberately practiced segregation. Justice Thurgood Marshall (who had argued the Brown case for the NAACP in 1954) disagreed, claiming that such reasoning was a "giant step backward" in the fight to desegregate schools. Metropolitan problems necessitate metropolitan solutions, he argued.[13]

No doubt the future will bring more cases on desegregation, as some people feel that not enough is being done and others become angered by what they perceive is excessive government interference in local school matters. What this section has emphasized is that the courts historically have waited for local districts to provide an equal education; they can only intervene when constitutional questions arise, and when an individual or group has filed an objection to the local practice.

Desegregation Remedies

When the courts rule that a local district is in violation, the district is given a reasonable amount of time to propose a plan for desegregation. Over the years a variety of remedies have taken account of the different conditions that exist in districts. Future educators should be concerned about these strategies, since they affect the classroom.

The essence of all desegregation remedies is that there must be some attempt to achieve racial balance. Desegregation plans involve movement, although not always busing. School districts may reapportion student enrollments to various buildings, pair schools, cluster schools, or build new facilities. Or a local system may decide to use a combination of strategies, one of which is busing. Desegregation plans recognize that some friction is possible initially, but they assume that the final results will benefit *all* students.

For years the simplest and often least expensive way to counter a segregated school population has been to redraw the district's *attendance lines* for various schools. (Of course, the same tactic was used to maintain segregation.) This remedy is tied to the concept that certain schools in the district should not become the minority schools. Some districts have attempted to maintain a profile of the community's population in each school. Thus, if the whites were 60% of the school enrollment, blacks 25%, and Hispanics 15%, then each attendance center was to have a 60-25-15 composition, plus or minus 5% to 10%. That plan has generally been found to be awkward. More likely, the local district and the regional agency in charge of overseeing that racial balance is achieved will work out a maximum percentage figure for minority students permitted in any one school. It may be determined that the black population of a city is 10%. Local and federal authorities agree that no more than 25% to 30% of any school's student population can be black. If it goes beyond that point, attendance lines have to be redrawn. In both the *Swann* decision and the later Pasadena, California, case, it was decided that a district is not required to redraw lines every year to make sure racial balance is achieved.[14]

This strategy has been attacked on several grounds. First, it seems not to work well in large metropolitan areas that have had to make numerous realignments. Citizens find it hard to keep up with the changes. Second, in a number of instances local or school officials have attempted to falsify racial population figures to preserve black and white schools. Shifts in populations in some cities make this plan hard to regulate even when officials are cooperating.

As buildings need replacing, districts can use *site selection* to ensure maximum desegregation. The assumption in such a plan is that an attractive new facility on the border between black and white neighborhoods will draw students from both groups. Some evidence suggests that smaller cities have been more successful than large cities in using this strategy.

One desegregation remedy that has worked well in some communities is the school *pairing* concept. Frequently called the "Princeton Plan" because it was first tried in that New Jersey city, it merges two neighborhood schools into sister schools. When buildings are paired, typically *all* the kindergarten to third-grade students from the combined school attendance areas go to one building, and *all* the students in grades 4 to 6 are placed in the other. This remedy is somewhat limited in scope because it requires two adjacent neighborhoods, black and white, with relatively similar student populations. It is popular, however, because there is minimal disturbance of the regular routine. Parents may find that their children still can walk to the second school, and that they need be less concerned about lengthy bus trips.

Large metropolitan districts have tried *open enrollment* as another technique for increasing desegregation. Students are free to attend any school in the system, with the stipulation that their presence in the school does not increase the percentage of majority students past a predetermined point. In the 1960s, when this plan was tried extensively, two problems emerged. First, some districts had not placed majority/minority quotas on the transfers. It was learned that more frequently the few white students still living in a predominately black neighborhood were the ones asking for the transfer. Second, in cities like Boston, open enrollment required the parents to pay the transportation costs (which could have been for subways rather than buses) if their children were transferred. The participation in such communities was minimal. Open enrollment plans have worked best when school administrators actively publicize and fully finance the programs.

An open-enrollment variation that is gaining much support is the *magnet* concept. Several schools in the district offer special programs or emphases. For example, one elementary school may institute a back-to-basics curriculum; a junior high school may offer a special science core of courses. One high school in the district might specialize in computer programming, while another is known for its fine-arts department. In those cities that have successfully adopted this model, students are able to attend the high school of their choice (assuming that it does not increase racial isolation) for all or part of the school day. Transportation costs are borne by the district. There has been much support of this type of program because it relies upon voluntary compliance by the residents of the community. The drawback to this plan is two-fold: the first is cost (transportation); the second is there is no real assurance that meaningful integration will occur in the buildings.[15]

The school desegregation plan that has provoked the greatest furor is busing. Usually it is undertaken to achieve better racial balance in the system and is done to conform with the order of the courts. Due to the problems in the past, it is usually not done unless it is the only alternative that remains. Advocates have argued that it can result in improved race relations. In addition, proponents claim that if busing is so harmful, why do we allow 21 million students a year to be be bused (when only 5% of the busing is done to comply with desegregation mandates)?

Those who oppose busing—they usually call it forced busing—believe that the costs outweigh the benefits. White and black parents are fearful that the long rides will upset their children. Some fear that their children will not be safe in predominately black schools. A few use the argument that busing costs taxpayers more (a weak argument since several studies have shown that desegregation bus routes are often more efficient that the routes designed to keep students segregated). A more valid criticism may be that only a small percentage of those eligible are bused.[16] The major fear about busing—expressed by

Chapter Fourteen

LUTHER   **By Brumsic Brandon, Jr.**

both white and black parents—is that the academic performance of their children will suffer.

A little-used but possibly increasingly viable option may be *metropolitanism*. The nation may see several school districts cooperating—probably one from the city with one or more from the surrounding suburban area. (You will recall that earlier the *Milliken* v. *Bradley* case from Detroit specified that one district could not be *forced* to aid another.) Such a plan might include some busing, sharing of special facilities, and exchange of faculty members.[17]

A question parents and educators frequently ask about desegregation is: What will it do to the performance of students in schools? Educators and politicians often ask a related question: Has the cause of desegregation been aided by these remedies? (Has segregation been slowed? Have feelings of trust and cooperation between groups been improved?) In response to the first question, virtually all studies that we know of conclude that the academic performance of white and black youngsters is not lowered because of desegregation programs. Moreover, such related matters as the students' self-concepts and their attitudes about schooling in general and their particular schools does not drop; in fact, it tends to rise for those students who move from the inferior school.[18]

Many individuals choose to ignore this data if it does not agree with their personal experience, or if it does not fit their personal biases. There is some evidence that desegregation remedies are not totally positive. Dr. James Coleman, a sociologist at the University of Chicago who directed several studies related to desegregation, has changed his position regarding the effectiveness of some remedies. He contends that desegregation has not improved the attitudes between whites and blacks. More importantly perhaps, his recent studies show that desegregation is counterproductive, because it has induced more whites to leave the school systems of the cities. Some researchers who have reexamined Coleman's data claim that it is flawed; they argue that desegregation still does work, and that it can reduce "white flight."[19]

The debate about desegregation will go on. According to one estimate, about 90% of the desegregation plans will work, but the 10% that don't will get an inordinate amount of attention in the media. It is difficult to forget the school riots in Boston, parent demonstrations in Pontiac, Michigan, or buses burning in Denver. What can be done to improve the odds that desegregation programs will work once they are mandated? Harvard psychologist and sociologist Thomas Pettigrew offers 10 suggestions, which you may wish to keep in mind if you are in such a situation:

1. Minority students are sometimes denied equal access to school activities such as student government or cheerleading squads. If provisions for equal access are not made, resentment is likely to grow.

2. Schools have to face the dilemma that they must prepare students for a labor market that is white, middle-class, and male-oriented; however, schools must also deal with the individual needs of their students.

3. Sometimes federal funds are cut when a desegregation plan occurs, because officials note that low-income students have been moved from certain buildings. Money for remedial programs is still needed to maintain educational services.

4. If students are to develop and maintain interracial friendships, the students should go to the same elementary, junior highs, and senior highs (i.e., consistent feeder patterns). Unfortunately, some districts disperse elementary students to a large number of junior highs, breaking the chances for continued relationships.

5. Research has shown that when a school staff reflects the racial composition of the student body, there is less likelihood of violence than if the minority teachers are underrepresented.

6. Districts should avoid token minority representatives in each school so that every building can say it is integrated. Meaningful patterns and equal treatment must be established.

7. Since integration is a cumulative process, it is important to begin desegregation with young children, before they are totally immersed in racism.

8. Schools may track disporportionate numbers of minority students into special education, vocational, and low-performance courses; schools should be very sensitive to such patterns.

9. The cultural bias of tests may foster segregation of racial groups. It is better to provide a variety of group learning experiences.

10. People tend to assume that minorities are poor, and to confuse race or ethnicity with class standing.[20]

ACTIVITY 14–2

Desegregation Today and Tomorrow

Prepare a position paper on what desegregation means to you now. Consult the sources cited in the "Notes" and "For Further Study" sections. Stress in your paper how you would respond if you were a teacher employed in a school that was desegregating. What would you do in your classroom?

SOCIAL CLASS BIAS AND THE SCHOOLS

Just as we recognized that race is an abstract term that does have real implications, likewise we can acknowledge that social class is an abstraction that, while difficult to document in the case of individuals, is associated with profound cultural differences. All Americans do not speak the same language (they have dialects), share the same values, have the same attitudes toward education, join the same clubs, prefer the same types of clothes, or share power.[21]

More significant for us is the conclusion of the educational researchers who argue that social class differences are even more influential than racial or ethnic differences when school performance outcomes are evaluated. After we discuss their general findings, we shall list some of the specific ways that social class is reflected in school practices, and in what ways it can influence the judgment of a teacher. Specific programs to overcome social class bias will be examined. Throughout the section the dominant issue is whether schools can (or should) be used to redistribute the chances for equal income.

The Case for Bias

Patricia Sexton in *Education and Income*, her 1961 study of Detroit, divided parents into income levels and then plotted the school performances of their children. She found high correlations between the income level and performance on achievement tests and placement in ability groups and curriculum projects. Students from lower-income homes were more likely to score lower on standardized tests. Moreover, Sexton noted that there were significant

differences in per-pupil spending amounts among the schools in this large district; those that had the higher parental income levels received more money per student than those schools that had a lower average parental income. Similarly, facilities for the children of the lower-income parents were poorer, and curricular materials less extensive.[22]

Her study, like others, was tied to the question that the courts were raising about the equality of educational opportunity: Do inequalities in education result in inequalities of opportunity? The U.S. Congress, as part of the 1964 Civil Rights Act, commissioned a major national study to answer the question. The chief researcher was James Coleman and, understandably, when the report was released in 1966 as *Equality of Educational Opportunity*, it was usually called the Coleman report.[23] It was widely assumed that the study would reveal that the different schooling outcomes among racial groups and the poor were attributable to the differences in their school facilities. To the surprise and consterna-

According to most educational researchers, social class differences are more important than racial or ethnic differences in determining academic performance levels.

tion of many, the report concluded that facilities, class size, teacher experience and training had relatively little impact upon schooling outcomes. Two factors identified as critical for success in school were the education or social class background of the student's family, and the social class composition of the school's students. Such conclusions made the study highly controversial.

Christopher Jencks of Harvard University, in the process of working on a book about the limits of schooling, decided to reexamine the findings of the Coleman report and to explore its policy implications. Jencks' results, reported in *Inequality*, agreed with most points developed by Coleman. He concluded that "school resources" such as class size, ability group, and curriculum have small and inconsistent effects on achievement. In this book and a succeeding one, *Who Gets Ahead?*, Jencks broadened the study to find out what in school, if anything, had an effect upon students' later economic successes.[24]

Incidentally, the Coleman and Jencks reports raised some questions about the accuracy and effects of data such as Sexton had collected in Detroit. Coleman found that schools attended by black and white children did not differ very much in terms of the inputs of education. In other words, schools are far more alike than they are different. If one adds that, based on their research, many school variables such as the number of library books or the age of the building do not appear to make much difference, should the conclusion be that schools are unimportant? In addition, are the researchers saying that the traditional belief that schooling is a vehicle for equal opportunity in society ("the great equalizer") is a myth? No. They agree that having schooling is far more important than not having schooling. Certainly students who complete high school are more successful, on most scales, than those who do not

complete school. When comparing high school graduates to each other, they are more alike than different. And what accounts for their post–high school accomplishments will most likely be *nonschool* variables. Should you want to predict what they will be doing 10 years after high school, you will have better success using their family social class background than data relating to their high school performance. In summary, they argue that America has exaggerated the importance of the school as a determinant of success in life.[26]

Social Class and School Practices

Individual studies confirm the pervasive influence of social class in the schools. While there is evidence that parents of all social classes value education to some degree, some do not make as much effort as others to encourage their children to persist in their school work. Middle-class families make more concerted efforts to encourage their children to do well in school, and they instill in them career goals that will require more extensive schooling. School attendance is closely correlated with social class background. Years of attendance, certainly, as well as daily attendance correlate highly with academic achievement. That, in turn, relates significantly to those who go to college.[27]

More specifically, the most common assessment techniques used in schools—grades and standardized tests—correlate highly with social class background. There is some evidence that certain school districts *predetermine* the quotas for A's, B's, C's, D's, and F's in various schools in the district, a policy that negatively affects lower-income students. Closely related to this practice is the self-fulfilling prophecy that teachers are likely to use in the classroom. Ray Rist has demonstrated how teachers teach more to and expect more of middle-class students than children who come from impoverished backgrounds.[28]

Participation in extracurricular events is also related to social class. Despite the stereotype of inner-city students being heavily involved in athletics, the National Federation of State High Schools Association reports that such districts have the lowest percentages of participation. Other activities such as student councils, newspapers, yearbooks, and school plays show a similar pattern of lesser involvement of students from lower socioeconomic backgrounds. It could be argued that some students cannot participate because their family circumstances require them to work.[29]

One of the most significant examples of the social class bias of schools is in the representation on school boards. Disproportionately, members of the upper-middle-class hold these elected offices. As Chapter 9 revealed, studies going back to the 1920s report the same findings— minorities, as well as members of the working class, are underrepresented on school boards. This lack of representation, as we shall see, has become a political issue for those who advocate more rights for the poor.

The problems of financing schools were discussed in Chapter 10. As the *Serrano* v. *Priest* case in California and the *San Antonio School District* v. *Rodriguez* case from Texas reveal, the property taxation as the chief method of raising funds for schooling favors wealthy districts. While the courts, both state and federal, acknowledge that the system is unfair, little has been done to eliminate the discrimination against the poor. In light of the quotation used to open this chapter (from *Brown* v. *Board of Education*), it is important to note another comment made in the *Rodriguez* ruling. It appears to some that the justices changed their minds, retracting their earlier statement that education is a fundamental right entitled to protection under the U.S. Constitution. In *Rodriguez*, the Supreme Court acknowledged that education is still crucially important but stated it was not a fundamental right guaranteed by the Constitution. In this case and in later cases at the state level, legislatures have been asked by the courts to reconsider their financial plans so that both the burden and benefits of education are available more equally to all.

School Remedies for Children of the Poor

The case that there was a discrepancy between the educational opportunities that the wealthy received and those that the poor had was convincingly made in Washington, D.C., during the early 1960s. The symbol of the acceptance of poverty as an issue was the popularity of Michael Harrington's book, *The Other America*, which concluded that one-fourth of the American population lived in poverty. In the wake of John F. Kennedy's death, Lyndon B. Johnson was ready to declare a "war on poverty" as part of his plan for a Great Society. The shrewd Johnson, who had been a teacher and who wished to be remembered as "the education President," believed that a major educational bill was needed if better educational opportunities were to be provided the children of the poor.

But passing federal funds for public education was difficult because education was seen as primarily the states' responsibility (see Chapter 9). Further, those who favored public funding of nonpublic schools usually joined forces with the states' rights advocates if federal bills did not include something for the nonpublic schools. A clever way was found to gain passage of the proposed Elementary and Secondary Education Act. Monies would be made available to school districts in the nation that had a certain number of persons below the poverty line. The compromise was that nonpublic schools were eligible for many of the programs and services under ESEA. For example, Title I of ESEA provided for remedial aid to schools. The amount of money a district received depended upon the number of families at the poverty level. How the money was distributed, however, once the district received it, was based on the criterion of "educational disadvantage." And, of course, the funds could go to both public and nonpublic schools. These guidelines for the ESEA of 1965 were so generous that 90% of the counties in the nation qualified for funds![30]

Compensatory Education Remedies. By far the most common type of remedy was the compensatory plan. Millions of federal dollars were distributed to the nation's schools under various ESEA provisions. By 1980, over $35 billion in ESEA funds had been allocated.[31] Title I and Title VII provided most of the monies. The general philosophy of these remedies was that students with low achievement levels were lacking educational advantages as a result of poverty. Districts proposed various programs to provide necessary services to educationally disadvantaged students. Such services ranged from meals before school to remedial specialists helping them during the school day to counseling after school. Programs for families as well as the students were instituted. Many of the compensatory programs begun in the 1960s are still being funded, although some have been phased out, and others have been modified significantly.

Remedial programs are the most common form of compensatory education, and the type of remedy on which most federal funds are spent. The funds have paid for, among other things, the services of remedial reading specialists, nurses, social workers, and tutors. Students from the inner city, children of migrants, and children who speak a language other than English are helped with problems that hinder their academic progress at school.

Because of the large expenditures, there is much concern whether these programs have been effective. Critics believe that there has been too much waste, that programs are not managed well, and that cognitive gains have not been sustained. Proponents disagree, pointing out that relatively little is spent per pupil, and that the most recent studies show better results than the earlier evaluations.[32]

Another type of compensatory remedy involves *cocurricular* and *curriculum* projects designed to enhance feelings of pride in the students. For example, students who otherwise might not be exposed to museums, theaters, and art galleries are taken to such places. In some communities, special efforts are made to involve parents in after-school evening programs. Examples of the curriculum projects include black history and ethnic heritage. The intent of such programs is to build a sense of worth in the students. The assumption of advocates of these plans is that school performance will be enhanced when students feel good about themselves and are proud of their heritages.

The third general compensatory plan emphasizes *preschool preparation.* The most famous prototype of this remedy has been Operation Head Start. In most Head Start programs, youngsters' verbal and social skills are developed so that they can better compete with students from more "enriched" homes. (See section in Chapter 12 on "Early Childhood Education.")

A key to success for compensatory programs, according to both proponents and critics, is the degree to which the participants feel it is really their program, rather than one provided for them by an alien authority. Teachers in such programs need to convince students that the programs are for them, and that they, the teachers,

There is much debate today whether the gains made in preschool compensatory programs will be sustained.

are sincerely interested in helping students achieve success.

Teacher Preparation Programs. Some contend that it is more effective to change the type of teacher who instructs children from poor and minority situations than to try to change students or their environment. However, in one 1965 survey of teacher education institutions, fewer than 10% of the programs made any special effort to train individuals for the unique conditions of urban schools. It is doubtful that today more than 20% of the teacher education programs prepare teachers of disadvantaged students in a way different than they prepare teachers of regular students.

The teaching profession is growing more supportive of specialized training. One example is found in the standards for accreditation of the National Council for the Accreditation of Teacher Education (NCATE). One of the standards indicates that teachers should have multicultural training. Not only are prospective teachers to receive information about various cultural groups, they are expected to experience working with members of various social, economic, and ethnic groups before they graduate.

One example of this type of training is the Cooperative Urban Teacher Education program in Kansas City, Missouri. A consortium of liberal arts colleges and a land-grant university provide funds to staff the program. The colleges' students who wish to teach in the inner city do their student teaching in city schools. Under the guidance of experts in urban education, sociology, and city management, participants learn about and work in a variety of urban settings (stores, churches, schools, and social service agencies) for 16 weeks, including their student teaching.

There have been some federally funded programs that encouraged individuals to prepare for inner-city teaching. One is the Career Opportunities Program. Another is the Teacher Corps. Both programs received more funding in the 1960s than they are now. On the whole, the results of the training appear to be good. Its chief problem is the limited number of persons who are prepared to teach under these programs.[33]

The Community Control Movement. Parents in large urban districts are likely to feel that they have little voice in setting educational policies. Even in smaller communities the poor often conclude that their opinions don't count when school goals are determined. Certain changes in the thinking of educational leaders since the 1950s, as well as federal legislation and state law provisions in the 1960s and 1970s, have increased the possibilities for more involvement by low-income parents as well as minority group members. The civil rights movement of the 1960s prompted educators in some major cities to call for more involvement by parents at the neighborhood school level. Aided by private foundation funds and governmental support, the process of decentralizing school gov-

Should you desire to teach in the inner city, we suggest you take a teacher education program which will give you experiences working in a multicultural environment.

ernance was tried in major cities during the same time.[34]

Neighborhood school boards were elected or appointed, and they were involved in decisions regarding curriculum, school policies, and selection of principals. The rationale behind such efforts included the belief that greater participation in school decisions by the parents would result in better schools. Many parents in the large cities had felt that the system was too big and unresponsive to their demands. By getting involved, the parents believed that the schools would be improved.

Provisions of most recent federal programs and state education actions require either advisory committees representing the community or boards of directors comprising those who live in the served neighborhood. In short, the government recognizes the right of parents to be involved with their children's education. To the teacher in the classroom, that should mean that parents' concerns must be given the greatest consideration.

Community control, as appealing as it is in theory, also has some drawbacks. Those programs that decentralized have found that less administrative red tape was not a natural outcome. In some cases, the creation of the local boards added new levels of regulations and procedures. Also, in some cases, costs increased. Local election turnovers have not increased. There is the fear that the local advisory groups at times have a parochial point of view; that is, they are so concerned about local issues that they lose sight of the total community's educational goals. Finally, there is little evidence to indicate that community control has significantly altered the academic performance of the students.

DEFINING EQUAL EDUCATIONAL OPPORTUNITY

This discussion on remedies for children of the poor and the earlier consideration of desegregation remedies referred to

Chapter Fourteen

Reprinted with permission from "Values and Schools," a cartoon essay by Elsa Bailey, *Colloquy*, January 1970. Copyright 1969 by United Church Press.

equal educational opportunity. It is a goal of American education for all its young, including minorities as well as those who are economically or educationally disadvantaged. A matter of concern for local districts, and for individual teachers, is how will we determine whether we have met the letter and the spirit of the law in our efforts to provide equal educational opportunity? What criteria should be used? Is it sufficient to have the criteria external— that is, based on factors that are related to the composition of the student body population? To what extent should our criteria involve school performance?[35]

Following are possible criteria to consider, some of which have been alluded to previously in the chapter. Some have argued that the most meaningful (objective) way to determine that equal educational opportunity is being provided is to insist that the district have a *racial balance* plan in force. Should that be modified to include a balance of socioeconomic levels at the district's schools? (What implications does this have for you as a teacher? If your classes included students from diverse racial, ethnic, and social class backgrounds, would you be fair to all of them? Would you have a self-fulfilling prophecy about certain students because

of their racial or economic backgrounds?)

Is spending an equal amount of *money* for each student in the district a better way to achieve equal educational opportunity (e.g., the *Serrano* case)? That also would be objective, and presumably easy to monitor. How does that rectify the needs of those who have received less in the past or those who need additional help now?

Some claim that the allotment of equal *resources* per student would be the more acceptable criterion. This would account for such factors as some students attending school in new facilities, or others having the benefit of teachers with better preparation. In short, some method would have to be determined to weigh the variables in education. Critics of this approach believe such a procedure would be difficult, if not impossible, to construct. How does one determine the value of such intangible resources as school tradition?

Another criterion of equal educational opportunity is the *perceptions* of the students and the community about their school. Studies done in some cities like Chicago suggest that certain inner-city schools that were comprised of low-income students had lower rates of vandalism and teacher turnover than did schools with high-income student populations. Students in the low-income schools had immense pride in their buildings, despite the poor physical appearance of the structure. Some evidence from the Coleman and Jencks reports might support this concept. Critics could contend that the measurement of pride would be difficult. Also, persons in the community might be misled about the actual performance of students.

Some hold that *results* are the schools' only important consideration. They would be less concerned about the techniques (which might include busing) than about the performance of students on standardized tests. They would monitor the dropout rate to see how it compared with schools that had higher income level families or different racial compositions. In their minds, equal educational opportunity occurs only when students perform at similar levels. Opponents of this point of view could argue that such a criterion does not realistically account for the difference that social class background makes.

ACTIVITY 14–3
Effective Equal Educational Opportunity Remedies

Throughout the chapter a number of remedies to aid equal educational opportunity have been mentioned. We have just considered some questions to think about in terms of measuring whether equal educational programs are working.

Read several journal articles or chapters in books about equal educational opportunities. Write a report on the success or failure of a remedy mentioned in your source(s), listing the criteria that the author(s) used to judge the effectiveness of the strategy.

Questions that you should also respond to include the following:

1. How would you have decided to evaluate the success or failure of the program? (Would you have used standardized tests, economic measures, comments made by participants in interviews, or some combination of cognitive and affective techniques of assessment?)
2. To what extent can the school be held accountable for nonschool environmental variables, such as social class?
3. Is it proper for schools to be concerned about the economic inequities in America? Is one of the functions of the schools to improve the income of its graduates?

A resource you may wish to consult is Richard H. Quay, comp., *In Pursuit of Equality of Educational Opportunity: A Selective Bibliography and Guide to the Research Literature* (New York: Garland Publishing, 1977).

SUMMARY

The call for equal opportunity has a long tradition in America. Writers and orators from Thomas Jefferson to Martin Luther King have made impassioned pleas for Americans to live up to our Constitution. Despite our ideals, we realize that there is much racism in the nation, slowing the efforts of the schools to offer equal opportunity for all. Likewise, there is the more subtle, but as potent, bias against the poor that prevents equal education.

The section on racism in the schools noted that the courts became more involved with school affairs over the years when the schools denied minorities the opportunity for equal education. A major

Chapter Fourteen

premise of the court action is that racial desegregation is required to achieve equality. A host of strategies have been attempted over the years to increase desegregation, in the North as well as the South. No remedy is without its flaws, but the point is that different remedies *have* succeeded in specific situations. There has been and will be debates over the application and effectiveness of specific remedies in specific situations.

The less publicly recognized issue of social class bias, many educators believe, may be a more serious matter. If it is true that many school practices reflect a bias in favor of those students from middle- and upper-middle-class homes, then equal educational opportunity is being denied. Again, a number of remedies have been instigated since the 1960s to attempt to give the parents of disadvantaged students greater input into school policies and to aid the students with their problems. There is much controversy about the effectiveness of compensatory remedies.

The problems of racism and social class bias do make an impact upon school districts and carry into the classroom. Teachers need to work with parents and students who may be victims of one or the other of these social ills. Individual teachers must determine how they will handle classroom situations related to race and social class. Achieving equal educational opportunity for all students remains a goal for tomorrow's teachers.

NOTES

1. This list of competencies was suggested, in part, by the staff of the Midwest Race Desegregation Assistance Center of Manhattan, Kansas. Alfred Lightfoot, *Urban Education in Social Perspective* (Chicago: Rand McNally, 1978), pp. 75–84 mentions additional skills needed.

2. Robert Terry presented this definition in an unpublished paper at a Human Relations workshop in Minneapolis, June 1978.

3. Charles Vert Willie, "Biological and Cultural Differences and Race-Related Behavior," in Charles V. Willie, ed., *The Sociology of Urban Education* (Lexington, Mass.: D.C. Heath, 1978), pp. 45–56.

4. U.S. Department of Commerce, Bureau of the Census, *Statistical Abstract of the United States, 1978* (Washington, D.C.: U.S. Government Printing Office, 1978), pp. 28–34, 35.

5. *Sourcebook of Equal Educational Opportunity*, 2nd ed. (Chicago: Marquis Academic Media, 1977), p. 4.

6. U.S. Commission on Civil Rights, *Statement on Metropolitan School Desegregation* (Washington, D.C.: U.S. Government Printing Office, February 1977), p. 6.

7. C. Vann Woodward, *The Strange Career of Jim Crow*, 2nd ed. (New York: Oxford University Press, 1966); Patricia Sexton, *Education and Income* (New York: Viking Press, 1961).

8. Terry Eastland and William J. Bennett, *Counting by Race: Equality from the Founding Fathers to Bakke and Weber* (New York: Basic Books, 1979).

9. *Sweatt* v. *Painter*, 339 U. S. 629 (1950).

10. *Brown* v. *Board of Education of Topeka, Kansas*, 347 U. S. 483 (1954). In 1979 Linda Brown asked that the case be reopened because her two daughters were not receiving an equal educational opportunity in Topeka.

11. *Brown* v. *Board of Education of Topeka, Kansas*, 349 U. S. 294 (1955).

12. *Alexander* v. *Holmes County Board of Education*, 396 U. S. 19 (1969).

13. *Swann* v. *Charlotte-Mechlenburg School District*, 402 U. S. 1, 15 (1971); *Milliken* v. *Bradley* 418 U. S. 717 (1974).

14. U.S. Commission on Civil Rights. *Racial Isolation in the Public Schools*, vol. I (Washington, D.C.: U.S. Government Printing Office, 1967) details some of the programs attempted in the early 1960s. The *Pasadena* v. *Spangler* case, 96 California State Court 2697 (1976), of course, is from a nonfederal jurisdiction.

15. Jane Power, "Magnet Schools: Are They the Answer?" *Today's Education* 68, no. 3 (September-October 1979): 68–70; Also important is *Keyes* v. *School District No. 1*, 413 U.S. 189, 208. In this 1971 decision involving the Denver, Colorado school system, the Court ruled that a city-wide desegregation plan could be instituted even though segregation did not occur in all parts of the city.

16. Nicholas Mills, ed., *Busing U.S.A.* (New York: Teachers College Press, 1979). For an alternative outlook on busing see Virginia Trotter, *Busing: Constructive or Divisive?* (Washington, D.C.: American Enterprise Institute, 1976).

17. Civil Rights Commission, *Metropolitan School Desegregation*. In the early 1970s, the Rockefeller Foundation gave $25 million to explore the possibility of large educational parks in metropolitan areas, which might enroll as many as 25,000 students from various racial and economic backgrounds. That remedy was never really tried and is rarely even considered now.

18. Harold B. Gerard and Norman Miller, *School Desegregation* (New York: Plenum Press, 1975); Elizabeth Cohens, *Desegregation: Past, Present, and Future* (New York: Plenum Press, 1979).

19. J. S. Coleman et al., *Equality of Educational Opportunity* (Washington, D.C.: U.S. Government Printing Office, 1966); James S. Coleman, "Racial Segregation in the Schools: New Research with New Policy Implication," *Phi Delta Kappan* 56, no. 2 (October 1975): 75–78; Thomas F. Pettigrew and Robert L. Green, "Urban Desegregation and White Flight: A Response to Coleman," in *New Perspectives on School Integration*, ed. Murray Friedman, Roger Meltzer, and Charles Miller (Philadelphia: Fortress Press, 1979), pp. 124–33.

20. Thomas Pettigrew, "Guidelines for Integrating Schools," Midwest Race Desegregation Assistance Center *Horizons* 2, no. 1 (January 1980): 1, 4.

21. Joseph Kahl, *The American Class Structure* (New York: Rinehart, 1957); Dennis Lawton, *Social Class, Language and Education* (New York: Schocken, 1968).

22. Sexton, *Education and Income*.

23. See note 19. Critical analyses of the Coleman Report can be found in a special issue of the *Harvard Educational Review* 38, no. 1 (Winter 1968), as well as in Frederick Mosteller and Daniel Moynihan, eds., *On Equality of Educational Opportunity* (New York: Random House, 1973).

24. Christopher Jencks, *Inequality* (New York: Harper and Row, 1972); Christopher Jencks et al., *Who Gets Ahead? The Determinants of Economic Success in America* (New York: Basic Books, 1979).

26. Jencks, *Inequality*, pp. 135–75. Donald M. Levine and Mary Jo Bane, eds., *The "Inequality" Controversy: Schooling and Distributive Justice* (New York: Basic Books, 1975) explores the implications and controversies surrounding Jencks' findings.

27. William Brookover et al., "Educational Aspirations and Educational Plans in Relation to Academic Achievement and Socio-economic Status," *School Review* 75, no. 1 (Winter 1967): 392–444; Gary Bridge et al., *The Determinants of Educational Outcomes: The Impact of Families, Peers, Teachers, and Schools* (Cambridge, Mass.: Ballinger, 1979).

28. John Touliatos et al., "Influence of Family Background on Scholastic Achievement," *Journal of Experimental Education* 46, no. 3 (Spring 1978): 22–28; Ray Rist, *The Urban School: A Factory for Failure* (Cambridge, Mass.: MIT Press, 1973).

29. Correspondence from the National Federation of State High Schools Association, Elgin, Ill., 19 June 1978.

30. Julie Roy Jeffrey, *Education for Children of the Poor: A Study of the Origins and Implementation of the Elementary and Secondary Education Act of 1965* (Columbus, Ohio: Ohio State University Press, 1978).

31. *Special Report on Mandated Studies* (Washington, D.C.: National Advisory Council on the Education of Disadvantaged Children, 1979); for descriptions of specific programs, see A. Harry Passow, "Compensatory Instructional Intervention," in F. N. Kerlinger and J. B. Carroll, eds., *Review of Research in Education*, vol. 2 (Itasca, Ill.: Peacock, 1974), pp. 145–75.

32. Robert J. Havighurst and Daniel U. Levine, *Society and Education*, 5th ed. (Boston: Allyn and Bacon, 1979), pp. 222–43; *New York Times*, 6 January 1980.

33. Lightfoot, *Urban Education*, pp. 175–78.

34. George R. LaNoue and Bruce L.R. Smith, *The Politics of School Decentralization* (Lexington, Mass.: Lexington Books/D.C. Heath, 1973), pp. 11–24; Mario Fantini, Marilyn Gittell, and Richard Magat, *Community Control and the Urban School* (New York: Praeger, 1970).

35. Mosteller and Moynihan, *Educational Opportunity*, p. 7.

FOR FURTHER STUDY

Bresnick, David; Lachman, Seymour; and Polner, Murray. *Black/White/Green/Red: The Politics of Education in Ethnic America*. New York: Longman, 1978.

de Lone, Richard H. *Small Futures: Children, Inequality, and the Limits of Liberal Reform*. New York: Harcourt, Brace Jovanovich, 1979.

Harvard Educational Review. Special issue on Equal Educational Opportunity, vol. 38, no. 1 (Winter 1968). Special issue on Perspective on Inequality. vol. 43, no. 1 (February 1973).

Hogan, John C. *The Schools, the Courts and the Public Interest*. Lexington, Mass.: Lexington Books/D.C. Heath, 1974.

Levin, Betsy, and Hawley, Willis D., eds. *The Courts, Social Science, and School Desegregation*. New Brunswick, N.J.: Transaction Books, 1977.

Madaus, George F.; Airasian, Peter W.; and Kellaghan, Thomas . *School Effectiveness: A Reassessment of the Evidence*. San Francisco: Jossey-Bass, 1978.

Chapter Fourteen

Miller, Lamar P., and Gordon, Edmund W., eds. *Equality of Educational Opportunity*. New York: AMS Press, 1974.

Persell, Caroline Hodges. *Education and Inequality*. New York: Free Press, 1977.

Rehberg, Richard A., and Rosenthal, Evelyn R. *Class and Merit in the American High School: An Assessment of the Revisionist and Meritocratic Arguments*. New York: Longman, 1978.

Rist, Ray C., ed. *Desegregated Schools—Appraisals of an American Experiment*. New York: Academic Press, 1979.

15

Offering Educational Options

Anyone who would attempt the task of felling a virgin forest with a penknife would probably feel the same paralysis of despair that the reformer feels when confronted with existing school systems.

Ellen Key, 1909

I hold that moulding of the young mind is criminal, whether the moulding is moral or religious or political. Free education must allow a free mind.

A. S. Neill

Although the nation's public school system is still widely supported (Chapter 11), its size, bureaucracy, and value system (or lack of one, in some people's view), seem to invite criticisms. You should realize that complaints, justified or not, will come de-spite concerted efforts of schools and teachers to meet the individual needs of students and to remedy discrimination. Society, as well as teachers and administrators, must wrestle with the validity of the charges against the schools. Some people ultimately will decide that the reforms they believe necessary cannot be accomplished inside the traditional school structure, and they will begin alternative schools.

The first section of the chapter acknowledges the criticisms of schools from a spectrum of liberal to conservative. After examining the diverse charges against the schools, the section highlights two reforms that have been instituted—performance contracts and the voucher plan. The second portion of the chapter discusses alternative methods of instruction that schools are already implementing in response to criticisms. They include open education, schools-within-a-school, schools without

343

walls, and the free school movement. You should gain some understanding of the problems associated with modifying the curriculum. Because every tenth elementary and secondary student in America attends a nonpublic school, it is important that we discuss the extent and focus of such schools. Religious schools and private schools are treated.

As you read the chapter, you may be surprised by the variety of schools currently available to students. You may find yourself considering whether you might or should teach in an alternative school. In addition, we ask you to reflect on two societal issues. First, are these choices of schooling any better than the conventional public school system? Second, can a culture that, by definition, must have certain common experiences and values, tolerate as many forms of education as we appear to have?

Once again, we ask you to think about the implications of the evidence and trends that are discussed here. We offer the following as just a few of the competencies that educators of the future must have.

Tomorrow's teachers should have *knowledge* of:

● major criticisms of the public schools;

● the variety of options available within public schools;

● the characteristics of free schools, such as Summerhill;

● trends in nonpublic education;

● provisions of the voucher plan.

Tomorrow's teachers should have *skills* in:

● working with educators from other systems;

● organizing subject matter so that it can be presented in different types of schools.

Tomorrow's teachers should be *disposed* toward:

● appreciating the variety of schools that America has supported throughout the country's history;

● being flexible as they work with students who come from a variety of schooling backgrounds.

After you have completed Chapter 15, you should be able to (1) state the major objections to American education of at least two critics, (2) describe briefly four options currently offered within public schools, and (3) identify two trends in nonpublic education.

ACKNOWLEDGING THE CRITICISMS OF SCHOOLS

Many of the criticisms leveled against the schools today—that they have taken over many parental responsibilities, that the curriculum is atheistic, that academic standards are low—were voiced in the 1940s and 1950s. Other criticisms today—that the effects of schools dehumanize—were loudly shouted in the 1960s. Some critics, upset by Vietnam and later by Watergate, protested that the schools were frauds, unable to teach students anything meaningful. So it is that criticisms from the 1940s through the 1970s are repeated, using new slogans like "back to basics," "humanizing education," or "individualization."

The backgrounds of the critics are as diverse as their complaints. Some are university professors; others, therapists or military officers. Some are linked with minority groups, the poor, or churches; others come from within the establishment. Politically, they range from anarchists to conservatives. Some have elaborately documented cases against the schools; others have been described as "young men agonizing in public over their discovery that the world is a difficult place."[1] Their differences in background and cause make

it difficult to link the critics precisely with the philosophical outlooks discussed in Chapter 11. You will, however, note some parallels as their basic criticisms are elaborated.

The Criticisms

The Call for Higher Standards. One group of critics has emphasized the lack of standards in the schools. Those cited here come close to the perennialist or essentialist points of view. In the main, they support the concept of training the mind as the goal of education. They believe that certain fundamental subjects must be mastered by all students. Student interest in the subjects is secondary in importance.

Although the call for higher standards is a constant one (and such groups as the Essentialist Committee for the Advancement of Education was founded in 1938), we focus on groups active in the post–World War II years. In that period the nation's schools experienced a depleted teaching staff, poor buildings and lack of materials, rapidly rising enrollment, and a rising resentment toward communist influence. Progressive education, in vogue for nearly half a century, was increasingly regarded as too permissive. A banner year for criticisms about the lack of rigorous standards was 1953, when Albert Lynd's *Quackery in the Public School*, Robert Hutchins' *The Conflict in Education*, Paul Woodring's

Let's Talk Sense about Our Schools, and Arthur Bestor's *Educational Wastelands*, appeared. After Sputnik was launched in 1957, Kermit Lansner's *Second-Rate Brains* (1958) followed.[2]

Arthur Bestor probably had the greatest impact. An American history professor who had taught at Columbia University's Teachers College, Stanford, and the University of Illinois, Bestor attacked the schools for their lack of academic training. For Bestor, the primary purpose of education was intellectual training—"the deliberate cultivation of the ability to think." Intellectual training could best be given through the academic disciplines, which were thought to be the best systematic method for solving problems.

Therefore, the task of public education, Bestor argued, was to provide to all citizens a basic education in history, English, science, mathematics, and foreign languages. Bestor urged reform of the schools in three areas: *control* of schooling (greater decision making by parents and liberal arts professors, and less by educational professionals); *teacher training* (more academic subject matter and fewer education courses); and *university control of teacher education* (rather than allowing departments and schools of education to determine requirements). Bestor became a leader of an organization to promote such a curriculum, the Council for Basic Education.[3]

Chapter Fifteen

Another widely read critic who shared some of these concerns was Max Rafferty. From 1969 to 1972, Rafferty served as the superintendent of public instruction in the state of California. Described as "a gadfly on the rump of education," Rafferty used his newspaper columns, books, and speeches to warn the public that the schools were controlled by educational professionals; progressive education doctrines were ruining the academic standards of students; a moral crisis was brewing; discipline was lacking in schools; teachers were spending too much time on frills; and schools were attempting to solve too many societal problems. Rafferty's solutions to the nation's educational ills included increased use of drill, memory work, tougher discipline standards, and more competitive activities.[4]

A recent critic of the perceived low standards in schools is Paul Copperman. As the operator of a private reading school in California, Copperman became upset with students' declining achievement scores and increasing school costs. He has called education today "entertainment" and a "literacy hoax," and he believes that giving teachers greater authority in the classroom and the students more rigorous doses of reading, writing, computation, science, and history will bring increased academic gains.[5]

The Need for a Humanistic Education. Bestor, Rafferty and Copperman, despite some obvious differences in style and interpretation, share the general viewpoint that academic standards must be higher. A number of other past and present critics disagree, arguing that the major problem with schools in America is that the curriculum and discipline standards are already far too rigid. Reflecting essentialist and progressive views, they hold that the individual needs of learners are central to education. They favor a broadening of the

curriculum and its constant renewal, so that it is relevant for students. For example, they ask that schools discuss women's liberation, and energy policies, and that students be taught how to cope with the rapidly changing future.[6]

Carl Rogers and William Glasser, a therapist and a medical doctor respectively, subscribe to this point of view. They claim that the goal of education should be the development of a healthy, self-directed independence, which is fostered in an environment that encourages students to set their own curriculum and determine their own grades.[7] Others from this perspective have argued that schools stifle good communication skills, because teachers are given authoritarian roles and expected to cover certain subject matter.

Neil Postman and Charles Weingartner in *Teaching as a Subversive Activity* are concerned about the passive, dull, almost fraudulent teaching practices they witnessed. They believe the task of education is to help students to be, in Ernest Hemingway's term, "crap-detectors." In succeeding books, *The Soft Revolution* and *The School Book*, they added to their earlier collection of suggestions for making classrooms more vibrant places where students would be allowed and encouraged to be more expressive. Postman, writing in *Teaching as a Conserving Activity* (1979), acknowledges that some of their ideas for increasing student opportunities were excessive, but maintains his belief in a student-oriented school.[8]

Herbert Kohl and George Dennison spoke from their own teaching experiences and wanted to make schooling less formal and more open to an ad hoc curriculum. Both wrote about their situations in New York City schools. Kohl taught in a Harlem school and found that he reached the students by foregoing the standard curriculum and helping them develop their own resources. His noisy classrooms and non-standard techniques disturbed some of the other teachers. Dennison, on the other hand, wrote about a school he started on First Street for 23 students who were judged delinquents in other schools. Dennison did away with report cards, tests, schedules, and rigid discipline techniques.[9]

Charles Silberman, an editor of *Fortune* magazine and a former college professor, illustrates how these critics see school problems. He conducted an extensive survey of American education under a Carnegie grant, and in *Crisis in the Classroom*, he concluded that there were two major deficiencies in American schools—lack of joy and mindlessness. Silberman called for teachers to be more humane, and he proposed a more open, interdisciplinary curriculum similar to that in the English primary schools.[10]

The most prolific of the humanist writers is John Holt. A private school teacher when he wrote his first book, *How Children Fail*, Holt called for more learner involvement, the use of the total community for educational ideas, and abolition of grades and compulsory attendance. More recently, Holt has branched into two related learning areas. He has been concerned about improving learning "networks," i.e., associations of groups and individuals who formally or informally help each other with learning tasks. Moreover, he has become increasingly convinced that the schools will not change radically, and that more people will have to educate their children at home if they wish a humane form of schooling.[11]

An Attack upon the Economic Values of Schools. While the humanists attribute the failings and faults of schools to the general ineptitude of well-intentioned teachers or the apathy and ignorance of communities, another group of critics believe that schools are deliberately organized by the establishment to maintain political and social status quo. These crit-

ics are somewhat like the reconstructionists who wanted the schools to solve social problems. Unlike Theodore Brameld, many of these critics do not attempt to retain democracy as a political system. Some would favor abolishing schools as we know them.

Two such writers active in the late 1950s and early 1960s were Paul Goodman and Edgar Friedenberg. Goodman, a social critic, often noted the connection between the industrial needs of the country and the types of training and conditioning offered in schools. Viewing the increasingly technological world, he favored informal learning centers that might offer, besides a liberal arts background, enough mathematics and sciences to prepare individuals to be "active, competent, initiating citizens who can produce a community culture and a noble recreation."[12]

Friedenberg, a sociologist and university professor, was appalled by the conditioning of students he found in his research studies. Skeptical that democracy works under the best of conditions, Friedenberg was disturbed by the dehumanizing conditions in schools, which he believed would virtually guarantee future citizens would not challenge the system.[13]

Revisionist historians such as Joel Spring, Michael B. Katz, Samuel Bowles, and Herbert Gintis have echoed the sentiments of Goodman and Friedenberg. These historians contend that their research on schools, federal and state educational agencies, and testing organizations shows how those in power subjugate the general public.[14] These critics prefer to describe and analyze why schools are the way they are, rather than suggest ways the schools might be reformed.

The radical critic whose works contain the most specific curriculum suggestions and teaching strategies is Jonathan Kozol. Politically involved throughout his teaching career in Boston, Kozol's disappointments with the slowness of the system to bring about justice for the poor turned him increasingly to a socialist point of view. Kozol states that those schools which are or appear to be innovative give a deceptive appearance of changing society: the schools do not teach students disloyalty to the country whose flag they fly, nor do they teach students how to challenge the country's corrupt economic system. In one of his later books he pays a glowing tribute to Cuban efforts to reduce illiteracy, because they have used a variety of methods, including peer teaching and community-based education, to achieve their results.[15]

Two Latin American reformers who share Kozol's political point of view are Ivan Illich and Paulo Freire. Illich, a Roman Catholic priest who founded a language study center at Cuernavaca, Mexico, also served a church in the United States and was a vice-president at Catholic University of Puerto Rico. Schools, Illich posits, have moved from being primarily educational agencies to being political-social units; that is, they provide "proper" political orientations and serve as "credentialing" authorities. Individuals receive their roles in society based on the type, length, and reputation of schooling they received. To save society and redeem education, nations must deschool themselves, which for Illich means that learning must be made voluntary and should be available from a network of sources.[16]

Freire, a South American priest, argues that schooling has been used to oppress people. Blending Marxist philosophy with some Christian beliefs, he developed in Brazil an adult literacy model that he claims offers individuals a vehicle for controlling their own destinies. His books tell educators to provide instruction in the basics that can be related to vocational skills.[17]

ACTIVITY 15–1
Critics of Education

The section you have just finished reading provides a general overview of the weaknesses of the American educational system, from the point of view of the critics. For your personal benefit, or for a class presentation or report, you might consider reading one of the books mentioned in the notes. Several other books by critics are mentioned below and others will be found in the section "For Further Study" at the end of the chapter.

For some criticism of the critics, you may find the following articles and books helpful:

Arthur Pearl, "What's Wrong with the New Informalism in Education?" *Social Policy* 1, no. 6 (March-April 1971): 15–23; Samuel S. Shermis, "Educational Critics Have Been Wrong All Along: Long Live Tradition," *Phi Delta Kappan* 55, no. 6 (February 1974): 403–6.

Jerry Farber. *The Student as Nigger* (North Hollywood, Calif.: Contact Books, 1969).

James Herndon. *The Way It Spozed to Be* (New York: Simon and Schuster, 1968).

A.S. Neill. *Summerhill* (New York: Hart, 1960).

Robin Barrow. *Radical Education* (New York: Wiley, 1978).

Mary Anne Raywid. *The Ax-Grinders: Critics of Our Public Schools* (New York: Macmillan, 1962).

Cecil W. Scott and Robert Burns. *The Great Debate: Our Schools in Crisis* (Englewood Cliffs, N.J.: Prentice-Hall, 1959).

Jonathan Kozol has gone beyond merely criticizing the American public school system. With others, he has founded a free school and engaged in various efforts to provide schooling opportunities for children of the poor.

Two Reforms: Performance Contracts and the Voucher Plan

The criticisms voiced about the schools have already resulted in at least two attempts, both federally funded, to restructure public education to better meet the individual needs of students. One of the two experiments, performance contracts, is now considered a failure. It could be called an inside reform, i.e., it brought private business management techniques inside the regular classroom. The second reform, the voucher plan, is an outside reform because it seeks to establish a variety of alternative schools within a community. While public tax funds would be used to finance the alternatives, the various schools would be under private control.

The prevailing sentiment of the advocates of these reforms was voiced as far back as 1859 by John Stuart Mill. Writing in *On Liberty*, he noted:

> An education established and controlled by the state should only exist, if it exist at all, as one among many competing experiments, carried on for the purpose of example and stimulus, to keep the others up to a certain standard of excellence.

Performance contracts were designed to raise achievement scores of students (very often in inner-city schools). The students were obviously not doing well in traditional school programs, and it was hoped that a new type of school climate would improve their performance. Perhaps the most unusual feature of this reform was that private companies were allowed to manage these programs.[18] One of the unique features of these programs was that students were often given tangible rewards for improvements in their reading and mathematics performances as measured periodically by standardized tests. The rewards ranged from S&H green stamps for perfect papers, to radios and toys for successful completions of unit materials, to television sets for being the best in the class.

In time, at least 30 private firms bid on performance contracts. In virtually all the contracts, reading and mathematics were the only areas in which the experimentation occurred. The major project in performance contracting involved 18 schools and 27,000 students. At hearings prior to the beginning of the experiment, the National Education Association and the American Association of School Administrators (AASA) announced their opposition, because they feared that the private companies running the experimental programs were inexperienced, and that the test measures were not conclusive. Those who favored performance contracting believed that the results would be no worse than from existing instruction available at the time, and they criticized the teachers and administrators for being so concerned about losing control of the school classrooms.

The experimental groups did improve their performance scores, although the evaluators concluded that their results were not significantly higher than the control students at the 18 test schools. The cost per pupil was lower in the experimental schools. While proponents argued that the reform was successful, the NEA, AASA, and the media tended to view it as a failure.[19]

The voucher plan first appeared at about the same time as the performance contracts. It was advocated by a wide spectrum of political and educational leaders, such as economist Milton Friedman and Harvard professor Christopher Jencks. To overcome the sameness of the curriculum of public and private schools, the critics argued that each family should be given a voucher for each of their school-age children, redeemable at a school of the family's choice. The advocates of this plan believe that persons and groups who might otherwise hesitate to start new schools would do so, knowing that vouchers for tuition were in the hands of families.[20]

As in the case of the performance contracts, strong criticism emerged. Opponents argued that the voucher plan was a vehicle to avoid integration, that it would result in the weakening of academic standards, that it was likely to result in public monies going to private religious schools, that it would produce elitist schools, and that it would have a negative effect on teacher tenure. Despite the criticisms, a modified voucher plan was tried in the Alum Rock Union School District in suburban San Jose, California, in 1972 and 1973. Because of numerous restrictions, it was never viewed as a true test.[21]

While performance contracts may be a thing of the past, voucher plans are still

being considered around the nation. What these two reform efforts should indicate to us is that the American school system is constantly under pressure to change. Numerous questions about any reform effort can and should be raised. For example: How should curriculum be determined? What about the performance level of students in alternative programs? To what extent should the professional educators' point of view be accepted?

PROVIDING ALTERNATIVES AND OPTIONS IN EDUCATION

Bombarded with criticisms as they have been since the 1940s, public education systems in the United States have attempted many innovations. It has been estimated that over 10,000 alternative schools have been attempted in two-thirds of the states. Before we examine the various types of alternative programs, the term *alternative education* as well as another receiving more usage, *options in education,* should be clarified. Mary Anne Raywid explains that:

> Although the terms 'alternatives' and 'options' are often used interchangeably, there are important practical differences. The term *alternatives* applies to an educational system in which more than one viable, attractive possibility is present (be this a matter of curriculum, purpose, environment, or something else). The term *options* attaches to the way in which choices are made within such a system. It is possible to have an alternatives system providing multiple educations, while reserving decisions on individual student placement to educators. In an options system, however, the choice is left to the student and/or his or her family.[22]

It is important to note, considering these definitions, that both private and public educators at times have used the term *alternative* loosely. If a public school system decides that there is one better way to do schooling, or if the founder of a nonpublic school advertises that his or her new school is a real alternative but in fact only substitutes one monolithic approach for another, they are not in fact providing a real alternative.

Generally speaking, what are the characteristics of alternative/options schools? (The emphasis here is on those options in public schools.)

1. They are open to all on a voluntary basis. In other words, the choices are real, and they are not a sham that allows certain schools in the district to be founded for specific racial or class clientele.

2. Their goals are comprehensive. Besides basic skills, most alternative schools have broader goals. Teachers are aware of the individual needs of the students, and in that sense the schools tend to be humanistic. However, schools in a system may nevertheless develop specific thrusts. One may be a traditional school concentrating upon basic subjects. Another may see its goal as building self-concepts for students who have been identified as having low self-images. Another may concentrate upon improving race relations.

3. They have a flexible curriculum and schedule. A feature of such schools is that they realize that individual students have different rates and ways of learning. The curriculum will be adjusted rather than having students accommodate the schedule.

4. They have smaller enrollments. Generally, alternative schools will have no more than 200 students. Many will have about 100.

5. More alternative schools are at the secondary level than at the elementary level.

6. The students of such schools are just as likely to be from working- and middle-class backgrounds as from upper-middle-class backgrounds. Certainly, this will depend in part upon the socioeconomic makeup of the district. Apparently, there is some reluctance of upper-middle-class parents to try something other than the traditional school that they feel is an appropriate model for education.[23]

This section highlights some forms of alternative/options education. The forms selected for review are found both in public and nonpublic schools, although two of them, schools-within-a school and schools without walls, are more likely in public schools, and open education and free schools are more likely to be available in the nonpublic schools. The section closes with a discussion of some of the research findings regarding these programs.

Open Education

Admittedly, this is a catchall category; it contains descriptions of four subgroups of programs that embody an open education philosophy—open schools, learning centers, continuation centers, and multicultural schools. Should you attempt to read about alternative education, you will find as we did that the most commonly used term is open education.

Open education may appear to be the least revolutionary form of alternative education. It often occurs in a traditional building with fairly recognizable classroom patterns. Simply put, open education schools provide individualized learning experiences throughout the building. Such schools want to "open" instruction by allowing greater involvement of students in choosing their curriculum, providing students more opportunities to research topics of their own interest, using multiage groups, and giving less attention to age- and grade-level units.

Open Schools. Public school systems that operate open education schools usually have them at one site, although they may be at several locations. In St. Paul, Min-

Chapter Fifteen

nesota, 500 students, kindergarten through 12th grade, go to school in a refurbished warehouse. The Murray Road School in Newton, Massachusetts also is in one building. In its particular program, students in the lower grades begin with more structured (and required) courses, but it allows increasingly open blocks of time for student selections. In North Haven, Connecticut, one elementary school in the system was identified as an open school. It adopted a curriculum used in British primary schools (which Charles Silberman so admired).

Learning Centers. Some districts concentrate special resources or a special form of instruction at one site. For example, Houston High School for the Health Profession is located at the Texas Medical Center in Houston, Texas. The Automotive Transportation Learning Center in St. Paul, Minnesota is meant for junior high students who wish to explore a mechanical curriculum.[24]

Continuation Centers. For students whose schooling has been, or is likely to be, interrupted by a job, pregnancy, or some other reason, some districts offer open education programs called continuation schools, dropout centers, or reentry programs. They are often located in a place other than the conventional school and may have a very informal atmosphere.

Multicultural Schools. Some school districts, usually in urban areas, believe that as part of their curriculum they should emphasize the contributions of various ethnic and racial groups to American life. One of the best ways to do this is to have a student body that reflects the composition of the community. A few of the multicultural schools have set quotas for student representation and faculty membership. The main purpose of such schools is to foster greater cultural awareness and appreciation. During part of the day, students may meet in homogeneous groups to explore their own heritages. In 1971 the Brown School was established in Louisville, Kentucky, part of a voluntary integration effort;

The Learning Center in St. Paul, Minnesota.

that is, students from any part of town could join it, and be exposed to its multicultural curriculum.[25]

Schools-Within-a-School

This type of alternative education is self-descriptive. Most frequently, it involves a school district operating a number of educational programs under one roof. The variety in the programs offered usually means that any one program is not large. Schools-within-schools usually belong to one of the types of open school formats that have been previously mentioned: the learning centers, the continuation schools, the multicultural curriculum programs, or open curriculum.

Quincy, Illinois, for example, developed seven curricula for their students: traditional, work-study, flexible, fine arts, career, special education, and individualized. Mamaroneck, New York, introduced such options as: small classes for educationally disadvantaged students, special classes for the gifted, a cooperative teaching program with a range of minicourses, and an enrichment program capitalizing on teacher specializations.

Occasionally, some district will use the term "schools-within-schools" to describe satellite programs run in other buildings that may be under the supervision of different principals, but that are still tied to the central administration. Thus, a district may have a conventional program in one building, a fundamental or traditional curriculum at a second site, and a free school (to be discussed) at a third.[26]

Schools Without Walls

Some educators, recalling the criticism that not enough use was made of the resources within a community, have developed schools without walls. The most famous has been the Parkway Program in Philadelphia.[27] The only qualification is that

the students from the Philadelphia area must submit an application form. Those students chosen for admission are drawn by lot. The central concept is to use resources of Philadelphia as much as possible. Trips are made to museums when natural history and zoological subjects are discussed. Foreign language instruction takes place in some of the barrios and ethnic neighborhoods. Discussions with insurance executives and drug company officials apply mathematics and the sciences to problems of everyday life. While Parkway was first (in 1969), other cities have developed similar schools: Metro in Chicago, Genesis (formerly Community High School) in Berkeley, California, and City School in Madison, Wisconsin.

Some of the basic assumptions and features of the schools without walls are that school buildings per se are unimportant, their teachers can be flexible and imaginative, and the organizational structure is loose-knit. As a result of general financial cutbacks in Philadelphia schools, Parkway experienced a temporary problem in 1979–80. The seniority system brought teachers to Parkway who did not really want to teach in that kind of system, but virtually all came to prefer it to a conventional school.[28]

The Foxfire type of school is also closely related to its community. Students in such schools are expected to identify the strengths of their communities and use them to bring about changes in their neighborhoods. They may develop television shows, write newspaper articles, interview political leaders, and investigate social problems. Foxfire programs, estimated to be in use at 200 schools throughout the country, have called this emphasis upon action a "lesson in empowerment."[29]

Free Schools

For those who have come to believe public schools cannot be sufficiently altered to be truly humane, the best choice may be a free school. "Free" refers to the opportunities students have in planning their curriculum, doing their assignments, and attending or not attending classes. It does not refer to their cost, as some free schools have tuition charges running to thousands of dollars.

In the discussion that follows, Summerhill, located in Leiston, England, is used as an example of a boarding school model. The focus is on the goals of these schools rather than on the specific details of how the schools were started or what occurs in the classroom. If you wish to learn more about methods for organizing free schools, there are a variety of books you can consult.[30]

Summerhill. Begun in 1926 by A.S. Neill, Summerhill has been the prototype for hundreds of other free schools. In his autobiography, Neill related how his strict Calvinist upbringing motivated him to start a different type of school. He decided that a free school, incorporating some of the techniques of psychoanalysis, would be effective. Filled with antagonism toward organized religion, convinced that society had harmful sexual attitudes, and sure that governments are too often petty and cruel, Neill acknowledged that he was a Peter Pan, trying to establish a never-never land free of "life-haters."[31]

The goal of schooling, Neill argues, is happiness: "Take care of the emotions, and the intellect will take care of itself." The role of the teacher is to work with the student, not control the student. Grades should not be given, attendance is not required, and dress codes are abolished. The arts are used extensively. To those who fear this would promote academic anarchy, Neill responds that it promotes freedom. Excessive behavior of students is controlled in democratic meetings of the entire community. There, each member, from the 6-year-old to the oldest teacher, has one vote.

Summerhill enrolled 50 to 75 students annually, with a teaching staff between 8 and 10. In the early years, the students were frequently delinquents referred from the courts or children with emotional problems. As the years passed, more and more children came because their parents liked the philosophy Neill espoused. While some of the students have been from wealthy homes, the sliding tuition scale Neill employed permitted Summerhill to have students from a wide range of socioeconomic backgrounds. In the late 1960s and early 1970s, about half of the students at Summerhill were Americans.

In America, at least 100 schools have indicated that the principles practiced at Summerhill have been a key factor in their programs. The American Summerhill Society and several other clearinghouses for alternative schooling have listed Summerhill-type schools in virtually all parts of the nation, and in rural as well as urban settings.[32]

The most frequently asked question about Summerhill is, "How well do the graduates do in the 'real' world?" As far as we know, there have been no research studies of those who attended Summerhill. One writer, who interviewed 60 former Summerhillians, found them to be contented with life and typically at work in some nonbusiness area.[33]

American Free Schools. Free schools in America are found in urban and rural locations. Some are day schools, while others offer boarding facilities. (Some public schools have provided a free-school option to students.) Free schools, more than open education schools, are likely to enroll white middle-class and upper-class students who rebel against traditional social structure. Others try to have individuals from all social classes and a range of ethnic groups. There are elementary and secondary free schools. In short, it is diffi-

An elementary-level free school. Would you like to teach in this informal situation?

cult to make generalizations about American free schools.[34]

Many were begun by parents upset with what they regard as the dehumanizing atmosphere of traditional schools. The parents, moreover, are critical of open education because they believe even in such programs the teacher retains too much control over the student's curriculum. In the free school the students should make all important curriculum decisions. A school that carried this philosophy to its logical conclusion was the Elizabeth Street Cleaners School. It was started in New York City in 1969 by a group of students (with their parents' blessing). They rented a former drycleaning establishment on Elizabeth Street and placed ads in the New York papers for teachers. The students interviewed the candidates and selected their instructors. Together, the students and teachers worked out a curriculum, grading system, and procedures for admitting future students.[35]

How have free schools fared in America? One estimate is that there were fewer than 10 in 1970, but more than 1,200 by 1975. Some sources indicate the average free school lasts only nine months; others maintain that the average is closer to 18 months, or two school years. Causes for the frequent demise of free schools appear most often to be financial problems, lack of structure by the teachers in the curriculum, or a clash between patrons and teachers about educational ideology. There is limited evidence on the academic performance of students in free schools, but it suggests that they perform at least as well as students in conventional schools.[36]

ACTIVITY 15–2
The Free School Movement

Read three articles or portions of two books on the subject of free schools. Select at least one article or book that is critical of the free-school approach. After completing your reading, write the answers to these questions:

Chapter Fifteen

1. What is a free school?
2. List several benefits students can receive from such an education that they could not gain in conventional schools. Do free-school advocates offer what you consider to be adequate proof that their schools work?
3. Can you describe some differences between free-school proponents?
4. What reservations, if any, do you have about free schools?
5. If you had the chance, would you teach in a free school? If you had children, would you send them to a free school?

See the references in the "Notes" and in the "For Further Study" sections for sources to consult. In addition, see Lawrence A. Cremin, "The Free School Movement: A Perspective," *Today's Education* 13 (September 1974): 71–74 and Suzanne S. Fremon, "Why Free Schools Fail," *Parents' Magazine* (September 1972), pp. 50–51, 96, 98.

Problems and Promises of Alternatives and Options

Students, parents, and educators who have been involved in starting alternative programs know that the cost is high, in terms of effort and energy, even if not in dollars. Are the typical problems that emerge too often insurmountable? Parents, in particular, also ask, whether it makes a difference academically if a child goes to a conventional school or a presumably more humane alternative school.

Alternative schools have had several persistent problems. There is often a stigma attached to them. The students who are participants in the optional programs may be perceived to be the disruptive, disturbed, or weird students who don't fit in the regular classrooms. Moreover, teachers and administrators in conventional schools, according to some alternative-school supporters, frequently put down the alternative schools, making it difficult for such programs to gain acceptance. Sometimes, when such programs are instituted, the new staff is not given sufficient time or resources to prepare adequately for the change. Most communities that have alternative schools have insisted that they cost no more per pupil than the conventional schools. While that is possible, problems often occur in getting the initial funding to cover start-up costs. When finances become a problem, often alternative programs that are seen as frills or extras are cut back. Finally, when early research findings concluded that most students in alternative programs did no better academically than students in traditional classrooms, some parents lost interest.[37]

Other evidence, however, suggests that alternative schools have much to offer. Generally speaking, students in alternative programs exhibit more creativity than those in conventional classrooms. Minority students, in some studies, perform better academically in classrooms. Pupils in alternative schools are more independent and interactive in problem solving and cause fewer disciplinary problems. Based on certain self-esteem and self-concept tests, students in open education programs show more maturity for their age than students in conventional schools. Some research studies conclude that underachieving students have benefited from optional programs.[38]

The major point of this section has been that there are a myriad of alternatives within and among schools. There are those critics who contend that these options are cosmetic, and that viable changes have been aborted. Nevertheless, the persistence and apparent growth of options seems to indicate that there is a growing acceptance of the idea that all students do not learn in exactly the same manner and that a diversity of educational environments should be provided.

GAINING AWARENESS OF NONPUBLIC EDUCATION

Predictions of the demise of nonpublic schools, like the rumors about Mark Twain's death, have been greatly exaggerated. While parochial school enrollments, like public school enrollments, have been falling, students in nonsectarian private schools have increased 60% since 1970 to 1.8 million.

Why the continuing interest in a nonpublic option, when most authorities in the 1970s projected a sharp decline in such schools? The explanation for attending nonpublic schools might be found in one or more of the following reasons: (1) moral and religious training, (2) intensive preparation for college, (3) the small classes and personal attention of faculty, (4) rigorous discipline (especially in the military academies), (5) transmission of specific ethnic or racial cultures, and (6) fear of racial integration.

Religious Schools

Many Americans believe that education has a religious dimension. Often the religious outlook determines the nature and severity of discipline that parents expect teachers to use. As Chapter 8 revealed, in the 1800s numerous groups, seeing that public education could not combine religion and education, began religious schools. Others believed it was unpatriotic for parents to send their children to a parochial or private school. The feelings against religious schools reached a high in the early decades of the twentieth century. In 1922 the Oregon legislature passed a law requiring that all students attend public schools. A Roman Catholic school and a military academy brought suit. In 1925 the U.S. Supreme Court ruled in *Pierce* v. *Society of Sisters* that parents do have the right to choose the type of education they wish for their children. The justices made clear in the same decision that a state does have the power to regulate all schools within its borders in such matters as health, safety, minimum academic standards, and instruction in specific disciplines.

In 1977 almost 80% of the nonpublic schools had a religious affiliation. Roman Catholic schools constituted 54% of all nonpublic schools. Enrollment in Roman Catholic schools was 68% of the total nonpublic student population.[39] Compare these percentages with those just one year previous in Table 15–1. What this reveals is a decline in Roman Catholic enrollment which is somewhat offset by the increase in Christian day schools.

Parochial Schools. Parochial schools are here defined as those schools with clear ties to a specific denomination or religious tradition. Teachers in such schools are usually of that faith and may be ordained or commissioned in a special teaching order. Usually most of the students are from that religious heritage. Financial support for the schools comes mainly from student tuitions and donations from local congregations.[40]

Chapter Fifteen

Table 15–1.
Religious schools: 1976

Affiliation	No. of schools	(%)*	Students	(%)*
Baptist	310	(2.1)	87,917	(2.1)
Calvinist	182	(1.2)	47,129	(1.1)
Catholic	8,986	(60.9)	3,110,972	(73.5)
Episcopal	304	(2.1)	73,774	(1.7)
Jewish	264	(1.8)	59,810	(1.4)
Lutheran	1,366	(9.3)	201,157	(4.8)
Seventh Day Adventist	517	(3.5)	46,998	(1.1)
Other	618	(4.2)	130,412	(3.1)
	12,547	(85.0)	3,758,269	(88.8)
Nonaffiliation	2,210	(15.0)	475,901	(11.2)
	14,757	(100.0)	4,234,170	(100.0)

*The percentage represents the portion of all nonpublic schools, including those such as the Christian day school, which are not affiliated with any denomination. From the National Center for Education Statistics, *Nonpublic School Statistics, 1976–1977*, mimeographed paper (1977), p. 2.

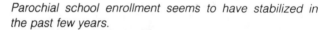

Parochial school enrollment seems to have stabilized in the past few years.

In fall 1964, Roman Catholic elementary and secondary schools' enrollments constituted approximately 90% of the nonpublic student population: more than 5 million K-12 students were taught by 171,200 faculty in approximately 13,000 buildings. In 1976, 3 million students attended approximately 9,000 Catholic schools, and represented almost 75% of nonpublic school enrollments.[41]

For a number of other religious groups, there has been in recent decades either a revival of interest or a new thrust in beginning religious schools. More than 80% of the Baptist, Presbyterian, and Episcopal schools now in existence as well as more than 95% of all Jewish day schools were founded after 1930. Christian day schools are the newest religious schools. Table 15–1 documents the commitment to "weekday" schooling by various denominations.

Christian Day Schools. In the 1970s a new phenomenon in the education world was evident—the rise of Christian day schools. Parents of students attending these schools are convinced that religion must be part of the curriculum. They are certain that the public schools are godless, that fundamental values instruction is missing, and that firm discipline is desirable. One newspaper writer estimated that 5,000 to 6,000 such schools with a student population of 900,000 had been reached. A more modest figure is suggested by the Association of Christian Schools International, which reported a membership of 763 schools with an enrollment of 93,576 students. This organization, however, does not include all the Christian day schools.[42]

What distinguishes these schools from parochial schools? Unlike the parochial schools, most Christian day schools are not tied to a specific denomination. Usually, a single congregation or a cluster of local churches sponsors the school initially.

Students and their parents sign a statement pledging support of fundamentalist or evangelical religious doctrines such as the inerrancy of the Bible, the sinful nature of humankind, the need for judgment and redemption, and the belief in the second coming of Christ. Parochial schools are much more likely to accept federal and state funds for milk and lunch programs, textbooks, and transportation costs than are the Christian day schools. In some states, teachers in parochial schools are fully certified by the state, and students are tested with the same instruments (standardized tests) as are used in the public schools. Fearful of state control, Christian day schools, as a general policy, avoid any entanglements with state governments.[43]

There are some similarities between the two types of schools. Teachers are expected to be models for appropriate behavior, including living up to specific moral codes. Special textbooks in such fields as history and science may provide a religious interpretation of world events and natural phenomena. Hair and dress regulations, based on biblical injunctions, are common. Both types of schools may offer extracurricular activities programs, albeit on a limited scale.

While it is difficult to predict what the future holds for religious schools, our opinion is that their future appears modestly bright. The general conservative climate in the country, the growing support for the tuition tax credit (see Chapter 10), and the voucher plan are just several indicators favoring the increase in such schools. Christian day schools, based on recent figures, would seem to be growing at a faster rate than parochial schools.[44]

Amish Education. As a result of religious persecution in Europe, the Amish immigrated to America more than 200 years ago. They settled in what became Pennsylvania, Ohio, Indiana, Wisconsin, Illinois, and Iowa, where they have continued to practice their agrarian life-style. Their interpretation of scripture demands that men and women have specific vocations; it dictates that personal and social problems are to be solved within the community of faith; and it holds that eight years of schooling are sufficient because they want to keep their children from worldly corruptions.

The last position puts them in conflict with compulsory attendance laws. Moreover, many of their teachers have not gone beyond the eighth grade. Their school curriculum, which emphasizes reading, writing, religion, nature study, and German, is often below the states' guidelines for mathematics and sciences.[45] The U.S. Supreme Court ruled in *Wisconsin* v. *Yoder* that Amish students could not be required to attend school beyond the eighth grade.

A series of questions raised by this case could be asked of all religious school education. Are students in such schools performing at an adequate academic level? Will the attitudes they gain from such schooling affect their loyalty to the nation? If our society is willing to tolerate some forms of religious education, what forms will it not tolerate? For those who want religious education, another question is whether religious schools have been effective in transmitting their faith. These questions have sparked lively debates that continue.[46]

Private Schools

Just as there is diversity among alternative and religious schools, so there is a variety of nonsectarian private schools. There are the traditional boarding schools, day schools, schools with special experimental programs, and programs for specific groups of students. This section will discuss the independent schools, the Montessori schools, and separatist/ethnic schools.

Independent Schools. The term *private schools* might prompt you to think of eastern boarding schools with a student body composed of daughters or sons of establishment families. Nonsectarian private schools prefer the term independent schools. There are an estimated 3,200 independent schools in the country. One organization that speaks for some of that number is the National Association of Independent Schools (NAIS).[47]

There is a long tradition of such schools— 17 of the NAIS member schools were founded before 1776. Phillips Exeter and Phillips Andover were academies; the Collegiate School of New York City started as an elementary charity school. While most of these schools increasingly emphasized preparatory studies and some became boarding schools, most independent schools are day schools.

One special branch of the independent boarding schools is the military school. The establishment of West Point (1802) and Annapolis (1850) stimulated the growth of such schools as Howe Military School and Culver Military Academy in Indiana. Most of the 17 military schools that are members of NAIS have a denominational affiliation and require some religious courses and/or attendance at church or chapel, as do most boarding schools.

The girls' boarding schools, which became popular in the 1800s, were inclined toward a finishing-school format (e.g., Miss Porter's, the Westover School) but increasingly moved toward a more academic program (such as Baldwin, Shipley, and the Bryn Mawr School).

Day schools flourished in the early 1900s. In New York City, traditional schools such as Trinity were complemented by independent schools that reflected John Dewey's progressive ideas—Dalton School and Lincoln School. Some of the day schools around the nation were called country day schools because they either were oper-

America has a long tradition of private schools which is likely to continue.

ated in suburban areas or were urban centers that maintained estates where they took students for weekend excursions.[48]

Today, independent schools are geared toward rigorous academic programs. Many have cutoff scores on entrance exams to exclude all but the highest-scoring pupils. A number of the independent schools have broadened their formerly narrow range of clientele and may have 10% or more of their students from minority groups.[49]

Montessori Schools. In the first decade of the twentieth century, Maria Montessori, Italy's first woman physician, tried out her educational ideas in a Rome slum with 50 children considered to be retarded and/or delinquent. As the children became more expressive, learned how to read and write, developed skills in problem solving, and improved personal health habits, others wanted to know Montessori's secrets.[50]

Her philosophy was that young children learn best through structured play activi-

ties. Students were encouraged to become independent thinkers and doers through the development of their cognitive reasoning abilities. Montessori created unique beads, rods, blocks, sandpaper letters, and puzzles. She trained teachers to be directors of learning and she set guidelines for certain mechanical tasks, such as washing hands, so that students would become better managers of their own affairs.

In the early twenties there was much enthusiasm for her ideas in America, but it waned. A rebirth of interest occurred in the 1960s, and since then an estimated 500 schools using her techniques have been started. Most of the schools only go through the nursery level, but a few elementary schools have been established. One of the most famous Montessori schools was the Whitby School, founded in 1958 in a renovated carriage house in Greenwich, Connecticut. Although the earliest schools were often begun by upper-middle-class families, a number of them do attempt to recruit children of various religious, social class, and racial backgrounds. Some public school teachers have adopted Montessori materials and methods, especially for kindergarten children.[51]

Separatist/Ethnic Schools. The story of privately controlled schools would not be complete without mention of two other special types of programs. Information on separatist and ethnic schools is meager and enrollment figures are unreliable; nevertheless, you should know something about them.

Separatist schools are designed to avoid court-ordered integration. After the U. S. Supreme Court ruled segregated public schools unconstitutional in 1954, numerous individuals who wished racial isolation devised plans to circumvent the decision. A favorite was some form of tuition grant to parents who could then use the state funds to pay for segregated schools. Such plans have been repeatedly declared unconstitutional. Yet, even without state aid, private segregated academies have sprung up. By 1977, one source estimated 4,000 such schools enrolled approximately 750,000 students. Whether a court decision in 1976 (*Runyon* v. *McCrary* 427 U.S. 160), which found that exclusion of students from private schools based on race was illegal, will affect the growth of such academies remains to be seen.[52] Another issue is the tax-exempt status of such schools.

In the North and in the urban centers of the West, groups such as the Black Muslims have begun weekday educational centers, some enrolling as many as 600 students. The curriculum of the schools has a religious basis, but their goals are also political. Instruction in Arabic and French may be included, and discipline is quasi-militaristic.[53]

ACTIVITY 15–3
Visit an Alternative School

Perhaps you find the descriptions of the schools mentioned in this chapter intriguing. Consider making a trip to one.

Report your general reactions to your class. Think about these questions as you observe the students and school:

1. Do the students come from the same social class background? Are different cultures represented?
2. Why did the school begin? What are its stated goals?
3. What is the future (enrollment/facilities/programs) for this school?
4. How do students, curriculum, and atmosphere of the school compare with a conventional school?
5. Would you want to teach in a school like this? Why or why not?

SUMMARY

America's educational landscape is dotted with a beneficial array of alternatives, according to some observers. Others, however, see a bureaucratic system producing conformists. For these critics, the schools of America—public, parochial, or independent—turn out the same kind of student—compliant, nonquestioning authority addicts.

There are other critics who believe that

the schools have allowed students far too much freedom already. They propose a more rigorous, subject-oriented school system that will concentrate upon building rational decision-making skills. Other reformers believe that the curriculum is still too inflexible and that teachers and the system treat students inhumanely. They believe that schools can be made more warm and friendly. The most radical critics suggest that no amount of modification can rectify the basic wrongs of the public system.

Despite what the radicals say, a number of other individuals believe the public schools can be improved. A variety of programs have been tried, including open education, schools-within-schools, schools without walls, and free schools. There is much discussion about the advantages and weaknesses of these alternative models. Possibly the only major point of agreement is that schools should provide more than one style of learning to service the variety of student needs.

Regardless of where you may teach, you are likely to find some nonpublic schools. The parochial system is still the largest type of nonpublic schools, but a growing number of religious schools are Christian day schools. There are varieties of independent schools also, from college-preparatory boarding schools to free schools.

Two issues were raised in the chapter. The first asks whether the new schools are better than the conventional schools. There is little to suggest that alternative schools are decidedly better or worse than traditional schools. It is impossible to judge how successful religious or private schools are, considering how much of their appeal is to the attitudes and values of their patrons. The second issue is coming to a head in America. We must decide soon whether much more tolerance will be granted.

NOTES

1. Robert J. Havighurst, "Requirements for a Valid 'New Criticism,'" *Phi Delta Kappan* 50, no. 1 (September 1968): 20–26.

2. Lawrence A. Cremin, *The Transformation of the School* (New York: Knopf, 1961), pp. 338–43, 347.

3. Ibid., pp. 343–46.

4. Max Rafferty, *Suffer, Little Children* (New York: Devin-Adair, 1962); *What They are Doing to Your Children* (New York: New American Library, 1965); *Max Rafferty on Education* (New York: Devin-Adair, 1968); William O'Neill, *Readin, Ritin and Rafferty: A Study of Educational Fundamentalism* (Berkeley: The Glendessary Press, 1969).

5. Paul Copperman, *The Literacy Hoax: The Decline of Reading, Writing and Learning in the Public School and What We Can Do About It* (New York: Morrow Quill, 1978).

6. Alvin Toffler, *Future Shock* (New York: Random House, 1970).

7. Carl Rogers, *Freedom to Learn* (Columbus, Ohio: Charles E. Merrill, 1969); William Glasser, *Schools Without Failure* (New York: Harper and Row, 1969).

8. Neil Postman and Charles Weingartner, *Teaching as a Subversive Activity* (New York: Delacorte Press, 1969); *The Soft Revolution* (New York: Delacorte, 1971); *The School Book* (New York: Delacorte, 1973); and Neil Postman, *Teaching as a Conserving Activity* (New York: Delacorte, 1979).

9. Herbert Kohl, *36 Children* (New York: New American Library, 1967); George Dennison, *The Lives of Children* (New York: Vintage, 1969).

10. Charles E. Silberman, *Crisis in the Classroom* (New York: Random House, 1970).

11. John Holt, *How Children Fail* (New York: Pitman Publishing, 1964); his other books include *How Children Learn* (1967), *What Do I Do Monday?* (1970), *The Underachieving School* (1969), and *Freedom and Beyond* (1972). The book on at-home instruction is *Instead of Education: Ways to Help People Do Things Better* (New York: Dutton, 1976).

12. Paul Goodman, *Compulsory Mis-Education* (New York: Horizon, 1964), pp. 7–12.

13. Edgar Friedenberg, *The Vanishing Adolescent* (New York: Dell, 1959), pp. 41–49; *Coming of Age in America* (New York: Random House, 1965).

14. Joel Spring, *The Sorting Machine: National Educational Policy Since 1945* (New York: David McKay, 1976); Michael B. Katz, *Class, Bureaucracy, and Schools* (New York: Praeger, 1971); Samuel Bowles and Herbert Gintis, *Schooling in Capitalist America: Educational Reform and the Contradiction of Economic Life* (New York: Basic Books, 1976).

15. Jonathan Kozol, *Death at an Early Age* (Boston: Houghton Mifflin, 1967); *Free Schools* (Boston: Houghton Mifflin, 1972); *The Night is Dark and I Am Far From Home* (Boston: Houghton Mifflin, 1975);

Chapter Fifteen

Children of the Revolution (New York: Delacorte Press, 1978).

16. Ivan Illich, *Deschooling Society* (New York: Harper and Row, 1971).

17. Paulo Freire, *Pedagogy of the Oppressed* (New York: Seabury Press, 1970); *Pedagogy in Process* (New York: Seabury Press, 1978).

18. Roald F. Campbell, *Performance Contracting in School Systems* (Columbus, Ohio: Charles E. Merrill Publishing, 1972).

19. Joan K. Smith, "Educational Innovations and Institutional Bureaucracy," *Journal of Thought* 9, no. 4 (November 1974): 219–29; G.D. Hottleman, "Performance Contracting is a Hoax!" *Educational Digest* 37 no. 1 (September 1971): 1–4.

20. George LaNoue, *Educational Vouchers: Concepts and Controversies* (New York: Teachers College Press, 1972); John Coons and Stephen Sugarman, *Education by Choice: The Case for Family Control* (Berkeley: University of California Press, 1978).

21. Denis P. Doyle, "The Politics of Choice: A View from the Bridge," in Institute for Contemporary Studies, *Parents, Teachers, and Children: Prospects for Choice in American Education* (San Francisco: Institute for Contemporary Studies, 1977), pp. 227–56.

22. Mary Anne Raywid, "Optional Schools: Pipedream or Probability?" *Viewpoints in Teaching and Learning* 55, no. 2 (Spring 1979): 41–51.

23. These characteristics have been compiled from the following sources: Vernon H. Smith, Robert Barr, and Daniel Burke, *Alternatives in Education: Freedom to Choose* (Bloomington, Ind.: Phi Delta Kappa, 1976); Mario Fantini, *Public Schools of Choice* (New York: Simon and Schuster, 1973); and W.C. Wolf, Jr. and Mike Barkhurst, "Initiating, Sustaining Alternative Schools," *Phi Delta Kappan* 59, no. 9 (May 1978): 635–36.

24. Smith et al., *Alternatives in Education*, p. 37; Susan S. Petreshene, *The Complete Guide to Learning Centers* (Palo Alto, Calif.: Pendragon House, 1978).

25. Smith et al., *Alternatives in Education*, pp. 95–96; Mario Fantini, "Alternatives in the Public Schools," in Terrence Deal and Robert Nolan, eds., *Alternative Schools: Ideologies, Realities, Guidelines* (Chicago: Nelson-Hall, 1978), p. 55.

26. J. Kock and L. Kock, "Seven Schools in One," *McCall's* 102 (June 1975), pp. 34–35; Paul Abrason, "How One Public School District Offers a Variety of Alternative Programs," *The American School Board Journal* 162, no. 10 (October 1975): 38–40.

27. John Bremer and Michael Von Moschzisker, *The School Without Walls: Philadelphia's Parkway Program* (New York: Holt, Rinehart and Winston, 1971).

28. James H. Lytle, "An Untimely (but Significant) Experiment in Teacher Motivation," *Phi Delta Kappan* 61, no. 10 (June 1980): 700–702.

29. *Des Moines Register*, "One Teacher's Lesson of 'Empowerment,' " 4 September 1979, reprinted from the *Washington Post*.

30. Jonathan Kozol, *Free Schools*; Samuel Yanes, *The No More Gym Shorts, Build It Yourself, Self-Discovery Free School Talkin' Blues* (New York: Harper Colophon Books, 1972); The Great Atlantic and Pacific School Conspiracy (Group), *Doing Your Own School* (Boston: Beacon Press, 1972). See also note 34.

31. A.S. Neill, *Neill! Neill! Orange Peel!* (New York: Hart, 1972).

32. The American Summerhill Society is now defunct. However, certain exchanges about alternative schooling are still in operation at the University of Massachusetts and Hofstra University.

33. Emmanuel Bernstein, "What Does a Summerhill Old School Tie Look Like?" *Psychology Today* 2 no. 2 (October 1968): 37–41ff. For a student's perspective, see Joshua Popenoe, *Inside Summerhill* (New York: Hart, 1970); William Matthias, "Summerhill," *Childhood Education* 58, no. 5 (April/May 1979): 265–67.

34. Allen Graubard, *Free the Children: Radical Reform and the Free School Movement* (New York: Vintage, 1972); Steve Bhaerman, *No Particular Place to Go: The Making of a Free High School* (New York: Simon and Schuster, 1972).

35. *Starting Your Own High School: Elizabeth Street Cleaner's Street School* (New York: Random House, 1972).

36. Wayne Jennings and Joe Nathan, "Startling/ Disturbing Research on School Program Effectiveness," *Phi Delta Kappan* 58, no. 7 (March 1977): 568–72; E. Cagan, "Individualism, Collectivism, and Radical Educational Reform," *Harvard Educational Review* 48, no. 2 (May 1978): 250–55.

37. Lyn S. Martin, *More Than Joy: What Does Research Say About Open Education?* (New York: Agathon Press, 1976); Bernard Spodek and Herbert J. Walberg, eds., *Studies in Open Education* (New York: Agathon Press, 1975); R. D. Barn et al., "Analysis of Six School Evaluations: The Effectiveness of Alternative Public Schools," *Viewpoints* 53, no. 4 (July 1977): 1–30.

38. Vincent R. Rogers and Bud Church, eds., *Open Education: Critique and Assessment* (Washington, D.C.: Association for Supervision and Curriculum Development, 1975), pp. 83–98; Smith et al., *Alternatives in Education*, p. 31.

39. National Center for Education Statistics, "Selected Statistics of Private Schools, Fall 1977," unpublished report, 27 January 1979, p. 2.

40. Technically, Catholic schools include parochial and diocesan schools as well as those operated and controlled by teaching orders. In this section, the term parochial is used for all Catholic schools as well as those affiliated with other religious denominations.

41. Martin A. Larson, *When Parochial Schools Close* (New York: Robert B. Luce, 1972); Gregory M. Holtz, "The Changing Catholic Schools," *The Education Digest* 16, no. 10 (April 1976): 816–23.

42. William J. Lanouette, "The Fourth R is Religion," *National Observer* 15 January 1977, pp. 1, 18.

43. Richard Ostling, "Why Protestant Schools are Booming," *Christian Herald*, July-August 1977, pp. 44–47. The evangelical groups have developed their own testing services.

44. Virginia Davis Nordin and William Lloyd Turner, "More than Segregation Academies; The Growing Protestant Fundamentalist Schools," *Phi Delta Kappan* 61 no. 6 (February 1980): 319–94.

45. John A. Hostettler, *Children in Amish Society* (New York: Holt, Rinehart & Winston, 1971); Albert Keim, ed., *Compulsory Education and the Amish* (Boston: Beacon Press, 1975).

46. Andrew M. Greeley and Peter H. Rossi, *The Education of Catholic Americans* (Chicago: Adline Publishing, 1966), especially pp. 191–98; J.T. Hiltz, "Effects of Independent Religion Study on Religious Interest in High School Sophomores," *Religious Education* 70, no. 4 (July 1975): 416–27.

47. Gil Sewall, "Private-School Boom," *Newsweek*, 13 August 1979, p. 83; *Private Independent Schools* (Wallingford, Conn.: Bunting and Lyon, 1979).

48. Otto Kraushaar, *American Nonpublic Schools* (Baltimore: Johns Hopkins University Press, 1972), pp. 74–78.

49. Leonard L. Baird, *The Elite Schools* (Lexington, Mass.: D.C. Heath, 1977), pp. 10–11.

50. Maria Montessori, *The Montessori Method* (New York: Schoken, 1974). See also Urban H. Fleege, "Montessori System of Education," in Edward Ignas and R. Corsini, *Alternative Educational Systems* (Itasca, Ill.: Peacock, 1979), pp. 151–99.

51. Paul Willcott, "The Initial American Reception of the Montessori Method," *School Review*, 76 no. 2 (June 1968): 147–65.

52. "Private Academies: A Thorn for Public Education," *Education U.S.A.* 19 (February 1977): 177; David Nevin and Robert E. Bills, *The Schools That Fear Built* (Washington, D.C.: Acropolis Press, 1976), p. 53. Otto F. Kraushaar, *Private Schools: From the Puritans to the Present* (Bloomington, Ind.: Phi Delta Kappa, 1976), p. 44; "Black-Run Private Schools Lure Growing Numbers in New York," *New York Times*, 5 April 1980.

FOR FURTHER STUDY

Avrich, Paul. *The Modern School Movement: Anarchism and Education in the United States*. Princeton: Princeton University Press, 1980.

Baird, Leonard. *The Elite Schools: A Profile of Prestigious Independent Schools*. Lexington, Mass.: Lexington Books, 1977.

Buetow, Harold A. *Of Singular Benefit: The Story of U.S. Catholic Education*. London: Macmillan, 1970.

Duke, Daniel. *The Retransformation of the School: The Emergence of Contemporary Alternative Schools in the United States*. Chicago: Nelson Hall, 1978.

Glatthorn, Allan A. *Alternatives in Education: Schools and Programs*. New York: Dodd, Mead and Company, 1975.

Gross, Ronald and Beatrice, eds. *Radical School Reform*. New York: Simon and Schuster, 1969.

Mays, Robert E. *Opening the Public School Curriculum*. Dubuque, Iowa: Kendall/Hunt, 1976.

Newman, Arthur J. *In Defense of the American Public School*. Berkeley, Calif.: McCutchan Publishing, 1978.

Rust, Vale D. *Alternatives in Education: Theoretical and Historical Perspectives*. Beverly Hills, Calif.: Sage Publications, 1977.

Taylor, Joy. *Organizing the Open Classroom*. New York: Schocken Books, 1972.

Vogel, Alfred T. *The Owl Critics*. University, Ala.: University of Alabama Press, 1980.

Epilogue
Your Future and Education

The educator must above all understand how to wait; to reckon all effects in the light of the future, not of the present.

Ellen Key, 1911

Human history becomes more and more a race between education and catastrophe.

H. G. Wells, 1920

Is teaching for you? What are schools for?
Teaching Today and Tomorrow opened with these two questions. Throughout the text, these two questions were asked again and again, sometimes directly, sometimes indirectly. By now you should have at least a tentative answer to these two fundamental questions which are central to an introductory course in education. In framing your answers, you have begun to develop your philosophy of education.

IS TEACHING FOR YOU?

Frequently, we have observed that students who contemplate a teaching career enter the initial course in education with high ideals. Recalling teachers who have made an impact upon their own lives, they focus on the influence that individual educators can have upon students. They often forget that teachers do more than relate to students on a one-to-one basis. Teachers are representatives of society, members of professional organizations, and participants in their communities.

One of our major purposes was to help you look at the "big picture" of what teaching has been like and what it is going to be tomorrow to aid you in making your own decision about teaching as a career. More specifically, we believe you needed information that would help you make a better self-assessment, tell you about the historical and current roles of teachers, describe the types of individuals choosing a teaching career, alert you to the activities of teacher organizations, expose you to classroom routines, and have you become aware of issues facing teachers as well as career opportunities.

Common sense dictates the beginning point for your consideration of teaching as a career—a self-assessment. Teaching is a profession that is based on effective human interactions. We are convinced that your effectiveness as a teacher is seriously diminished if you do not understand yourself. By looking at your personal priorities and needs in Chapter 1, you should be able to determine more precisely what type of educational situation would be best for you.

Then we provided you with descriptions of various historical roles that teachers have held, from disciplinarians to Jacks and Jills of all trades. Most, if not all, of these roles continue today, but there are also new expectations. Teachers of tomorrow will be expected to exhibit their concern for the personal needs of students as well as demonstrate ability to diagnose learning disabilities. They also will be asked by their peers to be concerned about the needs of the profession. Are you able to accept the roles described? Do any of them inhibit you? Do you believe that these roles are reasonable?

Before you began this course you may have wondered whether you would fit in as a teacher. Especially if you held teachers in high esteem, you may have wondered whether you would be accepted by those now teaching. We sought to answer your questions with some data and cautious generalizations about those who have become teachers in recent years. Teachers are likely to be from the middle class; they regard themselves as politically conservative; and they are average academically when compared with other college graduates. Such information, when coupled with descriptions of how teachers feel and act in the classrooms, should help you determine whether you fit the general profile of most teachers today.

While Part 1 focused on you as an individual contemplating teaching as a career and how your perceptions about teachers squared with reality, Part 2 addressed topics related to what teachers are facing today. It began with an overview of teacher education and the certification process. Then came the fundamental question many veteran as well as beginning teachers ask: "Will I be able to teach next year?" Analysis of the issues of teacher supply and demand concluded that there is likely to

be more of a demand than is generally predicted today. You should recall that there are increasing numbers of employment opportunities outside the classroom. Skills gained in teacher education may aid your chances for employment in a variety of careers.

Another point stressed in this part was that teachers do not operate in isolation. Teacher organizations are becoming increasingly powerful and making an impact upon educational policies as well as salaries. The political actions of teachers may change the shape of education in the nation. Can you accept the likelihood that you will be part of an organization that is run along the lines of a union?

Classroom routines of the future will not be the same as they are today. Granted, changes may occur slowly, but school districts are instituting new instructional techniques. While there will never be absolute agreement on what constitutes effective teaching, there appears to be a growing consensus about such matters as how students learn, the importance of class size, discipline procedures, and teacher attitudes towards students. There is also greater agreement on how to evaluate teachers. There also are concerted efforts to improve evaluation procedures of students' performance. Teachers in tomorrow's schools will have to become adept at devising their own measurement instruments as well as knowledgeable about the wide variety of assessment procedures that are available from regional and national sources.

Finally we singled out several educational trends in America with which tomorrow's teachers will have to cope. Our society has made a fundamental commitment to identifying and meeting the individual needs of students. Similarly, teachers are expected to promote equal educational opportunity regardless of race, class, or ethnic background. Even if you do not become a teacher in a desegregated school, you still have an obligation to make your students aware of the diversity of our society and our goal of equal educational opportunity for all students. The heated debates about the most appropriate forms of education appear likely to result in a growth of educational alternatives and options. If you become a·teacher, your own career may be in a school quite different from the one you attended.

WHAT ARE SCHOOLS FOR?

Part 3 focused on the second major question of the text. In providing you with information on the heritage, governance, and financing of schools, as well as descriptions of how educational goals are set and curriculum evolves, we wanted you to learn the rules of the game. We believe we would do you a disservice if you finished

Is teaching for you?

this course without an accurate picture of the ways schooling decisions are made.

You may be among those students who dislike or ignore history. One of the major misconceptions we have found among our students is their belief that what is happening now in American schools is brand new. It isn't. Most of today's vital issues and the proposed reforms for educational problems have been around before. We looked at some of the recurrent themes in American education, which reveal that the schools reflect society's needs and perceptions. Hence, schools are conservative. In Chapter 8, and in historical sections throughout the book, we offered our personal opinion that the public school cannot be simply categorized as the nation's chief instrument of salvation (as its advocates maintain), or a cruel hoax offering the downtrodden only the illusion of opportunity (as its critics argue). After considering both the positive and negative interpretations of the school, you must decide whether one outweighs the other.

At a number of points in the book, but most especially in Chapter 9, we asked you to consider the issue of control of public education. Is it true, as tradition has it, that America is unique because there is local control of education? Legally, each state, rather than the federal government, sets educational policies. In reality, however, a number of national forces—federal agencies, teacher organizations, foundations—also affect local decisions. Do you believe that local control will—and should—be maintained during the next several decades?

The educational system of the nation is a huge enterprise, involving approximately one in four citizens as students, teachers, or staff. That in itself suggests education is important in America. The fact that we raise over $80 billion annually in taxes for public schools is also revealing. We also looked at the "bottom line" regarding the financing of American schools. (Because there are often great disparities between rhetoric and reality, the "bottom line" will help you identify a person's or group's real priorities by seeing what they spend for different projects.)

Questions about the importance of education can be raised, however. Has schooling been a financial priority of the nation? Are teachers adequately compensated? What, if anything, should be done to rectify the disparities within and among states regarding per-pupil expenditures? Are sufficient efforts being made to reduce dropout rates? Many of these questions may not seem important to you now, but if you become a teacher you will find that many of the priorities in schools will hinge upon economic rather than pedagogical considerations.

If you become a teacher, you will be an agent for one of America's largest social institutions. You have learned about some of its historic instructional goals. You have gained some understanding of what the public thinks the school does well and what it should be in the future. Have you identified *what* it is, academically, that you personally think should be stressed? What is your opinion now about the relationship of the "basics" and what might be termed "social adjustment skills"? As you discovered, the accountability movement implies that tomorrow's teachers will have to be sensitive to curriculum demands of many groups. Districts will use both formal means, such as needs assessment, and informal methods for soliciting and receiving new goals for the schools. Do you believe that the school system has been responsive enough to public demands to alter the curriculum? What do you think you can do as a citizen or teacher to minimize curriculum censorship?

Those who become educators in the

coming decades will find new emphases in the curriculum. The curriculum has evolved since colonial times and there are now many more subjects and more kinds of specialized programs. Efforts to reform the curriculum are constant, even though few succeed. One of the current trends is an increasing use of educational technology. Teachers of tomorrow will use more television, computers, and simulations. Other areas that are receiving more attention in the 1980s include early childhood education, the basics, bilingual and multicultural education, and career education. Teachers must keep abreast of curriculum changes.

A conclusion that you should have reached is that the school is a complex system. Those who call for simple solutions to the complicated problems of schooling are deceiving themselves. In part this is due to the many publics that the school system must serve. One plan to reform school financing is not likely to be fair to all groups. Equal educational opportunity can be defined in many ways; remedies that work in one locale have been disastrous in others. Alternative forms of schooling may weaken rather than improve educational performance of students. The professional educators of the future have an obligation to improve the system, but they also have the responsibility to resist changes that have not been adequately assessed. An understanding of our schools and educational system is important not only to teachers but to all citizens in our country. What are schools for? What is your view of the school as a social institution?

In closing, we are reminded of a story told about a young boy who often served as a guide to tourists at the Notre Dame Cathedral in Paris. One group of visitors, seeking to learn how knowledgeable the youth was about the treasures within, asked him to describe the saints. Thinking of those depicted in the stained glass windows, he replied: "They are the people the light shines through." We believe that is also a good definition of an effective teacher—people whom the light of knowledge shines through.

We hope we have conveyed our view of teaching as an exciting, exhilarating, and yes, sometimes exasperating endeavor. It is a demanding profession. We hope greater awareness of the diversity of American schools may enable you to make a more intelligent decision about the kind of school in which you would be most effective. But we know, too, that teaching is not for everyone. Remember that your careful self-assessment of teaching as a career choice, regardless of the final outcome, will benefit not only yourself, but the students of tomorrow. If we have helped you reach a clearer decision, we shall feel that we have succeeded.

Part 4
Self-Assessment

Date ⎯⎯⎯⎯⎯⎯⎯⎯⎯⎯⎯⎯⎯⎯

1.0 Decision on Teaching as a Career

Since reading Part 4, my decision on becoming or not becoming a teacher has been—
( ) confirmed, because⎯⎯⎯.
( ) somewhat modified, in that⎯⎯⎯.

Epilogue

( ) drastically changed, because_____.
( ) made more difficult, because_____.

2.0 Philosophy of Education Statement

Now that the course is completed, reread each of your previous statements and comment again on all of the following points in terms of how your statements have been modified:

2.1 goals of education.

2.2 the curriculum.

2.3 the role of the teacher.

2.4 perceptions of learning.

2.5 educational policies and procedures.

3.0 The School as a Social Institution

3.1 Since reading Part 4, my general understanding of the school's role has—
( ) not been altered. I still believe the school to be_____.
( ) become more appreciative. For example,_____.
( ) become more critical. I now feel_____.
( ) been expanded. I now realize why the school_____.

3.2 Regarding the social relationships in the school, I have changed my views on (write about only those which have been altered, most likely 3.2.2 and 3.2.6 in this part):
3.2.1 student-student.
3.2.2 teacher-students.
3.2.3 teacher-teacher.
3.2.4 teacher-administrator.
3.2.5 administrator-school board.
3.2.6 school-community.

4.0 Information Gained

4.1 What specific information or concept(s) mentioned in Part 4 did you find most significant or interesting?

4.2 What information did you find least interesting?

5.0 Reflection on an Educational Issue (Select only one; be as specific as you can when you react to the issue, and include specific points made in class or in the book.)

5.1 (Chapter 13) To what extent can the school meet the individual needs of students, considering society's expectation that schools also socialize pupils?

5.2 (Chapter 14) What is equal educational opportunity? Is America providing equal educational opportunity for all students?

5.3 (Chapter 15) To what extent can America permit optional forms of instruction?

Index

Index

Index

Index

Index

Index

Index

Index